Ageism and Elder Abuse

Ageism and Elder Abuse

Edited by
Lynn McDonald and K.L. Sharma

RAWAT PUBLICATIONS
Jaipur • New Delhi • Bangalore • Hyderabad • Guwahati

ISBN 978-81-316-0431-1

Published by
Prem Rawat for **Rawat Publications**
Satyam Apts, Sector 3, Jawahar Nagar, Jaipur 302 004 (India)
Phone: 0141 265 1748 / 7006 Fax: 0141 265 1748
E-mail: info@rawatbooks.com
Website: www.rawatbooks.com

New Delhi Office
4858/24, Ansari Road, Daryaganj, New Delhi 110 002
Phone: 011 2326 3290

Also at Bangalore, Hyderabad and Guwahati

Typeset by M & M Pre Press Consultants, Trivandrum
Printed at Chaman Enterprises, New Delhi

Contents

Introduction

Lynn Mc Donald and K.L. Sharma

The term 'ageism' was coined in 1969 by Robert Butler, the first director of the National Institute on Ageing (US). He associated it with other forms of bigotry such as racism and sexism. He defined it as a process of systematic stereotyping and discrimination against people because they are old. As an 'ism' ageism reflects a prejudice in society against older adults.

But ageism is different from other 'isms' (sexism, racism etc.) for primarily two reasons: age classification is not static. Moreover everybody experiences ageism unless he or she dies at an early age. Secondly one can be an 'ageist' (i.e., he/she may stereotype other people on the basis of age) with respect to both others and oneself. This distinction distinguishes it from other 'isms' as it affects the self-concept and well-being of an individual.

Ageist attitudes are perpetuated in many ways, for example, in the lack of positive images of the elderly in advertisements and also in TV programmes, and in the widespread use of demeaning language about old age as can be noticed nowadays. In addition, business institutions perpetuate ageism, by frequently reinforcing ageist stereotypes by not hiring or promoting older workers even when they are physically and mentally fit. Another example is the use of state welfare funds, which is often targeted at children and adolescents, and women (who are of productive age group), excluding equivalent services for older adults—protective services such as, pension, geriatric physical and mental health services.

Human service professionals also perpetuate ageism. This is done covertly by denying or limiting services, by not including ageing issues in their schedule of activities. The same criticism can be made about training of professional social workers who receive little information about the ageing process although many of their clients will be elderly.

Underlying these attitudes are myths and stereotypes about old age which are deeply entrenched in all the societies who claim themselves to be modern. Even those who would not say that they are ageist probably have some ageist attitudes based on distorted or inaccurate information. The most common of these negative myths and stereotypes about ageing are: older people are sick and disabled, impotent, ugly, cognitively impaired, useless fellows, socially isolated, poor, senile and so on.

The evaluation of older adults on the basis of age or giving judgements on the basis of age means that they are not considered as members of in-group. The intentional mistreatment of or harm to another person is elder abuse. Anyone can be an abuser who comes in to the contact of an older person. He may be a neighbour, or anyone who has negative attitude towards elderly persons. Even a caregiver may be an abuser if she/he has such a negative attitude. Abuse can be verbal, psychological, emotional, financial and physical. Mostly elderly are abused by family members and relatives. Due to the fear of victimization, elderly people isolate themselves, and thereby become "a prisoner in their own home".

The book has two parts. The first part of the book on **Ageism** contains 10 papers. Jane Roberts in the paper *Age Bias in Social Work Practitioners: Implications for Social Service Programmes Managers* found that the knowledge of ageing of social workers was biased. Thus, the author has suggested strategies for administrators' reduction of ageism among staff. Kelly Joyce, John Williamson and Laura Mamo's paper *Technology, Science and Ageism: An Examination of Three Patterns of Discrimination* argues that there are three primary ways people use science and technology to produce ageist ideals and relations. The 'negative attitude' towards older persons and 'ideal of youthfulness' force old people to desire a youthful body. In this context the authors have discussed two examples: the example of Viagra and hormone replacement therapy. The rise of anti-ageing medicine and insistence on the view that all aspects of ageing are pathological is the proof of the emphasis on youthful body. This direct targetting of ageing body is the first kind of ageism. All the recent advances in technological and scientific designs are made keeping in mind the young people. For example, answering machines, computers, cell phones etc. are devised keeping in mind youthful able-bodied persons. As an example of the third type of ageism the authors have discussed the rationing of medical technologies. Finally, they have concluded that, these techno-scientific forms of ageism, limit individual's ability to fully participate in political and civic life.

The paper entitled *Ageism and Social Exclusion in the United States: Implications for Social Policy and Social Work Practice* by Yeon Shim Lee and Rashmi Gupta examines the issues associated with ageism and social exclusion and its effects on older people in the United States. They have reviewed the range of social policies (such as income transfer policies, medicare and medic-aid, employment and social services) and social work practice and their impact on social exclusion of older people. It also provides a comprehensive analysis of government policies and direct practices, their implications, and suggested strategies to cope with ageist attitudes.

Joan K. Davitt, in his paper *The Ageism Conundrum of Age-Based Public Policy: Examples from the US*, has emphasized that ageism in any form (positive or negative) is related to age stratification and age segregation in a society. This phenomenon generates a policy conundrum. Age-based policy may support ageist assumptions about older adults. The paper discusses two examples of age-based policy—employment/retirement and housing policy—in the US and their connections to ageism. The author has explained negative effects of both positive and negative forms of age discrimination and has given recommendations for change. He has argued that policy makers must be more conscious of this conundrum when designing age-based policies to prevent unintended support for ageist assumptions.

Douglas McConatha and Jasmin Tahmaseb McConatha, in their paper *Ageism and Modernization in Contemporary China*, address the relationships between age, ageism and modernization, focusing on the case of contemporary China. As China experiences its rapid rise into modernity, it could face considerable social and cultural challenges in regard to its large ageing population. They have discussed how China can potentially bridge the gap between the economic requirements of a technologically sophisticated economy and ongoing cultural heritage and necessity of honouring ones elders.

Arup K.Banerjee, in his paper *Ageism in Health Care: A British Perspective*, has shown that despite recent attempts to root out ageism, ageism is still there in health care in UK. He talks about three broad categories of ageism in health care: primary, secondary and tertiary. Denying an established and well validated treatment to an individual just because of chronological age is primary ageism. It is simply a denial of certain opportunities and facilities. The secondary ageism is about collective discrimination, such as, poor accommodation in hospitals, policies to avoid frail older patients with multiple pathologies. Such patients are not hospitalized or even seen by specialists. Tertiary ageism is about downgrading the specialty of elderly care. He also suggests the ways to encounter ageism.

D. Jamuna and P.V. Ramamurti's study *Perceptions of Ageism Across the Generations* empirically investigates the contemporary prevalence of ageism in the perceptions of young adults (20–40), the middle aged (40–60) and the old (60–80). The sample consisted of 120 rural and urban men and women in each of the three age groups. The tool consisted of a checklist of attitude towards ageism adapted from an inventory of attitudes towards the aged. Results indicate a high prevalence of ageism among the young compared to the middle aged and the old, though all age groups held negative attitudes towards ageing. Some strategies of debunking ageism have been suggested.

Indira J. Prakash's paper entitled *Psychological Issues in Ageism and Its Prevention* explores the psychological issues in the development and prevention of ageism. Is caregiving to parents or grandparents, a burden or a source of satisfaction? B. Devi Prasad and N. Indira Rani have argued on this issue in their paper *Older Persons and Caregiver Burden and Satisfaction in Rural Family Context.* They have reported that large percentage of subjects (women) reported satisfaction in caregiving and some women caregivers reported tiredness and worsening health due to stress arising out of their caregiving roles. They have also reported that higher age and lower income was found to bring down the caregiver satisfaction significantly. 'Caregiver stress theory' suggests that stressors on the caregiver cause the caregiver to lash out against the elder. Factors of caregiver stress are: lack of motivation for caregiving, lack of supportive services, lack of coping skills, lack of resources/ respite, isolation of the victim, and outside stressors (job, losses, etc.).

The last paper in this section is contributed by U.C. Jain and K.L. Sharma. In their paper on *Stereotypes of Ageing among School Students,* the authors found that majority of students have medium level of prejudices towards elderly people. Difference in the prejudices towards elderly between male and female students (of present sample) was also noticed. On the whole, the findings are suggestive to the prevalence of negative as well as positive stereotypes at moderate level amongst the young school students. The study suggests that at school level intervention is needed to impart correct information about the aged and the need of their care within the family system.

The second part of the book focuses on the theme **Elder Abuse.** It consists of 16 papers from different parts of the globe that examine various dimensions of abuse and neglect as they are manifested in the different regions of the world. As the number and percentage of individuals 65 and over have increased in developed and developing countries, it is likely that the prevalence and the incidence of elder abuse will increase too, although there is a paucity of data to support this observation. Unfortunately, the nature of this growing problem has generally remained hidden from public view for a number of reasons. For example, the factors that may prevent the abused or neglected older person from reporting abuse or denying the occurrence of abuse include shame, guilt, fear, retribution or hopelessness. The abused person may have a fear of being abandoned or being placed in a facility if there is an allegation of abuse. He may also be afraid of retaliation by the abuser. While older people may not want to report elder abuse or neglect, there is also the problem that there has been limited research on the incidence and prevalence of the issue mainly due to its later appearance in the abuse literature in the 1980s following the discovery of child and woman abuse.

Elder abuse, also called mistreatment or maltreatment, is harmful behaviour directed towards older persons by informal or formal caregivers who the older person loves, or trusts or on whom they depend for assistance. The destructive behaviour can cause physical, psychological and material injury to the older person resulting in unnecessary distress, suffering and sometimes death. Elder abuse usually occurs in one of two locations: in the elder's home, usually called domestic abuse, and mistreatment in nursing homes or other long-term care facilities referred to as institutional abuse.

Although there is considerable definitional disagreement about the type and nature of elder abuse, at least five categories have been identified with considerable disagreement about whether self-neglect or abandonment are forms of elder abuse. Physical abuse includes any act that involves the intentional infliction of physical discomfort, pain, or injury. Examples of physical abuse include such behaviours as restraining, slapping, kicking, cutting, or burning. Medical maltreatment is sometimes considered an example of physical abuse. Sexual abuse or assault covers non-consensual sexual contact of any kind with an older person such as unwanted touching, all types of sexual battery like rape or coerced nudity. Psychological abuse, sometimes referred to as verbal or emotional abuse, involves the intentional infliction of mental anguish or the provocation of fear of violence or isolation in the older person. Psychological abuse can take various forms, such as name calling, humiliation, intimidation or threats of banishment to a nursing home. Material abuse, often referred to as financial abuse, involves the intentional, illegal, or improper exploitation of the older person's material property or financial resources by the abuser. Material abuse can include fraud, theft or use of money or property without the older person's consent. Neglect generally refers to the intended or unintended failure of a formal or informal caregiver to fulfill any part of a care giving obligation. Examples include failure to provide an older person with the necessities of life such as food, water, clothing, shelter, medicine or comfort.

Most recently, three new studies in developed countries report on the prevalence of elder abuse. In 2003/4 the First National Survey on Elder Abuse and Neglect under the sponsorship of The Association for Planning and Development of Services for the Aged in Israel (ESHEL) and the National Insurance Institute examined the prevalence and severity of various forms of abuse and neglect from a victim's perspective. Findings indicate that 18.4 per cent of respondents were exposed to at least one type of abuse during the 12 months preceding the interview, the highest form being verbal abuse followed by financial exploitation. The UK Study of Abuse and Neglect of Older People, carried out by the National Centre for Social Research (NatCen) and King's College London (KCL), was commissioned by Comic Relief and the Department of Health. Over 2,100 people in England, Scotland, Wales and Northern Ireland took part in the survey between March and September 2006. Overall, 2.6 per cent of people aged 66 and over, living in private households reported that they had experienced mistreatment involving a family member, close friend or care worker, with the most common form being neglect followed by financial abuse.

In Spain, the First National Study of Elder Abuse in the Family in Spain, a random study carried out in 2006 found that 0.8 per cent of the interviewees had experienced abuse by family members in the last year, with the most common form being neglect and emotional abuse followed by financial abuse. In these three recent studies the rates vary substantially because definitions of elder abuse and neglect vary, cultures are different and, methodologies and timeframes for the occurrence of abuse differ and samples do not always accurately represent older people.

In terms of institutional abuse, a new study in Germany indicates that over 70 per cent of staff reported in a random survey that they had behaved at least once in an abusive or neglectful way towards residents over a one-year period. Psychological abuse and neglect were the most common forms of abuse reported by over 50 per cent of the sample.

Efforts to advance social action to end elder mistreatment at a national level and to develop national polices and legislation are at varying stages of growth around the world as seen in this special edition of the United States, has developed a full-blown national response to elder abuse at the state level that allows for the funding and reporting of elder abuse and has instituted at least three national organizations while other countries have been less proactive. In the light of this longer history, it is no surprise that the paper, *Elder Abuse and Mistreatment: A Life Span and Cultural Context* by Carey Wexler Sherman, Dorrie E. Rosenblatt and Toni C. Antonucci presents a new and innovative way to conceptualize the complexity of elder abuse using an intergenerational approach. The authors are of the view that the increased longevity is generally a positive development, but older adults and family members responsible for their care are often faced with associated problems due to such issues as chronic illness, family mobility and shrinking public and medical resources. Such factors strain the families' abilities to provide optimal care and increase the likelihood of elder abuse. The violation of a trust relationship, a defining feature of elder mistreatment, suggests that a consideration of social relations across the life span is useful for understanding elder mistreatment. Cultural expectations of intergenerational responsibility and assistance also influence perceptions of and responses to elder mistreatment. This paper examines social relations and culture as essential to a comprehensive understanding of elder mistreatment. Such understanding is critical to identifying risk, improving early detection, and providing sensitive intervention for elders in communities with increasingly diverse populations. Picking up a similar intergenerational thread, Ariela Lowenstein and Israel Doron, in their paper, *Intergenerational Justice: An Israeli Perspective,* emphasize the view that intergenerational equity is a central issue not only in gerontological theories but for the gerontological field at large. This paper describes and analyses the development of social welfare policies in Israel, in the context of intergenerational justice. The paper examines the developing themes of intergenerational justice in Israeli social policy, along with specific examples in old age with emphasis on the phenomena of elder abuse and neglect.

In Australia and Canada, various states and provinces have created mechanisms for dealing with elder abuse but there are no established federal policies about elder abuse per se. Both countries have national organizations dedicated to the termination of elder abuse which were established in the 1990s. In this issue three papers provide a window on Canadian responses to elder abuse and neglect. In keeping with the theme on legal issues, in the paper entitled, *Adult Protection Legislation: From Intent to Practice in Three Canadian Provinces*, Joan Harbison et al., discuss the problem of mistreatment and neglect and governments' responses in the form of adult protection legislation. Their study is based on three rural communities in Canada where this act has been operative for the last twenty years. The authors find that there is a complex relationship between the provisions of adult protection legislation and the provision of assistance. In addition, there are many issues with regard to respecting the rights and autonomy of older people. The paper *A Community Response to Financial Abuse of Older Adults* by Daphne Nahmiash and Rhonda Schwartz addresses one of the most prevalent forms of elder abuse observed in many countries. It addresses the phenomenon of financial/material abuse of dependent older adults who live in the community where they are cared for by a family member, friend or neighbour and those living in a residential/nursing home where they are cared for by paid care givers. The article focuses on describing the types of financial and material abuse that are perpetrated and also suggests how to avoid them. On a less travelled road in elder abuse, Peter Clark and Barry Goldlist, in their paper on *Protecting Vulnerable Older Adults in the Health Care System*, review the role of the Geriatric/Long Term Care Review Committee to the Chief Coroner for the Province of Ontario which has a mandate to improve medical care for the elderly in Ontario and decrease the occurrence of what could be construed as 'medical abuse'. The motto of the chief coroner's office, "We speak for the dead to protect the living," is most telling. The systematic review of problem cases in the care of the elderly with the creation and dissemination of annual reports has been an important method for improving the care of older people in Ontario and Canada.

In the United Kingdom, there is a national body called Action on Elder Abuse that has stimulated government responses to elder abuse. The paper in this volume, *The Abuse of Older People: The English Scenario*, by Arup K. Banerjee provides an interesting overview of abuse and neglect in the UK. The various types and aspects of 'abuse' are outlined and the approach to handling suspected cases of abuse is discussed. Various international guidelines are mentioned and the latest UK government actions are presented. The crucial need for more research in the field is emphasized—a case to be made for all countries—as is the importance of ongoing in-service education and training for professionals and carers. A number of regulatory measures recently taken by the UK authorities are mentioned. Above all, it is suggested that the need for an attitudinal change to old age will be of paramount importance. Norway has had parliamentary approval for services and a resource centre for research and information while France, Germany, Italy and Poland are at the point of recognizing the legitimacy of elder abuse and neglect. Included in this volume is a paper from Sweden, *Investigating Emotional Reactions to Elder Abuse: Pilot Study of a Triple Perspective Questionnaire* by Christen Erlingsson. The paper reports the results of a pilot study in Sweden examining lay persons' emotional reactions to a vignette concerning a potential elder abuse situation involving an elderly caregiver and his care receiving spouse. The participants rated emotional reactions from three different perspectives; how they themselves reacted, and how they thought the caregiver and the care recipient would each react emotionally. Emotional reactions were explored through questionnaire items of anger, impatience, shame, disgust, concern, embarrassment, compassion, irritation, a desire to help, insecurity, and fright. Results showed differences between participants' own reported reactions and the reactions they expected the older persons to experience. These differences were especially noticeable between questionnaire versions. Analysis also indicated differences in response patterns that were related to participants' gender and marital/cohabitation status. This pilot study reveals several fruitful avenues for refinement of the questionnaire and for further investigation of emotional reactions to elder abuse.

The Latin America Committee on Elder Abuse has drawn attention to the problem within Latin America and the Caribbean while in Buenos Aires, the organization, Proteger, works solely with elder abuse cases. In Brazil, the Ministry of Justice, Health and Welfare supports official training on elder abuse. In Chile, a law against family violence was passed in 1994 which clearly addressed abuse of the elderly.

Turning to Asia, there has been several studies by researchers in Japan, India and the Republic of Korea about elder abuse and the beginnings of national organizations to fight the issue. South Africa established a preventive programme on institutional abuse which was jointly sponsored by the government and the private sector in 1994 while the Nigerian Coalition for the Prevention of Elder Abuse facilitates the meetings of professionals working with older adults. This volume is particularly rich in reports from India and is the heart of this book for those struggling with the problems of abuse and neglect in India.

Looking specifically at India, many years ago, the elderly had a special place in the family and in Indian society. The elderly were loved, cared for and respected. Their thoughts and opinions were considered to be of immense value, something every young person would look up to. Over the years, however, there has been slow and gradual erosion of this view of the elderly. For a number of reasons, older adults have faced growing covert dissidence, a form of subtle defiance from the young and society in general which, in some instances, can lead to elder abuse or neglect. For example, through retirement or loss of productive capacity and hence the ability to be independent, older adults are exposed to a high risk of being abused and neglected. In some instances, living in long term care facilities due to frailty or the death of spouse may lead to depression, enhancing the chances of becoming a victim of abuse or neglect. In such situations the caregivers fail to recognize the problem or provide the victim with emotional support.

An important case on point are widows in India. Most of the widows in India face much insecurity and dependence in old age. They have been dependent on the earnings of their husbands and after the death of their husbands they have to search for alternative means of survival. Therefore, those who have lost their husbands are more prone to social isolation and a decline in status in the family. More traditional upper class Hindu society imposes very strict restrictions on a widow's lifestyle so that such an extreme transition into old age will surely be a major problem for many women. These women have to adapt to substantial changes in the patterns of their lives that they had previously pursued. The plight of rural widows is even worse than that of urban widows. Urban widows sometimes receive a retirement pension and life insurance benefits from their deceased husbands. In contrast, rural women rarely have this advantage because rural men do not easily find a job in the organized or core sector of the economy and cannot contribute to life insurance policies.

Following these themes, the paper *Determinants of Elder Abuse in Rajshahi City Corporation, Bangladesh: Evidence from a Micro-Level Survey*, by Md. Ismail Tareque et al., presents a disturbing finding that in Rajshahi City Corporation, 17 per cent of the elderly are abused. Their study shows that most of the abused elderly were the young old, widows and the illiterate. The overall finding of this study also suggests a close relationship of abuse with the family head, physical condition of the older person, living arrangements and educational background. The authors recommend that this knowledge needs to be utilized in developing suitable programmes addressing the abuse of the elderly in the country. The researchers emphasize the importance of replicating this research, and incorporating culturally specific findings into customized intervention strategies, an important suggestion, giving the ethnic diversity of India.

An important issue in understanding global elder abuse is that of cross-cultural differences. Addressing Asian communities in the United States, Rashmi Gupta and Anoshua Chaudhuri's paper, *Elder Abuse in a Cross-cultural Context: Assessment, Policy and Practice*, examines the concept of elder abuse in a cross-cultural context. The authors are of the view that elder abuse is evidenced in the form of silent treatment, neglect, social isolation, and exploitation. Practitioners often associate elder abuse with physical violence, but analysis of reported abuse in the United States demonstrates that financial abuse is more common. Elder abuse is widespread but it is often underreported as it is difficult to assess and prevent, especially in Asian communities in the United States and in South Asia. The importance in understanding the link between the countries of origin and the host countries in elder abuse is underscored in this study.

Selecting the caregiving theme, Roopalekha Jathanna P.N. and K.S. Latha in their paper, *Caregiving and Caregiver Stress: A Case Report*, examines the issues of elder abuse in a caregiver setting where patients suffer from dementia along with others with severe physical and psychiatric disabilities found in the data from their long term project. In addition, the stresses and strains experienced by informal caregivers of the persons with dementia are highlighted. K.S. Latha, in her paper entitled, *Elder Abuse and Neglect: A Review*, emphasizes the widespread and serious problems of elder abuse and neglect and the factors which contribute to elder abuse, the reasons why it is not reported by the victim, the characteristics of the abused and the abuser, manifestations of abuse and management issues thereby providing an excellent overview of the issues. U.C. Jain, in his paper *Elder Abuse: Outcome of Changing Family Dynamics,* traces the pattern of increasing elder abuse amidst changes in Indian family structures and functions. The short case studies reported by the author indicate that older adults are encountering both physical and psychological distancing in joint as well as in nuclear families. The paper also explores the possible solutions for such a grave social problem.

Moving to an institutional setting, Varsha Pandya, in her paper *Resolving Elder Abuse Complaints in Homes for the Aged: Relevance of an Ombudsman Programme,* provides information on the Ombudsman Programme in the US and other European countries for consideration of Indian stakeholders in the development of homes for the aged. The paper also provides alternative models, processes and potential pitfalls of these to guide the decision-making for programme development. According to Mala Kapur Shankardass, in *Critical Understanding of Prevalence of Elder Abuse and the Combating Strategies with Specific Reference to India,* elder abuse has only recently been a subject worthy of serious academic inquiry and concerted action in India—a situation seen around the world. However, absence of valid statistics and systematic collection of facts related to the problem contribute to it being still under-recognized and insufficiently acknowledged. Lack of conceptual and definitional clarity as well as underreporting comes in the way of finding ways and means to combat it. Understanding abuse of older people and finding solutions to deal with it is further complicated by social taboo among older people on discussing the subject and consistent denial by family members that abuse takes place in their homes. Yet another difficulty is that not all of the situations characterized as abuse fit into existing legal categories. Consequently, little attention is being given to elder abuse as a major social issue. Even less effort is being devoted to tackling the underlying causes of elder abuse and developing appropriate interventions and adopting combating strategies. This paper reviews the prevalence of elder abuse and strategies to end the abuse in the Indian context based on the author's research, academic interest and engagement with the subject as an activist.

Considering widows, Madhurima in her paper, *Elderly Widows as Victims of Physical Abuse: A Qualitative Study in the State of Punjab,* emphasizes that due to changing age pyramids, value systems and withdrawal of family support systems, domestic maltreatment of the elderly in India is emerging as an important social problem. The institution of joint family, caste and village community, which formed the building blocks of the traditional structure in India, assured economic and psychological security and high social status for the aged who are now at the mercy of their son(s). This problem can be better understood from a dependency framework as older widow's investment in the ideals of family are quite high. Their social reality has not been constructed outside family living. It comes as a rude shock to them when they are physically abused by their sons or have to leave their family to seek support from formal agencies as a last resort. The paper by Anupriyo Mallick entitled, *Narratives of Aged Widows on Abuse,* is fittingly based on in-depth interviews with elderly widows residing in various old age homes in Kolkata and its adjoining areas. The paper portrays the suffering and humiliation of the widows in terms of the abuse and neglect they experience and there is no more eloquent commentary on the tragedy of abuse and neglect than their own words.

Throughout the world, abuse and neglect of older persons is largely under-recognized or treated as an unspoken social problem. Regrettably, no community or country in the world is immune from this expensive, public health and human rights problem as witnessed in the articles that appear in these papers is exemplary in recognizing this transgression against older adults around the world and should be commended.

In the end, we would like to express our gratitude to all the authors who have contributed their papers for this volume. We deeply appreciate the continued keen interest and full cooperation of Rawat Publications, Jaipur in the publication of this book.

Lynn Mc Donald
K.L. Sharma

Part I

Ageism

1

Age Bias in Social Work Practitioners: Implications for Social Service Programme Managers

Jane Roberts

In a rapidly ageing worldwide population, many people remain quite viable, self-sufficient, and productive at advanced ages. In contrast to widespread beliefs about ageing and being old, many older people do not live isolated, functionally impaired lives typified by cognitive or personality declines, or by failing intellectual abilities (Maddox, 2001; Palmore, 2005). In fact, the individual uniqueness among older people along many dimensions is as pronounced as diversity among individuals at younger ages (Binstock, 1994). As has been well documented, the problem with inadequate or inaccurate information about ageing is its tendency to promote stereotypical thinking, which results in ageism or negative attitudes toward ageing (Palmore, 1998; Stewart, 2004). The purpose of this study was the examination of age bias in a professional population—social workers—who increasingly have direct and influential contact with a growing segment of the American population: older adults.

Researchers have suggested that those who work most closely with older people may be at risk of holding negative attitudes towards older people, due to their increased exposure to those who are ill and infirm (Lookinland and Anson, 1994). Many social workers are likely to work with older people or their families, at some time during their careers (CSWE, 2001). However, many of the studies on age bias were completed with samples of nursing and other medical students, but very infrequently with those not in a medical field, or with those who are no longer students and already practicing with older people. Many social work (and other) practitioners assist older adults who are not necessarily frail or incapacitated, and although some work in medical settings, they are not physiological medical professionals in the same way that nurses and physicians are. Rather, social workers primarily attend to behavioural and social aspects of the medical patient and the family. Therefore, this study examined ageism in a population of social workers, a population that is infrequently studied in that regard. The results of the study have important implications for managers and administrators who are charged with attracting, evaluating, and hiring competent staff.

Working definitions of 'management' vary, and are sometimes used interchangeably with the term 'administration', particularly in the field of social work. For the purposes of this study, I am using a definition derived from Robert Weinbach's writings on practical matters for social work professionals, which encompass an administrator's charge to "facilitate the accomplishment of organizational goals" (Weinbach, 1998). While a broad definition, this depiction of administrative function does include the ethical mandate to any social work organization's staff, to practice competently and within their areas of expertise. (It would be difficult to imagine an agency's goals being met in any other manner.) Thus, competent practice must currently include an understanding of ageing and of older people's needs, as social workers will encounter older people in most practice venues, whether or not the primary purpose of the agency is targeted to older individuals. Management is a proactive (rather than a reactive) endeavour (Weinbach, 1998) and as such, administrators need to make ageing knowledge and updates in gerontology content available to their staff by means of continuing education opportunities and other avenues to current knowledge. In so doing, administrators will provide resources for good service delivery.

In relating social services management principles to the need for continuing education in ageing matters, we can utilize typical categories of management functions to examine the areas in which a clear understanding of ageing is important. Five frequently-cited categories of management tasks are *planning, organizing, staffing, leading or guiding staff, and controlling management operations* (Weinbach, 1998). By engaging in these five functions, the social work manager can help to shape various aspects of the work environment to be inclusive of older individuals as clients or as participants in the lives of other clientele.

Upon entering the workforce, few social workers have had adequate education in understanding ageing processes or in practice concepts relating to ageing (Takamura, 2001). Even so, prior studies have repeatedly shown that academic education in gerontology alone does not promote a definite career choice of working with elders, although classroom education coupled with field experience does appear to promote such choice (Davis-Berman and Robinson, 1989). Some suggest that contact with older people, and life influences from that contact are related to positive attitudes toward ageing (Miller and Dodder, 1984; Palmore, 1998). It seems reasonable, then, that the type, frequency, duration or other aspects of prior experiences with one's elders may also have a similar effect upon one's biases or prejudices that have been formed around ageing. The field of social work is increasingly in need of practitioners who will work with older people, and any measures that can be undertaken to increase the likelihood of choosing to work with elders will be important. Even if social work administrators have employed social workers who are age biased, some steps can be taken to increase contact and experience with older people, such as promotion of intergenerational programmes or specific inclusion of older people in agency advisory panels, for example. Erdman Palmore, a leading researcher of age bias, suggests such contacts and programmatic focus as possible measures to combat age bias in communities (Palmore, 2005a).

In addition to the educational and work settings, another arena of experience or exposure to views of ageing is through media representations of older people, at least in Western venues. The United States is a youth-oriented society; print and electronic media (television, advertising, e-mail jokes, stories, urban legends) portray older individuals as largely dependent, cognitively impaired, or incapable of decision-making (Ferraro, 1992; Vasil and Wass, 1993). Knowing the importance of academic work, and general exposure to older people as influential in forming opinions and attitudes towards ageing, it was deemed relevant to undertake a study of social workers' age bias specifically in relation to contact and experiences with older adults.

The Research Questions

The research questions surrounding age bias were the following:

1. Is the prevalence of age bias towards older people among a deliberately selected sample of social work practitioners the same as age bias in the general population?
2. What contextual or experiential factors are related to knowledge of ageing processes? We see from a review of the literature that specific contextual or experiential factors explain variation in knowledge of ageing processes. Family and social-relational influences, television and other media influences, and care-related experiences were assessed to determine significant correlations with knowledge about ageing. I hypothesized that the more extensive the social and relational influences, the more accurate the knowledge of ageing, and therefore the less exhibition of biased attitudes.

Method

A purposive sample was sought from various types of agencies and social workers in individual practice, as well as public departments of social services. Social workers at these agencies can be assumed to have some degree of higher education in their fields. All respondents had achieved either a baccalaureate or master's level degree in the field or in a related field of study. Very few, 2 per cent, practised at the level of Ph.D. or DSW. Having identified the sample frame, the author then enlisted the cooperation of state professional social work organizations in providing their membership lists, which comprised a random sample that included practitioners who have opportunities to engage in direct practice with, or who do actually engage in work with, older adults. (The state organizations provided standard, randomized lists which they offer to researchers.)

US states with the highest percentages of populations of individuals over the age of 65 comprised the sample, as these states' current populations most closely typify the proportion of older individuals to be found in all states within the coming years. In part, these states were chosen as an approximation of projected future demographic conditions in most of the United States and perhaps globally. This choice allowed examination of public social workers' attitudes and experiences in environments in which they are highly likely to encounter elders in their work. Although this specialized selection decreased specification error by limiting demographic and other aspects of the sample selected, it also decreased, to some extent, the generalizability of findings to social workers in other states. Most importantly, however, it closely resembles situations that social workers and other practitioners are likely to encounter in the future, with regard to exposure to older people.

In determining sample specifications, effect size and power analysis factors were derived from the work of Cohen, a primary source for power analysis factors (Pedhazur and Schmelkin, 1997). Power analysis allows the strategic use of effect size, alpha or significance level, desired power, and *N*, or sample size (Pedhazur and Schmelkin, 1997). Fixing any three of the elements determines the fourth, in this case sample size. Therefore, a minimum of 150 respondents were targeted for the survey research, and an N of 367 was ultimately obtained.

Measures

Experience. An author-developed questionnaire was used in the absence of existing measures that would meet the study's purposes. Experience questions were based on elements of contact and experience with older people; questions were devised from concepts defined in previous studies by researchers studying influences upon age bias (Gergen, 1991; Menec and Perry, 1995). Known influences include family biases and preferences, media and other public influences, and experience with older individuals in caregiving and care-receiving contexts (Aday, 1996; Davis-Berman and Robinson, 1989). An example of an experience item is the following: "I have been involved in giving care to an older person (over age 65)". A four-point scale of Likert-type responses included (a) does not apply to me; (b) very slightly applies to me; (c) somewhat applies to me; or (d) very much applies to me. The experience scale was subjected to reliability measures and factor analysis.

Knowledge and age bias. The Facts on Ageing Quiz (FAQ), developed by Erdman Palmore (1998), was the instrument used to assess ageing knowledge and age bias. This well-established 25-item true-false instrument has been widely used to assess both knowledge of ageing facts and processes, as well as age bias, and is currently used in such studies despite its development (in its original version) nearly thirty years ago. The test contains 25 true-false questions pertaining to biological, social, emotional, and psychological traits of older people. (This instrument is also known as the 'FAQ1' because other versions have been developed over the years.)

Due to distribution of the surveys to social workers engaged in a variety of subfields such as adult services, children's services, and individual or family work, the non-specific distribution obscured, to some extent, the focus of the study as bias- or ageism-related. Table 1 shows the distribution of sample characteristics.

Results

The major dependent variable in this study's primary analysis is social workers' knowledge of ageing processes. Table 2 shows that social workers' knowledge of ageing and the derivative factor, age bias, are similar to those of the general population, and while it is not high in relation to the general population, any age bias is to be considered deleterious to effective practice in any profession.

The experience variables were identified from a factor analysis relating to the origination of knowledge about ageing, such as "Most of my attitudes about older people come from my family". The variable named a 'social-relational factor' was derived from survey questions regarding caregiving or care-receiving and elder individuals, and the elder alertness variable came from such questions as "Most older adults in my experience have been alert and oriented". Each of these questions was preceded by an instruction to use the age 65 as a guideline for 'older adult'—type terms, as 65 is often the age marker for older adults in the gerontology literature.

Tests of the Assumption of No Difference in Social Workers and General Population

Assumption. There is no difference in the prevalence of age bias among social work practitioners in comparison to the general population, as all people have varying early and ongoing experiences that produce biased or non-biased attitudes.

Table 1 State of Residence, Experience and Work-Related Activities

State of NASW membership	Academic education			Number of years in social work			Prefer social work with		Attended elder conference w/in older people		Belongs to ageing past 5 years		Have engaged in social work organization with older people	
		n	%		n	%	n	%	n	%	n	%	n	%
Florida	Baccalaureate	21	19	< 10 years	42	37								
	Master's	86	76	10-20 years	45	40	14	12	2	2	16	14	8	7
	Doctoral	5	4	> 20 years	24	21								
	Other	2	2											
Iowa	Baccalaureate	14	16	< 10 years	38	41								
	Master's	75	82	10-20 years	43	47	24	26	37	41	13	14	18	20
	Doctoral	0	0	> 20 years	9	10								
	Other	1	1											
Pennsylvania	Baccalaureate	12	16	< 10 years	32	42								
	Master's	62	82	10-20 years	33	43	17	22	37	51	11	15	16	21
	Doctoral	1	1	> 20 years	11	14								
	Other	0	0											
West Virginia	Baccalaureate	17	20	< 10 years	27	31								
	Master's	70	80	10-20 years	49	56	19	22	35	40	6	7	19	22
	Doctoral	0	0	> 20 years	10	12								
	Other	1	1											

Table 2 Age Bias by State in Relation to General Population

Age Bias by State	Per cent scoring an age bias	Per cent bias in general population	Per cent bias in social work population	Per cent bias in study population
Florida	37%			
Iowa	24%	33%	27–32%	29%
Pennsylvania	29%			
West Virginia	26%			

Table 3 Knowledge of Ageing, and Age Bias Scores

	Total n=367			Florida n=113			Iowa n=91			Pennsylvania n=76			West Virginia n=87		
	Mean	SD	Range	Mean	SD	Range	Mean	SD	Range	Mean	SD	Range	Mean	SD	Range
Knowledge (FAQ)	20.2	3.5	8–25	18.7	3.5	8–25	21.4	3.5	10–25	20.6	3.0	13–25	21.0	3.2	12–25
Scores	29	.45	0–1	37	.48	0–1	.24	.43	0–1	.29	.45	0–1	.24	.44	0–1
Age Bias	Age Biased 109	% 29		Age Biased 42	% 37		Age Biased 22	% 24		Age Biased 22	% 29		Age Biased 33	% 26	

Table 4 The Prediction of Age Bias from Experience Factors

Coefficients(a)

Model	Unstandardized Coefficients B		Standardized Coefficients Std. Error	t Beta	Sig.
1 (Constant)	14.740	1.223		12.048	.000
Value Source	.495	.121	.242	4.104	.000
Social-Relational	.029	.121	.012	.237	.813
Elder Competence	.168	.107	.093	1.577	.116

[a] Dependent Variable: Total FAQ score (Facts on Aging Quiz)

Model Summary

Model	R	R Square	Adjusted R Square	Std. Error of the Estimate
1	.300(a)	.090	.082	3.331

[a] Predictors: (Constant), Value Source, Social-Relational, Elder Competence

Approximately 30 per cent of this sample (n = 109) were found to be age biased, whether they held negative or positive bias. The assumption was supported by this analysis in that this sample exhibited a relatively high degree of age bias overall, but was consistent with that found in the general population and in social work practitioners. The percentage of social workers found to hold age bias in prior studies, has been between 27–32 per cent (Palmore, 1998). Table 3 shows that nearly 30 per cent of this study's sample responded incorrectly to subsets of negative ageism-related questions on the Facts on Ageing Quiz (FAQ), or to one or more of the five questions that indicated positive ageism. Thus, among social work practitioners who work with older people or who have the propensity to do so, age bias was found to exist to a degree similar to that of the general population.

Test of the Hypothesis: Contextual Factors Explain Variation in Knowledge of Ageing

A linear regression analysis predicted three specific contextual or experiential factors that explain variation in knowledge of ageing processes. Family and social-relational influences, television and other media influences, and care-related experiences were significantly correlated with knowledge about ageing. The more extensive the social and relational influences, the more accurate the knowledge of ageing. Table 4 shows that those with close relationships and those who perceived older people as oriented and alert did not score as highly on the FAQ.

Discussion

This study revealed two important aspects of age bias among the social work population represented by this sample:

1. age bias exists among social work practitioners,
2. family influences and television and other media significantly influence one's perception of ageing and risk for age biased attitudes.

Social work managers can have a direct and influential impact upon an organization's response to the rising need for expertise in ageing practice. The functional areas of social work administration outlined earlier can provide a structure to incorporate ageing issues into the day-to-day operations of the workplace. Ageism is detrimental to service provision because inaccurate assessments produce flawed service planning, but due to the rapid ageing of the population, practitioners will often encounter older people directly, if only as clients' family members. Current and non-biased knowledge about ageing is important, and managers must help staff accurately assess clients' needs and plan effective services. These findings suggest strategies for administrators' reduction of ageism among staff.

Application of Age Bias Findings to Management Functions

Planning and staffing functions. Having accurate knowledge of ageing will enhance social workers' ability to assess clients' actual change or decline (or growth and improvement), and will decrease the likelihood of basing interventions upon erroneous assumptions. Managers can plan for effective services by putting into place, adequate education and training in ageing issues to assure that staff skills are up-to-date and accurate. A more accurate assessment of clients' needs and capabilities will result in greater client autonomy and better services to older clients overall.

Nearly 30 per cent of the sample indicated age bias by responses to established measures of ageism. In 1987 fewer than 30,000 social workers engaged in professional work with older people or their families; however, by 2010, now only a few years in the future, 60,000 social workers will be needed for work with the same population. One condition fostering the risk of age bias among practitioners is the lack of students and faculty with interest in ageing work, as they often perceive work with older people as less interesting and less-valued than work with other populations. Many students indicate a lack of interest in gerontology specialization, and those who have felt interest perceived little faculty or curricular support (CSWE, 2001).

Organizing function. Perhaps one way of presenting ageing studies (both in ageing academic studies and in workplace continuing education) is the manager's attention to the practitioner's age, period, and cohort as a vehicle to understanding the current perspective. Culture (and 'culture' pertains to the workplace culture as well as larger societal culture) is integrally related to the ways in which people view themselves, their peers and significant others, and one's age or 'placement' in society due to various sociocultural factors. Thus, differences among practitioners of different ages, cultural or ethnic background, and education level as factors associated with early experiences, can also be taken into account as a programmatic consideration. Administrators and programme managers may be able to match interests, age and experience, and life values or perspectives when assigning work duties and when delegating work with specific client populations, or at least raise these possibilities for staff discussion.

Leading/guiding function. A simple initial solution to ageism is the provision of additional ongoing information and training for staff. This training can take the form of in-service education, ageing-relevant reading lists, support for return to academic coursework or seminars, workshops, intergenerational opportunities, and conferences dealing with ageing matters. Additionally, daily attention to ageing specifically when discussing family case material or when planning clinical interventions can be a managerial role, as would promoting collaborative projects with agencies and organizations attuned to ageing needs in the community.

Controlling agency operations. This function of management operations incorporates ideas from the preceding functions, such as hiring effective, competent staff, and maintaining continuing education opportunities and supporting these by allowing time for educational pursuits or agency-sponsored financial support for coursework. An assessment of the best 'fit' of various staff to client needs is an operations function. Some aspects of age bias or the potential for inadvertent bias could be important in agency recruitment and hiring practices. Specific questions regarding ageing knowledge and experience or prior work with elders may help the agency administrator designate work areas, choose work roles for incoming employees, or provide appropriate orientation and workplace updates. One might also review agency intake procedures and standardized forms to ascertain their reflection of a life-course perspective or attention to elder family members. Are ageing matters integral to the organization, or are they 'tacked on' and seemingly afterthoughts? The manager's operations tasks include an integrating function with regard to older clients.

Although any experience-related influences could be tempered by accurate ageing information in social work and other human services practice venues, the majority of human services students have received little ageing-related material. Thus, employees new to the workplace and to the profession are entering with a disadvantage in terms of preparation for a possible lifetime of work with an ageing population. The data from this study show that ongoing education and updating of basic knowledge about ageing processes and expectations can be integral to the effective practice of current clinicians, and that they are not important only for students. Thus, while inclusion of gerontology content in the social work curriculum is important, it may be even more critical to provide ongoing gerontological education for social work practitioners already in the field, as they are already engaging the burgeoning population of older individuals and their families. Perhaps another simple approach would be a greater emphasis upon specific orientation of new staff. This orientation could be provided by longtime employees who have had a good deal of experience in working with elders and their families. Regardless of the methods used to shore up skills for working with ageing clients, social work administrators can play an increasingly significant role in assuring that older clientele receive social work services based upon accurate, timely, unbiased assessments and plans of treatment.

References

Aday, R. (1996). Changing children's perceptions of the elderly: The effects of intergenerational contact. *Gerontology and Geriatrics Education,* 16: 37–51.

Binstock, R. (1994). Transcending intergenerational equity. In T. Marmor, T. Smeeding and V. Greene (eds.), *Economic security and intergenerational justice: A look at North America.* Washington, DC: Urban Institute.

CSWE (2001). *A blueprint for the new millennium.* Publication of the Council on Social Work Education, prepared for National Professional Conference.

Davis-Berman, J. and J.D. Robinson (1989). Knowledge of aging and preference to work with the elderly: The impact of a course on aging. *Gerontology and Geriatrics Education,* 10: 23–24.

Ferraro, K. (1992). Cohort changes in images of older adults, 1974–1981. *The Gerontologist,* 32: 293–304.

Gergen, K.J. (1991). *The saturated self: Dilemmas of identity in contemporary life.* New York: Basic Books.

Lookinland, S. and K. Anson, (1994). Perpetuation of ageist attitudes among present and future health care personnel: Implications for elder care. *Research on Aging*,12: 399–408.

Maddox, G. (2001). *The encyclopedia of aging* (3rd ed.). New York: Springer.

Menec, V. and R. Perry (1995). Reactions to stigmas: The effects of targets' age and controllability of stigmas. *Journal of Aging and Health*, 7: 365–83.

Miller, R. and R. Dodder (1994). An empirical analysis of Palmore's FAQ and the Miller-Dodder revision. *Social Spectrum*, 4: 53–69.

Palmore, E.B. (1998). *The facts on aging quiz: A handbook of uses and results* (48–50). New York: Springer.

——. (2005). Functional age. In E.B. Palmore, L.G. Branch and D.K. Harris (eds.), *Encyclopedia of ageism* (154–155). New York: Haworth Press.

——. (2005a). Reducing ageism. In E.B. Palmore, L.G. Branch, and D.K. Harris (eds.), *Encyclopedia of ageism* (25–26). New York: Haworth Press.

Pedhazur, E.J. and L.P. Schmelkin (1997). *Multiple regression in behavioral research: Explanation and prediction.* New York: Holt, Rinehart and Winston.

Stewart, J.T. (2004). Why don't physicians consider depression in the elderly? *Postgraduate Medicine*, 115: 57–59.

Takamura, J.C. (2001). Towards a new era in aging and social work. *Journal of Gerontological Social Work*, 36: 1–11.

Vasil, L. and H. Wass (1993). Portrayal of the elderly in the media: A literature review and implications for educational gerontologists. *Educational Gerontology*, 19: 71–85.

Weinbach, R.W. (1998). *The social worker as manager: A practical guide to success.* Boston: Allyn and Bacon.

2

Technology, Science, and Ageism: An Examination of Three Patterns of Discrimination

Kelly Joyce, John Williamson and Laura Mamo

Science and technology are central to the normative definitions and lived experiences of ageing. The design and use of technologies can enable ageing people to participate more fully in civic and political life. Alternatively, they can reproduce ageist practices and biases. As social products, technologies can be designed in a range of ways and put to a variety of uses, each of which redefines behaviours, perceptions and lifestyles associated with ageing.

In this paper, we discuss three ways, science and technology contribute to the social construction of ageist ideals and experiences. Drawing on literature in medical sociology, gerontology, and science and technology studies, we show how the medicalization of ageing bodies, the design of technologies, and health care rationing, all help produce ageism in contemporary life. These examples demonstrate the importance of putting science and technology at the centre of future empirical investigations of ageing and ageism.[1] Throughout this paper we focus on the United States, but we hope that the analysis presented here will foster similar analyses of developments in other countries and cross-national comparisons.

The Medicalization of Ageing

The twentieth century was marked by an increasing tendency to define mental, physical and emotional processes as illnesses. This trend, known as medicalization, was initially described by sociologists Zola (1972), Friedson (1970), and Pitts (1968).[2] In his canonical essay "Medicine as an Institution of Social Control", Zola noted how alcoholism, having trouble sleeping, pregnancy, and other behaviours and bodily processes once defined as socially unacceptable or normal, became redefined as illnesses by the 1970s. As additional aspects of life were redefined as medical problems, physicians and other health care professionals gained more control over the management and treatment of people. Zola (1972) expressed concern about the expansion of medicine's jurisdiction over new areas of life, noting that "the labels health and illness are remarkable 'depoliticizers' of an issue". That is, medical labels turn social issues (e.g. structural reasons for addiction, sleeplessness, and the like) into an individual 'illness' in need of a medical, not a political solution.

Medicalization affects all ages, but it has particular implications in an ageist society. In societies that position youthful bodies as the norm, the changes associated with ageing are ripe for being labeled pathological. As Zola cautioned, turning such processes into illnesses depoliticizes underlying cultural and structural causes. The opportunity to challenge the ageist bias that causes their very construction is lost.

Sociologists and gerontologists have spent years documenting the transformation of the emotional, mental, and physical changes associated with ageing into 'illnesses' (Cruikshank, 2002; Estes and Binney, 1989; Gubrium, 1986; Kaufman, 1994; Lock, 1993). For example, the biomedical construction of Alzheimer's disease redefined memory loss as an illness category during the 1960s and 1970s (Gubrium, 1986). What had been a normal component of ageing was reconfigured into disease through the creation and delineation of medical diagnostic categories.

This early work provides key insights into the way ageing was transformed into pathology. However, major transformations have occurred in the organization of biomedicine in the United States since this research. The last two decades witnessed the increasing privatization of health care as for-profit hospitals, clinics, and health insurance companies increased in number. The use of technologies grew in diagnostic and treatment practices, and care moved from the hospital to the home as hospital stays were shortened and the responsibility for care work, shifted to families and friends.

The medical knowledge landscape also changed. Medical technology, pharmaceutical companies and hospitals increasingly used direct to consumer and product placement forms of advertising to shape medical care. Simultaneously, patients gained more opportunity to educate themselves about biomedical matters as support groups and organizations were formed, self-help literature boomed, and medical search engines such as MEDLINE became available.

Working at the crossroads of medical sociology and science and technology studies, Clarke et al. (2004) offer a reconceptualization of the medicalization thesis in light of these broader changes. Drawing on a core science and technology studies idea that technologies—defined broadly as any application of knowledge (e.g., drugs, the built environment, and machines)—are central to daily life, the authors focus on the meaning and content of scientific knowledge and technological applications. Through this focus, Clarke and her colleagues emphasize the need to put technology and science at the center of analysis of new medicalization processes.

Clarke et al., suggest the term 'biomedicalization' be used to demarcate contemporary medicalization processes given the significant transformations in medical knowledge and practice. They outline five processes in particular that constitute biomedicalization: (1) the increasing privatization of biomedicine with for-profit companies and hospitals gaining in prominence; (2) the extension of risk and surveillance categories resulting in more and more healthy conditions being labeled as pre-disease or at the very least risky; (3) the escalating use of technology and science in clinical practice and home care; (4) the availability of new computer technologies, such as the internet, that change knowledge production and distribution; and (5) the production of new individual and collective health-related identities such as 'chronic fatigue syndrome' or 'fibromyalgia' (Clarke et al., 2003). Together these processes help produce the conditions needed to spur the expansion of biomedical categories and treatments into more and more areas of life.

Clarke and her colleagues' expansion of the medicalization thesis provides a theoretical framework for new considerations of the relations between ageism, economic interests, stratification, and medicine. To illustrate the ageist bias of biomedicalization processes, we offer two illustrative examples.

Case Study 1: Viagra

In research and clinical trials from 1989 to 1994, Pfizer Pharmaceutical researchers realized that UK-92480 (the early name of Viagra) increased blood flow to the genital region (Loe, 2004). After this finding, Pfizer continued to investigate the link between the substance and the production of erections. In 1998, the company received approval from the Food and Drug Administration to market and distribute the drug, now known as sildenafil or Viagra. Drugs, however, need a disease, and the disease needs to be recognized by both medical professionals and the public in order to garner widespread support. The medicalization of men's sexuality included a conceptual shift from impotence to erectile dysfunction (Fishman, 2007).

Shortly after Pfizer received FDA approval, Laumann et al. (1999) published an article in *JAMA*—one of the most prestigious medical journals in the United States. Laumann et al. found that 31 per cent of the 1410 men surveyed had sexual dysfunction. Within the context of the study, any man who reported ever having experienced premature ejaculation, erectile dysfunction, or low desire received the disease label. This broad definition of sexual dysfunction increased the number of potentially "sick" men and made sexual dysfunction sound like a pressing problem. Although the initial publication neglected to include financial disclosure information, it was later revealed that two of the authors (Laumann et al., 1999) consulted for Pfizer. Despite the expansive definition of sexual dysfunction and the economic relations between the authors and Pfizer, the article performed critical work in establishing sexual dysfunction as a serious public health problem.

Pfizer further promoted the disease and the drug by launching an aggressive advertising campaign. In 1997, the FDA clarified advertising requirements for pharmaceutical companies (Nordenburg, 1998). The new regulations allowed companies to market drugs directly to consumers on television and radio as long as certain adequate provision requirements were met (e.g., refer customers to physicians or pharmacists, provide a toll free number, or provide the name of a website or print ad that had more information). This change marked a shift from previous years during which a moratorium limited pharmaceutical advertisements on television and radio. Pfizer took advantage of the regulatory change and broadcasted advertisements that featured erectile dysfunction and its cure—Viagra—

on American airwaves. The *JAMA* article, advertisements, and news articles all helped 'educate' people about erectile dysfunction and the benefits of treatment.

The rise of Viagra redefined sexuality for old men and women. In the Viagra era "normal for males, as defined by Pfizer Pharmaceuticals and its experts, is having a consistently hard and penetrative penis, feeling eighteen again, and never having to worry about occasional problems with erections" (Loe, 2004). While this definition of normal is hard for men of any age to accomplish, it is particularly difficult for old men to embody. Purchasing and using Viagra is one way this ideal can be achieved. The redefinition of male sexuality affects women as well. Whether women enjoy penetrative sex or not, the existence of Viagra (and other similar drugs) raises "new concerns for women regarding marital obligations and sexual duty" (Loe, 2004). Female partners of Viagra users are now expected to be sexually active until death.

The biomedicalization of sexuality illustrates the connections between ageism, medicine, pharmaceutical companies and media. The rise of Viagra capitalized on ageist practices that position the youthful body as the norm. Creating an erection on demand and having frequent sex are activities commonly associated with younger bodies. Putting ageing bodies at the center would create a different ideal. However, old bodies are not privileged as the model for ageing sexualities. Instead, old men and women are expected to adjust their sexual practices to mimic youthful expectations and desires.

Case Study 2: Hormone Replacement Therapies

Ageism and medicine also intersect in the development and use of hormone replacement therapies. The use and marketing of hormones have a long history in the medical marketplace. Medical practitioners experimented with hormone supplements throughout the 1920s and 1930s, and the first estrogen pill, Premarin, was introduced in 1942 (Neel, 2002). Premarin, which is still prescribed today, is made from pregnant mares' urine—a fact that is evoked in the drug's name: Pre(gnant)Mar(e)in.[3] The pharmaceutical company Ayerst (now Wyeth-Ayerst) initially promoted the drug for a variety of conditions associated with ageing, including menopause.

Menopause was defined as unnatural throughout the 19th and 20th centuries in Europe and the United States. The Victorians viewed it as a sign of sin and decay, while early 20th century Freudians viewed menopause as a neurosis. During the 20th century, physicians, researchers, and pharmaceutical interests transformed the deviant status of menopause into a biomedical disease (Palmlund, 2006). Part of the broader trend of biomedicalization, the medical profession defined menopause as a deficiency disease, which helped give doctors control over this bodily process (Bell, 1987).

The definition of menopause as pathological and the promotion of Premarin and other hormone therapies intensified in the 1960s. Gynaecologist Robert Wilson (1962, 1966; Wilson and Wilson, 1963), a man who had financial ties to pharmaceutical industries, was a key supporter of both projects, published scientific articles in *JAMA* and the *Journal of the American Geriatric Society* as well as the popular book *Forever Feminine* to convince the public and medical professionals about the value of hormone replacement therapy. Illustrating the framing of menopause as pathological, Wilson called women who did not use estrogen replacement therapies "castrates".

Sales of Premarin and other estrogen replacement therapies steadily increased throughout the late 1960s and the 1970s. The Food and Drug Association's announcement in 1986 that estrogen replacement pharmaceuticals helped prevent the bone loss associated with osteoporosis, further fueled the market (Kling, 2000). Offering additional medical reasons to prescribe estrogen products, the announcement increased the perceived legitimacy of the drugs and prescriptions soared. By the 1990s, there were estrogen only and estrogen-progestin combination drugs available to "treat" menopausal symptoms. Millions of women used the drugs, and the multi-million dollar market thrived (Palmlund, 2006).

In 2002, the Women's Health Initiative's decision to stop a clinical trial on estrogen-progestin combination therapies (e.g., Pempro, Premphase) due to clear evidence of increased risk of heart disease, stroke, and breast cancer put a damper on the hormone replacement bandwagon. This announcement was soon followed by a second one. In 2004, the Women's Health Initiative halted a trial on estrogen alone therapies (e.g., Premarin) when it became clear that participants had an increased risk of stroke and blood clots deep in veins. Moreover, the study showed that the drug regime did not reduce the risk of coronary heart disease as had been claimed (NIH, 2005).

These studies (and the publicity that surrounded them) resulted in numerous women stopping their HRT use. However, the tendency to define menopause as pathology remains. As with the rise of Viagra and the biomedicalization of old men's sexuality, the definition of menopause as a pathological state arises in part from ageist ideas that use the youthful body as the point of contrast. Compared to menstruating, ovulating youthful women, menopausal women are defined as lacking. The visible changes associated with post-menopausal life (e.g., wrinkles, dry skin) are also interpreted through an ageist lens. In an ageist society, signs of ageing become signs of deviance. They should be avoided whenever possible.

Companies continue to look for new ways to capitalize on the desire to erase the changes associated with menopause. Despite the dangers associated with estrogen-alone and estrogen-progestin combination therapies, some women still use these drugs. Vitamins, minerals, and herbal remedies, such as black cohosh, are also promoted (see, for example, Cornforth, 2007) and bio-identical hormones represent a booming new market. Such hormones are made from yam and soy, and are considered to be more similar to the hormones a woman's body makes, than pharmaceutically produced ones. However, hormones produced from yam or soy derivatives are not *more natural* than pharmaceutical products. As Love Susan and Sue Rochman (2006) point out, "Premarin (estrogen alone) and Prempro (a combination of estrogen and progestin) are made from pregnant mares' urine, which also comes from a natural source."

Viagra and hormone replacement therapies are two examples that signal the biomedicalization of ageing. Many more examples abound. New diseases such as pre Alzheimer's or mild cognitive impairment are being invented and the disease categories associated with ageing are proliferating. Moreover, each disease identity comes with a corresponding treatment regime and an array of specialists. The creation and practice of such diseases enrols a range of actors including pharmaceutical companies, medical specialists, media outlets, patients, and consumers.

In the future, new research should explore how race, class, sexual orientation, and nationality shape the contours of biomedicalization processes. Biomedicalization is a stratified and uneven practice. As such, it can affect various groups in particular and locally situated ways. While some researchers document the uneven effects of biomedicalization processes (see, for example, Cruikshank, 2003; Lock, 1993; Martin, 1989), examination of this issue is all too rare.

Anti-Ageing Medicine: The New Face of Biomedicalization?

The biomedicalization of ageing reaches its logical conclusion in the rise of anti-ageing or age-management medicine. Within this emergent field all ageing becomes pathological. Physicians no longer aim to carve out aspects of ageing as disease. Instead, the process of ageing itself is something to be avoided at all costs.

Anti-ageing medicine proliferated in the 1990s (Mykytun, 2006). During this decade, physicians and other anti-ageing proponents tried to gain scientific legitimacy by creating professional organizations such as the American Academy of Anti-Ageing Medicine [A4M] and journals such as the *Journal of Anti-Ageing Medicine*. The A4M's full scale assault on ageing can be seen in their three basic rules of anti-ageing: "don't get sick, don't get old, and don't die". These rules, which are posted on their website, represent ageism at its most extreme.

The A4M and other anti-ageing organizations promote numerous tactics to help people reach the "triple digit lifespan". Stem cell research, nanotechnology research, and cancer treatment research all provide potential anti-ageing interventions. Anti-ageing clinics and practitioners can also encourage off label uses of prescription drugs such as human growth hormone. It is claimed that human growth hormone increases muscle mass, decreases fat, increases energy and sexual desire, and can therefore counteract the effects of ageing. Despite critical evaluation of these assertions by physicians (see, for example, Vance, 2003), about 20,000 to 30,000 Americans took human growth hormone as an anti-ageing medicine in 2004 (Maugh, 2007).

The desire to eliminate ageing is strong in an ageist society, and those who accept ageing as a normal component of the life course can have low status. Geriatrics medicine has traditionally emphasized ageing as a normal process. Guiding the ageing process is more important than using unnecessary medical interventions. Geriatric medical doctors are typically paid less than many other specialities and are not considered prestigious in a medical context where technological and scientific interventions are valued.

Not surprisingly, the number of doctors specializing in geriatrics medicine is small. Only 9 out of 145 medical schools in the United States have departments of geriatrics (Gross, 2006). Yet, even as geriatrics is a low-paid, low prestige profession, its twin—anti-ageing medicine—is growing rapidly despite the reservations and scepticism on the vast majority of American physicians.

Technology Design and Ageism

Technology design is another site where technology, science, and ageism intersect. While some technologies such as walkers or pill dispensers are designed for elderly users, most technologies are designed with a youthful, able-bodied person in mind. Although technological design does not determine which people use a technology or how they use it, built-in assumptions about ideal users can hinder full participation and equal access to a particular apparatus. The reliance on the youthful body in design practices can exclude old people from using computers, the internet, and other technologies that are now crucial for participation in political and cultural life.

Science and technology studies (STS) scholarship provides a useful framework for examining the relations between technologies and users. In the 1980s, scholars working in STS began to articulate the importance of analysing how designers—intentionally and unintentionally—have an ideal user in mind when they create technologies. In his classic essay "Do Artifacts Have Politics?", Langdon Winner (1980) examined an array of technologies (e.g., overpasses on Long Island, NY, machines used to make metal castings) to show how each had an imagined user embedded in it. For Winner, technologies have political qualities; design is one way where specific forms of power and authority are embodied.

During the same decade that Winner called for analyses of the politics embedded in artifacts, other STS scholars began examining how people use technologies in daily life. Pinch Trevor and Bijker Wiebe (1984), working within the social construction of technology (SHOT) approach, theorized users as key social groups that create multiple meanings of technologies. Feminist historian Ruth Schwarz Cowan (1987) also called for research that examined the junction between the consumer and his or her choices about technologies. Since this early work, STS scholars have produced a rich literature that analyses how users contribute to the social shaping of technology (see, for example, Moore, 1997; Oudshoorn and Pinch, 2003; Taylor, 2006). While STS rarely takes up ageing and ageism as a central concern, the focus on the relations between technologies and users provides an entry into such analyses.

For example, computers and internet sites are typically designed with a youthful body in mind. The movement of cursors on websites or documents requires precise hand-eye coordination, and the font size on many web sites is geared toward those who can read small print. Although people age in a variety of ways, these qualities are more commonly found in younger bodies. People who experience changes associated with ageing (e.g., changes in hand stability or vision) will not be able to use information technologies as easily as those who do not. Given that companies, governments and organizations use internet sites to distribute information in the United States, such design barriers are a concern. Cost and cultural familiarity influence computer use among old adults (Cutler et al., 2003; Selwyn, 2004), but technological design can also create a significant barrier.

Ageism also shapes the design of pharmaceuticals. Most pills are sold in standardized sizes. Standardized doses can affect all people, but it can especially harm older people. As people age, the liver's ability to process medication and the kidney's efficiency in eliminating it decline (*Consumer Reports on Health*, 2005). Thus, smaller doses may be more appropriate for old people—a fact ignored in the "one size fits all" approach to pill design.

Groups that traditionally advocate for the interests of the old have not called for action on design issues. For example, the American Association of Retired Persons (AARP), an American organization that represents approximately 38 million people aged 50 and over, recognizes that design bias exists. This recognition is done through technology: the AARP includes two links on its website that allow viewers to increase and decrease font size. It also discusses technologies aimed at older people in promotional articles such as "Life Online: Demystifying the Communications Gap". However, the AARP does not focus on the relation between design and ageism in its reports or advocacy campaigns. Moreover, even when the organization discusses technologies geared towards older people, it does not comment on the ageist designs of new or existing technologies. Instead, all new technologies (e.g., Skype, Vista) are discussed without giving any consideration to the biases of design.[4]

Despite the lack of action by the AARP and other organizations, some companies and non-profit organizations are designing products for ageing people. The Center for Research and Education on Ageing and Technology Enhancement at the Georgia Institute for Technology is one project that thinks about design through the bodies and abilities of older people.[5] Companies such as Life Solutions Plus and Marilyn Electronics sell dressing aids, arthritis aids, and other products aimed to ensure independent living. These types of products make it possible for people with different abilities to participate more fully in daily life.

Recent changes in cell phone design illustrate how technologies change when old people are the imagined user. Like computers and the internet, cell phones were initially designed with an able-bodied, youthful person in mind. The small buttons and print on cell phones demand precise hand-eye coordination and the lack of contrast between the text and background on the LCD screen requires visual acuity. Given these design constraints, it is not surprising that old people have not purchased and used cell phones to the same degree as younger consumers.

In recent years, however, cell phone companies changed the technologies to accommodate ageing users. In 2004, Tu-Ka, a Japanese mobile phone company, recognized that they were missing a potential market, and designed a phone with elderly users in mind (Nakamoto, 2004). The phone has large buttons, no LCD panel, and the buttons light up when it is time to use them. Shortly after Tu-Ka's release, Fujitsu, another mobile phone company, launched the Raku-raku (easy-easy) phone line (Lewis, 2005). While the phone's name recreates the ageist idea that old people need things to be "easy", its design takes changes in hearing and conversational styles into account. The Raku-raku phone instantly converts all incoming voices to a slower speed so that it is easier for listeners to understand what is being said.

Such changes in design practices challenge the ageist bias of many technologies. Nonetheless, until computers, pharmaceuticals, and other technologies that are central to daily life are reconfigured with the aged body in mind, design will be a key form of ageist discrimination. As long as younger people develop and market technologies to other young consumers, old people will continually be excluded from new technologies (Cutler, 2005).

Rationing of Health Care

The third key area that science, technology and ageism intersect is health care rationing. Age-related rationing can be direct or indirect (Adams et al., 2006). Direct ageism occurs when health care policies or guidelines clearly state that goods or services are unavailable to people of a certain age. This form of rationing does not take into account the varied ways people age and is less common as it tends to create controversy.

Indirect ageism takes place when clinicians' or organizations' ageist ideas influence clinical encounters and the provision of services. This form of ageism is difficult to recognize since it can occur behind the scenes in one-on-one encounters, and/or be coded as unrelated to age in health care policies. Nonetheless, patients are more likely to encounter this ageist practice than direct forms of discrimination.

For example, physicians' assumptions about age can cause them to disregard old people when they mention new physical or mental problems. When heard through an ageist lens, patients' knowledge about changes in their bodies and minds is dismissed as a normal part of ageing. Age biases may also prevent clinicians from presenting the full range of treatment options to elderly patients. Studies have shown that patients over 65 often do not get appropriate treatment for cancer, heart disease, and depression (Anti-Ageism Taskforce, 2006). Although financial access to health care, sexism, and racism can contribute to this pattern, it is also related to the intentional and unintentional ways, ageism shapes the clinical encounter.

Conclusion

National and local policies that invest in technologies and science have helped create what Robert Butler, calls "a revolution in longevity". Particular technologies and scientific knowledges such as the practice of antisepsis in medicine and the use of engineering and chemistry to create safer water supplies can extend life expectancy. The availability of better glasses, higher quality hearing aids, appropriate medications, and safe and reliable public transportation all contribute to one's ability to participate fully in life as we age.

In this paper we highlighted three ways science and technologies help produce ageism in contemporary life. Biomedicalization, technological design and health care rationing are three key sites where technologies, science, and ageism can co-produce inequalities. Future research should examine how national policies and ideologies contribute to these practices, highlighting differences and commonalities between nations.

Acknowledgements: We would like to thank Shari Grove, Mary Molineux, Shashwat Pandhi and Diane Watts-Roy for their contributions and suggestions.

Notes

1. This article builds upon Joyce and Mamo (2006). In this piece, Mamo and Joyce argue that it is time to "gray the cyborg" and put science and technology at the center of analyses of ageing. Drawing on a central assumption of science and technology studies, we argue that a focus on science and technology is crucial to understand ageing identities and experiences.
2. For good overviews of the medicalization thesis, see Conrad (1992) and Rosenfeld and Faircloth (2006).
3. Animal rights groups critique the treatment of the pregnant horses used to make Premarin and other similar hormone replacement pharmaceuticals. For example, People for the Ethical Treatment of Animals (PETA) challenge how the horses are kept in small stalls during their pregnancies as well as the fate of the foals born on the ranches. For a summary of PETA's evaluation of Premarin, see http: //www.peta.org/mc/factsheet_display.asp?ID=73
4. To view the technology related articles posted on the AARP website, see http: //www.aarp.org.
5. For more information on the Center for Research and Education on Ageing and Technology Enhancement's projects and publications, see http: //www.psychology.gatech.edu/create/index.htm.

References

Adams, A., Buckingham, S. Arber, J. McKinlay, L. Marceau and C. Link (2006). The influence of patient's age on clinical decision-making about coronary heart disease in the USA and the UK, *Ageing & Society*, 26, 303–21.

Anti-Ageism Taskforce (2006). *Ageism in America.* New York: International Longevity Center, USA.

Bell, S. (1987). Changing ideas: The medicalization of menopause, *Social Science and Medicine*, 24(6), 535–42.

Clarke, A., J. Shim, L. Mamo, J. Fosket and J. Fishman (2004). Biomedicalization: Technoscientific transformations of health, illness, and US biomedicine, *American Sociological Review*, 68, 161–94.

Conrad, P. (1992). Medicalization and social control, *Annual Review of Sociology*, 18, 209–32.

Consumer Reports on Health. (2005). Are you taking too much prescription medication? For many people, standard doses are excessive, *Consumer Reports on Health*, 17(8): 1, 3–4.

Cornforth, T. (2007). Natural menopause: Eight natural alternatives to reduce the symptoms of menopause. Retrieved February 22, 2007 http: //womenshealth. about.com/cs/menopaus1/a/naturalmenopaus.htm.

Cowan, R.S. (1987). The consumption junction: A proposal for research strategies in the sociology of technology. In W. Bijker, T. Hughes and T. Pinch (eds.), *The social construction of technological systems*. Cambridge, MA: The MIT Press.

Cruikshank, M. (2003). *Learning to be old: Gender, culture, and aging*. New York: Rowan and Littlefield.

Cutler, S. (2005). Ageism and technology, *Generations: The Journal of Western Ge*, 29(3), 67–72.

Cutler, S., J. Hendricks and A. Guyer. (2003). Age differences in home computer availability and use, *Journal of Gerontology*, 58B(5), S271–80.

Dey, A., J. Schiller and D. Tal (2004). *Summary Health Statistics for US Children: National Health Interview Survey, 2002*. Vital Health Statistics Series 10, Number 221. Hyattsville, MD: DHHS Publication No. 2004-1549.

Estes, C. and E. Binney (1989). The biomedicalization of aging, *Gerontologist*, 29(5), 587–96.

Fishman, J. (2007). Making viagra: From impotence to erectile dysfunction. In A. Tone and E. Sigal Watkins (eds.), *Medicating modern America: Prescription drugs in history* (pp. 292–52). New York: New York University Press.

Friedson, E. (1970). *The profession of medicine*. New York: Dodd, Mead.

Gross, J. (2006). Geriatrics lags in age of high-tech medicine, *New York Times*, October 18.

Gubrium, J. (1986). *Old timers and Alzheimers: The descriptive organization of senility*. Greenwick, CJ: Jai Press Inc.

Joyce, K. and L. Mamo (2006.) Graying the cyborg: New directions of feminist analyses of aging, science, and technology. In T. Calasanti and K. Slevin (eds.), *Age matters: Realigning feminist thinking* (pp. 99–122). New York: Routledge.

Kaufman, S. (1994). Old age, disease and the discourse on risk: Geriatric assessment in US health care, *Medical Anthropology Quarterly*, 8(4), 430–47.

Kling, J. (2000). The strange case of Premarin, *Modern Drug Discovery*, 3(8): 46–52.

Laumann, E., A. Paik and R. Rosen (1999). Sexual dysfunction in the United States: Prevalence and predictors, *JAMA*, 281(6), 537–1174.

Lewis, L. (2005). Mobiles to slow it down for the old, *The Times*, August 20, p. 11.

Lock, M. (1993). *Encounters with aging: Mythologies of menopause in Japan and North America*. Berkeley, CA: University of California Press.

Loe, M. (2004). *The rise of Viagra: How the little blue pill changed sex in America*. NY: New York University Press.

Lyman, K. (2000). Bringing the social back in: A critique of the biomedicalization of dementia. In J. Gubrium and J. Holstein (eds), *Aging and everyday life* (pp. 340–56). Malden, MA: Blackwell Publishers.

Martin, E. (1989). *The woman in the body: A cultural analysis of reproduction*. Boston, MA: Beacon Press.

Maugh, T. (2007). Growth drugs don't fight aging, researchers find, *Los Angeles Times*, A8.

McKee, K., S. Parker, J. Elvish, V. Clubb, M. El Nahas, D. Kendray and N. Creamer, (2005). The quality of life of older and younger people who receive renal replacement therapy, *Ageing and Society*, 25, 903–23.

Moore, L. (1997). 'It's like you use pots and pans to cook. It's the tool': The technologies of safer sex, Science, Technology and Human Values, 22(4), 434–71.

Mykytun, C. (2006). Anti-aging medicine: Predictions, moral obligations and biomedical intervention, *Anthropological Quarterly*, 79(1): 5–31.

Nakamoto, M. (2004). Mobile phones call on elderly users, *Financial Times*, October 9, p. 8.

National Institute of Health [NIH]. (2005). *Facts about menopausal hormone therapy*. NIH Publication No. 05-5200.

Neel, J. (2002). The marketing of menopause: Historically, hormone therapy heavy on promotion, light on science, *All Things Considered*, National Public Radio, August 8.

Nordenberg, T. (1998). Direct to you: TV drug ads that make sense, *FDA Consumer* 32(1), 7–10.

Oudshoorn, N. and Pinch (2003). *How users matter: The co-construction of users and technology*. Cambridge, MA: The MIT Press.

Palmlund, Ingar (2006). Loyalties in clinical research on drugs: The case of hormone replacement therapy, *Social Science and Medicine*, 63, 540–51.

Pinch, T. and Bijker Wiebe (1984). The social construction of facts and artifacts: Or how the sociology of science and the sociology of technology might benefit each other, *Social Studies of Science*, 13, 399–431.

Pitts, J. (1968). Social control: the concept. In D. Sills (ed.), *International Encyclopedia of the Social Sciences*, Volume 14 (pp. 381–95). New York: Macmillan.

Rosenfeld, D. and C. Faircloth (2006). Medicalized mascinities: The missing link? In D. Rosenfeld and C. Faircloth (eds.), *Medicalized masculinites* (pp. 1–20). Philadelphia, PA: Temple University Press.

Selwyn, N. (2004). The information aged: A qualitative study of older adults' use of information and communications technology, *Journal of Aging Studies*, 18(4), 369–84.

Susan, Love and Sue Rochman. (2006). Going natural: Are "bio-identical" hormones better than synthetics for menopausal relief?, *Ms. Magazine*, Spring, 63–64.

Taylor, T.L. (2006). *Play between worlds: Exploring online game culture.* Cambridge, MA: MIT Press.

Vance, M. (2003). Can growth hormone prevent aging?, *New England Journal of Medicine*, 348(9), 779–80.

Wilson, Robert (1962). Roles of estrogen and progesterone in breast and genital cancer, *Journal of the American Medical Association*, 182, 327–31.

—— (1966). *Feminine forever.* New York: M. Evans.

Wilson, Robert and T. Wilson (1963). The fate of non-treated post-menopausal woman: A plea for the maintenance of adequate estrogen from puberty to the grave, *Journal of the American Geriatrics Society*, 11, 347–61.

Winner, Longdon (1980). Do politics have artifacts? *Daedalus*, 109(1), 121–36.

Zola, I. (1972). Medicine as an institution of social control, *American Sociological Review*, 20: 487–504.

3

Ageism and Social Exclusion in the United States: Implications for Social Policy and Social Work Practice

Yeon Shim Lee and Rashmi Gupta

Elderly population is increasing due to advancements in medicine and improvement in health and so ageism is an issue that is affecting more and more people. Second, with the advancements in health care, more people will die of old age rather than die prematurely, which suggests that older adults inevitably become a threat to people's ability to manage death related fear. Earlier research on attitudes towards ageing reveals that as more prejudice is directed towards older people, the more people fear this aspect of life. The more people derogate the older people, the more the elderly people will reflect not only the future that inevitably leads to death, but also one in which old people are not culturally valued.

In American society old adults are seen as declining, dependent and evoke in others fear about their own death. Old age is a reminder of our own vulnerability and what makes life meaningful. American world view is based on productivity and growth and adherence and pursuit of these values promote self-esteem. Based on the world view that in old age people have to give up goals and aspirations such as athletics and having children as biologically it may not be feasible, this brings about reminders of losing a sense of meaning and moving towards death. This passage of seeing elderly, exposes people to their own existential dilemma's and fears which motivate most people to ignore, belittle and isolate the elderly. A wide range of pressure also affect people as they move into their 60s and beyond: for instance, economic deprivation stemming from the loss of income, due largely to retirement, problems arising from chronic health conditions, and hardship associated with the impact of changes in life course transition. Butler and Lewis (1973) furthermore draws parallels with these other forms of oppression, where ageism is described as "a process of systematic stereotyping of and discrimination against people because they are old, just as racism and sexism accomplish this for skin colour and gender".

One major effect of ageism is that the news media, the academics and the social environment in which the older adult lives perpetuates ageism as it depicts older adults as being dependent, needy and to be pitied. Over a life time of being bombarded with negative stereotypes about old age, the elderly internalize the negative messages and begin to use the negative self talk by remarks, such as "I forget where I kept my keys, I must be getting old" or "I do not have the strength that I used to have as I am getting older". This negative self-talk eventually becomes a self-fulfilling prophecy as we see that older adults start playing the part, especially in institutions as become dependent on the nursing staff to do basic things for them. Socially excluded from the normal activities of citizens in mainstream society, the aged often become marginalized and disenfranchised.

Demographic and Social Trends in the US

The US is an ageing society, with 12.1 per cent of its population aged 65 and over while children under 18 accounted for 25 per cent in 2005 (US Census Bureau, 2005). Like all the advanced industrialized countries, the US has experienced an increasing life expectancy, a decreasing mortality, a declining birthrate, and a rising immigration. By 2004, life expectancy had risen to 80.4 years for women and 75.2 years for men (National Center for Health Statistics, 2007).

The US has had an exceptionally high rate of an older population—nearly 35 million of the population is 65 or older in 2005, increased from 3.1 million in 1900 to 31.2 million in 1990. By 2050, one in every five Americans or almost 87 million of the population will be age 65 or over (US Department of Health and Human Services, 2004b). During the period 2010–2030, the majority of the older population will be Baby Boomers (those born between 1946 and 1964) as they begin to turn 65 in 2011. Individuals age 85 and over comprise the most rapidly growing

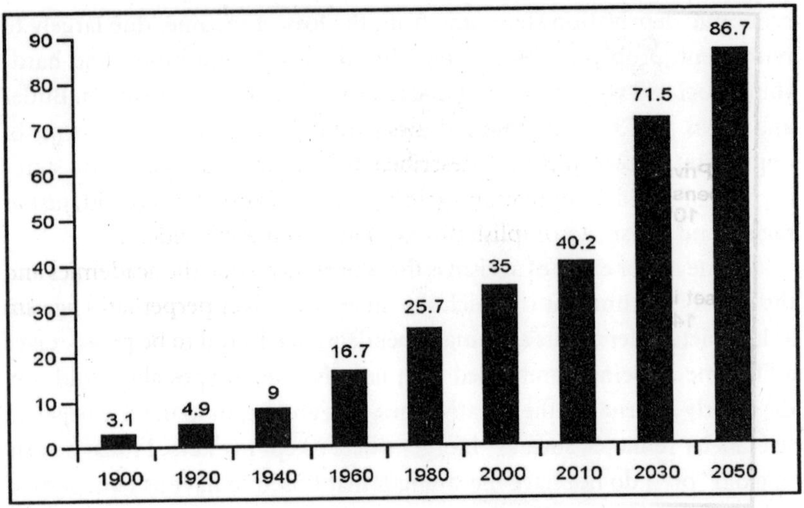

Figure 1 Number of Persons Age 65 and Over, 1900–2050 (Numbers in millions)
Source: US Department of Health and Human Services. Administration on Aging (2006). Snapshot: A Statistical Profile of Older Americans Aged 65+, p. 1. Retrieved January, 2006 from www.aoa.gov/PRESS/fact/pdf/Attachment_1304.pdf-2006-04-05

elderly group with approximately 4.2 million in 2000, nearly 42 times the number in 1900 (Federal Interagency Forum on Aging-Related Statistics, 2004). In 2005, women accounted for over 57 per cent of the population age 65 and over and 67 per cent of the population age 85 and over.

The US elderly population has become more diversified. In 2005, non-Hispanic whites made up about 81 per cent of the US older population (US Census Bureau, 2005). Blacks consisted of just over 8 per cent, Asians made up approximately 3 per cent, and Hispanics (of any race) accounted for roughly 6 per cent of the older population. However, the percentage of the older population among ethnic minority groups will more than double—from 17 per cent in 2000 to 38 per cent in 2050. The older Hispanic population is the fastest-growing ethnic group within the elderly population (US Department of Health and Human Services, 2003). The group is expected to be about 7 times larger in 2050 than it was in 2000 (13.4 vs 1.8 million) and is expected to be larger than the older black population by 2028. This demographic trend will have important policy implications in areas of retirement income, health care, employment, housing, and community social services.

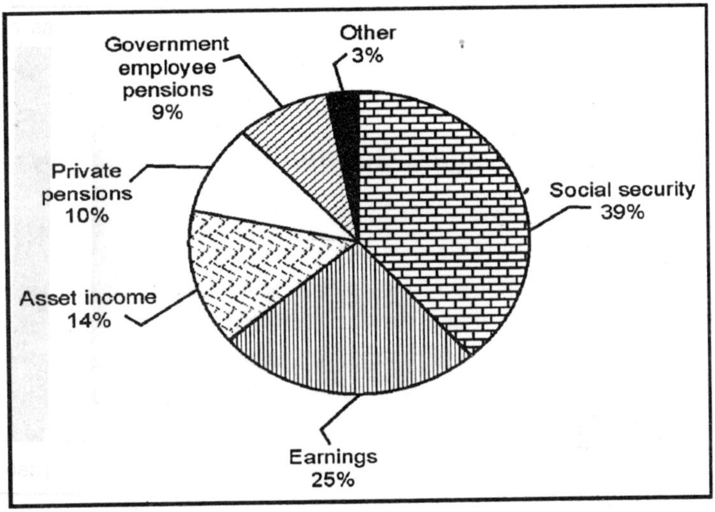

Figure 2 Income of the Aged Population: Shares of Aggregate Income by Source, 2002

Source: Social Security Administration (2004). Fast Facts and Figures about Social Security, 2004. Office of Research, Evaluation, and Statistics. Washington, DC: SSA Publication (No. 13–11785), p. 6.

Poverty and Income among the Elderly

The rate of the elderly age 65 and over living below the poverty line significantly dropped from 35 per cent in 1959 to less than 10 per cent in 2005 (US Census Bureau, 2005). In 2002, aggregate income for older people age 65 and over came primarily from six sources: Social Security (39 per cent), earnings (25 per cent), asset income (14 per cent), private pensions (10 per cent), government employee pensions (9 per cent) and other (3 per cent) (Social Security Administration, 2004). Social Security benefits have been the most common source of income. The proportion of the aged population with asset income was about 55 per cent in 2002. Home ownership is the largest asset type, accounting for 78.5 per cent of their median net worth in 2000 (US Department of Health and Human Services, 2004a). Although private pensions accounted for only a small proportion of total income, they more than tripled their share over the 40-year period, from 3 per cent in 1962 to 10 per cent in 2002. The percentage of the aged receiving government employee pensions has increased from 9 per cent to 14 per cent. Strikingly, the proportion of seniors who received earnings was significantly diminished from 36 per cent in 1962 to 22 per cent in 2002. Nearly one out of three seniors (31.5 per cent) earned less than $10,000 in 2002—albeit in employment.

Multiple Disadvantages: Gender, Race, and Class

Despite a decrease in poverty rate in the general aged population, certain groups have faced multiple disadvantages and remain excluded. They tend to experience discrimination and encounter a 'double jeopardy', because of the combined effects of age, gender, race, and class. This applies, for example, to women, and in particular, to women of colour and women without a spouse, to some minority ethnic groups, and to people living persistently on a low income. They are more likely to be poor and to lack health insurance and less likely to receive adequate earnings.

It is the conventional interpretation that women tend to earn less than men and these gender differences are particularly pronounced late in life. In 2004, 12 per cent of older women lived below the federal poverty line, compared with 7 per cent of older men (US Department of Health and

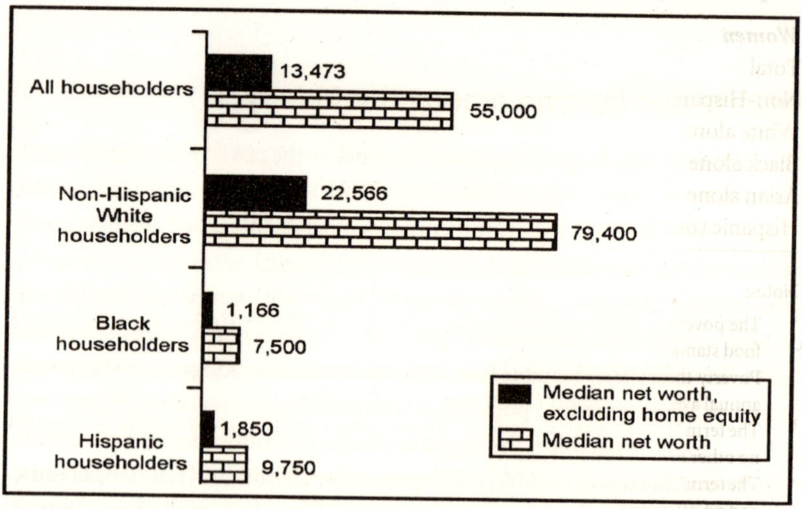

Figure 3 Median Net Worth and Median Net Worth Excluding Home Equity of Households by Race and Hispanic Origin of Householder, 2000 (2000 dollars)

Source: US Census Bureau (2003). Net Worth and Asset Ownership of Households: 1998 and 2000. US Department of Commerce. Economics and Statistics Administration. Washington, DC., p. 13.

Table 1 The population age 65 and over living in poverty[a], by selected characteristics, 2000. (Percentage)

Selected characteristics	65 and over	65 and over living alone	65 and over, married couples	65.74	75 and over
Both sexes					
Total	10.4	19.2	5.1	9.4	11.7
Non-Hispanic					
White alone[b]	8.3	16.1	3.8	6.9	9.8
Black alone[c]	23.8	37.2	11.8	23.3	24.4
Asian alone[d]	8.4	23.4	6.1	6.9	10.9
Hispanic (of any race)	21.4	44.1	16.0	20.2	23.1
Men					
Total	7.7	15.6	5.3	7.7	7.8
Non-Hispanic white alone	5.8	12.1	3.8	5.6	6.0
Black alone	18.1	30.2	11.3	18.1	18.2
Asian alone	6.8	-[e]	7.1	4.9	10.6
Hispanic (of any race)	19.3	37.2	17.0	19.0	19.8
Women					
Total	12.4	20.5	4.9	10.8	14.1
Non-Hispanic					
White alone	10.1	17.4	3.7	8.0	12.2
Black alone	27.4	40.6	12.3	27.2	27.7
Asian alone	9.6	25.3	5.2	8.7	11.1
Hispanic (of any race)	23.0	47.1	14.9	21.2	25.6

Notes:

a The poverty level is based on money income and does not include non-cash benefits such as food stamps.
Poverty thresholds reflect family size and composition and are adjusted each year using the annual average Consumer Price Index.

b The term "non-Hispanic white alone" is used to refer to people who reported being White and no other race and who are not Hispanic.

c The term "Black alone" is used to refer to people who reported being Black or African American and no other race.

d The term "Asian alone" is used to refer to people who reported being Asian as their race. The use of single race population in this report does not imply that this is the preferred method of presenting or analyzed data. The US Census Bureau uses a variety of approaches.

e Base is not large enough to produce reliable results.

Human Services, 2006b). In that same year, the median income for men age 65 and over was $21,102, compared to $12,080 for women. What is involved is cumulative effects of a relatively shorter work history of women and the economic, social and political inequalities women face throughout their lives. As a result, a significant number of older women are left in poverty, isolation, and invisibility.

Growing income disparities among diverse ethnic groups still persist. The median net worth of older white households ($79,400) is over 10 times greater than that of older black households ($7,500) in 2000 (US Census Bureau, 2003). Nearly one in four African American elderly age 65 and over lived in poverty, almost doubled the general aged population in 2002 (Federal Interagency Forum on Aging-Related Statistics, 2004). Black elderly women were at greater risk of poverty among all ethnic groups, almost three times more likely than non-Hispanic White women (27.4 per cent vs 10.1 per cent) in 2002. Similarly, elderly Hispanic people face a high rate of poverty (21 per cent). Substantial differences have also emerged in different household types. Nearly one in every five individuals age 65 and over who live alone lived in poverty in 2002 (19.2 per cent). The poverty rate among women age 65 and over who live alone (20.5 per cent) was nearly four times larger than that of married women at the same age group (4.9 per cent) in 2002.

Social exclusion rooted in marginalization and cumulative disadvantages must be understood in implementing services and socio-economic development strategies. Greater poverty gaps suggest considerable income disparities among certain population. A recent report from the Organization of Economic Cooperation and Development (OECD) revealed that the US had the highest income inequalities among nine countries and is the only country with larger income discrepancies among the elderly than the working age group (OECD, 2006a) .[1.]

This reflects the inadequacy of retirement income arrangements, further deepening already substantial inequalities existing in the course of an individual's employment.

Social Policies and Social Work Practice for the Elderly in the US

Attempts to confront social exclusion are the focus of a wide range of social policies and social work practice in the US. They are directly or indirectly formulated in all major social policies. This section examines several policies and social services that are of particular importance to the elderly.

Table 2 Impact of social protection on measures of relative income poverty among nine OECD countries in 1998 (%age)

	DEU	FIN	FRA	GBR	ITA	LUX	NOR	SWE	USA
Poverty headcount									
All groups									
Market income	31.5	29.9	30.5	31.8	29.2	28.7	22.8	29.0	24.5
After taxes and transfers	6.0	4.4	5.5	11.1	13.2	4.3	6.2	2.2	17.2
Children									
Market income	19.9	15.2	19.6	35.4	20.7	21.0	12.2	18.1	26.7
After taxes and transfers	4.0	3.6	5.4	16.9	17.8	5.5	3.3	0.9	22.8
Working age (18–64)									
Market income	20.4	22.1	21.2	22.2	21.9	19.6	13.9	18.6	16.8
After taxes and transfers	5.7	4.3	5.5	8.7	11.8	4.3	6.0	2.5	13.7
Old age(65+)									
Market income	85.1	87.5	84.1	64.8	67.8	78.2	74.1	80.2	58.5
After taxes and transfers	9.3	6.0	5.4	12.0	13.2	2.9	11.1	2.8	22.1
Poverty gap									
All groups									
Market income	24.3	22.2	21.0	24.01	19.2	19.4	14.9	25.0	14.5
After taxes and transfers	1.2	0.6	0.83	1.79	4.0	0.6	1.6	0.6	5.4

Note: The poverty line is defined as 50% of median household incomes using the "square root of household size" equivalence scale and expressed in annual terms. The poverty headcount is the share of each group living in households whose equivalized income falls below the poverty line. The nine countries studied are Germany (DEU), Finland (FIN), FRA (France), GBR (United Kingdom), ITA (Italy), LUX (Luxembourg), NOR (Norway), SWE (Sweden) and United States (USA).

Source: Organization of Economic Cooperation and Development (OECD) (2006a). An age perspective on economic well-being and social protection in nine OECD countries. OECD Social, Employment and Migration Working Papers. Paris, France, p. 18.

(a) Income Transfer Policies

Income transfer policies are primarily decisive influence on minimum standards of living for pensioners as they are likely to face low income as a result of retirement and more limited earning potentials. A strong interest in elderly poverty lies at the heart of a range of policies on income. In this regard, the proportion of older people living in poverty represents one of the key indicators of the impacts of such policies.

1. *Old Age, Survivors and Disability Insurance* (OASDI), often called Social Security, is the largest income maintenance programme in the United States. It is the cornerstone of US social insurance programme that was designed to replace, in part, the loss of income due to retirement, disability, or death of a breadwinner. Coverage is almost universal—nearly 96 per cent of the jobs in the United States are covered (Social Security Administration, 1997). It is also a work-related, compulsory, and contributory programme—workers finance the programme through a payroll tax that is levied under the Federal Insurance and Self-Employment Contribution Acts. Social Security is a pay-as-you-go system in which today's workers and employers pay for today's recipients.

In December 2003, 47 million persons were receiving monthly benefits totalling $470.8 billion (Social Security Administration, 2005). The majority of those beneficiaries were retired workers (63 per cent), and 12 per cent were disabled workers. The remaining 25 per cent were spouses, children, survivors, or dependents of retired or disabled workers. In December 2003, of all OASI beneficiaries, 85 per cent were aged 65 or older, with 8 per cent of those aged 62–64. Among DI beneficiaries (disabled workers and their spouses and children), only 0.9 per cent were aged 65 or older. In 2002, nearly 90 per cent of the aged population received Social Security benefits (Social Security Administration, 2004). Additionally, Social Security was the key source of income for 66 per cent of aged beneficiaries, providing at least 50 per cent of total income, and it was the only income source for 22 per cent. For older Americans in the lowest fifth of the income distribution, the receipt of Social Security benefits accounts for nearly 83 per cent of aggregate income.

A major impact of Social Security is reducing the proportion of pensioners experiencing poverty. Social Security kept 39 per cent of the aged population out of poverty in 2002 (US House of Representatives, 2004). The poverty rate for elderly people was lower than that of the general population in 2002 (10.1 vs 11.7 per cent). As recently as 1969, before the inception of the Social Security cost-of-living adjustments (COLAs), the poverty rates for the elderly again rose sharply, doubled that of the general population (25 vs 12 per cent). It is widely accepted that along with other existing social benefits, Social Security has made a significant contribution to reducing poverty among the elderly.

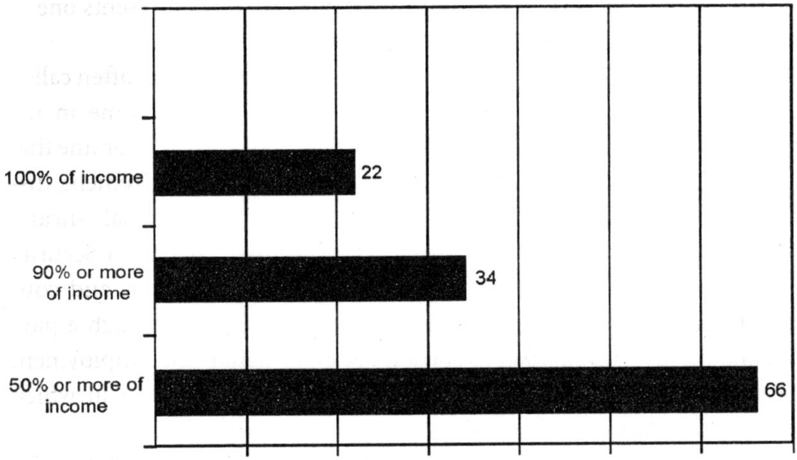

Figure 4 Reliance on Social Security, 2000: The Aged Receiving Social Security Benefits by Relative Importance of Benefits to Total Income

Source: Social Security Administration (2004). Fast Facts and Figures about Social Security, 2004. Office of Research, Evaluation, and Statistics. Washington, DC: SSA Publication (No. 13-11785), p. 7.

2. *The Supplemental Security Income* (SSI) is a means-tested, monthly cash payment for aged (at least 65 years old), blind, or disabled persons whose income is below a certain level (Social Security Administration, 1997). Unlike OASDI, it is a federally administered public assistance programme funded through general revenue taxes. Federally administered SSI payments varied by age group, ranging from an average of $491 for beneficiaries under 18 to $344 for those 65 or older, with an average of $417 (Social Security Administration, 2004).

In 2003, 29 per cent of the 6.9 million SSI beneficiaries were aged 65 or older, declined from 61 per cent in January 1974. Women are the largest group and constitute 70 per cent of the 2 million senior beneficiaries while accounting for 58 per cent of total SSI beneficiaries. A portion of older people receives SSI in combination with Social Security. In 2003, more than 57 per cent of SSI beneficiaries aged 65 or older also receive OASDI benefits. Other types of unearned income, such as veterans' pensions or income from assets, made up of 15.4 per cent of income of SSI beneficiaries age 65 or older. Only a small portion of their income is generated from earnings, about 1.4 per cent. Because of the low level of benefits and the stringent requirements for eligibility, aged beneficiaries of SSI were raised to only 75.8 per cent of the poverty threshold in 2002.

(b) Medicare and Medicaid

Combating social exclusion is an important feature of health and medical care, notably through developing health promotion schemes for older people and enhancing access to a variety of health and support services, and facilitating the participation of consumers in the design and management of care packages.

1. Medicare is the second largest social insurance programme in the US. The 1965 amendments to the Social Security Act established health insurance plans for persons aged 65, so-called "Medicare". The major objectives of Medicare were to provide elderly people with prepaid hospital and optional medical insurance. The current Medicare system consists of four parts: compulsory Hospital Insurance (HI), or Part A; a voluntary programme of Supplemental Medical Insurance (SMI), or Part B; the Medicare advantage programme, or Part C; and the Medicare Prescription Drug, Improvements, and Modernization Act of 2003 (MMA), or Part D. Although Medicare traditionally was made up of two parts (HI and SMI), Part C (established by the Balance Budget Act of 1997) expanded beneficiaries' options for participation in private sector health care plans. The MMA or Part D was added in 2003.

Unlike today's younger workers with no universal health coverage, nearly all older Americans have Medicare as their primary source of health insurance. In 2003, more than 41 million people were enrolled in one or both of Part A and B (Center for Medicare & Medicaid Services, 2004). Medicare offers acute care, inpatient hospital care, physician services, skilled nursing facility care, and hospice services. Yet a number of cost-sharing aspects of Medicare leave almost half of health spending to be covered by other sources. Many beneficiaries have supplemental insurance to fill these gaps and to obtain services not covered by Medicare: an employer sponsored retiree health plan, private "Medigap" insurance, or Medicaid (if the person is eligible).

Table 3 Percentage of Medicare enrolled age 65 and over who reported problems with access to health care, 1992–2000

Reported Problem	1992	1993	1994	1995	1996	1997	1998	1999	2000
Difficulty in obtaining care	3.1	2.6	2.6	2.6	2.3	2.4	2.4	2.8	2.0
Delayed getting care	9.8	9.1	7.6	6.8	5.5	4.8	4.4	4.7	4.8

Medicare has achieved important policy goals, such as providing greater access to health and medical care for the elderly people, preventing institutionalization, and contributing to user satisfaction. According to the Federal Interagency Forum on Ageing-Related Statistics (2004), only 2.9 per cent of older people enrolled in Medicare reported difficulties in obtaining health care services in 2000. Despite the important progress made in health care services, the limitations from a social exclusion perspective are still evident. A particular concern was heightened with a rapid increase in health care costs. Moreover, average costs were substantially higher for people with lower incomes, for people at older ages, and for people with multiple chronic conditions. There is also concern about the imposition of cost-containing features, precipitating more stringent requirements, and higher out-of-pocket costs for the elderly. Another area of concern relates to non-institutional social services for people who are chronically ill but not covered by Medicare. More progress should be made in areas such as improving preventive care for the elderly, developing a continuum of home- and community-based long-term care services, and addressing inclusive, universal health care coverage to all.

2. Medicaid is a means-tested public assistance programme and offers medical and health related services for individuals and families with low incomes through direct payment to suppliers of the programme. It is the largest source of funds for medical care and related services to America's poorest people, covering about 14 per cent of the population (US House of Representatives, 2004). Medicaid is a cooperative endeavour between federal and state government and hence it is financed by shared federal and state funds. Within broad federal guidelines, states determine eligibility

standards and establish type, amount, and duration of services. Medicaid policies are, therefore, complex, and vary among states. Unlike Medicare, Medicaid is a means-tested programme. Assets and resources are tested against established thresholds determined by each state. Yet states must cover 'categorically needy' individuals (which usually include recipients of SSI and families with dependent children receiving cash assistance) and certain low-income Medicare beneficiaries.

Although almost half of the recipients of Medicaid are children, the greatest single outlay goes to the aged population. The elderly comprised 11 per cent of all Medicaid recipients in 2002, but they made up approximately 26 per cent of the Medicaid budget (Center for Medicare & Medicaid Services, 2004). Payment for long-term nursing home care alone accounted for 37 per cent of the Medicaid budget. Medicaid has become the de facto subsidy for the middle class, covering elderly parents of current middle class who spend down their assets (Karger and Stoesz, 2006). States find this programme a costly burden even with the federal government absorbing 50 to 83 per cent of the cost. Medicaid has led to important gains in health promotion and health care utilization. However, there are also drawbacks that tend to have a disproportionate impact on the elderly, prone to social exclusion. For example, important gaps exist in coverage for the elderly and disabled (i.e., limited long-term care) and in the low eligibility limits set for Medicaid coverage. Such weaknesses become even more apparent when states cutback in Medicaid coverage because of lower state revenues.

When older people are placed in health care settings being inactive is promoted and reinforced by younger staff who outline in many ways on how older people should behave. Older people avoid doing things when they are placed in nursing home/or hospital setting as they are unsure on how to behave. Attitudes of hospital staff will influence the way patients feel about themselves and can promote negative images. As older people avoid new activities they become less active. Their belief in the negative attitudes of the hospital employees becomes a self-fulfilling prophecy. As they become less active they also lose self-esteem and become depressed.

(c) Employment

Discrimination from employment and gainful activities epitomizes a key component of social exclusion. At one level, such exclusion relates to a lack of economic security and income adequacy in retirement. Such exclusion has impacts on both individual elderly and the communities where they live. At another level, there is growing recognition of the current trends underscored significance of employment opportunities for older workers: increasing life expectancy, rising financial strain associated with costs of living and health care, and mounting debates on the waste of human capital as a result of structural discrimination in employment based on age. The magnitude of the age discrimination is highlighted by recent statistics revealing that between 1977 and 2002, lawsuits awarding monetary benefits due to age discrimination in the workplace have exceeded an estimated $861 million from 1992 to 2004 (US Equal Employment Commission, 2007).

Employment and ageism: In general, it has been found that employers think that older adults are less productive, have less relevant skills, are resistant to change and new technology, are less trainable, leave employment sooner so that training them has a lower rate of return, and are more prone to absenteeism and ill health (Taylor and Walker, 1993, 1995; Tillsley 1990; Trinder et al., 1992). Ageism and discrimination in recruitment is, therefore, evident in the widespread use of overt and covert upper age limits in job advertisements and in training and promotion opportunities, as well as exit policies.

To counter act these beliefs a large body of industrial gerontological research argues that age is a poor proxy for performance (Doering et al., 1983; Grimley Evans et al., 1992). As a result, the aim of recent goverment-backed campaigns against ageism, and much academic literature, is being done to persuade employers that discrimination against older employees is not only irrational but also commercially damaging. An argument against ageism and discrimination against older workers can lead to a sub-optimum use of human resources, including a poor return on investment in human capital. A second view from a broader labour perspective is the use of older workers as a contingent labour force or 'reserve army' to be drawn into the labour market as and when conditions demand. This has repercussion on the older adult employee for whom mobility to another job may not be feasible given the family commitments and having a settled lifestyle. In a research, students were asked to rate the employability and work performance of older adults. A majority of the students rated 'resistant to change' as one of the major problems of old age. Women faced 'double jeopardy' of age and sex, as ageing women are perceived to be unproductive, ineffective, intellectually rigid and asexual and having a marked decline in job performance (Martens, et al., 2004). Ageist attitudes with regard to the labour market, early mandatory retirement can be perceived both as working for and against the interests of younger people. It may be viewed as enhancing the employment prospects of younger people, but at the same time, it has the potential to adversely affect dependency ratios.

The Age Discrimination in Employment Act (ADEA) of 1967, signed into law by President Lyndon Johnson on December 15, 1967, protects most workers from ages 40 to 69 from discrimination in hiring, job retention, promotion, terminating, and wages of workers. Since 1978, it has prohibited mandatory retirement in most sectors, with phased elimination of mandatory retirement for tenured workers, such as college professors, in 1993. The ADEA was later amended in 1986 and again in 1991 by the Older Workers Benefit Protection Act (Pub. L. 101–433) and the Civil Rights Act of 1991 (P.L. 102–166). The ADEA applies only to employers with 20 employees, thus offering less protection. An age limit may be legally specified in the circumstances where age has been shown to be a "*bona fide occupational qualification* (BFOQ) reasonably necessary to the normal operation of the particular business" . In practice, BFOQs for age are limited to the obvious or when public safety is at stake (for example, in the case of age limits for pilots and bus drivers). Legislation to eliminate the '70 cap', applied to those who reach 70 and are not covered by the ADEA, has failed in Congress, despite reform efforts and the powerful advocacy by such groups as the American Association of Retired Persons and the Gray Panthers.

(d) Social Services

Social services are another essential component of policies devised to cultivate social inclusion. It has a direct role in meeting the needs of older people and in helping the involvement of older people in mainstream social activities. The clearest expression is viewed in the Older Americans Act (OAA) of 1965, a primary source of social services for the elderly.

Older Americans Act (OAA) of 1965: Since the elderly comprises a larger segment of the voting population, they have attracted the interest of politicians more than other minority groups. On July 14, 1965 the Older

Americans Act (OAA) was signed into law by President Lyndon Johnson. It established the Administration on Ageing within the Department of Health, Education, and Welfare. Title XVIII covering Medicare and Title XIX covering Medicaid were also signed into law in 1965. The OAA was directed to provide older Americans with increased opportunities for participating in the benefits of American society. The objectives of the OAA encompassed: (1) an adequate income in retirement in accordance with the general standard of living, (2) the accomplishment of the best possible physical and mental health without regard to economic status, (3) the provision of suitable, adequate, and affordable housing, (4) opportunities for employment with no discriminatory personnel practices because of age, (5) the pursuit of meaningful activities in civic, cultural, and recreational opportunities, and (6) efficient community services that provide access to low-cost transportation and social assistance. The major government agency responsible for administration of programmes is Administration on Aging (AoA), an agency of the US Department of Health and Human Services (DHHS). The Act created an 'ageing network' at the federal, regional, state, and local levels. Nationwide there are more than 27,000 service provider agencies to provide the needed services and programmes to the elderly. Notwithstanding its achievements of greater social integration, there are some concerns about the relatively low level of funding and vulnerable groups within the older population who are less likely to claim benefit entitlement than others (for instance, the oldest groups, ethnic minority groups, and older people in rural and deprived urban areas).

Conclusion

This present study critically examined government policies and social work practice responding to ageism and their impacts on social exclusion of older people in the US developing policies and social services to tackle social exclusion have been a crucial element of government interventions. Recently, more attention has been paid to this issue, largely emerging out of concern for a rapidly increasing ageing population. The major policies and ageing services to alleviate institutional barriers were highlighted and reviewed.

1. Implications for Social Policy in Ageing

The review of this study indicates that the impact of policies on social inclusion in the US has been uneven. Policy has been relatively successful in combating certain types of problems that help eliminate stereotypes and myths about older people and age-related changes. Among the major successes are the decrease in elderly poverty, the rise in income among older people, the improvements of health and medical care, and the focus on dismantling age discrimination in employment. On the other hand, it has been less effective in mitigating inequalities and disparities, whose effects have been accumulated over the life course into old age. These experiences of marginalization and multiple disadvantages were more pronounced in groups, such as older women (especially, women of colour), those with low income, and ethnic minority groups.

Despite the implementation of a broad array of policy packages, legal and practical supports for older Americans are still comparatively weak. Many would insist that there has been no comprehensive policy regarding the elderly and the diverse needs of the elderly have rarely been the predominant factor in decision-making. Moreover, US policy has focused on poor elderly far more than it has on the elderly in general, and on antipoverty policy, stressing social assistance and means-tested benefits as its primary strategy with exceptions of Social Security and Medicare. Dire statistics reveal the immediate needs for comprehensive safety-net measures and social protection system for older people. Three types of policy development would be suggested:

(a) Reforming social security and pension systems along with labour market measures: As the baby boomers move into retirement, escalating expenditures on social security will be likely to be financed by taxes on a smaller number of workers. Public spending on Medicare is projected to mount even more rapidly. Furthermore, with insufficient average public pension entitlements, a current pension system is mainly characterized by strong link between earning histories and pension entitlements, all of which significantly widens income inequalities among the elderly. Reform efforts should be translated into three systematic objectives (OECD, 2006b): (i) the promotion of long-term financial maintainability of social security, (ii) an adequate income in retirement, and (iii) encouragement of older workers to carry on working. A large stride could only be made when such reform begins with labour market policies, such as providing incentives to alleviate existing early retirement or raising effective retirement age.

(b) Strengthening measures to challenge ageism in the labour market: Eradicating barriers in the labour market requires effective actions by government, employers, and older workers, which addresses the full range of issues preventing older people from working. It is vital to expand the scope and quality of employment opportunities available to older workers. Carefully designed policies that allow flexibility in incorporating income from employment and pensions will more adequately enhance financial security for the elderly. Employers' personnel practices will also be key factors in determining the employment opportunities of older workers. Encouraging employers to participate more actively in adoption of anti-discrimination policies is not only a sound economic strategy, but also a good strategy in the long term. The US could learn from recent development in France and Germany where employers have received subsidies to recruit and train older workers (Frerich, 1995; Taylor and Walker, 1993).

(c) Developing comprehensive social protection agenda: A shift in emphasis from means-tested to universal entitlements is likely to be more effective and inclusive way of ensuring minimum standard of living for all older people. The full potential benefits of policies aiming at social inclusion will only be realized if proactive safety measures adequately address considerable variations and complex differences, not only between age groups, but also within elderly groups, particularly, those facing 'double jeopardy' who still remain excluded from key services and benefits.

2. Strategies to Cope with Ageist Attitudes

One response to ageism that older adults have used is direct confrontational responses, such as retaliating directly to the offender or reporting it to the Equal Employment Opportunity Commission (EEOC). This stance can mitigate the effect of perceived discrimination on psychological distress because confrontation can alter the situation and reduce the sense of helplessness and victimization. However, confrontation might exacerbate the distress due to ageism because direct responding can contribute to instigation and escalation of conflict and hostile interaction. Also, confrontation may not be an option available to relatively powerless groups, such as visible minority immigrants. Serious outcomes can result, for instance, fear of losing a job, inadequate social support at work place, and lack of institutional sanctions for reporting ageist incidents militate against confrontational responses to ageism. Forbearing responses include passively accepting the experiences or not reacting may be the most viable method of recourse for older adults. Forbearance may reduce the association between ageist attitudes and depression because it might help avoid direct hostilities. However, it could contribute to further distress because the situation is not altered and the sense of helplessness and victimization may be amplified.

Ageism can be dealt with in a number of ways, such as policy changes (Braithwaite, 2002), using the media to portray favourable images of the elderly (Palmore, 2001), with education about ageing, and death, and with contacts with older adults. Another way to reduce ageism would be learning how to cope with the fears of our own ageing and mortality. Research on death education has shown mixed results, as in some studies participants stated that their death anxiety was reduced and in another study death education brought about increased levels of death anxiety. Finally, there is limited research on the meaning and effects of ageism and its other forms of disadvantage and discrimination. There is paucity of research on people with cognitive impairments which would contribute to health care research.

At the macro level a way to reduce ageism may be to broaden our values in what makes life meaningful. In Asian cultures older adults are valued for their wisdom and close relationships with the elderly are respected (Gupta and Pillai, 2002). The clearest conclusion is that a shift from Western values that emphasize rugged individualism and capitalism to collectivism where older people are appreciated, will be one of the key hallmarks of social inclusion agenda of the aged for the 21st century.

■ Notes

1 The nine countries studied were Finland, France, Germany, Italy, Luxembourg, Norway, Sweden, the United Kingdom, and the United States. To examine income inequality among different age groups, Gini measures were used for individuals using equivalised household incomes for working-age (18–64) and old-age (65+) groups. The United Kingdom showed that the basic and

means-tested pension elements indeed helped to reduce inequalities among the elderly. To a lesser extent, social protection systems in the Nordic countries also presented an equalizing effect, although income discrepancies there were already comparatively limited among the working age-group.

References

Age Discrimination in Employment Act of 1967. P.L. No. 90–202, 81 Stat. 602.

Braithwaite, V. (2002). Reducing ageism. In T.D. Nelson (ed.), *Ageism: Stereotyping and prejudice against older persons* (pp. 311–38). Cambridge: The MIT Press.

Butler, R.N. (1969). Ageism: Another form of bigotry. *Gerontologist*, 9, pp. 243–46.

——. (1980). Ageism: A foreword. *Journal of Social Issues*, 36, pp. 8–11.

Butler, R.N. and M.I. Lewis (1982). *Aging and mental health: Positive psychosocial and biomedical approaches* (3rd edn). St. Louis, MO: C.V. Mosby.

Center for Medicare and Medicaid Services. (2004). Brief Summaries of Medicare and Medicaid. Retrieved November 2006 from http://www.cms.hhs.gov/publications/overview-medicare-medicaid/default3.asp.

Doering, M., R.S. Rhodes and M. Schuster (1983). *The ageing worker: Research and recommendations.* London: Sage Publishers.

Federal Interagency Forum on Aging-Related Statistics (2004). Older Americans 2004: Key Indicators of Well-Being. Federal Interagency Forum on Aging-Related Statistics. Washington, DC: US Government Printing Office.

Frerich, F. (1995). *Current developments in labor market policy for older workers in the Federal Republic of Germany.* Institute of Gerontology. University of Dortmund.

Grimley Evans, J., M.J., Goldacre, M.,Hodkinson, S. Lamb, and M. Savory (1992). Health Abilities and Well-Being in the Third Age. The Carnegie Inquiry into the Third Age. Research Paper 9. The Carnegie UK Trust, Dunfermline.

Gupta, R., and V. Pillai (2002). Cultural influences on perceptions of caregiver burden among Asian Indians and Pakistanis. *The Southwest Journal on Aging*, 17(1/2), 65–74.

Karger, H.J. and D. Stoesz (2006). *American social welfare policy: A pluralist approach* (5th edn). Boston: Allyn and Bacon.

Martens, A., J., Greenberg, J., Schmel and M. Landau (2004) Ageism and death: Effects of mortality salience and perceived similarity to elders on reactions to elderly people. *Society for Personality and Social Psychology*, 30(12), 1524–36.

National Center for Health Statistics (2007). Deaths: Preliminary Data for 2004. Centers for Disease Control. Retrieved January 2007 from http://www.

cdc.gov/nchs/products/pubs/pubd/hestats/prelimdeaths04/preliminary-deaths04.htm.

Older Americans Act of 1965. P.L. 89–73, 79 Stat. 218.

Organization of Economic Cooperation and Development (OECD) (2006a). An age perspective on economic well-being and social protection in nine OECD countries. OECD Social, Employment and Migration Working Papers. Paris, France.

——. (2006b). Older workers: Living longer, working longer. *DELSA Newsletter Issue* 2.

Palmore, E.B. (2001). The ageism survey: First findings. *The Gerontologist*, 41, 572–80.

Practice guide—http://www.scie.org.uk/publications/practiceguide09/overview/gaps.asp. Retrieved 2/9/07.

Social Security Administration (1997). *Social security programs in the United States.* Office of Research, Evaluation, and Statistics. Washington, DC: SSA Publication (No. 13–11758).

——. (2004). *Fast Facts and Figures about Social Security, 2004.* Office of Research, Evaluation, and Statistics. Washington, DC: SSA Publication (No. 13–11785).

——. (2005). *Annual Statistical Supplement, 2004.* Office of Research, Evaluation, and Statistics. Washington, DC: SSA Publication (No. 13–11827).

Taylor, P. and A. Walker (1993). Employers and older workers. *Employment Gazette*, 101, 8: 371–78.

——. (1995). Utilising older workers. *Employment Gazette*, 103, 4, 141–51.

Tillsley, C. (1990). The impact of age upon employment. *Warwick Papers in Industrial Relations*, 33, University of Warwick, Coventry.

Trinder, C., G. Hulme and U. McCarthy, (1992). Employment: The Role of Work in the Third Age. The Carnegie Inquiry into the Third Age. Research Paper 1. The Carnegie UK Trust, Dunfermline.

US Census Bureau (2003). *Net Worth and Asset Ownership of Households: 1998 and 2000.* US Department of Commerce. Economics and Statistics Administration. Washington, DC.

——. (2005). *Fact Sheet: United States, 2005 American Community Survey, Data Profile Highlights.* Retrieved January 2007 from http://factfinder.census.gov/servlet/ACSSAFFFacts?_event=&geo_id=01000US.

US Department of Health and Human Services. Administration on Aging (2003). *Snapshot: A Statistical Profile of Hispanic Older Americans Aged 65+*. www.aoa.gov/prof/Statistics/minority_aging/Facts-on-Hispanic-Elderly.pdf.

——. (2004a). *Statistics: A Profile of Older Americans: 2003, Special Topic: Net Worth of Older Households.* Retrieved December 2006 from http://www.aoa.gov/PROF/Statistics/profile/2003/16.asp.

——. (2004b) Statistics: Aging into the 21st Century-Demography. Retrieved

December 2006 from http://www.aoa/prof/Statistics/future_growth/aging21/demography.asp.

——. (2006a). *Snapshot: A Statistical Profile of Older Americans Aged 65+*. Retrieved January, 2006 from www.aoa.gov/PRESS/fact/pdf/Attachment_1304.pdf-2006-04-05.

——. (2006b). *Statistics: A Profile of Older Americans: 2005*. Retrieved December 2006 from http://www.aoa.gov/PROF/Statistics/profile/2005/10.asp.

US Equal Employment Commission. (2007). *Age Discrimination in Employment (ADEA) Charges, FY 1997–FY 2006*. Retrieved February 2007 from http://www.eeoc.gov/stats.

US House of Representatives (2004). *Committee on Ways and Means*. Green Book. Washington, DC: US Government Office.

4

The Ageism Conundrum of Age-Based Public Policy: Examples from the US

Joan K. Davitt

Ageism is defined as "the process of systematic stereotyping of and discrimination against people because they are old" (Butler, 1969). Implied in this view is a negative image of older persons. Older adults are thus believed to be unattractive, asexual, less intelligent, unemployable, unproductive, senile, rigid in thought or manner, and/or old fashioned (Butler, 1969; Atchley, 2000). When a person acts on their ageist beliefs, they discriminate against individuals due to their age (Atchley, 2000).

However, age discrimination can be positive or negative (Kapp, 2001). In other words, age may be used as a criterion for inclusion or exclusion. For example, if a grocer offers a 5 per cent discount to senior citizens, this is a form of discrimination by age, but as it benefits older adults, they are included. Many US public policy programmes (e.g., Medicare, the Older American's Act) originally or currently discriminate by age; one must be a certain age to be eligible. On the other hand, negative age discrimination reflects exclusionary tendencies, e.g., refusing to hire older workers.

One can argue, however, that ageism supports both forms of discrimination by age. The key to ageism is that older adults are judged not as individuals but as members of a social category with certain traits (Quadagno, 2002). That judgement can generate both positive and negative consequences. Age discrimination and ageism are interlaced with each other but also with the tendency to divide our society by age strata with age-graded roles and opportunities (Atchley, 2000). Examples of age stratification can be seen in our educational systems, in employment and in practices of labour decommodification. Ageism and age stratification can also contribute to age segregation, the systematic limiting of interaction (social, physical and emotional) across age strata. Age segregation in turn reinforces ageism and age discrimination. In other words, the more a society focuses on age stratification, the more likely it is to segregate by age, which reinforces misunderstandings of individuals in other age strata and can lead to stereotypes and age discrimination.

This dynamic relationship between these social phenomena generates a policy conundrum. Age-based public policies may exacerbate ageist beliefs about older adults which may then generate the need for additional public policies to counteract negative forms of age discrimination. In this paper, I offer two examples of this in existing US policy on employment/retirement and housing. The employment example demonstrates the relationship between age stratification and ageism. The second, from housing policy, provides an example of the connection between age segregation and ageism. In both cases, I highlight the negative effect of discriminatory practices on both the elderly and society.

Ageism and Age Stratification in Employment/ Retirement Policy

The Social Security Act was enacted in 1935 to respond to the widespread economic distress caused by the depression. The Act included provisions for unemployment compensation, aid to needy children, blind and aged, and child welfare and maternal health services (Derthick, 1979). However, the main provision related to older adults was that of Old Age Retirement Insurance. This programme enabled eligible older adults to leave the labour force with an adequate income for their retirement. The emphasis on a retirement scheme as the major component of the legislation was useful during this time for several reasons. First, older workers could be more easily constructed as deserving of relief because they had worked all of their lives. Also given the greater number of physically challenging and labour intensive manufacturing jobs and higher rates of medical morbidity at that time, older workers as a class were more likely to have a harder time managing in the labour market. By giving them an adequate income, the government could decommodify these workers, thus freeing jobs for younger workers. And, they could reduce the elderly's financial dependence on family for income security once they left the labour market. In this way, older workers were an expedient political group. They were deserving due to their years of labour, their physical health status in relation to manual labour and the boost this would bring to the economy overall.

While granting access to economic security, however, this Act may have inadvertently increased negative stereotypes about older workers' capabilities and productivity levels (Koff and Park, 1999). This programme reinforced negative stereotypes of older citizens as being dependent, vulnerable, and physically frail or mentally incompetent and unproductive. Given the type of labour market when the Social Security retirement programme was created many older adults may have needed the release from the labour force. For many older workers, years of physically grinding manual labour in factories or construction certainly negatively affected their health status as they aged, making it more difficult for them to perform in such demanding work settings.

However, demographic changes in the US began to render this image obsolete. First, medical advances reduced morbidity and mortality allowing people to live longer on average and with greater active life expectancy. Likewise, technological advances shifted the nature of work in the US resulting in fewer physically demanding jobs in manufacturing (Akabas and Gates, 2006). Thus, the idea that most older workers could not perform the tasks required in this technologically advanced economy grew outmoded.

In fact, research on older workers confirms that job performance is not necessarily affected as one ages. Studies have shown that older workers, on average, do not lack aptitude compared with younger workers, (Schwartz and Kleiner, 1999), plus they tend to be more motivated, loyal and have a solid work ethic. They also have been shown to be more willing to work flexible schedules and to offer valuable mentoring skills from invaluable years of experience (Lockwood, 2003).

However, cultural lag resulted in a slower shift in attitudes and beliefs about the elderly and their productivity in relation to employment, requiring government intervention to counteract negative age discrimination in employment. Although efforts had been under way since the 1950s to eliminate arbitrary age discrimination in employment, it was not until the late 1960s that legislation was officially enacted.

ADEA

Passage of the Age Discrimination in Employment Act in 1967 (ADEA, P.L. 90–202, 29 U.S.C. §§ 621–634, regulations at 29 C.F.R. § 1625) was influenced, in part, by the civil rights movement and by shifting morbidity and longevity patterns in the US. In fact, a provision in the Civil Rights Act of 1964 instructed the Secretary of Labour to study "the factors which might tend to result in discrimination in employment because of age and to make recommendations for legislation to prevent arbitrary discrimination in employment because of age" (Civil Rights Act of 1964).

The Secretary of Labour reported in 1965 that there was widespread age discrimination in employment (US Department of Labour, 1965). Age discrimination is based on negative stereotypes about older worker's productivity levels and abilities, rather than on dislike or intolerance towards older workers, as is the case in racial discrimination (Querry, 1995–1996). The labour report exposed the injustice of using group traits rather than individual abilities to judge a person's employability (Querry, 1995–1996). The report emphasized discrimination in hiring practices and mandatory retirement based on an arbitrary age limit (Frolik, 1999).

In passing the legislation, however, Congress went beyond the report by covering all employment practices. ADEA prohibits arbitrary age discrimination in hiring, termination, promotion, compensation, terms/ conditions, and privileges of employment (Querry, 1995–1996). It also restricts employer's ability to "limit, segregate, or classify his employees in any way which would deprive or tend to deprive an individual of employment opportunities or otherwise adversely affect his status as an employee, because of age" (ADEA). Private employers with more than 20 employees, employment agencies, and labour unions, as well as federal employers are covered under this Act (Kapp, 2001). Originally, ADEA made it illegal to discriminate in employment practices against employees age 40–65 (Tichy, 1991). This upper age limit was raised over time to 70 in 1978, and eliminated for all but academics in 1986 and for academics in 1993.

The explicit purpose of the ADEA stated in the Act's preamble was: "to promote employment of older persons based on their ability rather than age; to prohibit arbitrary age discrimination in employment; to help employers and workers find ways of meeting problems arising from the impact of age on employment" [29 U.S.C. § 621(b)]. The implicit goal was to enable those older workers who preferred or needed to keep working to do so. It was not intended to mandate work for older workers or retirees.

Age discrimination is generally based on false assumptions about older workers capability rather than outright intolerance, which is the case in racial discrimination. Thus, Congress allowed for certain employer exemptions against an age discrimination claim. These include: (1) where age is a bona fide occupational qualification reasonably necessary to the normal operation of a particular business, (2) where the action is based on reasonable factors other than age (RFOA), (3) to observe the terms of a bona fide seniority system, (4) to observe the terms of a bona fide employee benefit plan, or (5) to discharge or otherwise discipline an individual for good cause [29 U.S.C. @ 623 (f)] (Koff and Park, 1999; Tichy, 1991).

In some cases age may be a factor in one's ability to safely perform the job, such as police officer or firefighter and can thus be used as a qualifying criterion for such employees (Kapp, 2001). Also employers can require medical exams for applicants over age 40 but only when it is directly related to the specific work to be performed and when exams are required for all applicants regardless of age (Tichy, 1991). Under ADEA employers can use a reasonable factor other than age such as an individual's disability to hire, fire or promote employees, as long as age is not used as a proxy for the RFOA. Likewise, employers can promote a younger employee over an older employee due to greater seniority of the younger employee. In addition, the employer cannot establish a mandatory retirement system, but can legally offer a retirement incentive as long as it is voluntary (Kapp, 2001; Tichy, 1991). An employer is allowed to fire or refuse to hire/promote based on an individual's qualifications or actual job performance, but cannot use chronological age as a proxy for job performance.

Problems with ADEA abound. First, the act does not clarify the term arbitrary (Querry, 1995–1996). Second, ADEA has had little effect on hiring decisions, as such discrimination can be very difficult to prove (Jolls, 1996). Third, Harper (1993) contends that ADEA and the Older Worker's Benefit Protection Act of 1990 do little to protect workers in relation to retirement incentives. Exit incentives can and have been used by employers "to defeat the intent if not the letter of the ADEA" (Frolik, 1999: 67). Employers offer retirement incentives as a way to reduce the workforce through attrition rather than forced layoffs. Older workers in most cases cost employers more for a variety of reasons (service time, higher health care costs, etc.). Thus it benefits the company more, to reduce the number of older workers (regardless of productivity levels) than to reduce the number of younger workers (Harper, 1993). "Conditional age-based exit incentives can be used to achieve precisely what the ADEA seeks to eradicate: the age-based elimination of productive older workers who would prefer continued employment to retirement" (Harper, 1993: 69).

Finally, recent case law in this area has made it difficult for older workers to win a claim around the use of age proxies (e.g., years of service) [Bailey, 2001; see also Hazen Paper Co. v Biggins, 507 US 604 (1993]. In the Biggins case the Supreme Court held that age and years of service are "analytically distinct" and thus cannot necessarily be considered age-based. This decision has also enabled employers to use reduction in force strategies to eliminate older (and generally more costly workers) from their payrolls. According to Minda (1997) these strategies are largely immune to ADEA litigation as they are generally couched in economic necessity for the employer, and thus are considered "reasonable factors other than age". Although there may be a correlation between age and seniority, pension status, or wage rates, the Supreme Court has ruled that these correlations do not always hold and thus are not age proxies [Hazen Paper Co. v Biggins, 507 US 604 (1993)]. Such case law developments have made it increasingly difficult for older adults to sustain an age discrimination complaint in the face of downsizing, and cost-reduction strategies.

"Decisions in the wake of Hazen Paper have demonstrated simply that where there is a tenuous connection between the proxy and actual age discrimination, and the plaintiff fails to demonstrate that the employer's explanation is unworthy of credence, the employer should prevail (in the absence of other evidence)" (Bailey, 2001: 15), However, where the proxy has a direct connection to age, as in the case of Medicare eligibility, courts have found that this cannot be allowed as a reasonable factor other than age (RFOA) [see Erie County Retirees Ass. v County of Erie, 220 F.3d 193 (3d Cir. 2000); Minda, 1997].

The intent behind this legislation was to promote a different construction of older workers as a class. In other words, assumptions should not be made about the productivity level of an employee simply due to chronological age, but rather the employee's actual ability to perform the job should be the major relevant criterion. However, employers have long held different opinions about older workers, some based on biased attitudes about productivity levels. The fact that an upper age limit was part of the original legislation speaks volumes to the degree that ageism infiltrated thinking in the US at that time. Such attitudes still prevail, albeit to a lesser degree.

However, there is also an economic incentive to eliminate older workers which complicates the ageism argument. Older workers tend to cost employers more in terms of wages and benefits. Add to that a technologically advanced industrial sector that requires much less skill, craft, or experience to complete job tasks, and older workers may become redundant. This scenario is bolstered by the fact that workers age 62 and over in the US have an available source of income, through social security, if they leave (or are forced out of) the labour market. However, that income source has come under increasing scrutiny and criticism in the past few years. Opening the door for possible reduction in or elimination of this age-based programme.

The US and other western democracies are concerned about their ability to maintain entitlement programmes such as social security in light of the rapid ageing of the population. Such increased pressure on entitlements increases pressure to raise the retirement age or reduce benefits. Also private employment-based pensions in the US are experiencing major financial shortfalls and many are filing for bankruptcy, thus eroding the private income that retirees will receive in the future. Likewise, health care costs continue to rise and recent policy changes in the US have increased out-of-pocket expenditures for retirees in the Medicare programme. All of these factors may generate pressure in the future for older workers to continue working to supplement retirement income. However, with ageism still rampant in the US, can older workers actually remain in the workforce? Will ageism come full circle in this vicious policy cycle? We started with the need to decommodify older workers to stimulate the economy and prevent their financial dependency. This, however, contributed to negative assumptions and stereotypes about older workers as a class, making it harder for older workers to maintain or obtain employment. Now the potential erosion of the social security benefit may mean that older workers will need to remain in the labour force longer than they have in the recent past. But ageism in our society will continue to make it very difficult for older workers to remain in the labour market. It is a conundrum indeed.

Americans with Disabilities Act: Added Protection Against Employment Discrimination

Until 1990 older employees who had adverse action taken against them (firing, failure to promote, etc.) due to RFOAs had little recourse (Hood, 1998). However, in 1990 Congress passed the Americans with Disabilities Act (ADA P.L. 101–336, 104 Stat. 327 (1990), 42 U.S.C. 12101–12213 (1994)) and this may help those older workers who are terminated for health reasons. This would be the case whether age is used as a proxy for health status (e.g., as a bona fide occupational qualification) or whether health status alone is the 'reasonable factor' given (Kapp, 2001).

The ADA (specifically Title I) prohibits public and private employers with 25 or more employees from discriminating "against a qualified individual with a disability because of the disability of such individual in regard to job application procedures, the hiring, advancement or discharge of employees, employee compensation, job training, and other terms, conditions, and privileges of employment". [42 U.S.C. § 12112 (a)]. A disabled person is defined under the Act as one who either: (1) has an actual physical or mental impairment that substantially limits one or more major life activities; (2) has a record or past history of an impairment ...; (3) is regarded as having an impairment ... [42 U.S.C. § 12102(2)(A, B, C)]. A qualified individual with a disability is defined as a person "who can perform the essential functions of the job with or without reasonable accommodations" [42 U.S.C. § 12111(8)]. Such accommodations can include reassignment or restructuring of the job, providing special aids or training, and access to employer provided facilities such as cafeterias, lounges, and fitness centers [42 U.S.C. § 12111(8)]. The employer must provide these accommodations unless they can show that it would "impose an undue hardship on the employer" (Kapp, 2001; Hood, 1998).

According to Kapp (2001) and Hood (1998), an older worker with arthritis prior to ADA could be terminated under the "reasonable factors other than age" exemption of the ADEA. "Now, however, that same employer may be liable under the ADA if it could reasonably accommodate her arthritis on the job" (Hood, 1988: 8). Employers can no longer simply use health as either a BFOQ or a RFOA to fire or demote an older worker. Under ADA employers now have to explain why they could not accommodate the older worker's health condition (Hood, 1998) (see www.eeoc.gov/docs/accommodation for further guidelines on the ADA).

Ageism and Age Segregation in Housing Policy

The second example of a public policy conundrum related to ageism can be found in housing. There are two critical policies which support the concept of age segregation in housing policy. The first is related to government subsidized housing for the elderly, referred to as section 202. The second is the senior-only exemption of the Fair Housing Act Amendments of 1988. We will first look at government sponsored housing policy and then analyze the housing exemption.

Federal Housing Programme

The first seniors-only housing programme referred to as section 202 was created by the National Housing Act of 1959. This programme focused on assisting the financially needy elderly who were independent and ambulatory. "While housing projects included some special features for older people, such as emergency call buttons, few services were tied to the complexes." (Pynoos and Nishita, 2005: 245). The programme was not focused on providing nursing homes or other assisted living facilities. Rather, policy makers were more concerned with the economic need of many elderly who could not find affordable housing on their limited and fixed incomes. The rent for these units was (and is) subsidized, residents pay 30 per cent of their income for rent and the remainder is paid by the programme. Instead of folding low-income senior applicants into existing, age-integrated housing programmes, a separate, age-segregated housing programme was created.

Assumptions behind this age-segregated housing included: seniors preferred to live in age segregated environments; age segregated communities were safer for seniors; age segregated communities would provide quantitatively and qualitatively better opportunities for social interaction and mutual support on age-related issues like poor health or retirement (Nelson, 2003; Pynoos and Nishita, 2005).

The Fair Housing Act Exemption

The Fair Housing Act of 1968[1] prohibited discrimination in the sale, rental or financing of housing on the basis of race, colour, religion, or national origin. The act's purpose was to promote residential integration and reduce segregation especially by race (Nelson, 2003).[2] The Fair Housing

Act Amendments of 1988 (FHAA, P.L. 100–430, 102 Stat.1619 (1988) 42 U.S.C. §. 3601–3619) also made it illegal to discriminate on the basis of disability and family status. Adding family status invalidated the 'adults only' restrictions of many housing complexes (Kapp, 2001) which made it very difficult for families with children to find adequate housing in decent neighbourhoods with appropriate amenities. "Congress included familial status as a protected class because of evidence that housing discrimination against families was pervasive and often affected minority families disproportionately" (Nelson, 2003: 4). This practice was believed to be a smoke screen for racial discrimination.

However, the FHAA provided an exemption for senior housing defined as: federal or state housing designated by HUD as being designed for the elderly; "housing intended for and solely occupied by persons age 62 or over; housing intended and operated for occupancy by at least one person age 55 or over per unit. Under this third and least restrictive option, a housing complex had to meet three additional criteria: 80 per cent of the units must be occupied by someone age 55 and over; management must publish and follow policies which demonstrate intent to provide housing for persons age 55 and over"; and housing complexes were required to show that significant facilities and services designed to meet the physical and social needs of older adults were provided [Kapp, 2001: 18; Napolitano, 1999; (42 U.S.C. § 3607(b)(2)(C)].

Many age-segregated condominiums, cooperatives, mobile home parks and other complexes, however, did not provide such services. Absent clear regulations on what "significant facilities and services" meant, the courts narrowly construed the exemption rule (Napolitano, 1999). This forced complexes to provide services or lose their exemption, resulting in increased condo/coop fees which were particularly problematic for lower-income seniors. Thus, housing and senior advocacy groups pressured Congress to rectify the problem. Congress enacted the Housing for Older Persons Act in 1995 (P.L. 104-76), which eliminated the facilities and services requirement and established a four-prong test to determine exempt status (Kapp, 2001; Panjwani, 1995). The test requires that the housing be intended and operated for older persons; 80 per cent of units are occupied by at least one individual 55 or over; the provider has policies and procedures to show the housing is for older residents; and the provider complies with HUD regulations (Panjwani, 1995).

One problematic with section 202 and this exemption and the four-prong test is that it unintentionally reopens the door for 'adult-only' apartment complexes, in this case senior-only. Although senior-only housing is a positive form of age discrimination, because seniors are included, does such segregation promote ageism? First, ageist opinions and attitudes held both by the general population and internalized by the elderly influence the perception that age segregation is a better condition under which to live and that it is preferred by most if not all elderly. However, if we replaced the word age with race, would we be so comfortable making this argument? By separating age groups in communities the everyday opportunities for interaction across generations are necessarily reduced. Such interaction is essential to the development of understanding and awareness of diverse groups. The critical questions are: by maintaining segregation do we support ageist attitudes/beliefs (e.g., older adults are old fashioned, set in their ways, do not like children and teens, etc.); by reducing interaction across generations do we generate additional misconceptions and false assumptions due to lack of contact?

Another problematic with the exemption affects older adult grandparents/relatives raising their grandchildren/other kin. Increasingly the US is seeing grandparents and other older relatives play a much larger role in the upbringing of children. In many cases grandparents become the sole caregiver for the child (children). "More than three million children in the US live with older relatives, and in at least one million homes a grandparent is the sole or primary caregiver" (ABA, 1998). A grandparent or other older adult surrogate parent who resides in senior-only housing can be evicted if their grandchild/niece, etc., comes to live with them due to the senior-only exemption.

This can affect them whether they live in federally subsidized housing or in private senior-only housing complexes. Ironically, this is more likely to affect African American and Hispanic older adults. Data from the US Census show that 4.2 per cent of white children under age 18 lived with a grandparent while 13 per cent of African American children and 7.5 per cent of Hispanic children lived with a grandparent (US Census, 2000 as cited in Nelson, 2003). The emotional, physical and financial stress of moving can be very difficult for an already stressed family unit in these circumstances, given that the majority of grandparent caregivers are single, female and low income. Interestingly, the overall intent of the FHA and its later amendments was to increase residential integration by race, disability status and family status. However, by maintaining age-segregated housing we may further exacerbate other forms of segregation and housing discrimination, especially by race, not to mention, complicating difficult kinship care situations.

Furthermore, the focus of the original federal elderly-housing programme and the elimination of the significant services and facilities requirement for senior-only housing complexes combines ageism with ableism. Until passage of the ADA heightened our awareness of ableism, many senior-only communities had strict policies about seniors with disabilities residing in the complex. Persons with disabilities, including older adults' housing rights are protected via the ADA (Titles II, public services, and III public accommodations), section 504 of the Rehabilitation Act (29 U.S.C. § 794) and the FHAA which made it illegal to discriminate in the sale, rental, terms, conditions or privileges of sale/rental or in the provision of services or facilities because of a handicap of the buyer/renter, someone intended to live in the property, or someone connected with that buyer/renter (Kapp, 2001). Individual home sellers and owner occupied buildings with four or fewer rental units are exempt from the policy. The FHAA focuses on the denial of residency or placing conditions on residency, refusal to make reasonable accommodations to policies, practices, and services, and refusing to allow residents to make reasonable accommodations to the dwelling or common areas to allow a person with a disability to have full enjoyment (US Department of Justice and Department of Housing and Urban Development, 2004).

The FHAA may be applicable in cases where independent living complexes or communities refuse to rent to seniors in a wheelchair or with other disabilities. Several courts have ruled that tenant selection standards even in senior housing can not exclude seniors with a disability [US v Cisneros, 818 F. Supp. 954 (N.D. Tex. 1993)]. "Because FHAA extends coverage to almost all multifamily dwellings, both Independent Living Communities (ILCs) and Assisted Living Communities (ALCs) fall under the scope of the Act and are therefore in violation of the Act if the resident selection process considers the existence of a disability" (Ziaja, 2001: 4). Providers may be exempt from this policy if they can show that the discriminatory policy is fundamental to the nature of the facility and such a change would instil an undue burden related to accommodation on the facility.

Finally, the FHAA may also prohibit certain state or local regulations (e.g., zoning and fire safety codes) which restrict certain types of housing operators from admitting residents with certain disabilities. For example, one federal court found on behalf of a plaintiff who applied for admission to a public housing authority apartment. She was denied an apartment due to her "inability to live independently". The court found that this provision violated the FHAA [Cason v Rochester Housing Auth., 748 F. Supp. 1002 (W.D.N.Y. 1990); Ziaja, 2001].

Age segregation in a housing policy is problematic for several reasons. First, it may promote ageism by reducing intergenerational interaction. Second, the idea that independent seniors do not want to live around less-ambulatory older adults only reinforces ageism. It is a form of internalized ageism where the older adult is avoiding an image of older adults who are viewed as less valued. This fear of being around someone who is 'less able' is supported by and endorses many negative stereotypes that comprise ageism (e.g., unproductive, incompetent). Further, age-segregated communities are less able to adapt to changing societal needs such as the increase in grandparents raising grandchildren.

Conclusion

There are no easy solutions to these policy conundrums. I would argue that we may have greater flexibility in altering housing policy. First, a focus on universal design in new construction and rehabilitation of existing housing, holds tremendous promise in terms of making housing safe and accessible to all regardless of ability (Pynoos and Nishita, 2005). This could enable integration of housing complexes for all types of people. We can continue to support the economically needy elderly by expanding existing housing voucher programmes, enabling them to find affordable, decent, and safe housing. Of course, housing integration is a very sensitive topic and these changes would not be easy to make. It would require major cultural reprogramming to open minds to the benefits of residential integration (whether by age, race, ability, etc.).

But if we were to eliminate all age-based policy what might we be looking at? If we eliminate the age-based component of social security benefits, what would happen to those older workers who cannot continue to function adequately in the labour market? We could potentially expand the existing social security disability benefit and apply it to all age groups in order to cover those older workers who are no longer able to contribute in the labour market. The dilemma for this option is that such a programme would be much more expensive to administer (due to subjective functional eligibility assessments). Programme efficiency would plummet, running the risk of increased cost for the programme or at best the same costs to cover fewer people. This might erode support for the programme or it might increase stigma attached to the programme recipients. The other dilemma is that until we eliminate ageism in society, we continue to run the risk that older workers (no matter how able) will be discriminated against in the workplace.

In this paper, I have shown how both positive and negative age-discrimination in public policy can support ageism. It is not my intention to argue that age-based public policies should be eliminated. Rather, it is my goal to highlight the potential that policy has in supporting ageism either directly (negative discrimination) or indirectly (positive discrimination). Policy makers must consider this conundrum when designing or enacting policy to proactively prevent the continuation of ageism.

I am also not suggesting that public policy is the sole contributing factor to ageism. On the contrary, ageism is a social construction that is generated by, but also embedded in the people and structures of society. So, we must work on a cultural level to counteract ageism as well. However, if we continue to employ age-based public policy without consideration of the potential to support ageism and the prospects of unintended consequences, we may never escape the vicious cycle.

Notes

1. Originally Title VIII of the Civil Rights Act of 1968.
2. FHA was amended in 1974 to include sex as a protected class (Nelson, 2003).

References

AARP (1997). *A Profile of Older Americans.* Washington, DC: Author. At: http:/www.research.aarp.org/general/profile99.pdf.

Akabas, S. and L. Gates (2006). Older Adults and Work in the 21st Century. In B. Berkman and S.D. Ambruoso (2006). *Handbook of social work in health and aging.* New York, NY: Oxford University Press. pp. 181–190.

American Bar Association (1998). *Facts About Law and the Elderly.* Chicago: Author.

—— (2004). *Legal Guide for Older Americans: The Law Every American Over Fifty Needs to Know*. Washington, DC: Author, available at www.abanet.org/aging/chapter/home.html.

—— (1998). *National Handbook on Law and Programs Affecting Senior Citizens*. Chicago: Author.

Atchley, R.C. (2000). *Social forces and aging: An introduction to social gerontology*. Belmont, CA: Wadsworth, Inc.

Bailey, J.C. (2001). Age Discrimination Models of Proof after Hazen Paper Co. v. Biggins. 9 *The Elder Law Journal* 175.

Butler, R. (1969). Ageism: Another Form of Bigotry. *The Gerontologist*, 9, 243–246.

Carlson, E. and K. Dyke (2002). Opportunity or Obligation?: Flexibility in States' Admission and Retention Laws may give consumers the right to demand facility accommodation of medical conditions. *Assisted Living Today*. June 2004.

Derthick, M. (1979). *Policymaking for social security*. Washington, DC: The Brookings Institution.

Frolik, L.A. (1999). *Aging and the law: An interdisciplinary reader*. Philadelphia, PA: Temple University Press.

Harper, M.C. (1993). The Effect of Conditional Age-Based Exit Incentives, Coercion, and the Prospective Waiver of ADEA Rights: The Failure of the Older Workers Benefit Protection Act. 79 *Virginia Law Review* 1271.

Hood, C.K. (1998). Age Discrimination in Employment and the Americans with Disabilities Act: A Second Bite at the Apple. 6 *The Elder Law Journal*. 1.

Jolls, C. (1996). Hands-Tying and the Age Discrimination in Employment Act. 74 *Texas Law Review* 1813.

Kapp. M.B. (2001). *Lessons in law and aging*. New York, NY: Springer Publishing Company.

Koff, T.H. and R.W. Park (1999). *Aging public policy bonding the generations*, 2nd Edition. Amityville, NY: Baywood Publishing Company, Inc.

Lockwood, N.R. (2003). The Aging Workforce. *HR Magazine*. 48(12). pp. 1–12.

Minda, G. (1997). Opportunistic Downsizing of Aging Workers: The 1990s Version of Age and Pension Discrimination in Employment. 48 *Hastings Law Journal* 511.

Napolitano, N. (1999). The Fair Housing Act Amendments and Age Restrictive Covenants in Condominiums and Cooperatives. 73 *St. John's Law Review* 273.

Nelson, J. (2003). The Perpetuation of Segregation: The Senior Housing Exemption in the 1988 Amendments to the Fair Housing Act. 26 *Thomas Jefferson Law Review* 103.

Panjwani, A.D. (1995). Beyond the Beltway: Housing for Older Persons Act of 1995. *Journal of Affordable Housing and Community Development Law* 5:1. 197.

Pynoos, J. and C.M. Nishita (2005). The Changing Face of Senior Housing. In R. Hudson (ed). *The new politics of old age policy*, Baltimore: Johns Hopkins University Press, pp. 244–264.

Quadagno, J. (2002). *Aging and the life course: An introduction to social gerontology* Boston, MA: McGraw Hill.

Querry, T.J. (1995–1996). Note: A Rose by any Other Name No Longer Smells Sweet: Disparate Treatment Discrimination and the Age Proxy Doctrine After Hazen Paper Co. v Biggins. 81 *Cornell Law Review* 530.

Schwartz, D.A. and B.H. Kleiner (1999). The Relationship Between Age and Employment Opportunities. *Equal Opportunities International*, 18(5/6). 105–10.

Tichy, G.J. (1991). The Age Discrimination in Employment Act of 1967. 34 *The Catholic Lawyer* 373.

US Department of Justice and Department of Housing and Urban Development (2004). *Reasonable Accommodations Under the Fair Housing Act.* Washington, DC: Author.

US Department of Labour (1965). *The Older American Worker: Age Discrimination in Employment.* Washington, DC: Author.

Ziaja, E. (2001). Do Independent and Assisted Living Communities Violate the Fair Housing Amendments Act and the Americans with Disabilities Act? *The Elder Law Journal* 313.

5

Ageism and Modernization in Contemporary China

Douglas McConatha and Jasmin Tahmaseb McConatha

Improved nutrition and expanded access to health care have triggered a global increase in life expectancy. This spike means that greater numbers of older adults continue to live healthy and productive lives—often well into their eighties. In the 21st century, later adulthood can be a healthy, productive, and satisfying time of life (Baltes and Carstensen, 1996; Diener, Diener and Diener, 1995). These improvements, though, are often undermined by a widespread ageism that has an ongoing negative influence on how older people perceive themselves and are treated by others (McConatha, Volkwein, Schnell, Leach and Riley, 2003). Prejudice and discrimination against older adults—ageism (Butler, 1989) is similar to racism and sexism. If one lives long enough, he or she may well become a target of age discrimination.

In the past, the percentages of the general population over the age of 65 have been higher in Western societies, a statistic that reflects better nutrition, health care, and sanitation available in technologically advanced nations. In the next 50 years, however, dramatic demographic and lifestyle changes are expected to take place in many parts of the non-Western world. By the year 2040, for example, demographers expect there to be 400 million elders in China (Jackson and Howe, 2004). Many of these elders may lack access to health care in a society that, up until recently, held the Confucist's idea that "a person should respect their elders and that the older one is, the more respect one deserves".[1]

Contemporary China presents an example of the positive and potentially negative consequences of modernization. In many ways, modern China is a contradiction. Since the late 1970s, China has experienced a remarkable economic growth—roughly 7 per cent per year. Although the economic changes brought on by the boom have in many ways improved the lives of Chinese citizens, the dramatic growth has not resulted in a concomitant growth in the job market. This disconnect has partially devolved from the realities of doing business in state owned enterprises, which have had to close or downsize, which, in turn, means that they have had to lay off millions of workers. Older workers are really caught in a bind, for once they have been laid off, these workers are often denied long promised pensions and health care support. These losses have a negative impact on the quality of their lives in later adulthood.

Such treatment of elders in a place like China flies in the face of modernization theory. Cowgill (1986) has suggested that a systematic relationship exists between ageing and modernization. According to this theory, people in less technologically advanced societies, who tend to be considered 'old' at a younger age, tend to wield more economic and social power than do older adults in more industrialized countries (Cowgill, 1986). As China experiences its rapid rise into modernity it could face considerable social and cultural difficulties in regard to its large ageing population. How can one bridge the gap between the economic requirements of a technologically sophisticated economy and ongoing cultural heritage and necessity of honouring one's elders?

The connection of an expected sharp rise in the population of Chinese elders to the social and economic side effects of its transition to a modern society may well result in additional complexities: job loss, a dip in status, and a decline in pensions and health care benefits. In such a climate, one can anticipate a parallel growth in the fears and anxieties that are common in contemporary industrialized societies. In fact, this dilemma of rapid modernization may result in a crisis which must be faced by China's elders.

Ageing in the Middle Kingdom

Overall population growth in China is expected to show a concomitant rise in the number and percentage of Chinese elderly. The number of people over 60 in China exceeded 90 million at the end of 2001, accounting for about one half of Asia's over-60 population and one fifth of the world's total, according to the report from the Chinese Academy of Sciences. Experts have urged relevant sectors of Chinese society to take measures to improve social welfare and medical care systems for senior citizens. As in the United States (US), the burden of care for this group is being magnified by the expanding number of two earner families thus reducing the home care now available. Again, as in the US, the community and institutional facilities needed to help ease this burden are currently inadequate.

More than 70 per cent of China's seniors are financially supported and looked after by their families and less than 17 per cent of them enjoy pensions, with the number decreasing. About 70 per cent of seniors are concentrated in rural areas and almost wholly depend on support from their children because of the lack of a social welfare system for older people in rural regions. Those who are childless or do not live with their children make up 25.8 per cent of the total elderly population. In Beijing, the rate is 34 per cent. These people and those not being cared for by their families may be a heavy burden on the economic resources of the nation as it begins to invest in infrastructure development (McConatha et al., 2004). *The New York Times* recently reported: "The government, state banks and companies and foreign investors collectively spent $200 billion in the first 11 months of last year on basic infrastructure projects, one quarter more than they spent in 2001, according to the State Statistics Bureau. That represents about 15 per cent of China's gross domestic product, or about the proportion that the US spends on health care" (*NY Times*, January 13, 2003).

Statistics also show that the number of Chinese people older than 60, about 11 per cent of the country's current population, is increasing at a rate of 3.2 per cent per year. The Vice-Minister of Civil Affairs, Li Baoku has stated that this huge ageing population brings various social and economical problems to China that must and will be addressed. According to Zhang Wenfan, president of the Chinese Old-age Association "the elderly will be a big burden for China through the year 2050 when that population will reach 400 million, accounting for 25 per cent of the total"(*Beijing Times*, August 21, 2002).

Given these statistics, China aims to gradually set up a series of networks for the aged, including social endowment assurance programmes and a looking-after service by 2010. But the honour accorded to the elderly in China can and should be an object lesson to the US. Many gerontological experts in China agree that respecting and providing for the elderly is a traditional virtue of the Chinese people and will be continued. But help will be needed. China plans to support its ageing population through a combination of family programmes and a modern pension system. Nevertheless, based on experience in the US and elsewhere around the world, ageism may develop into a pernicious issue in China as the society modernizes. With regard to the rising electronic global village, it may be possible to assist China in its process of modernization through the selective and careful application of technology, particularly through the use of the Internet and other electronic media designed to help the elderly maintain their elevated status.

Ageism

China does not have a history of ageism. In fact, most Asian nations have had a long history of honouring their elders and pride themselves in the veneration shown to their 'Honorable Elders' (see Palmore, 2001; McConatha et al., 1991). As modernism becomes a part of the daily lives of the people of a new China it is possible to forecast a dramatic change in this ethos that may result in increased ageism and negative stereotyping.

Age is, of course, both a biological and social classification. It helps organize an individual's self-image, identity, and social role expectations across the life span (Crawford, Bryan and Luszcs, 2000). Attitudes towards ageing provide a framework for understanding one's own ageing experiences as well as providing a template for age grading of a society's older adults. Studies have found that children and young adults often have negative perceptions of ageing, these negative attitudes tend to emerge from ageist stereotypes (Hepworth, 1995; Hamilton and Sherman, 1994).

Ageism has been found to be widespread around the world. As a set of beliefs and practices, ageism fosters a biased way of understanding older men and women and the ageing process (Butler, 1989). Negative views of ageing are systematically internalized. They influence self-image and increase fear and anxiety associated with one's own ageing. Images equating youth with positive physical and psychological attributes are prevalent in contemporary societies, whereas positive images of older men and women are still scarce (McConatha, Schnell and McKenna, 1999).

Changes in lifestyle, improved health care, and increased life expectancy have resulted in an increasing number of older adults who have challenged the traditional images of old age. However, studies indicate that older adults continue to be perceived as depressed, unattractive, ill, disabled, lonely, deteriorated, and even ready to die (Haught et al., 1999). These images reinforce societal attitudes that 'old age' is something to be denied and feared. Comparing the ageing self to the culturally constructed ideal of youth can result in a diminished self-image (Dumas, Laberge and Straka, 2005). Studies focusing on women's self concept, for example, have found that once women are no longer perceived as "youthful," they are more likely to develop negative attitudes about themselves and anxiety about ageing (Dumas, Laberge and Straka, 2005). Considering her personal ageing experience, Simone de Beauvoir (1972) explored ageism and its classic influences on the process of ageing. In her book, *The Coming of Age*, de Beauvoir writes poignantly about the painful ways in which widespread ageism negatively influences self-image.

While there are a number of ways in which people attempt to maintain a 'youthful' self, eventually the signs of age catch up and it becomes impossible to deny the ageing process. When the physical signs of ageing become impossible to ignore, people then may attempt to distance themselves psychologically from their own ageing. When faced with images of older adults they tend to think, "I will stay young, at the very least on the inside". Andrews (1999) refers to this obsession as 'trying to pass'. 'Trying to pass' triggers even more ageing-related anxiety and frustration because it is a battle that ultimately cannot be won. It can result in spending the last years or even decades of life in denial.

Ageing and Anxiety in Other Cultures

Lasher and Faulkender (1993) have discussed anxiety and fear about ageing as contemporary worldwide cultural phenomena. Perceived differences between older and younger people cannot be reduced to biological differences alone. These differences are socially and culturally constructed; they are reinforced through a culturally constructed system of values and beliefs. Although negative views of 'old age' and the ageing process are pervasive, culturally specific factors influence these. Cross-cultural research can help explain the importance of culture as an essential ingredient in understanding social behaviour (Singelis, 2000). Significant differences tend to exist between Western and non-Western societies; however, studies have found that even a comparison of attitudes towards ageing in two Western countries such as Germany and the US also yields many differences.

There are considerable sociological similarities that link Germany and the US. There are also significant cultural differences as well. German companies, for instance, can publicly state that they will lay off workers older than fifty-one years of age. The German media portrays the increasing number of older adults as a threat to the well being of society. This portrayal fuels potential intergenerational conflict. A popular German weekly '*Die Woche*' even featured a headline "War to the Old" (October, 1995). Another weekly magazine (*Focus*, June 1996) summarized discussions about pensions and long-term insurance with the headline "Old Against Young: How the Old Steal the Future From the Young" (Thimm, Rademacher and Kruse, 1998). Such media coverage is likely to reinforce negative views of ageing and further promote negative stereotypes of older adults.

Germany also faces one of the steepest declines in birth rates of any advanced nation (Cockerham, 1997). By the year 2040, there are expected to be 56 people over the age of 65 for every 100 people between the ages of 20 to 64. This proportion is considerably higher than in the United States. As the German population continues to 'age' a growing number of older men and women will become eligible for old age benefits, increasing pressure on the government to continue to provide extensive services to an increasingly larger segment of the population. Germany has a comprehensive system of social welfare system based on a history of paternalism dating back to the 1880's and the social policies of old imperial Germany. Germany was the first country to introduce a system of universal health insurance and old age pensions in the late 19th century (Cockerham, 1997). The current system in Germany creates a readiness on the part of its citizens to claim and use the welfare benefits to which they feel entitled (Smith, 1987). A welfare society rests on the assumption that the gainfully employed support those who are unable to work. This social contract, however, can only be sustained if the labour force can support the increased number of retired people.

In the US the arguments over Social Security benefits have often employed highly negative images of older people as 'Greedy Geezers'. However, recent studies in the United States indicate that only a small percentage of people, 13 per cent of three thousand people between the ages of 18 and 64 who were questioned believe that older men and women have too much power (Reinemer, 2001). By contrast the majority of people surveyed indicated that older men and women are not 'Greedy Geezers' using up resources. In fact, they stated that rather than cut services, Medicare should expand to pay for long term care (Reinemer, 2001).

Ageing is often associated with physical and psychological decline as well as the psycho-social variables above and thoughts of ageing can result in considerable fear and anxiety. Lasher and Faulkender (1993) define ageing anxiety as "combined concern and anticipation of losses centered on the ageing process". Fear and anxiety about the ageing process can begin early in life. Mosher-Ashley and Ball (1999), for example, explored the attitudes of college students towards their own ageing and older adults. In comparing the attitudes of business, psychology, occupational therapy, and nursing majors in the United States, they found that although older adults were seen as knowledgeable and enjoyable to be with, they were also perceived as having physical problems and being dependent on others.

In a similar study in Nigeria, Baiyewu et al. (1997) explored caregiver attitudes of those who lived at home with an older person. Overall, Nigerians in the general population tended to have positive attitudes towards older adults, however, caregivers had the most positive views; while hospital workers had the poorest. The researchers concluded that negative attitudes towards ageing are less relevant for those who are emotionally close to an older person. Thus the quality of the contact with an older person appears to be influential in determining attitudes towards ageing. Schwartz and Simmons (2001) suggest that attitudes towards older adults may be improved by ensuring favourable contact conditions.

Similar to China, Turkey is also a country in transition. Contemporary Turkey has struggled with industrialization and modernization and the ageing population has not received significant research attention. Turkey has, until recently, had a 'young' population (Imamoglu and Imamoglu, 1992). Given the recent increase in the older adult population, however, there is a need to address factors that effect the ageing process in Turkey. According to World Fact Book (July 1998 estimation), 31 per cent of the population of Turkey is between 0–14 years, 63 per cent are between the ages of 15–64, and only 6 per cent are over the age of 65. Current life expectancy in Turkey is somewhat comparable to the US, 72 years for men and 75 years for women.

Turkey tends to be a traditional, Islamic culture, with a collectivist orientation (Aykan and Wolf, 2000), a society which focuses on close-knit family relationships. Like in many countries, children or other relatives are expected to provide for the needs of older adults. Despite recent social change and an increase in urbanization, parents continue to support their children often well into adulthood. By the same token, children continue to emphasize respect for parents and to assume responsibility in caring for them in old age (Imamoglu and Imamoglu, 1992). An extended multi-generational family has generally been considered the ideal family in Turkey (Sunar, 1988).

Studies that have addressed attitudes towards ageing in Turkey have found conflicting results. Imamoglu and Imamoglu (1992) studied the life situations and attitudes of the Turkish older adults in relation to the age and gender of the respondents. They compared Turkish respondents with those of a comparable Swedish sample. In the Turkish sample, the researchers included 166 females and 282 males, with a mean age of 62.4. Surprisingly, Turkish respondents, although they reported more frequent contacts with family and other social connections, expressed more negative attitudes towards ageing. They also felt lonelier and less satisfied with their life than the Swedish sample. As a consequence, contact with older family members may decrease somewhat.

Bacanli, Ahokas and Best (1994) explored stereotypes of older and younger adults in Turkey and Finland. Turkish respondents reported shorter life expectancies and defined 'old' as occurring at an earlier age than Finnish participants. Women in both countries also reported lower life expectancies than actual life expectancies. Men's life expectancies were more realistic. The researchers suggested that compared with men, women appeared to be less optimistic about getting older.

There are significant cultural differences between Turkey and the United States, which extend to attitudes towards ageing and older adults. Although changes noted previously are beginning to take place in Turkey, studies would indicate that older adults still hold considerable prestige and are valued and respected. They also tend to have somewhat more intergenerational contact and closer extended family relationships than in the United States (Aykan and Wolf, 2000; Bacanli et al., 1994). However, education and contact appears to have a significant influence on attitudes towards ageing. Educational institutions in the United States have provided extensive education programmes on ageing and gerontology. Young adults have the opportunity to learn about the ageing process and gain more realistic views about later adulthood. These programmes have not yet been offered in Turkey.

The results of a recent study of attitudes about ageing in Turkey and the US (McConatha et al., 2004a) support the notion that ageism still appears to be widespread. This study focused on a comparison between young and middle-aged adults from the United States and Turkey. Significant differences between country were found with regard to attitudes towards ageing. Given the collectivist nature of Turkish society and the fact that older adults tend to have higher status in that society, it was anticipated that Turkish participants would have fewer concerns about the ageing process than participants from the United States. Surprisingly, however, Turkish participants appeared to be psychologically more concerned about ageing. This concern may well evolve from the social and economic transitions taking place in contemporary Turkey (Gerlin, 2002). Sunar (1988) discussed two conflicting themes which emerged in Turkish students' views about their older family members. The first focused on more positive attributes such as respect, gratitude, affection, and responsibility. The second tended to be more negative and focused on impatience with their dated ideas and attitudes. These negative views may increase as the older adult population increases, unless economic circumstances improve and more realistic views of the ageing process are presented through education programmes.

There are, as of yet, few countries in which extensive education programmes are geared towards increasing awareness of the ageing process. There are also few education and social service programmes in place to help meet the needs of older adults. Lack of access to accurate ageing related information can result in increased fear and anxiety of ageing and concerns about later adulthood. As the population of older adults grows around the world, it will become increasingly important to address concerns regarding ageing and the needs of older adults in order to avoid an epidemic of 'ageism' (McConatha et al., 2004b).

Contradictions of Modernization

The process of globalization will play an increasingly important role in how ageing and older adults are viewed. The global economy and technological advancement will, in many ways, help define ageing and attitudes towards older men and women in the 21st century. Changes in roles and attitudes are likely to influence the entire developmental process and extend to the arenas of employment, health care, lifelong learning, and social services in many developing countries as well as in developed nations (Weaver, 1999; McConatha, 2002).

Changing social structures are also likely to create new opportunities for older adults. For example, older adults can play an important role as educators. Increased life expectancy and changing demographics are also likely to create new concerns for an increasing older adult population. Some studies have suggested that more collectivist countries which have previously held their elderly in high regard may begin to experience ageism as a result of diminishing resources (McConatha et al., 1991).

China faces many challenges as it turns towards an emblem of the modern nation state. As the younger population continues to expand and the number of available workers grows, the number of older Chinese leaving the workforce will increase. Well before the second half of this century, the number of elders in their 6th and 7th decade will triple. The 80+ population will expand eightfold to 100 million individuals (Future Watch, 2004). However, 20 years before this happens, there will be a sharp decline in the number of working age adults creating a dependency ratio in the later half of the 21st century that has yet to be seen in modern times, dropping from a high of 8: 1 in 1980 to less than 2:1 by 2040. Within a single generation "this transformation that took the United States and Europe 150 years to experience, will occur in China in just one generation" (Jackson and Howe, 2004).

The causes of this 'time bomb' are clear: falling fertility rates (less than 1.0 per cent in some major cities), the one-child policy and growing affluence. What is not set in stone are the ways in which various segments of Chinese society will respond to these abrupt changes. Among the issues and institutions most affected by these shifts are Chinese attitudes towards the elderly, the family and other informal caregivers, the social status of the elderly, retirement programmes, and of course, health care.

Modernization theory predicts a fall in status of the elderly as society advances. In China, however, the strong tradition of Confucianism may require a rethinking of both the theory and the role of the elderly in a modern society. As technology advances and tools for living and working transcend the physical limitations set in the past by bio-physical changes in the body, there may well be a continuation of the high status of older

Chinese family members. Certainly there will be more older individuals using the tools that today seem linked to youth cultures as these 'children' will be the very ones making up the youthful lower end of the ageing spectrum by 2050.

One consequence of the growth in the dependency ratio will be the increased burden upon families and other informal structures to help sustain and care for this expanding population. As we have seen in Japan in the last two decades, the number of two income earners required to support families in many modern economies leaves little time for family home care (McConatha et al., 1991). This will leave many elderly Chinese at the mercy of local, provincial or national programmes. Most researchers do not see these entities stepping up to the plate to address this problem.

Much of the status of the elderly has to do with societal attitudes towards the population. Attitudes may indeed remain stable as mentioned above, but the government might be wise to consider undertaking systematic programmes to assure that this is the case. Without an enduring high regard for the oldest in the society, China may be faced with the necessity of creating a US-like Medicare programme to care for these individuals in order to circumvent the extraordinary costs associated with national care for an elderly population abandoned or ignored by family members.

Early during this rapid growth of elders in the population, retirement programmes must be reconsidered. As mentioned at the outset, the decline of state supported pensions has created an immediate problem for the Chinese. There are solutions, however. Privatization of pensions and contributions by companies can offset some of this problem. If private companies do not create (or at least contribute to government run) pension programmes, the situation in China will become dire. As it modernizes and privatizes its economy, it is essential that the unfunded liabilities of dealing with 400 million senior citizens be addressed head on.

And finally, as with the United States, health care is a major problem of the 21st century. With China expecting to have 30 per cent of its population over 60 by 2050, concerns over health care will grow even more. As the population grows more urban, more elderly and more ill, new programmes will be needed in order to train geriatricians who can meet the expanded needs of this population. Traditional Chinese medicine has many 'remedies' which can address the concerns of older men and women. What it does lack, at present, are the human resources and facilities to treat individuals who will live well beyond the life expectancies of the past. Traditional healing systems may not be able to deal with the chronic and debilitating illnesses of old age like Alzheimer's disease, most cancers or stroke.

Conclusions

The 21st century has been called the "The Century of China". Certainly economic developments and the rapid and successful modernization and even commercial privatization has resulted in considerable changes. But there are still many challenges China needs to face. Rapid modernization and related changes in Chinese society have raised social and gerontological concerns expressed in this paper. There are a number of positive signs. Life expectancy has risen from a mere 41 years in 1950–55 to over 70 by 2004. An annual GDP of 7 per cent or more portends a rosy economic outlook for the near term, and its 'Open Door' programme which began in 1978 has ushered in many reforms that have improved the live of many Chinese citizens regardless of age.

However, there are also concerns on the horizon for today's Chinese elderly population. China can be a model for changing social structures resulting from modernization. During the next few decades, China must address these concerns and decide how it plans to cope with demographic and social trends that will have a profound impact on today's older adults as well as its future elders. If the social, health and retirement policies that are capable of addressing these looming crises are met with the planning and foresight that greeted the economic transitions of the last few decades, then China may indeed remain the Middle Kingdom for the middle aged and beyond.

■ Note

1. http://www.bergerfoundation.ch/glossaire/chine/glossary_tao_confu.html

■ References

Andrews, M. (1999). The seductiveness of agelessness. *Ageing & Society*, 19 (3), 301–18.

Aykan, H. and D.A. Wolf (2000). Traditionality, modernity and household composition. *Research on Aging, 2, 395–422.*

Bacanli, H., M. Ahokas and D.M. Best (1994). Journeys into cross-cultural psychology. In Bouvy, A. and F.J.R. van de Vijver,(eds.), *Stereotypes of old adults in Turkey and Finland.* (pp. 307–319). Lisse, Netherlands: Swets & Zeitlinger.

Baiyewu, O., A.F. Bella, J.D., Adeyemi, B.A., Ikuesan, E.A., Bamgboye and R. Jegede (1997). Attitudes to aging among different groups in Nigeria. *International Journal of Aging and Human Development,* 44, 283–92.

Baltes, M. and L Carstensen (1996). The process of successful ageing. *Ageing and Society,* 16, 397–422.

Beijing Times. 21 August, 2002. Downloaded and translated 19 February, 2003.

Butler, R.N. (1989). Dispelling ageism: The cross-cutting intervention. *Annals of the American Academy of Political and Social Science,* 503, 138–47.

Cavanaugh, J.C. (1997). *Adult development and aging* (3rd ed.). Pacific Grove, CA: Brooks/Cole Publishing Company.

Cockerham, W.C. (1997). *This aging society* (2nd ed.). New Jersey, NJ: Prentice Hall.

Cowgill, D.O. (1986). *Aging around the world.* Belmont, CA: Wadsworth.

Crawford, J., J., Bryan and M. Luszcz, (2000). The executive decline hypothesis of cognitive aging: Do executive deficits qualify as differential deficits and do they mediate age-related memory decline? *Aging, Neuropsychology and Cognition,* 7(1), 9–31.

de Beauvoir, S. (1972). *The coming of age.* Patrick O'Brian (trans.). New York: C.P. Putnam Sons.

Diener, E., M. Diener and C. Diener (1995). Factors predicting the subjective well being of nations. *Journal of Personality and Social Psychology,* 64, 851–64.

Dumas, A., S. Laberge and S. Straka (2005). Older women's relations to bodily appearance: The embodiment of social and biological conditions of existence. *Ageing and Society,* 25(6).

Future Watch (2004). Paying for the Aging Revolution in China. Monograph, The Center for Strategic and International Studies.

Gerlin, A. (2002, November 1). Turkish party is favored, feared. *The Philadelphia Inquirer,* p. A25, A26.

Hamilton, D.L. and S.J. Sherman (1994). Stereotypes. In R.S. Wyer, Jr. and T.K. Srull (eds.), *Handbook of social cognition* (2nd ed.). Hillsdale, NJ: Lawrence Erlbaum.

Haught, P., R. Walls, J. Laney, A. Leavell and S. Stuzen (1999). Child and adolescent knowledge and attitudes about older adults across time and states. *Educational Gerontology,* 25(6), 501–18.

Hepworth, M. (1995). Positive ageing: What is the message? *Sociology of health promotion*, New Jersey: Routledge.

Imamoglu, E.O. and V. Imamoglu (1992). Life situations and attitudes of the Turkish elderly toward institutional living within a cross-cultural perspective. *Journal of Gerontology, 47, 102–08.*

Jackson, R. and N. Howe (2004). The Graying of the Middle Kingdom: The Demographics and Economics of Retirement Policy in China. *CSI and The Prudential Foundation.*

Kahn, J. (2003, January 13). China gambles on big projects for its stability. *The New York Times*, p. A1.

Lasher, K.P. and P.J. Faulkender (1993). Measurement of aging anxiety: Development of the anxiety about aging scale. *International Journal of Aging and Human Development, 37*(4), 247–60.

McConatha, J. Tahmaseb, L. Rieser-Danner, P.D. McConatha, V. Hayta and T.S. Polat, (2004a). A comparative analysis of Turkish and US attitudes toward aging. *The Journal of Educational Gerontology, 30*(3), 169–83.

McConatha, J. Tahmaseb, L. Rieser-Danner, K. Harmer and V. Hayta, (2004b). Life satisfaction in three countries. *Psychological Reports, 94,* 795–806.

McConatha, J. Tahmaseb, K. Volkwein, F. Schnell, E. Leach and L. Riley (2003). Attitudes toward aging: A comparative analysis of young adults from the United States and Germany. *The International Journal of Aging and Human Development,* 57(3), 203–15.

McConatha, D. (2002). The e-quality theory of aging: Using the internet to improve the lives of the elderly in Roger Morrell (ed.), *The Older Adult and the World Wide Web.* New Jersey: Lawrence Earlbaum Co.

McConatha, J. Tahmaseb, F. Schnell and A. McKenna (1999). Description of Older Adults as Depicted in Magazine Advertisements. *Psychological Reports, 85, 1051–56.*

McConatha, P.D., Tahmaseb J. McConatha and B. Cinelli, (1991). Japan's coming crisis: Problems for the honorable elders. *Journal of Applied Gerontology,* 10, 224–35.

Mosher-Asley, P.M. and P. Ball (1999). Attitudes of college students toward elderly persons and their perceptions of themselves at age 75. *Educational Gerontology,* 2, 89–103.

Palmore, E.B. (2001). The ageism survey: First findings. *The Gerontologist,* 41(5), 572–75.

Reinemer, M. (2001). *NCOA survey heralds new age of old age.* (http.www.//noca.org.publications/inno1_01/myths.html) Retrieved 5/2/02.

Schwartz, L.K. and J.P. Simmons (2001). Contact quality and attitudes toward the elderly. *Educational Gerontology,* 2, 127–38.

Singelis, T. (2000). Some thoughts on the future of cross-cultural social psychology. *Journal of Cross-Cultural Psychology*, 31(1), 76–91.

Smith, T. (1987). The polls: A report. The welfare state in cross-national perspective. *Public Opinion Quarterly*, 51(3), 404–421.

Sunar, D. (1988). Attitudes of Turkish students toward elderly relatives. *Journal of Cross-Cultural Gerontology*, 3, 41–52.

Thimm, C., Rademacher, U. and L. Kruse (1998). Age stereotypes and patronizing messages: Features of age-adapted speech in technical instructions to the elderly. *Journal of Applied Communication Research*, 26(1), 66–82.

War to the Old. (1995, October). *Die Woche.*

Weaver, J. (1999). Special issue: Aging education: Preparing for the 21st Century. *Educational Gerontology*, 25(6), 475–78.

World Fact Book. (1998). Turkey. Available: http:/www.tradeport.org/ts/countries/turkey/wofact.htm.

6

Ageism in Health Care: A British Perspective

Arup K. Banerjee

There are three common forms of prejudice in society: racism, sexism and ageism. Whilst the first two are fought hard by the victims and perpetrators reprimanded, the last one gets ignored by most, including the aggrieved! Furthermore, such prejudice and negative attitude to old age and the aged, can be caused by the elders themselves. How often it is said by an older individual, "you can't do anything for me doctor—it's my age; don't waste time on me".

Health care is an integral part of day-to-day social life and the professionals there are also members of the same society with similar attitudes and prejudices.

Let's look into the types of age prejudice which can and do exist within such a global scenario. This can be divided into three broad categories: primary, secondary and tertiary (Banerjee, 1998, 2003). Primary ageism is evident when someone is denied an established and well validated treatment to an individual just because of chronological age. Examples of such ageist discrimination will be quoted and discussed later. Denial of certain opportunities or facilities also could be counted within this category. Secondary ageism is about collective discrimination, e.g., poorer accommodation in hospitals for older and frailer patients, policies to avoid frail older patients, with multiple pathologies, being admitted to hospital or even to be seen by a specialist doctor. The story goes that once the Director of Medical Education, a pathologist himself, in a district hospital had suggested dumping the outdated medical books from the main hospital library to the local Geriatric Department, commenting "for older people old books are quite adequate!" Such remarks, even jokingly made, do, not only, reflect bad taste but a dangerous underlying attitude! Tertiary ageism is about downgrading the specialty of elderly care and those who are committed to it. A fully trained excellent nurse working in a Rehabilitation Unit for Older People or even in a stroke ward, is frequently looked down upon by her colleagues working in more glamorous areas e.g., operating theatres or maternity units. A highly qualified physician in geriatric medicine with a metre long list of peer reviewed publications and several monographs, is often labeled as a 'clinical undertaker' or a 'social activist'!

The overall attitude to old age is partly responsible for this. This is the era of youthfulness and rat-race—as faster as possible, time for ignoring and being indifferent to the past. Everyone is running all the time; whether they are going anywhere is, however, questionable. Older people are 'history'; they are no longer financially productive, politically powerful or sexually presentable. Therefore, they do no longer matter. Yes, by all means, be kind to them and give them food and shelter, but that is all; they are no longer full members of the society. Leave them to spend time with God! They are second class citizens with third class status! Accordingly, the special needs for the old and the infirm remain unmet. The shelves are too high in the supermarkets, corner shops and local post offices close down, no rest provisions for the weak and infirm in hypermarkets with mile long alleyways! Anti-ageing creams (although these are useless) are advertised by 21 old dolly-birds; one rarely sees an older model in a clothing brochure. How often does one see a special page for senior citizens in a newspaper similar to those for children?

Sadly, the health professionals reflect the overall social attitude to older people and are not immune to 'ageism' themselves. A survey among different categories of hospital staff in four large hospitals revealed a significant level of 'ageist' attitude to older patients, born mainly out of ignorance. Those with specialized training in elderly care were, however, more positive to ageing (Hanley, Khan, Kumar and Banerjee, 2004). Fortunately not all is bad and unhelpful. In the UK, older people can travel free in public transports during the off-peak hours, receive additional payments for heating in winter along with other benefits—some means—tested. But these are 'official' state measures, often paid out of the lifelong contributions made by all. This is due to the country's welfare system; it does not impart a positive attitude to old age!

Despite a welfare state with health care 'free' at the point of delivery and a state pension for all retired citizens, the working class people face significant financial hardship after retirement. Those with personal savings and/or additional occupational pensions are somewhat better but a large proportion of the retired people depend on a state pension grossly inadequate for a reasonably comfortable living. Costs of heating and other utilities have been steadily increasing at a much faster rate than inflation, but the annual increase in state pensions remain pegged at the minimum possible level. Accordingly poverty is increasingly evident among the ordinary older people. 'Wealthism' comes into the equation; money empowers people, poverty weakens! A poor old person is more likely to be discriminated exactly the same way as a poor young person often is.

In the UK, privately purchased care with the aid of health insurance system is very common but chronic on-going problems are not usually 'covered' by the insurers, so (a) the old cannot afford private health care anyway, and (b) quite often those available are of no great usefulness to many of them who are chronically sick or demented. This must be an example of 'ageism' in a very broad sense. On the other hand, although a few, there are very rich retired people too, enjoying a very happy living.

Rationing of medical care is inevitable in one form or another. All medical personnel make decisions each day on withholding certain forms of treatments from certain categories of patients. Withholding gall bladder surgery from a person of a BMI of 46 is not rationing, it is a safe clinical practice! Or discontinuing antibiotics from a terminally ill patient likely to die within a few days is also a sensible clinical practice. However, when a 75 year old is denied anti-cancer drugs or renal dialysis without any valid clinical reason, that amounts to rationing. Interestingly, such treatment could then be 'purchased' in the private market by a 'rich' 75 year old! It is, perhaps, difficult to comprehend such a scenario in countries like India where there is no such 'cradle to grave' National Health Service provision at the taxpayers expense. Individuals need to 'pay' for their care anyway.

With the steady increase in costs of medical care, expensive medicines, complex advanced techniques etc., constant debates are taking place whether chronological age should be considered in the overall measurements of cost-effectiveness (Harris, 2006). Quality Adjusted Life Years

(QALY) have been used as an argument to deny certain medications or treatment to older people. Demarcation between rationing and age discrimination becomes difficult in such circumstance (Gold et al., 1996). As mentioned earlier, it is likely that some form of age-based ' rationing' will be introduced in an increasing number of areas but that should be done overtly with everyone's knowledge and consensus. There must not be any place for personal prejudice or dogma in health care.

Severe unscrupulous rationing or denial of care can, in some instance amount to 'negligence'. The victim, if not well informed or vocal, may not appreciate such 'neglect' and protest such denial. More knowledge, better user-friendly information and advocacy should ultimately be able to rectify such serious face of ageist discrimination in health care. Fortunately such situation does not arise often.

Let us now look at a few specific areas of ageist approach to the provision of care.

A report published by the Royal College of Physicians of London had identified the general inequity in the provision of both non-invasive and invasive cardiological services to older people and had recommended some restorative actions (RCP Report, 1991). The media had been fairly open and critical of any such discriminatory practice. Despite such publicity and campaign, the situation is not yet perfect; cardiac catheterizations are often denied to older patients. Coronary care units also follow ageist policies on admissions to the units and on thrombolysis (Dudley and Burns, 1992). Subsequent to the Government's National Service Framework for Older People (DOH, 2001) and an unequivocal stand against all forms of ageist practice within the NHS, things are beginning to improve. A survey of a number of critical care units, looking after seriously ill cardiac patients, failed to note any ageist bias in their patient selection (Hubbard et al., 2003). This, however, could not confirm whether there were any choices made among the overall patient population prior to surgery or even their referrals to specialist centers. Improvements have also been occurring in CABG, angioplasty, valve replacements etc., according to a reported survey (Lawson-Matthew, 1995). It may be difficult to understand this anomaly between the young and the old in countries like India where such medical care is largely dependent on peoples' ability to pay; it would be interesting to find out whether any such discrimination exists in the 'free' state sectors.

Provision of renal services, e.g., CAPD and transplantation is also restricted towards older people; according to the official government sources. About two-thirds of patients above 70 with renal disorders are refused dialysis or transplantation. The Welsh Health Department has recently released guidelines for renal services (2006) attempting to overcome any ageist discrimination. Unfortunately, shortage of donor kidneys is also a major problem here. Younger Asian communities have been implicated as larger net recipients, yet refusing to donate their organs.

In the cancer service also, such discrimination has been observed. Only a miniscule number of older subjects are seriously investigated for a correct diagnosis; even fewer ultimately receive any curative treatment (Turner et al., 1999). The British Thoracic Society had commented on the inappropriate and unfair handling of elderly lung cancer patients most of whom are denied treatment (Agnew, 1997). Expensive anti-cancer measures, medications etc., are considered as wasteful on older patients who are unlikely to have a longer life span anyway! Explanations are offered, highlighting the possible 'toxicities' and 'complications' in older patients. Even the media in the UK are becoming increasingly aware of such discriminatory practice in cancer care. Critical comments have been made on the 'exclusion' of over 70s in the large bowel cancer screening programmes, thereby 'missing' nearly 25 per cent of such cancers in the community. It seems such an exclusion was necessary to fit in with inadequate national health care resources 'prioritized' for younger individuals! (*The Daily Telegraph*, September 13, 2006)—was it rationing or discrimination?

Although cerebrovascular disorders or strokes occur in people of all ages, these are more common in older people with equally devastating clinical, social and fiscal consequences. Sadly it is broadly considered as an 'old person's disease' with a lower priority in national resource allocation. The British Stroke Association, the major national charity promoting higher standards in stroke care and research/training, has enough evidence of ageist discrimination towards and within it (Stroke Association, 2004). Since the publication of the Governments Service Framework (NSF for older people, 2001) with stroke as one of the target areas, the situation has somewhat improved; although it is far from satisfactory and remains patchy and fragmented (RCP Sentinel Stroke Audit, 2004). A more recent report (Young, 2006) has identified discriminatory practice in the field of stroke prevention. Transient ischaemic attacks, a well-known precursor of a full stroke, still remain under-investigated and subsequently under-treated without any clinical justification (Fairhead and Rothwell, 2006).

Stroke disorders, if to be handled appropriately for a better outcome, warrant special knowledge and expertise; an effective multi-professional team is essential. A 'cure' for stroke is not yet available; certain measures, if properly taken, may, in some instances result in a better outcome. Accordingly, everything possible should be done to reduce its incidence. Aggressive treatment of TIAs are therefore so important.

Mental health care including for Alzheimer's disease (AD) has also been criticized on their unfairness to older clients. Whilst Alzheimers is principally a disease of old age, other mental conditions in older people do not always receive the fullest possible attention or assessment either (Burns *et al.*, 2001). The overall facilities and care provisions for Alzheimers are usually inadequate. The scientific evidence for the efficacy of the new treatments for AD, remains controversial; it would therefore be inappropriate to make any claim for ageist practice in this respect. But non controversial social care and support for the caregivers are also grossly inadequate. Had this condition affected the younger population or children, the sceanario would have probably been totally different.

In the UK, where the health care is provided from the general taxation resources by the state, 'evidence-based' clinical practices tend to get priority and fundings. Accordingly clinical trials and credible clinical research become closely linked with the delivery of care. One of the difficulties with the clinical practice of old-age medicine (not widely known in the subcontinent) is lack of such research-based evidence in many areas. Anecdotal practice becomes commonplace which cannot stand scientific evaluation or scrutiny. Even more dangerous is the practice of prescribing medications to older individuals with multiple pathologies, by extrapolating their safety and usefulness only on younger trial subjects. In 1997, at a survey of all the published papers in four well-known peer-reviewed British journals, nearly 30 per cent of those were found to exclude older subjects without any apparent reason (Bugeja, Kumar and Banerjee, 1997). A similar survey undertaken a few years later (McMurdo et al., 2006) had only shown a small improvement in such 'ageism' in research. It had been suggested that all researchers and trialists ought to remain aware of this issue with revisions of their protocol designs. Multiple co-morbidities and medications might be the reasons for such behaviour in the usual practice of research (Bene and

Liston, 1998). With the health care delivery becoming increasingly dependent on 'evidence' accrued from research activities, exclusion of older subjects or avoidance of research on ageing and age-related disorders, must be unethical warranting a change in research practice.

In a resource-limited publicly accountable health care system, some elements of prioritization and targeting are bound to occur. It can be argued that application of measures and methods of 'unproven' value is also incorrect and unethical. But that is not the issue here. Methods of reconsidering or rationing care provisions through deference, delay, dilution and discharge, are becoming increasingly common; and this is disadvantaging the older people more than any thing else (Banerjee, 1998).

Education and specialized training in elderly care and in medicine of old age is encouraged in the West; although its extent and depth remain somewhat questionable. The antagonists claim that there was nothing special about old age or older people—they are all adults! I remember a similar argument against paediatrics, during my medical student days in Calcutta; 'well' used to say the Professor of Medicine "children are little adults—place them in cots and give them small quantities of medicines."

Today, it is unthinkable for a sick child not to be looked after by personnel without specialized qualifications in childhood medicine or nursing. Failure to provide tailor made specialized and effective care also amounts to 'indirect negligence' and reflect age prejudice. Inclusion of a comprehensive training package in geriatric medicine within the undergraduate medical curriculum has been accepted in the UK for more than 30 years with nearly 40 academic centres around the country. Specialized nurse training has also been on going for many years; so in the fields of therapy services, social work and many other areas. Despite all these, problems still exist. As mentioned earlier, general attitude to old age still remains largely negative. The three factors which are likely to be the 'drivers' of health care throughout the globe are: (a) technological advances and innovative medications; (b) demographic changes, and (c) consumerism. Perhaps it is this last factor which will change the 'attitudes and actions' of the professionals and the state in due course. In this country, doctors are no longer on the driving seat—the patients are gradually taking over that role. Choice, information, empowerment, decision-sharing etc. are now the hot terminologies and the professionals, particularly the medicos, are expected to comply with these. The General Medical Council is increasingly being 'run' by layities and doctors' self-regulatory system is slowly being taken over by the general members of the public. As a result, hopefully, individual views and/or prejudices on age or any particular form of treatment or on the venue of its delivery, etc., will all change.

In countries like India, where large amount of health care is still purchased by the individual patients or their relatives, such 'consumerism' already exists. Accordingly chances of any blatant ageism are unlikely. The apparent lack of 'specialization' in this area and inadequacies of appropriate service provisions for older people, however, do look like 'discriminatory', at least to an outsider. Poor understanding of the ageing process, influences of ageing over illnesses and vice versa, widespread polypharmacy on older patients, poor or non-existent rehabilitation infrastructures, virtual absence of long-term specialized care facilities, are not in keeping with the twenty-first century global scenario. Many might label these as 'ageist'! Training for health professionals of all kinds, in these areas, are at best patchy and at worst, non-existent! In many situation, the older people are nothing but a commercial commodity!

So, what needs to be done about ageist behaviour and practice in health care, whichever country it might exist and whatever form it might take. In the UK, the National Service Framework for Older People has commenced to address this problem as their number one target; "all forms of discrimination on the basis of chronological age must be rooted out of health care practice". This kind of official stance is a good start but such 'ambitions' must result in concrete outcomes with change of practice. In societies with largely patient purchased 'private' health care with or without medical insurance arrangements, the insurance policies often discriminate against the old with 'exclusion' clauses for conditions likely to affect the aged, e.g., the chronic disabling disorders. This is expected, as the 'profit' margins on such conditions are nil; insurers making a loss instead. The state can only take corrective action through official actions and by legislation if necessary. In the UK, at long last, such an Age Discrimination Act (2006) has been passed by the national parliament against a lot of opposition by commercial employers and agencies. Although this is primarily against discriminatory practice in employment, this is bound to have implications for health care as well. For the health care areas, a National Director (called the 'Tsar') for Older People's Services has been appointed by the government, with responsibility for the overall 'care' of older people.

'Consumerism' will be an effective pathway for a non-ageist health service. All professionals are characteristically scared of 'complaints' and 'convictions', legalistic hassles etc. Even if nothing can ultimately be established and they are 'cleared', their reputation gets tarnished by bad publicity! Pressure from patients and their relations querying the medical 'decisions' of certain inactions towards an elderly patient or inadequate treatment resulting in delayed or no improvement, will begin to be questioned. Better information on age and related problems will enable the consumers to ask questions and to seek reasonable answers. Unexplained deaths or sufferings would no longer be accepted as simply a feature of old age and God's will!

The best and most plausible approach would be better education and training for all health care personnel; hopefully this alone would correct the negative attitude towards old age and its resulting ills.

The world population is ageing at a very fast rate. For the first time in history, there are more over 65s than under 15s in the UK. Each year, the human longevity is increasing by about three months. Like discriminations on the basis of race and gender, discriminatory practice in health care towards older individuals is unethical, immoral and wrong. This message is spreading loud and clear in this country. It needs to reach the rest of the globe.

The children are our future and must be looked after well and carefully nurtured. The elders are our heritage and history; they should also be looked after and respectfully heeded. Ageing is not a disease and unlike HIV/AIDS, can not be 'cured' and is, biologically speaking, universally 'fatal'. Like AIDS, however, some of its undesirable effects can be 'prevented' and 'treated'. Looking after its elders properly, enriches the intrinsic values of a society. Let us do it.

Summary

Despite recent attempts to root it out, discriminatory practice on the basis of chronological age is still widespread in the British health care system. The National Service Framework for Older People and the appointment of a Tsar for Older People's Services have been steps in the right direction. As ageism is born out of a general negative social attitude to the elders, an educational approach is likely to be more effective. As the East is rapidly copying the West in virtually everything, the plight of elders are likely to deteriorate in the subcontinent with elders being increasingly undervalued. Consumerism in health care as well as better financial prowess might prevent discriminatory behaviour in medical practice. Examples of such age discrimination in the UK in a variety of clinical settings have been cited and discussed. As ignorance tends to be the basic of all forms of discrimination, wider specialization with greater knowledge of ageing and elderly might be the way forward.

References

Agnew, T. (1997). Why lung cancer is neglected, *Health and Ageing*, 55–56.

Banerjee, A. K. (1998). Ethical dilemmas facing the practising geriatrician, Proceed. Royal College of Physicians of Edin, 28, 4–14.

—— (2003). Ageing and the challenge of the age, *Ind J Gerontol*, 17, 213–30.

Bene, J. and R. Liston (1998). Clinical trials should be designed to include older people, *Brit Med J*, 316, 1905.

Bugeja, G., A. Kumar and A.K. Banerjee (1997). Exclusion of older people from clinical research, *Brit Med J*, 315, 1058.

Burns, A., T. Denning and R. Baldwin (2001). Care of older people: Mental health problems. *Brit Med J*, 322, 789–90.

Department of Health. (2001). *National service framework for older people*, London: DOH.

Dudley, N. and E. Burns (1992). The influence of age on the policies of admissions and thrombolysis in coronary care units in the UK, *Age Ageing*, 21, 95–98.

Fairhead, J.F. and M.R. Rothwell (2006). Underinvestigation and undertreatment of carotid disease in the elderly patients with transient ischaemic attack and stroke: Comparative population based study, *Brit Med J*, 333, 525–27.

Gold, M.R., J.E. Siegel and L.B. Russell (1996). *Cost effectiveness in health and medicine*, New York: Oxford University Press.

Hanley, M., M. Khan, A. Kumar and A.K. Banerjee (2004). Attitude to ageing is often negative, *Health and Ageing—The Clinician*, 9, i–ii.

Harris, J. (2006). NICE is not cost-effective, *J Med Ethics*, 32(7): 378–80.

Hubbard, R. E. et al. (2003). Absence of ageism in access to critical care, *Age Ageing*, 32: 382–87.

Lawson-Mathew, P.S. and K.S. Channer (1995). Reporting on Reports—Cardiological interest in elderly patients, *J Royl Coll Physcns*, London, 29: 11–14.

McMurdo, M.E.T., Miles, D.W. and N. D. Gillespie, (2005). Including older people in clinical research, *Brit Med J*, 331: 1036–7.

RCP Report. (1991). Cardiological intervention in elderly patients, *J Royl Coll Physcns*, London, 25, 197–205.

Turner, N.J. et al. (1999). Cancer in old age—is it adequately investigated and treated? *Brit Med J*, 319, 309–12.

Young, J. (2006). Ageism in services for transient ischaemic attack and stroke (Editorial). *Brit Med J*, 333: 508–09 .

7

Perceptions of Ageism Across the Generations

D. Jamuna and P.V. Ramamurti

Ageing is an inevitable lifelong process, marked by stages of life, like infancy, childhood, adolescence and adulthood. Each stage is identified by relevant developmental tasks, appropriate skills, responsibilities and opportunities. Old age is the last of these stages. The objective of the science of gerontology (ageing) is to find answers to certain questions such as why we become old? What happens when we become old? What are the needs and concerns of old age? and how people look upon old age?

Fear of growing old may be a universal and natural apprehension for many. The fear may be minimal in some social groups and exaggerated in those that nurture ageism. Ever since Butler (1975) introduced the concept of ageism, the word has become ubiquitous. Ageism simply refers to the negative stereotype of the elderly and their behavioural manifestations. Such an attitude, then, may lead to a denial that we are ageing and it may also lead to an aversion for the aged, who are living symbols of what we will become. Furthermore, one's reaction and adjustment to changes in middle age and fear of growing old surely affect one's reaction and adjustment to old age.

Ageing is also a socially constructed phenomenon. In many societies, one's age partially determines the roles we play. It is to state that older people may be less active not because of their biology or the ageing process but because they are expected to present an image of inactivity. Social roles sometimes do not permit the aged to be active and involved. Age norms constrain people to behave in given ways. Age norms form a social clock that works alongside the biological clock that limits and guides behaviour through our individual life cycles.

The increased life expectancy in India is leading to four generation families. The interaction of intergenerational families can be a source of great personal enrichment, but it can also produce tension and conflict among the generations in the family resulting from differences in perceptions and values. These value differences may be a source of age prejudice or ageism with in the family. Social and technological change may be a major factor in causing age prejudice, primarily because, the more rapid these changes, the greater the possibility of value conflicts. However, some basic value orientations may remain fairly constant across several generations.

Negative stereotypes of the aged abound and are often harsh. Stereotyping can be direct and it can be subtle. Certainly, some old persons may fit all the negative images. However, individual variations are seen. Tuckman and Lorge (1967) were among the first gerontologists to study stereotypes and found that old people were perceived as being set in their ways, unproductive, rigid, uncouth, a burden to their children, and in their second childhood. Other studies on stereotypes and attitudes, reported similar findings that young people viewed as bound to the past, and old age as an unpleasant experience.

On the other hand, some studies on young children and high school students have shown positive attitude towards the aged (e.g., Anantharaman, 1981; Kullai Reddy, 1984, 1990). Nevertheless, we need more studies on attitudes towards old age to be more specific in explaining how negative images affect the elderly. The negative stereotypes of the aged must be disproved if we are to have a favourable picture of older people. A second way is to debunk the stereotypes. They are to be countered with accurate information.

Ageism in employment and careers in different job categories is common for both sexes. Discrimination based on age is severe for older workers. Most old persons are denied employment because of their age. The type and reasons for discrimination against the older worker vary. In some instances, stereotypes about older workers have been a part of the discriminations on the job against the elderly.

It is clear from the above that ageistic attitudes prevail in different age groups and in work situation. The negative attitudes towards aged, and ageing in the society reinforce ageism and nurture ageistic practices in different spheres of the society. Prevalence of ageism is dependent upon a whole gamut of factors like age, gender, educational level, type of family, the nature of interaction with the elderly, and personality. An attempt was made through this study to ascertain how different age and gender groups of the present population perceive ageism.

The present study had the following objectives:

1. To study the nature and prevalence of various stereotyped perceptions of the elderly.
2. To study the variation in these stereotyped perceptions as per age group (the young adult, the middle aged and the older persons) and gender groups.
3. To suggest means of countering these ageistic views.

Methodology

The study attempts to investigate the prevalence of ageistic images in the young, the middle aged and the older persons. A total sample of 240 men and women were drawn by a multi-stage random sampling technique from rural and urban areas of two districts (Chittoor and Kadapa) consisting of 80 in 20–40 age group; 80 in 40–60 age group; and 80 in 60+ years. A check list of characteristics of the elderly was adapted from the standardized inventory of attitudes towards the aged (Ramamurti, 1968). The checklist consists of 25 negative characteristics of aged and ageing. The test retest reliability of the checklist was 0.86 (interval of 15 days with N = 60). The inventory was in Telugu, the regional language and responses to statements recorded. The subjects were individually interviewed and the significance of the study was explained to them to ascertain their cooperation.

Results and Discussion

Ageism portrays a set of negative discriminatory attitudes and related behavioural manifestations towards the aged in a society. The elderly suffer many indignities. To realize the first objective, data on perception of ageism in the young, middle aged and the elderly subjects, was scored. The perceptions of these groups were analysed content-wise (i.e., statement wise). Also, the age differences in the perceptions were analysed to gain an understanding of the three generational dispositions towards ageism.

The percentage of men and women holding the negative perception in each of the age and gender categories were worked out (see Table 1). It could be seen that there were considerable variations in the percentage of persons holding the negative perceptions.

Table 1 Percentage of Men and Women in Each of the Three Age Groups Endorsing Each of the Characteristics of Older People

Particulars	20–40		40–60		60–80	
	Men	Women	Men	Women	Men	Women
1. Forgetfulness	34	30	64	62	80	78
2. Frequent illness	31	38	61	58	60	65
3. Weak	62	60	54	51	70	74
4. Wrinkled skin	28	31	51	48	58	61
5. Bald and grey hair	61	65	68	70	54	46
6. Dirty, smelly	28	30	21	24	13	17
7. Constipation	17	19	27	29	40	42
8. Chronic diseases	36	31	31	34	60	52
9. Falling tendency	44	42	49	52	51	47
10. Slow in work	60	64	60	54	70	64
11. Burden to family	55	51	64	66	70	72
12. Poor vision and hearing	56	60	52	50	32	24
13. Dull taste and smell	28	31	55	57	35	34
14. Short tempered, no patience	25	20	41	39	40	42
15. Authoritative, critical	61	67	44	54	20	18
16. Of no use to others	72	69	54	59	50	58
17. Conflict with the young	74	67	36	35	31	35
18. Rigid	51	53	48	46	21	19
19. Spiritual, religious and godly	59	60	57	62	55	64
20. Superstitious	66	70	49	51	30	34
21. Not fit to modern living habits	78	80	61	63	50	47
22. Not fit for sex life	49	47	64	66	46	44
23. Living in their past	55	51	32	34	32	30
24. Spoil grandchildren	29	31	55	59	18	21
25. Always dosing, wake up early	26	29	45	47	54	60
Gender Average	47.2	47.5	49.7	50.8	45.4	46.3
Age Group Average	47.4		50.5		45.9	

There were no substantial variations between the genders in these perceptions in most of the 25 characteristics listed. The averages of negative perceptions for the 25 characteristics listed, showed for men and women in the 20–40 age group were 47.2 and 47.5; in the 40–60 age group were 49.7 and 50.8; in the 60–80 age group they were 45.4 and 46.3, respectively.

Taking the averages of the per cent of population holding negative views for the age groups it is seen that negative views of ageing were less (45.9) in the older age group (i.e., 60–80) compared to the young and middle age groups (47.4 and 50.5). It is noteworthy that the older age group also attributed ageistic (negative) perception to old age and the views were only a shade different compared to the young and middle aged groups. It means that nearly a majority of the total population held negative views of the aged.

Since there were considerable variations in the percentage of the three age groups holding negative views among the different ageistic characteristics listed, it would be interesting to go into the details of the perception of the different characteristics. If we consider the young adult group, the characteristics that carried a moderate to high per cent of the population were: weakness, baldness and grayness, slow in work, burden to the family, poor vision and hearing, authoritative and critical, they were of no use to others, conflict with the young, rigid, godly and religious, superstitions, not fit to modern life and rooted in their past.

The characteristics endorsed by a fair number of middle aged persons were: forgetful, frequent illness, weakness, wrinkled skin, falls, slow in work, burden to family, poor vision and hearing, poor taste and smell, authoritative and critical, no use to others, spiritual and godly, rigid, superstitions, not fit for modern life, and spoil grandchildren by overprotecting them.

The characteristics mostly endorsed by the old themselves were forgetfulness, frequent sickness, weakness, wrinkles, baldness and grey hair, constipation, falling tendency, slow in work, burden to family, worthlessness, spiritual and godly, not fit for modern life, sleepiness, and waking early.

The characteristics endorsed by all the three groups were weakness, baldness and grey hair, slow in work, a burden to family, being of no use to others, spiritual and godly, not fit for modern life. These views were held by more than 40 per cent of the groups. It is interesting to note that none of the characteristics were totally endorsed by any age group but only by the majority (at most).

Several of these characteristics have some truth (but not the whole truth) on which they are based. Yet, the old are stereotyped into that characteristic. For instance, not all old people have these characteristics, only less than a majority have these characteristics, e.g., constipated bowels, frequent illness, dirty, smelly, short tempered, critical, authoritative, conflict with the young, rigid, spiritual and godly, superstitious, etc. It is seen that these characteristics can be found in individuals of other age groups as well and not only in the older persons. Also, some of these characteristics do not show up until late in the old age, with many in the young old group (60–75) not showing these characteristics. These facts suggest that some of these characteristics are used as criteria for 'exclusion' or marginalization of the aged, and putting them in an 'out group', i.e., social distancing by ascribing 'minority group status'. It is something that hints at 'not me' anyway but 'he/she' has these !

Stereotyping and labelling seem to fulfil a human need to structure and organize situations. Yet, stereotyping is usually inaccurate. When we generalize by putting people into categories, we tend to oversimplify reality and information and try to emphasize a few characteristics that are accepted as an 'adequate' description. Stereotypes can lead to strong emotions, such as hatred.

It is therefore necessary to devise intervention strategies to debunk these views of the older persons. One way to debunk this is to draw attention to the older people who have made significant contributions in their old age. Another way to debunk negative stereotypes is to counter them with accurate information. For example, the myth persists that the aged as a group suffer cognitive decline. More specifically, certain common beliefs are that (1) the mental faculties of aged decline, and (2) aged are senile, child-like and out of touch with reality. The older people are said to decline in intelligence, learning ability, and many. However, longitudinal studies on older persons over many years have found little overall decline in intelligence scores. Other studies show that aged individuals are just as capable of learning as younger people although they may take sometime to learn new things. Longitudinal studies by Baltes and Schaie (1974, 2003) on intelligence in the 21–70 age range subjects show that two out of four measures of intelligence increase with age. It is to conclude that general intellectual decline in old age is largely a myth. The researchers found 'crystallized abilities' (verbal comprehension, numerical skills, induce reasoning etc.) and visualization (the ability to organize and process visual stimuli) increase with age even to the 70's. Number of studies show little overall decline in intelligence with age. The reason is that the design of IQ tests have been particularly responsible for stereotyping old people as declining in intelligence. Tests to measure only those abilities are inappropriate for tapping the wisdom of the aged. Studies show that those who exercise their minds keep themselves mentally alert (Baltes and Schaie,1974, 2003; Birren and Schaie, 1996).

Research by providing evidence to the contrary is necessary and needs to be documented as evidence to debunk the stereotypes. By using the print and electronic media, and school curriculum the positive aspects need to be projected. Television shorts and cartoons can be developed depicting the positive aspects and usefulness of older people and discrimination they experience due to the incorrectness of stereotypes of the older people. In families too, parents may promote in their children respect and regard for older people. If these are consistently carried out, in due course, the attitudes towards older people would tend to become positive.

References

Atchley, R.C. (1977). *The social forces in later life.* Belmont, CA: Wadsworth.

Anantharaman, R.N. (1981). Perception of old age by two generations. *Jr. of Psychological Researches,* 25: 46–50.

Baltes, P. and Schaie, W. (1974). Aging and IQ: The myth of the twilight years. *Psychology Today,* 35–40.

——. (2003). New frontiers in the future of aging: From successful aging of the young–old to the dilemmas of the fourth age. *Journal of Gerontology,* 49: 123–35.

Birren, J.E. and Schaie, K.W. (1996). *Handbook of the psychology of aging.* San Diego, CA: Academic Press.

Butler, R.N.C. (1975). *Why survive?* New York: Harper and Row.

Kullai Reddy, L. (1984). A Study of Attitudes Towards Ageing and Their Relation to Problems of Adjustment. MPhil. thesis, S.V. University, Tirupati.

——. (1990). A Study of Some Factors Related to Attitude Towards the Aged in an Indian Population. PhD Thesis(Unpublished), S.V. University, Tirupati.

Ramamurti, P.V. (1968). A Study of Some Factors Related to the Adjustment of Urban Aged Men. PhD Thesis, S.V. University, Tirupati.

Tuckmen, J. and I. Lorge, (1967). Inventory of attitudes toward old people. In M.E. Shah and M. Wright, (eds.), *Scales for the measurement of attitudes,* New York: McGrand.

8

Psychological Issues in Ageism and Its Prevention

Indira Jai Prakash

When Robert Butler, the Grand Old Man of Gerontology, coined the term 'ageism' in 1968 (Butler, 2005) to identify age stereotypes, not many empathized with the term. Most thought it was another of the 'isms' that crops up in literature. Nearly forty years down the line, this particular 'ism' has been experienced by millions of people. Research evidence is accumulating that ageism is universal and omnipresent. This is evident by the fact that Palmore and colleagues thought it fit to publish an *Encyclopedia of Ageism* in 2005. This book lists more than 135 topics from A to V—Abuse in Nursing Home to Voice Quality—all related to ageing and age stereotypes (Palmore et al., 2005).

Psychologists need to examine the reasons for ageism and ageist attitudes. Palmore (1990) discusses the most common of these negative myths and stereotypes about ageing. Most young people, sometimes old people themselves, believe that old age is synonymous with sickness and disability. Statistics contradicting this that only 5 per cent of 65+ are institutionalized is often overlooked. Even physicians assume that sexuality is unimportant in old age (Butler, 1975). Culture of youth worship finds old age ugly. When factors such as motivation and learning style are taken into account, chronological age does significantly influence learning ability. Yet, people consider all old people as senile. Mental illness is neither common, nor inevitable, nor untreatable in the elderly population (Prakash, 2000). Nor are all the old people dependent and useless. Studies of employed older people under actual working conditions generally show that they perform as well as, if not better than, younger workers on most measures. Yet, employers may hesitate to hire an older person (McCann and Giles, 2002). Consistency of output tends to increase with age, and older workers have less job turnover, fewer accidents, and less absenteeism than younger workers (Riley and Foner, 1968).

Unlike sexism or racism, ageism is not constant in the sense, age classification is not static. Everyone, if he or she lives long enough, will join the rank of the 'aged' one day. One moves ahead progressively in the life cycle and hence age classification is continuously changing. As a result, people may hold ageist stereotypes against others when young and may develop attitudes towards self as they age. Ageism occurs in consume-based and economy-focused society where older people who cannot work are seen as 'disposable citizens' or as having outlived their usefulness to the economy.

Psychologists show that ageism is perpetuated not only by the media, but also by medical and other services. Woolf (1998) in a comprehensive article discusses different reasons for the development of ageism. The first factor that is postulated to contribute to ageism is the fear of death in Western society. Western civilization conceptualizes death as outside of the human life cycle (Bulter and Lewis, 1977). As such, death is experienced and viewed as an affront to the self. Death is not seen as natural and inevitable part of the life course. This can be contrasted with Eastern philosophy where life and death are all part of a continuous cycle. The argument is that since age and death are often associated, the fear of death gets translated as dislike of ageing. This may not be very convincing as even in Eastern culture where death is not 'expected' to be feared, ageism is seen. Indians with their concept of an eternal soul are also prone to ageism.

Kastenbaum (1973) hypothesizes that ageist attitudes and stereotypes serve to insulate the young and middle-aged from the ambivalence they feel towards the elderly. This ambivalence results from the fact that the older adult is viewed as representing ageing and death. Butler (1969) states: "Ageism reflects a deep seated uneasiness on the part of the young and middle-aged—a personal revulsion to and distaste for growing old, disease, disability; and a fear of powerlessness, 'uselessness', and death" (p. 243). This represents the most commonly argued basis for ageism (as cited by Woolf, 1998). Young centred culture is another factor considered responsible for ageism (Traxler, 1980). Persons who are dependent on physical appearance and youth for their identity are likely to experience loss of self-esteem with age (Block, Davidson and Grumbs, 1981). In societies where productivity is emphasized, once again, old age and dropping out of workforce is valued negatively.

Gray Panthers (2006) is an intergenerational organization dedicated to promote social justice for all identified different types of ageists. The Pretenders are those who refuse to believe in ageing and think that it is all in one's head. The Discriminators are quick to point out the realistic limitations of ageing. The Exceptionalists perceive themselves as productive and useful to society while their peers are in bad shape, useless and boring. The Colonists are usually politicians who preface any word related to ageing with the possessive noun such as 'out senior citizens', 'my elderly'. The Patronizers are happy as long as the old are in their place and are left there. Gray Panthers argue that none of us is immune to ageism. Ageism percolates society and we are all ageists.

Consequences of Ageism

Any discrimination whether it is due to gender, race of age will have similar consequences. The group discriminated against assumes the characteristics of a minority group. It starts internalizing the negative images attributes which affects self-esteem. The stereotyped views of the dominant group may consist of a set of behavioural expectations and prescriptions. In general, the consequences of ageism are similar to those associated with all attempts to discriminate against other groups: persons subjected to prejudice and discrimination tend to adopt the dominant group's negative image and to behave in ways that conform to that negative image (Palmore, 1990).

Robert Butler (1969) explained that ageism allows the younger generations to see older people as different from themselves; thus they subtly cease to identify with their elders as human beings. Ageism often intersects with and can be reinforced by other kinds of discriminations such as racism, sexism, and 'able-bodied-ism' (where preference or greater social value is given to people who do not have impairments or disabling conditions).

Palmore (1990) identifies four common responses of elders to these prescriptions and expectations: acceptance, denial, avoidance, and reform.

All of these responses can have harmful effects on the individuals. For example, an elderly person who 'accepts' the negative image may 'act old' even though this may be out of keeping with their personality or previous habits. This may mean that they stop or reduce social activities, do not seek appropriate medical treatment, or accept poverty. In essence, this internalization of a negative image can result in the elderly person becoming prejudiced against him/herself, resulting in loss of self-esteem, self-hatred, shame, depression, and/or suicide in extreme cases.

'Denial' of one's status as an elderly person can also have negative consequences. One example, lying about one's age may not seem significant, but it can further erode morale. Another example is the attempt to 'pass' for a member of the dominant, younger group by undergoing cosmetic surgery, having hair transplants, or using widely advertised anti-ageing products such as hair dyes, skin creams, cosmetics, etc. While these practices are widespread, the quest for eternal youth can become inappropriate and, ultimately, self-defeating for those who attempt to stop the natural ageing process entirely. 'Avoidance' of ageist attitudes may also take many forms. Examples include moving into age-segregated housing, self-imposed isolation, alcoholism, drug addiction, or suicide. The 'reform' response, is the antithesis of the avoidance response in that the person recognizes the discrimination and attempts to eliminate it. This attempt may be an individual one or a collective one through membership in an advocacy group such as the powerful American Association of Retired Persons.

Ultimately, stereotypes are dehumanizing and promote one-dimensional thinking about others. Elders are not seen as human beings but as objects, who therefore, can be more easily denied opportunities and rights. Stereotypes are accepted, perpetuated and reinforced in language, in medical practice, in policy and programmes not just in individual relationships. For example, elders are frequently misdiagnosed or denied medical treatment because they are seen as 'old' and, therefore, incurable. Elders are also frequently denied employment or promotion opportunities because they are 'old' and less productive. Such discrimination is also evident on the social policy level where the elderly are blamed for having medical problems and consuming public resources rather than seeing them as having human needs requiring appropriate social responses. Seeing people as objects also increases the likelihood that they may be subjected to abuse and other cruel treatment. Elder abuse is closely related to ageist attitudes.

Devaluing human beings on the basis of age goes against the basic principles of civic society.

Fighting Ageism

If ageism is so rampant how does one fight it? Perhaps the first step is to recognize the phenomenon itself. Defining what constitutes ageism itself creates some awareness regarding its effects. One needs to recognize the ageists as well. Then one has to develop strategies at individual and social level to counteract it.

Rodeheaver (1990) suggests that in order to counteract ageism, changes must be made in the systems which perpetuate it. Media, popular culture, business institutions, government and medical system all of them perpetuate stereotypes. Individuals with ageist attitudes are part of such systems. Therefore, changing individual ageist attitudes is a fundamental approach to reducing ageism. A firm step in this process is identifying personal attitudes which are ageist in nature. This can be difficult since most people will deny that they are prejudiced. However, until a person is aware of his or her own attitudes, little progress can be made.

Another approach which can modify ageist attitudes is personal contact with older adults. This is often an effective way to prevent or reduce the development of ageism, especially among young children. It is a well known fact in social psychology that contact and frequent interaction reduces prejudices. Many innovative intergenerational programmes have been created which not only benefit children, but also the older adults. Prakash (2003, 2004) reports some such studies carried out in India. Using drawings depicting older people, attitudes are elicited in children. Then psychoeducational programmes are carried out to change the attitudes in the positive direction. During these programmes, positive aspects of ageing can be emphasized so that the children will have a balanced picture of the older adults—and of themselves as they grow older adults' oral history by students. Schools could contribute in their own way by including ageing issues in curricula. Encouraging school students to do small projects involving older people helps forge a link between the two generations.

Many older people have sought more active and vigorous ways of combating ageism. They aim at social action and reform. This approach is particularly effective when directed at institutions. Gray Panthers which have watchdog committees to monitor and respond to negative media images of older adults is a good example of what collective force of people can achieve. Civic groups and churches can also be effective advocates along with other institutions in the community.

The Canadian Network of the Prevention of Elder Abuse (n.d.) gives some tips. They are as follows:

1. Identify the myths and misinformation.
   Recognizing the myths that abound about older people can be very revealing. The quiz developed by Palmore (1977) is a handy tool in this regard. When people can sift facts from fiction they would be taking the first important step towards better understanding of ageing.
2. Go beyond the stereotypes. People should recognize that labels like seniors or elders do not really give comprehensive understanding of the persons. It has to be recognized that older people are heterogeneous. Each person has to be looked upon as an individual.
3. Learn more about ageing. Correct information about ageing is one way to resist negative stereotypes.
4. Learn about ageism and discrimination. One needs to learn about how discrimination manifests in several areas of life. Also useful is to know the interactive effect of different types of discriminations.
5. Listen to seniors who have experienced ageism. Perhaps nothing can be more enlightening than finding out from people how and in what context they have experienced ageism. Experiential accounts help in better understanding.
6. Monitor media and respond to ageist material. Old people are often portrayed negatively by mass media. Just as now feminist groups monitor and protest against negative media portrayal, older people also need to register their protests.
7. Speak up about ageism. At an individual level each one of us must take the role of a teacher. Older persons should tactfully point out when others use ageist language or display such attitudes.
8. Watch out for own language. Very often old people themselves use ageist idioms, words and images. One has to be more observant of this trend.
9. Talk openly about ageing issues and ageism. Like other forms of discrimination, ageism has to be taken out of the cupboard and thrown

up in broad daylight. Being silent about such incidents is an indirect way of accepting it. The more unvoiced the concern, more appropriate it appears to behave in ageist way.

10. Build intergenerational bridges to promote understanding. Often people are ageist because they do not know better. Generation gap has to be addressed for harmony among people.
11. Provide support for organizations that address ageism. Nowadays, as awareness has spread, older people are organizing themselves to fight ageism. Organizations that address the issue of discrimination should be strengthened. Size and adequate finance add to the clout of such organizations.
12. Push for changes from your elected representative. People should educate the politicians whom they elect. Keeping them informed of key ageing issues is a way of influencing policies and change ageist policies.

Gray Panthers, the most influential advocacy group has its own set of tips to combat ageism. Their plan says that the hardest part in fighting ageism is to accept the fact that we are all ageists. To stamp out ageism, they say "quit complimenting people on how young they look". Promoting intergenerational sharing, not blaming age for everything (old as disorganized, young as poor planners, for example) and taking the media to task for ageist reports also helps. There is a difference between laughing with and laughing at elderly. Knowledge and approaching every person as an individual are two important weapons to fight ageism. Palmore (2005a) suggests both individual actions and group actions for fighting ageism. Individual action consists of getting facts, eliminating own prejudices, avoiding ageist jokes, terms, language, and acting appropriately when faced with ageism. Group actions are more powerful and may take the form of rallies, lobbies, passive resistance, supporting political campaigns and so on. In another article, Palmore (2005b) lists strategies for reducing ageism. They are: testing ageism (determine level of prejudice); education, propaganda and exhortation; slogans that are catchy; listing benefits of ageing; using religion, media and personal contact; setting models of successful ageing, and even therapy to counteract negative effect of ageism. Social structure changes in economy, government, family, housing and health care are also recommended by him.

Ultimately, it appears that people who are growing older need to actively fight ageism. Otherwise, they will be living out a 'self-fulfilling prophecy'—a prophecy that has been created and fed by social stereotypes and prejudices. Awareness, activism, advocacy and active ageing are the weapons to fight ageism. No country, no culture is free from ageism at present. In the future, this trend may increase as old people become a noticeable presence in the population. Hence, there is a need to educate people regarding ageism and ageist attitudes. Active or productive ageing encourages people to remain healthy and independent as long as physically possible. Mental attitudes of hardiness, openness to new experience and self-esteem help people retain their dignity in spite of societal attitudes. It also gives them the necessary strength and motivation to fight ageism.

References

Block, M.R., J.L. Davidson and J.D. Grambs (1981). *Women over forty: Visions and realities.* New York: Springer.

Butler, R.N. (1969). Age-ism: Another form of bigotry. *The Gerontologist*, 9: 243–46.

——. (1975). *Why survive? Being old in America.* New York: Harper & Row.

Butler, R.N. and M.I. Lewis (1977). *Ageing and mental health.* St. Louis: C.V. Mosby.

——. (2005). Foreword: Encyclopedia of Ageism. E.D. Palmore, Laurence Branch and D.K. Harris (eds.), *Encyclopedia of ageism.* New York: The Haworth Press.

Canadian Network for the Prevention of Elder Abuse. (n.d.)

Kastenbaum, R. (1973). On death and dying: Should we have mixed feelings about our ambivalence toward aging, death and the completion of being? Paper presented at an interdisciplinary meeting of Boston Society of Gerontologic Psychiatry, Boston, cited by Woolf.

McCann, R. and Giles, H. (2002). Ageism in the workplace: A communication perspective. In T. Nelson (ed.), *Ageism: Stereotyping and prejudice against older persons.* Cambridge: The MIT Press, 163–200.

Palmore, E. (1971). Attitudes toward aging as shown through humor. *The Gerontologist*, 11: 181–86.

——. (1977). Facts on aging: A short quiz. *The Gerontologist*, 17: 315–20.

——. (1990). *Ageism: Negative and positive.* New York: Springer.

——. (2005a). Changing strategies. In E.D. Palmore, Laurence Branch and D.K. Harris (eds.), *Encyclopedia of ageism.* New York: The Haworth Press, 60–62.

——. (2005b). Reducing ageism. In E.D. Palmore, Laurence Branch and D.K. Harris (eds.), *Encyclopedia of ageism.* New York: The Haworth Press, 259–60.

Palmore, E., Laurence Branch and D.K. Harris (eds.), (2005). *Encyclopedia of ageism.* New York: The Haworth Press.

Prakash, Indira J. (2000). Issues in mental health and psychological well-being of older persons. In M. Desai and S. Raju (eds.), *Gerontological social work in India: Some issues and perspectives.* Delhi: B.R. Publishing Corporation, 243–59.

——. (2003). *Aging: Diverse experiences.* Bangalore: Bangalore University.

——. (2004). *Ageing: Emerging issues.* Bangalore: Bangalore University.

Riley, M. and A. Foner (1968). *Aging and society,* Vol. I, An inventory of research findings. New York: Russell Sage Foundation.

Rodeheaver, D. (1987b). When old age became a social problem, women were left behind. *The Gerontologist,* 27: 741–46.

Traxler, A.J. (1980). Let's get gerontologized. Developing a sensitivity to aging, the multi-purpose senior centre concept. A training manual for practitioners working with the aging. Springfield, IL: Illinois Department of Aging.

Woolf, L.M. (1998). *Ageism: An introduction.* Webster University.

9

Older Persons and Caregiver Burden and Satisfaction in Rural Family Context

B. Devi Prasad and N. Indira Rani

The growing number of aged population as a result of the increase in the life span of the individuals, and the continuing preference of older persons to stay with their young are some of the reasons which led to the emergence of caregiving as an important aspect of family life (Bali, 1999). In India, home-based care, with family members as primary caregivers still remains as the first and often the only option for a majority of the elderly (Puri, 2004). So, the most common type of living arrangement for the elderly in India is found to be living with married sons and their families (Prakash, 1999). According to 2001 Census, the aged (60+) in India constitute 7.4 per cent of the total population whereas for Andhra Pradesh it is 7.6 per cent. There is an 11.8 percentage increase in the population of the older persons over the earlier decade, which was 6.54 per cent. According to Census, 2001, nearly 75.0 per cent of the elderly live in villages. The dependency ratio of the elderly is reported to be higher in the rural areas as compared to urban areas (NSSO 52nd Round). Therefore, family care-giving emerged as an important area of study.

One of the outcomes of caregiving is caregiver stress and burden. Several questions come to our mind when we think of caregiving and caregiver burden in family context. Who are the primary caregivers of the older persons in Indian family context? Which factors are associated with caregiver stress or lack of it? What measures are used to assess these variables and so on. Studies show that caregiver stress is reported to be associated with such variables as family income, age of caregiver, kinship relationship, caregiver's attitude and certain attributes of the care recipient, i.e., the elderly (Jamuna, 1997). It is found that women are traditionally caregivers in Indian families (Prakash, 2001, 1999) especially in rural communities (Jamuna, 1997; Chakrabarthi, 1999; Sharma, 2003). Also women report greater levels of stress as they are often engaged in the caregiving of two generations—rearing their own children and providing long term care to the elder relatives which results in great cost to their well-being both physical and psychological (Prakash, 1999; Hirst, 2005). Caregiver stress was reported to be high among daughters-in-law followed by spouse and daughter (Jamuna, 1997). Thus, there is a clear 'feminization of caring'. For men, the most common caregiver was the wife followed by daughter-in-law and in the case of women, it was mostly the daughter-in-law followed by the daughter (Prakash, 1999; Sharma, 2003). The other stressors which affect the quality of caregiving were work demands, availability of social support, health status of the caregiver (Jamuna and Ramamurthi, 1999), and the changes and modifications which have been taking place in interpersonal relationships as a result of changes in external realities (Vijaykumar, 1999).

Another important aspect in studies on caregiving is caregiver satisfaction. Compared to the literature on the burden of caregiving, studies are sparse focusing on the rewards and gratifications of elder care (Decalmer and Glendenning, 1997). Davies (1980) observed that caregiver satisfaction is possible only when the recipient of care was seen as a valued person rather than as a problem. Similarly, Cartwright et al. (1994) observed that caregiver satisfaction is also dependent upon the meanings ascribed to care, i.e., perceiving caregiving as a satisfying and pleasant relationship and of finding rewards in the several acts of care giving.

Caregiver burden is one of the most studied topics in gerontological literature. However, fewer studies are done on rewards and satisfaction of caregiving than on caregiver stress. Therefore, it was thought that a study based on a large and a systematic sample of caregivers in a rural family context would yield meaningful comparison and conclusions on both caregiver burden and caregiver satisfaction. Moreover, the social and psychological stress experienced by family caregivers in the family context is an important area of study. Though several scales have been developed to measure caregiver burden and stress, not many scales are available to measure these aspects in Indian context. Hence, there is a need to identify and standardize independent measures of the caregiver burden and caregiver satisfaction on an Indian sample. Thus, the purpose of the present study is to examine the discriminating capabilities of two measures, i.e., in measuring the caregiver burden and satisfaction and to explore how age, sex, income of the caregiver affect the different variables relating to care giving.

Objectives

1. To assess the burden and satisfaction experienced by the caregivers of the older persons in Indian rural family context.
2. To use and compare the two measures, i.e., Burden Assessment Scale (BAS) and Caregivers Reaction Assessment (CRA) scale in measuring the caregiver burden and caregiver satisfaction among the sample respondents.
3. To find out the association between the caregiver burden and caregiver satisfaction with relevant variables such as age, sex, income etc. of the caregivers.

Method

Sample

Seven villages in three panchayats from a predominantly rural mandal (Padmanabham) of Visakhapatnam district, Andhra Pradesh formed the setting for study. A census sample of these villages was taken and 822 elderly of both sexes were enumerated. From this sample, 300 caregivers who were having at least one older person (60+years) living with them under their care for a period of 6 months or more prior to the date of study were selected using a systematic sampling method. Thus, the median duration of stay of the older person with the caregiver came to be 31.5 years (range: 1 year–60 years). When there are more than two older persons in a family, one *referent* elderly was chosen by using a random procedure method. The caregiver responded to the interview keeping this referent elderly in mind.

Tools Used

An interview schedule was used which covered: (a) socio-demographic variables such as age, income, education, occupation and so on of the caregiver and the elderly, (b) the Burden Assessment Scale (BAS), and (c) the Caregiver Reaction Assessment (CRA) Scale. Both the measures were translated into Telugu. The reliability of the Telugu versions was determined by test-retest method by administering the test to 22 elder caregivers in an urban setting. The alpha coefficients for the pre- and post-tests came to be 0.81 and 0.87 for BAS and 0.52 and 0.72 for CRA respectively.

Explanation of the Measures Used

The Burden Assessment Scale (BAS)

The BAS developed by Reinhard and Horwitz (1995) is a 19-item questionnaire with response options on a 4-point Likert-type scale (from *not at all* to *a lot*). It is a unidimensional scale. Ten items measure objective burdens (such as missed days at work), and nine assess subjective burdens (such as feelings of guilt). Objective burdens are those that alter an activity or resource, whereas subjective measures are measured by affect or perspective. Thus, missed days at work or school, reduced leisure time, and changes in personal plans are objective burdens, and feelings of shame, guilt, and worry are subjective burdens. The total burden score, which taps both objective and subjective dimensions, is calculated by summing response values for all items. Scores range from 19 to 76 with higher scores indicating greater levels of burden. In the present study the alpha coefficient for the Burden Assessment Scale (BAS) is 0.78.

The Caregiver Reaction Assessment (CRA)

Given et al. (1992) developed this multidimensional scale, which is a 24-item measure with response options on a 5-point Likert-type scale. The response options range from strongly agree to *strongly disagree.* Two questions from the original scale (22 and 23) were deleted as these questions were found to be repetitive and eliciting similar answers from the respondents caused confusion to the interviewer and the respondent. The measure assesses five dimensions of caregiver reactions. They are impact on schedule

(5 items), caregiver's esteem/satisfaction (6 items), lack of family support (4 items), impact on health (4 items), and impact on finances (3 items). Five items (3, 7, 13, 15, and 19) are reverse scored. Total scores range from 22 to 110 with higher scores indicating greater burden or stress. The alpha coefficient for the Caregiver Reaction Assessment (CRA) is 0.71.

Findings

Profile of the Caregiver and the Elderly

Table 1 gives the socio-demographic details of the sample caregivers. As can be seen, around 64 per cent of the sample caregivers are women. The mean age of caregiver is 43 years (SD = 15.6). The age range is 16–75 years. Women caregivers are slightly younger (mean = 42.9, SD = 14.84) than men (mean = 43.2, SD = 16.87). Majority of them belonged to backward castes (68.7 per cent), followed by other castes (19.3 per cent) and scheduled castes (12 per cent). More women are found to be illiterate as compared to men and nearly 86 per cent of the caregivers are married. More than half (53.7 per cent) reported their family as extended type, i.e., having two generations with unmarried extended relatives. The mean family income came to be Rs. 1730 per month (SD=278.8) with a range between Rs. 100 and Rs. 3,000. As regards the duration of stay of the elderly with the caregiver, around half of them reported the duration to be 16–40 years. Of the older persons who were under the care of the sample caregivers, around 59 per cent are women who are slightly younger (mean = 67.0 SD = 6.44) to men (mean = 67.5, SD = 6.77). In terms of marital status, around half of the elderly (51 per cent) are married followed by widowed (48 per cent).

Relationship with the Elderly

Coming to the relationship of the caregiver to the elderly, of the 300 sample caregivers, 25.7 per cent are wives, 23.3 per cent are sons followed by daughters-in-law (22 per cent) and daughters (13 per cent) and husbands (8 per cent). The remaining 8 per cent are other relatives. When enquired who takes care of the older person when she or he falls ill, the relationships figured were: wife, son, daughter, daughter-in-law and husband (in the case of women elderly), in that order.

Table 1 Profile of the Sample Caregivers

Variable	Men (n=109)	Women (n=191)	Total
Sex	*36.3*	*63.7*	—
Age			
Below 30 years	32.1	27.8	29.3
31 to 57 years	37.6	51.8	46.7
58 years and above	30.3	20.4	24.0
Marital status			
Married	86.2	86.4	86.3
Unmarried	9.2	3.1	5.3
Widowed	3.7	7.9	6.3
Divorced	0.9	0.5	0.7
Separated	—	2.1	1.3
Religion			
Hindu	97.2	100.0	99.0
Christian	2.8	—	1.0
Caste			
Backward Caste	71.6	67.0	68.7
Other Castes	17.4	20.4	19.3
Scheduled Caste	11.0	12.6	12.0
Educational level			
Illiterate	67.0	84.3	78.0
Primary	17.4	10.5	13.0
Secondary	13.8	5.2	8.3
Inter and above	.9	.3	0.3
Professional	.9	.3	0.3
Family type			
Nuclear	16.5	28.8	24.3
Joint	25.7	19.9	22.0
Extended	57.8	51.3	53.7
Duration of stay of the elderly			
Up to 15 years	14.7	31.4	25.3
16 – 40 years	58.7	46.6	51.0
41+ years	26.6	22.0	23.7
Income			
Below Rs. 1000	18.3	28.8	25.0
Rs.1001 to Rs. 2000	57.8	48.2	51.7
Rs.2001 and above	23.9	23.0	23.3
N = 300	100.0	100.0	100.0

Comparison of the BAS and CRA Measures

To begin with, a strong positive relationship between burden assessment scale (BAS) and the caregiver reaction assessment score (CRA) can be seen by examining the scatter diagram (Figure 1). There is a discernable pattern concentrating along the regression line which confirms the close association (r =. 563, p < .000) between the two scores.

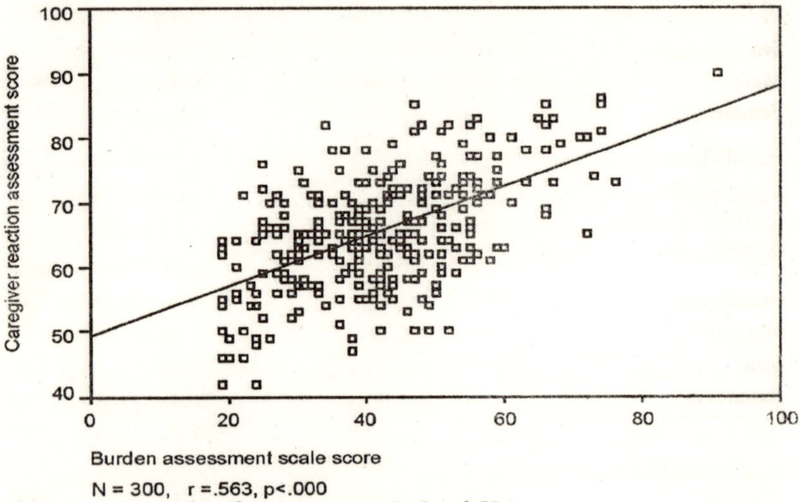

Figure 1 Scatterplot of two measures—BAS and CRA

Next, Table 2 shows the means of BAS and CRA scores obtained on certain key variables such as age, sex, income, and type of family of the caregiver. As can be seen, both the measures showed a similar trend in reflecting the differences on all the variables. Thus, with the increasing age of the caregiver, the caregiver stress also increased. Women caregivers reported higher levels of burden and stress (66.2 on CRA and 43.1 on BAS) as compared to male caregivers. Further, an inverse relationship is seen in the case of family income and the mean scores on these two measures i.e., the lower the income, the higher the stress levels reported.

In terms of type of family, caregivers from nuclear family background reported higher levels of stress on both CRA and BAS.

As the caregiver reaction assessment scale is a multidimensional measure, an attempt is made in Table 3 to study the relationship between sex and the different dimensions of CRA measure. In this measure, of the four (4)

Table 2 Comparison of BAS and CRA Scores of the Caregivers

Caregiver Variable	BAS		CRA	
	Mean	SD	Mean	SD
Age				
Below 30 years	36.1	11.6	60.8	8.5
31 to 57 years	42.8	11.7	66.2	7.8
58 years	46.2	14.0	69.6	8.2
Sex				
Male	39.1	10.8	64.2	7.3
Female	43.1	13.6	66.2	9.4
Family income				
Up to Rs.1000	50.5	14.1	70.5	8.8
Rs.1001 to Rs.2000	38.5	10.4	63.7	7.7
Rs.2001 and above	38.9	12.1	63.8	8.8
Family type				
Nuclear	46.2	13.4	69.0	8.9
Joint	39.9	13.5	64.4	8.7
Extended	40.3	11.8	64.2	8.2

sub-scales, caregiver esteem or satisfaction covers the rewards of care giving. The rest of the sub-scales are: the impact of caregiver's stress on the work schedule, family support, health and financial resources of the caregiver. The numbers of items in the original scale are given in the table. The responses to agree and strongly agree are combined and shown (Table 3).

As a whole, a large percentage of caregivers expressed satisfaction about the caregiving role played by them. More specifically, the trend shows that on caregiver esteem sub-scale, a slightly less percentage of women, as compared to men, expressed satisfaction about their caregiving role. At the same time, more men, i.e., 76 per cent reported resentment for having to take care of the elder relative than women caregivers (57 per cent). Similarly, with regard to impact on health, more women caregivers reported tiredness and worsening health because of stress arising out of their caregiving roles. Moreover, on all other sub-scales, more women reported interruption of schedule, constraints on social interaction, less visiting of relatives, and strain on financial resources. On the whole,

Table 3 Impact of Care Giving on Caregivers Esteem, on Schedule, Finances, Health and Family Support

Item	Item No.	Agree/Strongly agree		
		Men (103)	Women (191)	Total (300)
Caregiver esteem				
Privileged to care for . . .	1	97.2	88.4	91.7
Resent having to take care of . . .	7	76.1	57.0	64.0
I really want to care for . . .	9	97.2	89.0	92.0
Not able to do enough for . . .	12	86.2	79.6	82.0
Caring makes me feel good . . .	17	87.2	78.5	81.6
Caring for . . . is important to me	20	94.5	89.5	91.3
Impact on schedule				
My activities are centred around . . .	4	18.4	33.5	28.0
Have to stop work in the middle . . .	8	12.9	24.6	20.3
I visit family/friends less . . .	11	11.9	12.5	12.3
Have to eliminate things from schedule . . .	14	5.5	16.2	12.3
Difficult to find time for relaxation	18	5.5	16.7	12.7
Lack of family support				
Others have dumped caring for . . .	2	38.5	39.8	39.3
Very difficult to get help from family . . .	6	19.3	25.6	23.3
My family works together to care for . . .	13	11.0	22.0	18.0
Since caring for . . . my family abandoned	16	3.7	1.0	2.0
Impact on health				
Since caring tired all the time	5	12.9	27.2	22.0
My health gotten worse since caring for . . .	10	7.3	12.0	10.4
I have enough physical strength to care for . . .	15	7.3	16.7	13.3
I am healthy enough to care for . . .	19	15.6	18.8	17.7
Impact on finances				
My financial resources are adequate . . .	3	37.6	41.4	40.0
Caring put financial strain on family . . .	21	28.5	41.9	37.0
It is difficult to pay for the health needs of elderly . . .	24	34.0	46.6	42.0

the reason for lower percentage of women expressing satisfaction over caregiving and reporting of higher levels of burden on other scales could be because the major burden of caring the elderly is actually shouldered by women rather than by men.

Relationship between Caregiver Stress and Key Variables

From the above discussion, it is found that caregiver stress is correlated with sex and age of the caregiver, and family income. To explore the relationships further, correlations between BAS and CRA scores, and the variables namely age of the caregiver, family income, including duration of stay of the older person with the caregiver—were explored. The values are shown in Table 4.

Table 4 Inter Correlations between BAS and CRA Scores and the Variables of the Caregiver

	Family Income	Duration of Stay	CRA	BAS
Age of the caregiver	–0.070	0.74**	0.44**	0.33**
Sig. (2-tailed)	0.224	0.000	0.000	0.000
Family income	—	–0.014	–0.18**	–0.19**
Sig. (2-tailed)		0.804	0.001	0.001
Duration of stay		—	0.39**	0.30**
Sig. (2-tailed)			0.000	0.000
CRA			—	0.56**
Sig. (2-tailed)				0.000
N= 300				

** Correlation is significant at the 0.01 level (2-tailed).

As can be seen, there is a strong and statistically significant correlation between the age of the caregiver, the duration of stay, and the scores of the two measures, though there is no significant correlation with family income. While the age is positively correlated to both the scores (i.e., BAS and CRA), an inverse but weak relationship is seen between family income and the caregiver stress ($r = -0.19$ for BAS and $r = -0.18$ for CRA, both significant at $p < 0.001$). Thus, this accounts for the stronger relationship between age of the caregiver and caregiver stress than with family income. It can also be seen that the duration of stay is strongly correlated with the scores of the two measures.

Now, the next step is to find out which of the three variables, that is, age of the caregiver, family income, and duration of stay of the elderly with the caregiver—are related to caregiver stress and which explains most of the variation in the caregiver stress?

As the duration of stay of the elderly is found to be positively correlated with age of caregiver (r =0.74, p <0.000) and with the scores of the two measures, partial correlations were run controlling for the age of the caregiver. Then, the relationship between duration of stay with the BAS (r = 0.08, p <0.16) and CRA (r = 0.10, p<0.06) scores disappeared. However, the association between caregiver's age and BAS(r = 0.17, p <0.00) and CRA(r = 0.2, p <0.000) was still strong and was statistically significant even though duration of stay was controlled. That is, with the increasing age, the caregiver is likely to face more caregiver stress, irrespective of family's economic background. And, the caregiver burden is not related to the length of stay of the elderly with the caregiver.

Relationship between the Sub-scales of CRA and Key Variables

An attempt is made to analyse the relationship between the sub-scales of CRA and the key variables, i.e., age of the caregiver and family income.

The data in Table 5 show the correlations between the five sub-scales of CRA and the two variables. It can be seen that the age of the caregiver shows strong and positive correlation with the four areas i.e., impact on health, schedule, lack of family support, and impact on finances. While the age has a strong association with the impact on health, there is a strong negative

Table 5 Inter Correlations between Family Income, Age of Caregiver by Caregiver Satisfaction and Other Sub-scales of CRA

Variable	Caregiver satisfaction	Impact on health	Impact on schedule	Lack of family support	Impact on finances
Age of the caregiver	0.041	0.419**	0.280**	0.208**	0.241**
Sig. (2-tailed)	0.474	0.000	0.000	0.000	0.000
Family income	–0.016	–0.153**	–0.065	–0.125*	–0.174**
Sig. (2-tailed)	0.788	0.008	0.26	0.03	0.00
Caregiver satisfaction	—	–0.411**	–0.304**	–0.374**	–0.247**
Sig. (2-tailed)	—	0.000	.000	0.000	0.000
N=300					

** Correlation is significant at the 0.01 level (2-tailed).

* Correlation is significant at the 0.05 level (2-tailed).

correlation between the caregiver satisfaction and impact on health. Similarly, family income is also inversely correlated with the impact on health. This indicates that, as the age of the caregiver is increasing the impact of stress relating to caregiving on their health is increasing. With regard to family income, it was found that, the lower the income, the greater the negative impact of caregiving on health.

Impact on work schedule also shows positive correlation with caregiver's age and inverse relationship with caregiver satisfaction, thus indicating that higher disruption of the daily routine results in lower caregiving satisfaction and that the impact will increase with the age of the caregiver. In terms of lack of support, again with the increase in the age of caregiver, the chances of counting on family support to help to take care of the elderly seems to become less frequent. Similarly, caregiver satisfaction appears to come down significantly with the financial constraints experienced because of caregiving and this impact appears to scale up with the increase in the age of the caregiver. More importantly, it was found that both the age of the caregiver and family income are weakly related to caregiver satisfaction.

It may be recalled that the age of the caregiver and the family income were found to be strongly associated with the two measures of caregiver stress and burden. To explore the relationship further between, caregiver's age and family income with the caregiver stress, stepwise regression analysis was done. It is observed that both the variables, i.e., caregiver's age and family income put together explain 14 per cent of the BAS score, whereas caregiver age itself contributes up to 11 per cent. In the case of CRA, both the variables were found to explain 22 per cent of the variation, whereas the age of the caregiver is found to contribute up to 19 per cent variation of CRA scores. Both the relationships were significant for BAS and CRA at $F(2,297) = 24.97$, $p < .000$ and $F(2,297) = 41.41$, $p < .000$, respectively.

Conclusions

In the present study, the sample caregivers from rural family context are middle aged (mean age=43 years), predominantly illiterate, poor (mean income=Rs. 1730 pm) and are mostly from extended households. Most of the caregivers of the elderly are wives followed by sons, daughters and daughters-in-law.

A significant finding is that the sex of the caregiver is one of the strong explanatory factors for caregiver stress and women reported higher levels of caregiver stress as compared to men. This may be probably because the major burden of caring the elderly is actually shouldered by the women who are the conventional caregivers in the family. Though a considerable number of caregivers expressed satisfaction over caregiving role played by them, only a small percentage of women expressed their satisfaction about their caregiving role. The caregivers from nuclear households reported higher levels of burden as compared to joint or extended households.

Next, the caregiver burden was found to increase with the increase in the age of the caregiver. Similarly, caregivers from lower income households reported higher levels of burden and it decreased as the income level of the caregiver increased. Further analysis revealed that the age of the caregiver was an important contributing factor than the family income. That is, with the increasing age, the caregiver is likely to experience more stress irrespective of their income levels. Also, evidence shows that the lower the income of caregivers, the greater the impact of caregiving burden on health of the caregiver. And that is found to bring down the caregiver satisfaction significantly.

Coming to the comparison of the two measures used in the study i.e., BAS and CRA, they reflected similar trend with reference to differences on sex, age, and income variables. Therefore, it can be concluded that these two measures are able to capture the caregiver stress and burden in a similar manner. Hence, either of the measures can be used effectively in studying the stress relating to elder care. Next, as compared to BAS, CRA being a multidimensional scale could bring out the impact of stress on such specific dimensions as health, family support and financial strain. Furthermore, except with the sex of the caregiver, the caregiver satisfaction did not emerge as a strong factor either with income or with the age of the caregiver.

References

Bali, A. (1999). Well being of the elderly. *Social Change*, 29(1 and 2) March–June, 64–76.

Cartwright, J.C. et al. (1994). Enrichment processes in family care giving to frail elders. *Advances in Nursing Science*, 17(1): 31–43.

Census of India. (2001). Office of the Registrar General, Ministry of Human Resource Development, New Delhi.

Chakrabarti, P. (1999). Continuity and change in elder care in rural India. *Ageing and Society*, vol. X, nos. III and IV.

Davies, A.J. (1980). Disability, home care and the care-taking role in family life. *Journal of Advanced Nursing*, 5: 475–84.

Decalmer, P. and F. Glendenning (eds.) (1997). *The mistreatment of elderly people.* Second edition. London: Sage.

Given, C.W., B. Given, M. Stommel, C. Collins, S. King and S. Franklin (1992). The caregiver reaction assessment (CRA) for caregivers to persons with chronic physical and mental impairments. *Research in Nursing and Health*, 15: 271–83.

Hirst, M. (2005). Carer distress: A prospective, population based study. *Social Science and Medicine*, 61: 697–708.

Jamuna, D. and P.V. Ramamurti (1999). Contributants to good care giving: An analysis of dyadic relationships. *Social Change*, 29: (1 and 2) March–June: 138–44.

Jamuna, D. (1997). Stress dimensions among caregivers of the elderly. *The Indian Journal of Medical Research. Spl. issue: Aging in India*, pp. 381–87.

NSSO (1997). National sample survey. Socio-economic profile of aged persons. National Sample Survey Organization, Government of India, New Delhi, 52nd Round.

Prakash, Indira Jai (2001). On being old and female: Some issues in quality of life of elderly women in India. *Indian Journal of Gerontology*, vol. 15 (3 and 4): 333–41.

——. (1999). Adult women and the aging process. *Ageing and Society*, vol. X, nos. III and IV.

Puri, S. (2004). Supporting family care of older persons, a paper presented at the National Consultative Meeting on Emerging Issues in Care of Older Persons in India, 4th November.

Reinhard, S.C. and A.V. Horwitz (1995). Caregiver burden: Differentiating the content and consequenes of family care giving. *Journal of Marriage and the Family*, 57: 741–50.

Sharma, K.L. (2003). Health status and caregivers of elderly rural women. *Indian Journal of Gerontology*, vol. 17(1 and 2): 157–66.

Vijayakumar, S. (1999). Elderly in the changing traditional family structure: Indian scenario. *Social Change*, vol. 29 (1 and 2), March–June: 72–89.

10

Stereotypes of Ageing among School Students

U.C. Jain and K.L. Sharma

Human cognition is characterized by its capacity of categorization. Whatever is perceived is labelled in certain category pre-existed in the form of a cognitive schema which, is formed as a product of earlier learning. This categorization often leads to develop a number of stereotypes which guide our thinking, perceptions and actions towards the objects and human beings. Stereotypes are based on false generalizations of group characteristics to the individual level, which we share as members of social group. Once we label an individual belonging to certain category (e.g., caste, class, race, age) we are prone to attribute all those group characteristics to the individual member which may or may not be existing with the person. In this paper we are concerned with the stereotypes about the aged persons which are, in general false, but considered by perceivers as 'true'.

In recent years gerontologists have coined a term 'ageism' to refer the discrimination based on chronological age (Butler and Lewis, 1969). Ageism is a process of systematic stereotyping against the old people held not only by the younger and middle aged persons but also internalized by the older persons themselves. As stereotypes are formed on the basis of social interaction to simplify our perceptions and opinions about others, it becomes difficult to change them. However change is needed to present the correct images of the person(s) belonging to other category. For example, stereotypes about the aged present highly negative images of the aged persons as senile, suffer from memory loss, impotent, mentally declined, look ugly, sick and disabled, rigid and authoritarians etc. Such stereotypes lead to prejudices and discrimination (Palmore, 1990). Stereotypes about aged are not only held by younger and middle aged persons but the aged subjected to prejudice and discrimination tends to adopt the negative images and behaviours very much similar to the stereotypes about them. Thus, a vicious circle is created. Many of these stereotypes about old age are misconceptions. For example, believing that impairment is an inevitable part of ageing, older people cannot contribute to the household, workplace or community and so on and so forth. On the contrary in the present era better medical care has made persons above 60 years of age the fastest growing section of the society. The national policy recognizes that 60+ age group as a huge untapped resource. Their abilities should be boosted to enable them to have a healthy and cheerful life.

Several studies on ageism (e.g., Allen et al., 1980; Boone, 1985, Butler, 1969; Butler and Lewis, 1982; Sharma, 2002) have documented the prevalence of stereotypes about aged in developing and developed countries. Several social processes, such as communication, negotiation, advertisement, movies are involved in constructing and maintaining ageist attitudes. For example, commercial advertisements on anti-ageing drugs, availability of housing complex for aged and life insurances etc. depict older people in stereotypical ways. Indian religions and philosophical schools have characterized old age as the time for disengagement from the family and society to pursue spiritual goals which indirectly support the ageism by suggesting a secluded lifestyle different from the active members of the society. These socio-cultural processes create a set of expectations concerning the desirable behaviours of the aged.

Ageism has several consequences for elderly persons, particularly, for their behaviours in the society and family. In a study (Palmore, 1990) four common behaviours were noted in the aged, in response to the stereotypes held by the society. These include acceptance, denial, avoidance and reform. Such responses may result in depression and its attendant's physiological consequences. Government policy for the retirement of employees on reaching at certain age may contribute to prevailing ageism in the sense that, one is declared as not fit for the job any more. For many aged persons retirement brings depression due to reduced income and engagement. For many of them retirement brings idleness and boredom as they start believing that in old age everything turnout badly and failure is to be expected.

In fact retirement should be linked with the physical fitness rather than age. Retirement may be considered marginalization and stigmatization of elderly people due to society's misconceptions, intolerance and lack of awareness.

A number of controversies exist in the literature on ageism. For example, some thinks that ageism is not a cross-cultural phenomenon as in primitive societies it does not exist. Others think that it is universal and the differences are due to different methodology used in the studies (Sharma, 2002). India has had a long tradition of reverence to the older people and the younger generation feel obligation to have the blessings and guidance of the older persons. However, due to increasing trend of free market economy and its attendant consequences on the lifestyles of younger generation ageism is likely to be enhanced in India. Another important contributor to ageism seems to be increasing population of the older people (as per the 2001 census 7.7 per cent of the total Indian population is of the people 60 plus years) and high-rise pricing trend. In the present circumstances the older persons are vulnerable to abuse, neglect and exploitation (Datta, 2006).

The present study intends to explore the prevailing stereotypes among the high school students towards aged persons, for it is relatively easier to correct the negative stereotypes at this developing age before the stereotypes become deeply rooted. In the context of coeducation it is expected that both the male and female students will have somewhat similar stereotypes.

Method

The Help Age Questionnaire taken from Gastron et al. (2001) was translated in Hindi and back translated in English to assure the accuracy of the Hindi translation. The questionnaire has 15 items comprising nine items as erroneous (ageist) and six items as correct. The respondents must mark the items, according to their own criteria, which they consider to be true and which false. The scoring of the items involved two criteria: quantity and quality. Quantity can be judged by the number of errors committed in marking the items which, indicates the level of lack of knowledge and prejudice about ageing. The quality can be assessed by combining different correct and incorrect responses.

Sample: One hundred students equally drawn from the 10th standard of a school located in a neighbourhood of lower middle class families at Bhopal (Madhya Pradesh, India) whose age ranged from 14–16 years served as participants in this study. The questionnaire was administered in the classrooms instructing the students about the aim of the study to know their opinions described in the items. They were told to mark each item as true or false as per their opinions.

Procedure: Following Gatsron et al. (2001) the coding of each item as correct/incorrect was established. A table of the sum of lack of knowledge or prejudice was constructed. Subsequently, incorrect responses were grouped together to determine the level of prejudices: High, Medium, Low and no prejudice (criteria 1).

Responses were also categorized in the following dimensions to evaluate the prejudices as per criteria 2:

Dimension 1: Sexless—adding the responses on items 9 & 10
Dimension 2: Uselessness—adding the responses on items 1 & 15
Dimension 3: Homogenisation by age—adding the responses on items 12 & 13
Dimension 4: Normal decline neglect—adding the responses on items 2, 7 & 11
Dimension 5: Ineffectiveness and lack of performance—adding the responses on items 6 & 8

Results

The incorrect responses were counted for each item and the percentages of the participants were calculated for each incorrect response. The data are shown in Table 1.

It is clear from the Table 1 that percentages of incorrect responses on item 1, 4, 6, 7 and 14 are in high proportion showing that majority of the older persons are incorrectly perceived as senile, lesser effective workers, and rich than younger persons. These stereotypes are shared by both male and female students. The percentage of female students is greater than male students for these stereotypes. On the other extreme on items 2, 11 and 15 female respondents endorsed more correct responses than

Table 1 Percentage of Incorrect Responses

Item (F = False T = True)	Male	Female
1. (F) The majority of the elders are senile	66.66	71.64
2. (T) All five senses tend to decline with age	15.16	14.93
3. (F) The height of a person tend to decrease with age	39.39	23.88
4. (T) Older adults have more chronic illnesses that limit their activities than younger persons	21.21	19.95
5. (F) Older people have more damages in the home than younger persons	57.57	43.28
6. (F) The majority of older workers cannot work as effectively as younger workers	63.63	73.13
7. (T) Usually it may take somewhat longer to learn something in old age	24.25	16.42
8. (T) The majority of the elders are healthy enough to carry out their normal activities	36.36	38.41
9. (F) The life expectancy of women is about the same as of men	36.36	26.86
10. (F) Older widows are likely about the same as older widowers	42.42	44.77
11. (T) Reaction time in the majority of the elders tends to slowdown in comparison of the reaction time in the majority of younger persons	09.00	17.92
12. (F) Usually the majority of the aged resemble each other	42.42	41.79
13. (F) Healthy elderly naturally withdraw from participation in community life	39.39	37.31
14. (F) The majority of the elders are more rich than younger persons	63.63	50.74
15. (T) The majority of the elders have any job or want to work	30.31	17.42

incorrect. Similarly, male students also showed correct responses on the items 2, 4, 7, 11 and 15, however, in comparison to female students more erroneous responses were obtained on the item 15 for male students. Thus, aged are correctly perceived for having all the five senses tend to decline with age, older adults have more chronic illness that limits their activities

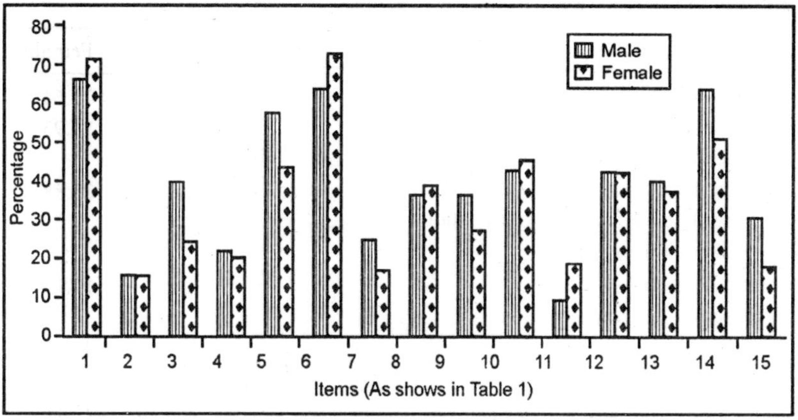

Figure 1 Percentage of Incorrect Responses

than younger persons, they take longer time to learn, majority of the aged have slow reaction time, and that majority of the aged want to work or have jobs. On other items majority of the responses reflect prejudicial.

The distribution of prejudices in high, medium and low categories is shown in the Table 2. It is clear that 27.27 per cent male respondents and 40.29 per cent of the female respondents fall in the low level of prejudice category. Similarly, 45.45 per cent of male students and 37.31 per cent female students show medium level of prejudices against older persons. It is interesting to note that only 27.27 per cent of male and 22.38 per cent of female students possess high level of prejudices. Overall female students expressed less prejudices than male students.

Table 2 Level of Total Prejudice (in %)

Level of Prejudice	Male	Female
High	27.27	40.29
Medium	45.45	37.31
Low	27.28	22.30

To assess the quality of the prejudice further analysis was conducted considering the incorrect and correct items. The results are shown in the Table 3.

Table 3 Quality of Total Prejudice (in%)

Type of Prejudice	Male	Female
Decrease in height	39.39	23.88
Without chronic illnesses	78.78	80.05
Homogenization by age	40.90	39.55
More injuries than younger persons	57.57	43.28
Ineffectiveness and lack of performance	63.63	67.36
Normal decline neglect	83.83	83.57
Sexless	39.39	35.81
Uselessness	68.17	76.86

1. Item 3 marks reference to a person's height. More than one-third of the respondents endorse the prejudice that the height of a person tend to decrease with age. In fact decrease in height is not a question of age in itself but a result of certain pathology like osteoporosis.

2. Item 4 deals with chronic illnesses in older persons which, is a fact, however, near about 80 per cent of the respondents denied this showing a positive prejudice.

3. This type of prejudice is derived from the combination of items 12 and 13 indicating that older people are very much alike and are healthy but do not participate in community life. Roughly 40 per cent of the respondents hold this prejudice.

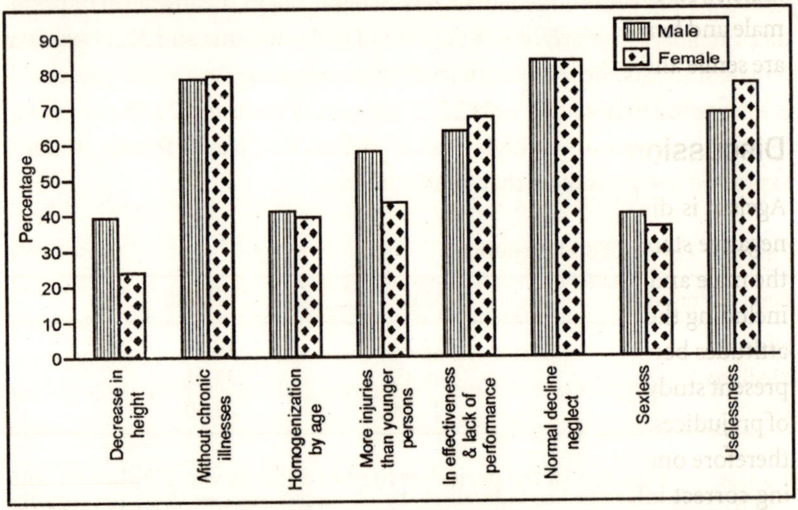

Figure 2 Quality of Prejudice

4. Item 5 deals with a prejudice that older people have more damages in the home than younger persons. It is a fact that older people are careful in moving than younger persons and hence have lesser possibilities of meeting accidents than younger persons.

5. This type of prejudice is obtained by combining item 6 and 8. The former refers to the unproductivity of elders and later to difficulty in doing normal activities due to health problems. The prejudice is because of labour market, high unemployment, and policy of retirement among other factors.

6. This type of prejudice represents the combination of items 2, 7, and 11 indicating decline in the senses, slowness in learning and slowness of reactions in order. All these items were keyed as true but as many as 84 per cent of male and female students responded incorrectly on these items, perhaps in order to present a positive picture of elderly and thus showed prejudice in the positive direction.

7. Items 9 and 10 make reference to the average life span for men and women and proportion of widowhood in men and women. A sizable responses 36–40 per cent were incorrect, showing lack of differentiation in men and women older persons.

8. This type of prejudice is reflected on the combined responses to the items 1, and 15 showing problem of senility and participation in labour market. As many as 70–76 per cent responses were in correct showing that male and female students wrongly believe that majority of the older people are senile and they do not want to work.

Discussion

Ageism is discrimination and prejudices towards elderly people. Mostly negative stereotypes towards aged are noted without much differences in the male and female students selected in the present study. A recent study including the three age groups also noted not much differences in ageistic attitudes between male and female samples.The significant finding of the present study is that only a lower percentage of the students hold high level of prejudices. Majority of the students have medium level of prejudices and therefore one can expect that these prejudices can be alleviated by providing correct information regarding the characteristics of the aged population. It is also observed that majority of these students have regards for their elderly family members and therefore if stereotypes are corrected at this stage during schooling, the goal of utilizing the wisdom of the aged as a rich human resource for the enrichment of the society and the betterment of the aged population can be achieved. In a recent study (Jamuna and Ramamurti, 2007) it is noted that the degree of prejudices towards aged are more in the younger adults as compared to the middle aged and old, thus it is reiterated that, at the school level, intervention is needed to impart correct information about the aged and the need of their care within the family system. The results of the present study must be taken with caution because of the small size of sample drawn from a particular school mostly serving the educational needs of lower middle class students. Nonetheless, the findings are suggestive to the prevalence of negative as well as positive stereotypes at moderate level amongst the young school students.

References

Allen, J. et al. (1980). Ageism and racism: Two issues in social work, education and practice. *Journal of Education for Social Work*, 16(2): 71–77.

Boone, D.R. (1985). Ageism: A negative view of aged. *ASHA*, 27: 51–53.

Butler, R.N. (1969). Age-ism: Another form of bigotry. *The Gerontologist*, 9: 243–464.

Butler, R.N. and M.I. Lewis (1982). *Ageing and mental health.* (3rd ed.), St. Louis, MO: CV Mosby.

Datta, A. (2006). Greying citizenship: The situation of the older persons in India. *Indian Journal of Gerontology*, 20, 3: 285–98.

Gatsron, L., H. Andres and J. Vujosevich (2001). Ageism at school: Images and stereotypes of ageing and the old age in Argentina. *Indian Journal of Gerontology* 16(1 and 2): 161–80.

Jamuna, D. and P.V. Ramamurti (2007). Perception of ageism across the generations. *Indian Journal of Gerontology*, 21, 2: 198–205.

Palmore, E. (1990). *Agism: Negative and positive.* (2nd ed.), New York: Springer.

Sharma, K.L. (2002). Images of ageing. *Indian Journal of Gerontology*, 16, 3, 4: 286–97.

Part II

Elder Abuse

11

A Community Response to Financial Abuse of Older Adults

Dephne Nahmiash and Rhonda Schwartz

The paper will first explain the prevalence of the overall phenomenon of abuse in general against older adults. Definitions will be addressed next, including the difficulties in arriving at a common terminology. We will then focus on financial and material abuse which is the most common type of abuse reported in Canada. We will present a brief review of the literature which highlights how financial abuse has been described and some attempts to prevent the problem throughout Canada and the USA. A brief discussion on the probable causes will follow including why seniors do not report such crimes. Next, we will present a case study of a small community's attempts to educate seniors about the possible incidents of abuse in the home and on the street using a community development model based on the principles of empowerment. Finally, we will draw some conclusions from the study and the model which could be useful for other community organizations in the prevention of such abuse.

Prevalence

Why are we talking about financial/material abuse towards older adults right now? Is the phenomenon more prevalent than it was? It is important to note that such crimes against older adults are not a new phenomenon. In fact, a recent study from Greece (Pitsiou, Darrough and Spinellis, 1995) notes that "ancient Greek history reveals clear cases of selfish carelessness or coarse insolence toward the old and offers instances of children taking over their parents property . . . without proof of incapacity in the elders" (p. 45). We also note that all types of abuse and neglect of older adults have only come to the attention of researchers and practitioners in the past three or four decades. However the first national Canadian study notes that approximately one in 25 older persons (over the age of 65) are victims of abuse and neglect (Podnieks et al., 1989). Similar estimates have been made for the United States (Select Committee on Aging, 1981). In the past three decades more and more countries have been identifying the problem and finding ways to bring it to the public attention. A British study observed that work on abuse of older adults has been reported in 22 European countries (Council of Europe, 1992), even though much of the work is still in the formative stages. One author has compiled research from ten countries in different parts of the world from international and cross-cultural perspectives (Kosberg and Garcia, 1995). The same authors conclude that the problem will probably augment as a worldwide social problem as populations are ageing rapidly and the number and proportion of older adults are increasing, especially the oldest of the old.

In spite of all this, few studies have actually measured the incidence or prevalence of the phenomenon. Of those studies which have attempted to measure the problem, the descriptions vary according to the methodology used. For example, it is difficult to distinguish in the studies between incidence and prevalence of cases. North American studies however, do seem to agree that between 3 and 5 per cent of persons over the age of 65 years are victims of abuse and/or neglect (Podnieks et al., 1989; Tatara, 1993). In the United States alone, this represents over one million persons. Thus, we can say that abuse of older adults is a serious social problem and practitioners should be aware of its existence in order to identify, treat and prevent it. Authors have also noted in all studies that the phenomenon of abuse and neglect is extremely taboo among the older population and rarely reported. The reported estimates of 3–5 per cent are probably underestimated since most cases are hidden and difficult to find. For this reason, it is extremely important that doctors and health care professionals become familiar with the signs and symptoms of suspected abuse. Next, we will define what we mean by the terms 'abuse' and 'neglect' of older adults and what we mean by 'caregiver abusers'.

Definitions of Abuse and Neglect

Definitions of abuse and neglect are problematic, since there are no agreed-upon intrinsic or extrinsic definitions nor are there standardized conceptualizations of the phenomenon as yet, although several authors have attempted this, including Hudson and Johnson (1986) from the US and Stones (1991) from Canada. Definitions are nevertheless important to give a clear understanding of the problem in question and differentiate that area of concern from others. One of the main reasons why definitions differ is that their meanings are interpreted differently by each researcher, depending upon the purpose of the study. Some people use the word 'mistreatment' and others use the term 'abuse and neglect'. The World Health Organization offers the following general definition of abuse: "a single or repeated act, or lack of appropriate action, occurring within a relationship where there is an expectation of trust, which causes harm or distress to an older person" (WHO, 2002). In the same document, relationships of trust are referred to as those between a senior and a family member (immediate or extended) and friends, but also include those in which an older adult relies on someone for care or services in a paid relationship, for example, a financial advisor, home care provider or medical professional. A Canadian framework for defining abuse and neglect is described in the EAST tool, which contain 71 items grouped into the following nine categories (Stones, 1995): physical assault, excessive restraint, putting health at risk, failure to give care by someone acting as a paid or unpaid caretaker under pressure, humiliating behaviour, abuse in an institution, material (includes financial) exploitation and verbal humiliation. Stones found high agreement among seniors and professionals on items that indicate greater or lesser abuse and the items rated as most abusive by seniors were mainly examples of physical abuse. However, most researchers have opted to use the following definitions to operationalize the types of abuse and neglect encountered (Podnieks et al., 1990; Pillemer and Finkelhor, 1988; Pillemer and Wolf, 1986; Kosberg,1988). They are as follows:

Physical abuse: hitting, burning, assault, rough handling

Sexual abuse: any form of assaulting the person in a sexual way or forcing them to perform or engage in any sexual activity against their wishes.

Psychological abuse: when an older person is subjected to repeated or chronic verbal assaults which insult, threaten, humiliate or exclude. This also includes lack of affection, social isolation or denying the person the chance to make or participate in decisions which are in their own interests are included.

Material/financial abuse: misuse of money, possessions or property. This includes fraud or using an older adult's funds for purposes contrary to their needs and interests.

Passive or active neglect: the withholding of items or care necessary for daily living, and can be intentional (active or physical) or non-intentional (passive).

Self-neglect has also been identified as a form of abuse. It consists of a person's failure to provide adequate care for him/herself. This form of abuse is different from the others in that there is no abuser involved. However relatives or others may be aware of the problem and fail to help.

Violation of a person's rights has also been recognized as a form of abuse. This consists of forcing a person to do something against their wishes or preventing them from making their own decisions, such as forcing them to go to a nursing home. Other authors include this as part of psychological abuse.

Social, systemic or collective abuse: a societal form of abuse. It includes ageism and other ways of treating elderly persons which affect their personal dignity and identity. This type of abuse was highlighted in a British study, which pointed out that abuse and neglect are socially structured through a range of policies and professional ideologies relating to dependency in old age (Biggs et al., 1995).

A knowledge of all types of abuse and neglect is important in this study of financial abuse as rarely do we find only one type of abuse present against older adults (Nahmiash, 1997).

Finally, it is important to note that multicultural or aboriginal groups may define abuse and neglect in different ways. This is particularly relevant to this article as the case study example was done in a multicultural community in Montreal. Most studies ignore these cultural aspects and seem to assume that all older adults are similar in their attitudes and perceptions. Primary prevention programmes, such as the one cited in the case study, need to pay attention to these aspects as each society and group has different standards and norms about what constitutes abusive and neglectful behaviour. Most standards and norms regarding financial and material abuse are laid down in the criminal code or the charter of rights of the country, but other types of abuse may be defined by common consensus of the society or group. Psychological abuse and neglect or self-neglect tend to mostly fall into this latter category. Having defined the different types of abuse and neglect, we will now focus specifically on financial and material forms of abuse.

Examples of financial/material abuse of older adults from case studies

The following case studies describe incidences of financial and/or material abuse and also hint at some possible causes and explanations for the abuse.

An 83-year-old father is abused by his son who persuaded him to sign over his house with a promise to take care of his father. After the father no longer owned his home he told the interviewer that the son "sold his house, he told me he'll invest his money in something . . . so he had to buy some stocks (Did you know about this and agree to it at the time?)" No, I was too stupid . . . everybody took advantage of me. And I feel that he took advantage of me and now he doesn't need me so he doesn't bother with me". The father told the interviewer how powerless and isolated this made him feel (Nahmiash, 1997). The case also hints at the abuser's explanation for his actions which can be noted as money or material possessions being a fair exchange for care in his son's eyes.

A daughter and son-in-law (both substance abusers) also took over their mother's property. They told the interviewer it was a gift and put the house in their own names. She describes it this way. "She (the daughter) broke into my house. She used her key . . . and stole . . . out of my purse". The daughter justifies her behaviour by stating: "I have heard how she . . . had to pay off her mortgage and how I've never paid her back. I didn't ask her to do that and I have no intention of paying her back. She did what she did. It was her choice and to me it was a gift . . . I will say she did give a lot materially, but all unsolicited. There were times when I did ask, yes, but the majority of time it was all unsolicited and it was the way my mother kept control. "

It is interesting how the daughter feels no remorse for her abusive behaviour towards her mother but justifies it and blames her, which conforms with Tomita's (1990) neutralization theory that abusers often justify their crimes.

A third example shows how some young stepchildren stole from their elderly father. "The kids started stealing from me and then . . . would tell me to go ahead find out who is stealing . . . money . . . clothes, from the bureau, from their mother's purse . . . and they would do charity work and steal from the donations . . . overwrite them then sometimes they would say "You're not my father" and I was the one giving everything. I paid all the expenses . . . and I didn't like the stealing."

The abusive stepdaughter also went to see a legal counsellor to get advice about how much money she was entitled to, from her stepfather. She said that "she could take half of everything, half of my (the stepfather's) savings, half the furniture . . . the insurance . . . I felt I was betrayed by the oldest girl. She kept asking and she thought "well this is the way I'll take her (the girl's mother) away from him. " In this example, we see how the child's explanation for her abusive behaviour was to get back her mother from her stepfather who she felt was too old and senile to fight back. "Now look, you're going cuckoo, you're losing it. You're going senile . . ." sort of like telling me you're not thinking properly. "

Thus, the girl justifies her behaviour through ageist comments which support Robert Butler's (1987) conclusions that in some cases, old age is equated by society with powerlessness and uselessness as a result of disease, disability and uselessness. Butler (1987) defines ageism as "reflecting a deep-seated uneasiness on the part of the young and the middle-aged, a personal revulsion to and distaste for growing old, disease, disability and a fear of powerlessness, uselessness and death" (p. 243).

Ageism was also described as the only cause in the following case example concerning financial and material abuse: A young couple bought a house and moved next door to a couple of older adults. Subsequently they went to extraordinary lengths to abuse and get control of part of the property and land belonging to the older couple. The case was brought to court by the 78 year old lady whose husband was disabled. She fought back bravely for over two years using the criminal justice system with little success. The only explanation for the behaviour of the abusers seemed to be that the older couple was, in the opinion of the younger, too old to fightback. The abused lady describes her experience as follows: In response to the abusers saying "You know we have a right to do these things. We are young and work hard", the abused lady replied: "I said Mister; we have worked all of our life. This is our home . . . He (the neighbor) would do crazy things so we couldn't get out. It was like that for three years . . . We were stuck. They hosed us in our yard, spat in our yard, waited for us at 10:00 at night . . . She started to mark the property with white paint . . . They built a fence . . . We tolerated, we endured. If it would have been somebody young, that would have thrown them. They would have had to face them, but they knew they were dealing with a crazy old woman . . . and (an) old man so they took advantage of it. They've hurt my health and made me incur expenses . . . I believe its going to go up to $10,000 because they know we were old . . . and to be gone soon".

This example demonstrates how ageist attitudes can directly contribute towards abusive behaviour and how a younger couple can justify such behaviour by such attitudes. Furthermore, the ageist attitudes were condoned by the very societal protection system, i. e., the criminal justice system, put in place to protect them, since after three years, the older couple did not resolve the case against the abusers and asked to be placed in a nursing home. The lady finally states, "How can it (the criminal proceedings) take so long, cost so much and make me suffer (she was hospitalized on account of the lengthy court proceedings)?" Her conclusion was "There is no justice".

How do we know if an older person is a victim of financial abuse?

Most seniors are reluctant to report abuse or neglect of any kind especially if it is perpetrated by a family member. The reasons for this include the fear that they will lose the important relationship they have with that person and the fear of their family's reactions to the abuse being made public or ashamed of what is happening and their inability to prevent it. Abuse of older adults is like all forms of violence: it is kept as a well guarded family secret. They also find it difficult to ask anyone outside the family for help. One victim of abuse expressed it this way: "Tell the Doctor what happened . . . I didn't think Doctors were interested in this, you know, family affairs. " Another stated, "I know sometimes you have to have someone to talk to but this woman was outside the family". A third person put it this way, "Some things are better not said . . . I was really scared to tell anyone . . . I just kept it to myself. "

In spite of the reluctance of victims to talk about financial abuse, there are some signs of abuse which friends, neighbours and health and social service practitioners can be aware of to detect whether abuse is occurring or not. If they do observe such signs, they need to ask further questions about the missing objects or money.

Here are some examples of the signs:

- Loss of money, bank books or cheques;
- The signature on checks does not resemble that of the older adult;
- Bank statements are no longer coming to the person's home;
- Sudden unexplained or large withdrawals from the bank;
- Sudden inability to pay bills or buy food or clothing;
- Receives incorrect change from person purchasing food or goods;
- Loss of jewellery, silverware, paintings, furniture or sculptures;
- Unprecedented transfer of money or property;
- Someone is pressuring the person to sign legal papers (such as a will, a power of attorney or a joint deed to the house);
- A new will is drawn up and the older person did not agree to change it;
- The older adult is not being allowed to make decisions or speak for him or herself;
- The person is not in close contact with family or friends;
- The person is afraid or worried when money is mentioned; and
- Power of Attorney or mandate is improperly obtained (from someone who is mentally competent).

Review of the literature concerning financial abuse

There is not a great deal of Canadian literature in scientific journals specifically about financial abuse but this brief review will document a few of the points emerging from the existing articles. Financial exploitation was noted to be the most frequently reported form of elder abuse by older victims of abuse in the large national study done through telephone surveys by Podnieks and her colleagues (Podnieks et al., 1989). However, in the Pittaway (Pittaway et al., 1995) study from 489 files of elder abuse cases, financial abuse was only observed to be the third largest form of abuse representing 26. 6 per cent of the abuse and neglect cases. (Psychological and physical abuse were the most frequent.) Finally, the Project Care study (Reis and Nahmiash, 1995) showed that financial abuse was the second most frequently documented among abuse cases.

In 1992, Spencer began a two year study in British Columbia investigating financial abuse among 200 seniors. She found that 8 per cent of older adults had been financially abused, losing, on an average, approximately $20,000 each (Spencer, 1994). Some forms of abuse, in particular financial abuse, constitute crimes and fall under criminal and civil legislation acts. As well, approximately one quarter of all crimes against older adults are committed by family members, usually a spouse or adult children. The consequences of abuse usually lead to depression and serious health problems associated with highly stressful living conditions. In the case of financial abuse, loss of housing, poverty and other economic costs are also related [Federal/Provincial/Territorial Committee of Officials(Seniors)2005]. Abuse and neglect has been found to significantly shorten the lives of older adults. Substance abuse problems (including gambling) and mental health problems are factors occurring in up to one third of cases [Federal/Provincial/Territorial Committee of Officials(Seniors) 2003]. Many forms of abuse also involve tangible and intangible social and economic costs, such as costs to health care, community services and the justice systems (Spencer, 1999), as well as to the older victims themselves. However the exact costs cannot yet be measured due to the lack of consistent definitions being used, the lack of standard services for abused older adults, the lack of reliable data and the lack of standardized information collection practices [Federal/Provincial/Territorial Committee of Officials(Seniors), 2005].

In spite of the dearth of scientific studies on financial abuse over the past few decades, a surprising amount of programmes have recently been established across Canada to prevent and intervene in cases of abuse and neglect. Abuse and neglect have been identified and prioritized by the Federal Government of Canada and most provincial and territorial governments as an important social and public health problem or as part of overall family violence prevention programmes. As well, World Elder Abuse Day is observed across Canada to offer widespread education and public awareness about elder abuse. A number of prevention, education and intervention approaches exist, though few have been evaluated scientifically to measure their effectiveness. Prevention approaches include models, such as the Community Response Networks in British Columbia, Alberta Elder Abuse Awareness Network, the Ontario Network for the Prevention of Elder Abuse and the Quebec Network against Elder Abuse. We can also note that many provinces, for example, New Brunswick and Nova Scotia, have produced manuals and educational materials for the prevention of fraud and scams and other forms of financial abuse which have been used widely across Canada. Most provinces have strategic plans to provide programmes, such as outreach, education and public awareness campaigns.

In terms of interventions, the main approaches used have been adult protection models, domestic violence models, advocacy programmes, integrated models and coordinated community approaches sometimes based on multidisciplinary teams offering a range of services, such as home care. Several provinces provide emergency shelters, crisis intervention or family therapy service programmes for victims of elder abuse. As well, some provide assessment and counselling teams, telephone hot lines and support groups.

It should also be noted that programmes are offered in the Yukon and the North West Territories to offer emergency shelter and education to victims of abuse.

The principle laws enacted in Canada to help victims of crimes, such as financial and material abuse are as follows: adult protection laws (primarily in the Atlantic provinces), adult guardianship, human rights laws (in Quebec), family violence statutes and criminal law. An innovative community legal clinic for low income seniors offering legal advice and services is the Advocacy Center for the Elderly established in the 1980s in Toronto [Federal/Provincial/Territorial Committee of Officials(Seniors)2003].

In spite of these available laws to intervene in cases of financial abuse, a recent study showed that most health care practitioners and seniors do not use the legal recourses and are not informed about them even though legal services could resolve most of the cases. In fact, there was agreement that financial abuse cases would be more likely to be resolved through the justice system than cases of other types of abuse (Noreau et al., 2007).

In spite of all of the above programmes and interventions, few articles if any, have evaluated the innovative community approaches to prevent financial abuse and neglect from occurring. For this reason we will next present a small evaluated Canadian community project to demonstrate how information can be provided to seniors with measurable outcomes for success.

Community Case Study: "Partners Against Crime"

Background and Context

In the west end of Montreal, a small community-based organization, Notre-Dame de Grace Community Committee on Elder Abuse (NDGCCEA), designs and implements programmes with the objectives of providing education about abuse of older adults to help reduce the incidence of this abuse occurring. During 2001–2002, they compiled and analysed statistics to explore which crimes were reported as most frequently perpetrated against older adults in the area. The study was undertaken by the community service police officers from the local police station, who sit on the board of this organization. The area of Notre-Dame de Grace had a population of 64,675 residents, of whom 12,945 persons were over the age of 60 years (CLSC NDG/Montreal Ouest, 2003). As well, since 1996 there has been an increase in the number of people who are 85 years and older in the area. This population group will continue to increase in number and represents the most vulnerable group in the community. We should also note that the proportion of people over 65 years in the area is 18 per cent higher than in the overall Montreal region. A high number of the residents are low-income, and the areas of low cost housing are at increased risk for criminal activity and security problems (Plamondon and Nahmiash, 2006), according to the police and the residents, creating a higher-risk situation. The case study also examined who were the perpetrators of such crimes against older adults as well as the types of crimes reported. The results of the study showed that 166 crimes were committed against 166 seniors during this period, representing 5.5 per cent of the total number of seniors in the area of Notre-Dame de Grace at the time of the study. Nearly 20 per cent of the crimes against older adults were perpetrated by young persons, most of whom were between the ages of 15–16years. It was also noted that this percentage (20 per cent) represents a total greater than the total percentage of youths in this age category (between 14 and 25 years) in the population of this area (14.3 per cent). The average overall age of perpetrators was 37 years for males and 39 years for females. However, this percentage includes a few persons who were over 60 years of age which elevated the average age of the group. The types of crimes reported and perpetrated against older adults fell mainly into two categories. The first included thefts and breaking and entering (clearly forms of financial abuse), while the second category included assaults and assault with a weapon or threats against older persons, including purse snatching. Fraud and other types of financial abuse were also reported. Even though the crimes against older adults are relatively few compared to the overall crimes in the area, few crimes against seniors are actually reported due to fear and lack of awareness of those in the community who can provide assistance to them. In fact, some seniors feel forced to move to another community to avoid what they perceive as dangerous environments, thereby removing them from their familiar surroundings and creating a new insecure and isolated situation (Brillon, 1987). It has also been reported that the impact of such crimes on older adults (particularly older women) is far more severe than on younger adults (Brillon, 1987). The fear and insecurity of becoming a victim contributes to social isolation, depression and loss of mobility, which all affect the physical and psychological health of the seniors. These factors all contribute to a cycle of fear, vulnerability and increased risk of becoming a victim.

A second small qualitative study found that a number of unreported incidents were also observed by members of the NDGCCEA (reported by a local bank representative and a legal expert) which show how financial experts have a difficult time assessing when financial abuse occurs:

An elderly client, who has substantial savings in her account, appears frequently before a bank teller and is visibly confused. Friends sometimes accompany her. The bank teller does not have enough knowledge to be able to judge the mental capacity of the client to assess whether she is competent to decide to make the withdrawals from her account or if she is being influenced by her companions.

A son accompanies his elderly mother to the bank every month at which time all money is removed from her account. Bankers are limited regarding what they can do when they suspect an elderly client may be financially abused due to the fact that the client is a fully capable person who has the right to make her choice.

An elderly person sends a neighbour to perform all her banking needs through the ATM machine by giving the neighbour her bank card (and PIN number) and money to deposit.

Following the study, it was decided to develop a programme to run over a period of one year,whose goals included the prevention of crimes against older adults by empowering them with the necessary skills, information and tools to in order to raise their awareness and knowledge of potentially abusive situations. The organization had previously been successful in offering (and continues to offer) educational workshops in high schools to address the issue of ageism among 14–15 year old youths, and to provide positive experiences with older adults and positive images of older adults (Joining Generations, 2001).

Objectives

The project "Partners Against Crime: A Programme to Help Prevent Financial and Material Abuse" (NDCCEA, 2007) involved a collaborative partnership with the NDGCCEA, local community police officers, Tandem Montreal (an organization which provides security services to the community), a representative of the Royal Bank and students from the McGill School of Social Work. The project was presented in five low-income housing units in the area of Notre-dame de Grace, with each building having approximately one hundred tenants.

The specific objectives of the project were to:

- provide seniors with the knowledge, skills and tools to safeguard their finances, property and person;
- reduce fears and insecurities so that their safeguarding measures would be appropriate;
- reduce fears and insecurities to increase the chances that they will report crimes/abuse to the appropriate authorities; and
- provide past victims with the knowledge, skills and tools to prevent further incidents (since a high number of such victims are repeat victims).

It was hoped to meet the objectives by empowering seniors with the knowledge and skills that would prevent them from becoming victims. It has been observed that education is not only about acquiring information, but is also about changing attitudes, behaviours and values. Thus, education is one of the most significant primary preventative interventions in elder abuse and neglect (Gallagher, 1993; Podnieks et al., 1989; Podnieks and Bailey, 1995).

Description

The project was designed and adapted from an unpublished model entitled "Community Organization Process" from the CLSC NDG/Montreal Quest with the following steps:

- Development of a preliminary understanding of the needs of the community and the problems defined by the community, based on a previous study done by Plamondon and Nahmiash (2006), exploring the needs and characteristics of tenants living in low-income housing units (Plamondon and Nahmiash, 2006).
- Assessment and analysis of the articulated needs in relation to the well being of and potential risks towards the residents in the buildings;
- Project development and planning phase—included establishing priorities, adjustment of project goals, determination of target population (selection of residences), definition of project activities and strategies, definition of indicators of success (measurement tools), definition of implementation procedures, definition of evaluation procedures and determination of resources required for implementation.
- Project implementation phase—included development of partnerships and joint community actions, provision of technical and supportive assistance to facilitate community participation and capacity building;
- Evaluation analysis and dissemination of the project—included production of reports and recommendations, DVD's and presentations to scientific conferences and journals.

The project provided three educational presentations in five different buildings about banking issues, safety on the street and safety in the home for a total of fifteen two-hour sessions. Time and dates were selected based on the recommendations of the Tenants' Committees in each building. Included in each presentation were theatrical comedic skits performed by animator/actors. The use of theatre was based on the rationale that an animated production with interactive dialogue would have a greater impact on the senior audience's memory and understanding of the concepts and skills associated with the prevention of financial/material abuse as the use of drama or drama skits as educational tools has proven to be very effective amongst seniors (Podnieks and Bailey, 1995). The aim was to empower seniors to make appropriate decisions and be aware of potentially risky situations. Furthermore, the empowerment would reduce fear and anxiety, enabling them to attend to their normal daily activities, a crucial aspect of their well being. The presentations would sensitize the participants to the issues of elder abuse in a learning environment which would help them to feel less vulnerable, powerless and fearful. To evaluate the effectiveness of the project an objective evaluator was hired to design and administrate pre- and post-questionnaires for each presentation at each locale in an effort to determine how much was learned by the participants.

Empowerment concepts and community development principles which support the community case study.

Some underlying concepts and principles underline the work of the NDGCCEA and this project. They are as follows-:

This small qualitative project described above in the case study is based on the hypothesis that powerlessness in older adults is due to inadequate financial and material resources, as well as unhealthy attitudes towards older adults, and may contribute to their being in abusive and neglectful relationships with their caregivers. The project draws on the ecological approach of Bronfenbrenner (1989), Seligman et al. (1995) and Schiamberg and Gans (1999) which provides a framework for studying the contextual interactions between the individual, interpersonal and environmental risk factors leading to abusive and neglectful behaviour in older adults in a family context.

Bronfenbrenner (1989) states that studies of the context, environment and resources present in a person's life course can affect whether or not the person will be in a position of helplessness and powerlessness which can lead to an outcome of abuse and neglect. Seligman's profound work with children found that an individual's learned explanations of behaviour are influenced by whether they learn pessimistic explanations (which produce hopelessness and passivity in the face of failure) or optimistic explanations (which see failures as challenges). He also demonstrates that such learned explanations and responses are produced by the environment in which a child is raised. Additionally, significant events in a person's life span, such as the death of a parent, physical abuse, severe parental strife or sexual rejection during adolescence can change the person's optimistic world view to a pessimistic one (Seligman et al. 1995). Few researchers have attempted similar studies in relation to older adults. This project attempted to change some learned behaviours of the seniors to prevent abuse from occurring, through giving them information and knowledge about other alternative behaviours to choose from, when they are at home and on the street or in other areas such as restaurants.

However, maximizing resources to persons who are powerless, oppressed and have unequal access to such resources has often been also stated to be an important goal in empowerment concepts (Kieffer, 1984). The relationship between absence and presence of resources has been noted to be relevant in studies related to care giving as influencing coping strategies and outcomes of continuity of care (Vezina and Roy, 1996). For example, studies have noted that less assistance is offered by the health care providers in the public sector in cases where there is a family member available, despite the fact that such expectations create a considerable burden for the family (Garant and Bolduc, 1992). For this reason handouts containing information about assistance and resources were distributed to the senior participants after the project was completed. The seniors were personally introduced to community police officers, bank and security representatives to enable them to feel less fearful about using these resources.

Powerlessness in this project is conceptualized as a continuous interactive process between the abused persons, the abusers and their environment. This relates closely to Seligman's definition of a pessimistic world view in which depression is often present. Depression has been observed to be often present in abusive and abused older adults (Paveza et al., 1992). Powerlessness is expressed through attitudes of self-blame, a sense of generalized distrust, a feeling of alienation from resources and a sense of hopelessness and discouragement (Kieffer, 1984).

Empowerment is conceptualized as an outcome of intervention or personal strategies to assist an abused older adult in moving out of this process of powerlessness. Empowerment is defined as a process of helping people assure or reclaim control over their destinies, which entails maximizing their confidence, skills and abilities and making informed decisions that are in their best interests, having access to choices and available, accessible resources and options (Health Canada, 1993) for the attainment of both personal and collective goals (Nahmiash, 1997). Empowered persons would express an optimistic world view and would have mastery and control over their lives as opposed to suffering from depression and feeling they have no control.

The project focuses on whether or not it was possible to empower the seniors through knowledge and information in order to prevent them from becoming powerless in a potential situation of abuse.

Evaluation

The goal of the evaluation was to assess whether the project objectives were met. This implied assessing the impact of the presentations on the senior's knowledge as to whether they learned the appropriate behaviour to adopt when confronted with situations which may present a risk of financial/material abuse.

A secondary objective was to assess the appreciation of the participants for the presentations concerning their perception of whether their knowledge of appropriate behaviours had improved and whether they would recommend these workshops to family members, friends or neighbours.

Methodology

Three questionnaires were developed, one for each of the three sessions. They were based on the information submitted in advance by the presenters. The questionnaires were on one page, contained a limited number of questions that could be answered rapidly, were easy to understand, mostly multiple choice, written in large characters to facilitate reading and allowed the possibility to determine whether participation in the sessions had an impact on the participants' answers. These included a comparison between before and after, and provided an assessment of the participants' level of appreciation of the training.

Each questionnaire had 5–6 questions on the topic of the presentation and two demographic questions on the age and sex of the participant. Each had a unique identifier to enable the evaluator to make comparisons individually. The questionnaires were handed out at the beginning and end of each session in the same manner to everyone who participated.

Results

To determine whether participation in the project changes the participant's answers in a statistically significant way, we gave for each of the nominal variables a choice of answers called optimal, that is, the choice of answers to which the participants should adhere in the post-test. Following the selection of these 'optimal' answers, we recoded the multiple level variables into binary variables on the basis of 'good' and 'bad' answers. The statistical analysis was based on these new variables. The ordinal scale variables and binary variables were analysed with respect to the three categories of the presentation themes—banking issues, prevention of financial abuse in public places, and prevention of financial abuse at home.

- In total, 176 participants completed one to three questionnaires. Of these, 78 per cent were women and 14.2 per cent were men. Only 13 respondents (7.4 per cent) did not indicate their sex. Ages ranged from less than 50 years (1.1 per cent) to over 90years (5.1 per cent). Most participants (64.2 per cent) were between the ages of 70–89 years, which reflects the average ages of persons living in the low-income housing units.
- The majority of participants appreciated the reception they received (100 per cent), the presentations (98.4 per cent), the question and discussion periods (97 per cent) and the environment (94.5 per cent).
- Over 75 per cent of participants stated they learned a lot or a great deal from the sessions.
- The majority of participants (over 90 per cent for each session) would be prepared to recommend the presentations to their friends or neighbours and family members.
- 22–24 per cent stated they knew someone who had been a victim of financial abuse.
- A question regarding the importance of leaving a will showed that the session significantly improved the participant's awareness of the problems that dying without a will could engender on the post-test. Similarly other questions improved, such as how to carry a purse safely at a restaurant or in a grocery store.
- Occasionally, the questionnaires demonstrated that the content of the presentations was not clear enough to ensure participants chose an 'optimal' answer on the post-test. An example was the question asking what they would do if someone called and claimed to be a bank employee or if someone knocked on your door. These two questions drew a variety of answers on the post-test.

Limits

Some limits of the project were observed. Not all participants attended all three sessions, which was compensated for, as each session was organized as a separate session. Not all the participants at the sessions completed the questionnaire for the following reasons: they arrived late to the session, they left early or they were reluctant to divulge any personal information (even though confidentiality was ensured). In addition, due to literacy, language or vision problems, several did not wish to complete the questionnaires despite the offer of assistance. The analysis also showed that some of the questions might have been ambiguous, lessening the participants' chances of answering correctly.

Overall we can conclude, through the quantitative and qualitative analysis of the results of the study, that the sessions had a positive impact on the participants who had no prior knowledge of the appropriate behaviours to adopt in the particular situations of potential financial abuse. A high percentage of seniors showed a significant increase of their understanding of which behaviour to choose in most situations presented following the presentations. In addition to the formal written questionnaires, verbal feedback from participants was also solicited. The feedback from participants was extremely positive in terms of their comprehension of the presentations, their questions regarding the issues and their comments about how they would act in future potentially abusive situations. They were also pleased to have had the opportunity to interact and converse directly with those responsible for their safety, and felt empowered to make informed decisions, protect themselves and refer, when necessary, to these experts. Some remained behind to discuss their personal experiences with the presenters during the break for the refreshments. Finally we can conclude that crime prevention is difficult to demonstrate in this type of community setting, at least quantitatively. Based on our analysis, though, we can confirm that most of the seniors would modify some of their behaviour and actions concerning banking issues, safeguarding their home and walking on the street to ensure the safety of themselves and their property. Some of the feedback was also useful to the presenters to modify the content of their own presentations with future groups of seniors.

Some Overall Reflections About the Prevention of Financial/Material Abuse

We would like to make a few observations following this project, which may be applicable for all communities, worldwide, in the prevention of financial abuse. As societies continue to age with seniors living longer and becoming more vulnerable, there will probably be a greater incidence of financial and material abuse perpetrated against them by persons in a position of trust. The prevention of violence is not the sole responsibility of specialized agencies but a responsibility of whole communities, who can participate in the prevention of such violence by empowering the seniors in the community to protect themselves and by promoting respect among other members of the community. We found the concepts relating to empowerment and community development techniques to be valid and essential. The concept of community participation was essential to building effective partnerships with other organizations to provide a concerted, standardized approach to information-sharing. By bringing the seniors together in groups, they were aware that they are part of a community and not just isolated, powerless individuals. They participated readily in the group discussions, finding their voices. As well, the project enabled the seniors from a multicultural, urban milieu to be aware of their rights and provided them with the skills, knowledge and choices to assist them in making optimal decisions when confronted by potential abusive situations.

We demonstrated that seniors, though vulnerable because of physical and psychological losses, were able to integrate new knowledge and information by giving them the resources, energy and power to make optimal choices and decisions for their security and safety. Furthermore, the group was enabled through the empowerment process of the project to present a brief to the Ministry of Health and Social Services about their insecure living conditions and ways to improve them. This step is the final phase of the Ninacs (1995) empowerment model entitled "Critical Awareness" in which the person or group becomes aware that they are not the only persons with the problem, but that the individual and collective problems are influenced by the way in which society is organized and that the solution to the collective problems comes through social and political systems. Through social change strategies, they can achieve resolution to their collective problems.

References

Biggs, S., C. Phillipson and P. Kingston (1995). *Elder abuse in perspective.* Rethinking ageing series. Buckingham, Philadelphia: Open University Press.

Blunt, A.P. (1993). Financial exploitation of the incapacitated: Investigation and remedies. *Journal of Elder Abuse and Neglect,* 5(1): 19–32.

Brillon, Y. (1987). *Victimization and fear of crime among the elderly.* Toronto and Vancouver: Butterworths.

Bronfenbrenner, U. (1989). Ecological systems theory, in R. Vasta (ed.). *Annals of ethics development* (pp. 127–249). Greenwich, CT: Jai Press Inc.

Butler, R. (1987). Ageism, in G. Maddox (ed.), *The encyclopedia of aging.* New York: Springs Publishing Co., 1–25.

CLSC NDG/Mtl.-O (2003). Profile Socio-Economique, et Sanataire de la territiore du CLSC NDG/MTL.-O, Report of CLSC NDG/Mtl-O. Montreal, Que.

Council of Europe. (1992). *Violence against elderly people.* Brussels.

Federal/Provincial/Territorial Committee of Officials(Seniors)2003. An Environmental Scan of Abuse and Neglect of Older Adults in Canada: What's Working and Why. Unpublished report prepared for the Federal/Provincial/Territorial Ministers Responsible for Seniors: Ottawa.

—— 2005. A Review of the Social and Economic Costs of the Abuse of Older Adults. Unpublished Report prepared for Federal/Provincial/Territorial Committee of Officials(Seniors): Ottawa.

Gallagher, E. (1993). Victoria Elder Abuse Project: Final Report. Victoria, British Columbia Health Research Foundation.

Health Canada. (1993). *Older Canadians and the abuse of seniors: A continuum from participation to empowerment.* Ottawa, Family Violence Prevention Division.

Hudson, M. and T.F. Johnson (1986). Elder abuse and neglect: A review of the literature, *Annual Review of Gerontology and Geriatrics,* 6(1): 81–132.

Kieffer, C.H. (1984). *Citizen empowerment: A developmental perspective.* Binghampton, NY: The Haworth Press, Inc.

Kosberg, J.I. (1988). Prevention of elder abuse: Identification of high risk factors prior to placement decisions, *The Gerontologist,* 28(1): 43–49.

——. (1998). The abused elderly men, in J. F. Prevratil and T. Tatara (eds.), *Understanding and combating elder abuse in minority communities,* pp. 225–42. Philanthropy Services Inc.

Kosberg, J.I. and J.L. Garcia (eds.), (1995). *Elder abuse: International and cross-cultural perspectives.* New York: The Haworth Press.

Nahmiash, D. (1997). Powerlessness and abuse: A descriptive qualitative study which explores abuse and neglect of older adults in the community in relation to the social context. Doctoral dissertation, Quebec, Laval University.

National Seniors Council. (2007). Elder Abuse in Canada: Preliminary Overview of the Issue, August 2007. Unpublished report prepared for the National Seniors Council, Ottawa.

NDGCCEA (2007). Partners Against Crime. Unpublished report prepared for Joint Management Committee of the National Crime Prevention Strategy Le Ministere de la Securite Publique du Quebec.

Noreau, P., M. Lithwick and D. Thomas. Social work and the use of judicial recourse in the intervention of elder abuse. Presentation given to the Elder Law Conference, Vancouver, B.C.

Novartis Foundation for Gerontology. (2001). *Joining Generations*. Report published on website of Novartis Foundation for Gerontology, Geneva.

Paveza, G.J., D. Cohen, C. Eisdorfer, S. Freels, T. Semla, W.J. Ashford, P. Gorelick, R. Hirschman, D. Luchins et P. Levy (1992). Severe family violence and Alzheimer's disease: Prevalence and risk factors, *The Gerontologist*, 32(4): 493–97.

Pillemer, K.A. et D. Finkelhor (1988). The prevalence of elder abuse: A random sample survey, *The Gerontologist*, 28(1): 51–57.

Pillemer, K.A. et R.S. Wolf (1986). Major findings from three model projects on elderly abuse, in K.A. Pillemer and R.S. Wolf (dirs.), *Elder abuse: Conflict in the family*, (pp. 197–217). Dover, Mass.: Auburn House Publishing Co.

Pitsiou, V., E.N. Darrough and C.D. Spinellis (1995). Mistreatment of the elderly in Greece, in J.I. Kosberg and J.L. Garcia (eds.), *Elder abuse: International and cross-cultural perspectives*, (pp. 45–64). New York: The Haworth Press.

Pittaway, E., E. Gallagher, M. Stones, D. Nahmiash, J. Kosberg, E. Podnieks, L. Strain and J. Bond (1995). *Services for abused older Canadians*. Ottawa: Family Violence Prevention Division, Health Canada.

Plamondon, L. and D. Nahmiash (2006). Portrait de la vulnerabilite et des risques dans la population vivant en HLM, *Vie et vieillissement*, 5(1) hiver, pp. 27–36.

Podnieks, E., K.A. Pillemer, J. Nicholson, T. Shillington and A.F. Frizzell (1989). *National survey on abuse of the elderly in Canada*, Toronto: Office of Research and Innovation, Ryerson Polytechnical Institute.

Reis, M. and D. Nahmiash (1995). *When seniors are abused*. Toronto: Captus Press.

Schiamberg, L.B. and D. Gans (1999). An ecological framework for contextual risk factors in elder abuse by adult children. *Journal of Elder Abuse and Neglect*, 11(1):70–103.

Select Committee on Aging. (1981). *Elder abuse: An examination of a hidden problem*. Washington, DC: US Government Printing Office, pp. 99–502.

Seligman, M.E.P., L.P. Kamer and S. Nolen-Hoeksema (1995). Explanatory style across the life span: Achievement and Health, in R.M. Lerner, E.M.

Hetherington and M. Perlmutter (eds.), *Child development in life-span perspective* (pp. 91–114). Hillsdale, N.J.: Erlbaum.

Spencer, C. (1993). *Diminishing Returns: An examination of financial decision making, financial resonsibilities, and financial abuse among seniors in B.C.*, Gerontology Research Center. Simon Fraser University, Vancouver, B.C.

——. (1994). New directions for intervention research on abused older adults, in M.J. McLean (ed.), *Abuse and neglect of older Canadians: Strategies for change*, (pp. 143–55). Toronto: Thompson Educational Publishing Inc.

——. (1999). Exploring the Social and Economic Costs of Abuse in Later Life. Health Canada, Violence Prevention Unit, Ottawa .

Stones, M. (1991). *A lexicon for elder mistreatment.* Written for St. John's provincial work committee, Newfoundland.

——. (1995). Portée et définition des mauvais traitements et de la négligence à l'endroit des personnes âgées au Canada, (pp. 159–74), in MacLean (ed.), *Mauvais traitements auprès des personnes âgées: stratégies de changement.* Montreal: Éditions Saint-Martin.

Tatara, T. (1993). Understanding the nature and scope of domestic elder abuse with the use of State aggregate data: Summaries of the key findings of a national survey of State APS and aging agencies, *Journal of Elder Abuse and Neglect*, 5(4): 35–59.

Tatara, T. and J.F. Prevratit (eds.), (1998). *Understanding and combating elder abuse in minority communities*, (pp. 19–24). Philanthropy Services Inc.

Tomita, S.K. (1990). The denial of elder mistreatment by victims and abusers:The application of neutralization in theory. *Violence and Victims*, 5(3): 171–84.

Vezina, A. and J. Roy (1996). State–family relations in Quebec from the perspective of intensive home care services for the elderly. *Journal of Gerontological Social Work*, 35, (3/4): 149–64.

Wahl, J. (1990). *Elder abuse: The hidden crime.* Advocacy Center for the Elderly, Toronto, Canada.

WHO (2002). *World Report on Violence and Health* (Definition developed by Action on Elder Abuse in the United Kingdom) World Health Organization: Geneva, Switzerland.

12

Protecting Vulnerable Older Adults in the Health Care System

Peter Clark and Barry Goldlist

Originally formed in November 1989, the Geriatric/LongTerm Care Review Committee (GLTCRC) has just completed its eighteenth full year of operation. The Committee is an advisory committee to the Chief Coroner that conducts independent reviews of deaths of elderly persons in both acute care and long-term care facilities in Ontario. The Committee is chaired by a Regional Supervising Coroner and includes respected health care professionals including a dietician, family physicians, geriatricians, an emergency room physician, and a local coroner. When indicated (i.e., geriatric psychiatry, gastroenterology, infectious disease) have assisted the Committee with case reviews.

In 2007, cases were referred to the Committee from a variety of sources including local coroners, Regional Supervising Coroners, and the Office of the Chief Coroner. In the previous years, cases had been reviewed at the request of advocacy groups and long term care facilities.

The Committee conducts an independent review of the available records relevant to the specific case and then prepares a final report including recommendations, where indicated, which are forwarded to the local community for discussion and implementation with the aim being to prevent future deaths in similar circumstances.

Committee case review statistics for the last 10 years are included in Table 1:

Table 1 Cases Reviewed by GLTCRR

Year	Number of cases reviewed	Total number of deaths	Number of cluster investigations with (# of deaths)
1998	18	18	0
1999	15	15	0
2000	20	25	1 (6)
2001	30	30	0
2002	21	21	0
2003	17	17	0
2004	25	38	Homicide Review
2005	28	28	0
2006	27	27	0
2007	17 (not complete)	17	0

Committee members have participated in the following activities over the years:

1. regular monthly meetings,
2. regional Coroners' reviews,
3. liased with individuals, government ministries, acute and chronic care, general and psychiatric hospitals, public health departments, long-term care institutions, medical and nursing associations, advocacy groups, Ontario and American Coroners and medical examiners, the Chief Coroner of the other Canadian provinces and territories, the International Association of Coroners and Medical Examiners and various professional gerontological associations,
4. published a number of articles in the medical literature, and
5. provided independent expert evidence at inquests.

The types of recommendations generated for the years 2002 through 2006 are shown in Table 2:

Table 2 Types of Recommendations Generated for the Years 2002–2006

	2002	2003	2004	2005	2006
Total number of cases	21	17	25	28	27
Medical/nursing management	13(28)	7(16)	14(26)	12(24)	10(30)
Communication/ documentation	8(12)	9(10)	9(16)	7(9)	(6(8)
Use of drugs in the elderly	(6(17)	4(8)	7(10)	5(8)	8(14)
Admission/discharge/ transfer procedures	6(10)	4(8)	3(3)	3(4)	3(5)
Determination of capacity and consent for treatment/DNR	2(2)	3(4)	2(2)	2(3)	0
Use of restraints	0	0	0	0	1(4)
The Ministry of Health and Long-Term Care	0	2(4)	6(10)	1(1)	0
The acute and long-term care industry	0	0	6(12)	6(9)	0
The Office of The Chief Coroner	4(4)	8(8)	10(10)	7(9)	9(9)

A number followed by a bracketed number [i.e., 10(30)] indicates that there were 10 cases with a total of 30 recommendations made relevant to the topic area.

As was the case over the previous years, the Committee noted that the "Medical/Nursing Management" section was the number one topic area for recommendations generated over the last five years. The "Use of Drugs in the Elderly" section has now replaced the "Communication/ Documentation" section as the number two topic area for recommendations generated in 2006.

In 2006, the Committee reviewed four cases in which no recommendations were generated.

Further analysis of the "Medical/Nursing Management" section revealed a number of common and recurrent themes leading to requests for independent review by the Committee. These themes include the following:

1. constipation and obstipation,
2. prevention and management of "bedsores",
3. use of diagnostic labels including "cancer" and "ALC" (alternate level of care), and
4. management of the elderly in the emergency room setting.

Similarly, common and recurrent themes in the "Use of Drugs in the Elderly" section include the following:

1. use of psychotropic drugs,
2. use of anticholinergic drugs, and
3. use of narcotics including Meperidine Hydrochloride.

The following four case studies are examples of some of the recurring issues being reviewed by the Committee:

CASE 1

Issues

1. emergency room management of the elderly, and
2. constipation in the elderly.

History

This is the case of an 89-year-old woman who was admitted to a licensed long-term care facility (LTCF) from her home on November 23, 2002 at the age 86 years. Her past medical history was extensive. In the LTCF, she underwent a number of investigations. She appeared to be doing well until May 17, 2005 when she fell which resulted in fractures of her vertebral spine.

Following the fall on May 17, 2005, the woman initially refused an assessment of her injury. She was assessed in the emergency room (ER) of a general hospital (GH) the following day where investigations revealed the presence of multiple fractures of her vertebral spine. The physician's section of the ER record included a section for vital signs which was blank. While the woman's vital signs may have been recorded in another section of the ER record, the Committee could not determine if the ER physicians were aware of an elevated temperature. In the Committee's experience, the recording of a patient's vital signs on the physician's portion of the ER record would ensure that the physician is aware of any abnormal vital signs. The recognition of the presence of abnormal vital signs would then allow the ER physician to investigate the reason(s) for the abnormal vital signs. Although this did not appear to be a factor in this woman's death, the ER management of an 89 year old patient with compression fractures may well differ if there is an unrecognized and undiagnosed comorbidity such as a febrile illness. On both ER visits, the woman's vertebral spine fractures were recognized and she was returned to the LTCF.

Upon her return to the LTCF, the woman's mobility was limited by the presence of pain. It would have been reasonably anticipated that her fracture related pain would respond to common analgesic medications. Her pain was initially managed by intermittent dosing with short acting Opioids in combination with Acetaminophen.

Codeine containing preparations were discontinued on May 25, 2005 following which her pain was mainly managed with Oxycet. There is evidence in the literature which supports this pharmacologic approach given that 10 per cent of caucasians are unable to convert Codeine to its active metabolites. Sustained release Opioids were not prescribed and, based on her sporadic and infrequent use of analgesics, the Committee believed that this was a reasonable therapeutic approach. In addition, this was respectful of her often expressed wish not to take medications.

In the elderly, the development of constipation is frequently multifactorial. Some of the known risk factors include the following:

1. presence of pain,
2. use of narcotic containing medications to control the pain,
3. presence of pre-existing large bowel disease,
4. decreased oral intake,
5. dehydration,

6. decreased mobility, and
7. age (>55 years).

In this particular case, an additional factor may have included a tendency to under-report or minimize symptoms. The woman did self report her bowel movements and was known to refuse initial investigations and medications from time to time.

On May 22, 2005, the woman was started on a 10 day course of a stool softener, Docusate Sodium, which resulted in her passing stool on almost a daily basis until the medication was stopped. Thereafter, her bowel movements were less frequent, generally once every third day. The Opioid medications were stopped altogether on June 26, 2005. Over this time period, prophylactic, sustained laxative therapy was not administered. In the Committee's experience, a regular prophylactic bowel management regimen should almost always be commenced in the elderly when narcotic therapy is initiated for the purpose of minimizing the risk for the development of constipation. This should include such items as patient education, counseling and management of toileting activities, lifestyle factors such as fluid and fibre content, and pharmacologic treatment.[3] In this particular case, Lactulose (a laxative) was ordered by the most responsible physician to be given on a "prn" basis if the woman became constipated. Lactulose is an excellent choice for the prevention of opioid-induced constipation.[4] While the physician did specify the purpose of the Lactulose, the Committee wondered if the medical and nursing health care professionals appreciated that the woman's change in stooling frequency from May to June was an indication that she was becoming constipated. As well LTCF residents are often unable to express their symptoms accurately.

The woman was found sitting in a chair in her room on July 2, 2005 complaining of abdominal pain. The nursing staff noted the presence of a fever. On July 3, 2005, she was found lying in her bed with similar complaints and a fever which resulted in her being transferred to the ER of the GH where she was subsequently admitted.

She was seen in consultation by a surgeon. Following the initiation of antibiotic therapy, she was taken to the operating room where she had an exploratory laparotomy with resection of the rectum, drainage and a colostomy. The surgeon noted the presence of an area of necrosis on the left lateral wall of the mid rectum with a perirectal abscess cavity which communicated with the rectum. The postoperative diagnosis was a perforated rectum.

The surgical pathology report read as follows:

> Diverticulosis with perforated acute diverticulitis and pericolic abscess formation. Negative for malignancy.

An addendum to the report read as follows:

> The surgeon informed me that the perforation occurs in the mid rectum. There is a large amount of hard stool in the intestinal lumen. Since diverticular disease rarely, if ever, involves the rectum, other causes of rectal perforation have to be entertained. In light of the clinical findings as well as the focal mucosal necrosis adjacent to the perforation, it is likely that stercoral ulceration is the cause of the perforation.

Post-operatively, the woman was admitted to the intensive care unit (ICU) where she was managed with ventilatory care, fluid support, and antibiotics. On July 5, 2005, she was transferred out of the ICU. A clear fluid diet was commenced three days later. By July 15, 2005, the woman was up in a chair and appeared to be improving.

At 1000 hours on July 18, 2005, the woman suddenly became unconscious. Immediate medical assessment was obtained. Her son was present at her bedside and requested no further investigation or treatment. Comfort care measures were instituted. It was the opinion of the treating physician that she had likely suffered a cerebrovascular accident (stroke). 40 minutes later at 1040 hours, death was pronounced. A post-mortem examination was not performed.

Recommendations

1. Health care professionals should be reminded that constipation and obstipation are common, preventable, and treatable medical conditions that affect the elderly. Untreated, these conditions can be devastating and may even result in death. Once obstipation is suspected, aggressive investigation and treatment should be considered on a case by case basis.

As with many geriatric syndromes, obstipation may present either typically (abdominal pain, fecal incontinence) or atypically (confusion, delirium). Health care professionals should be especially wary of elderly patients who have constipation/obstipation or who have associated systemic symptoms (tachycardia, fever). In these cases, the ordering of laboratory investigations and an EKG should be considered on a case by case basis.

The occurrence of overflow incontinence should alert the treating health care professionals to the possibility that the patient has developed faecal impaction with overflow incontinence. Faecal impaction can be difficult to treat and should be treated vigorously when present. Careful abdominal and rectal examinations should be performed. The findings of soft stool or no stool in the rectum does not absolutely rule out the presence of faecal impaction.

In these cases, an abdominal flat plate X-ray and/or a CT scan should be ordered to rule out the possibility of a higher impaction that cannot be detected on rectal examination and/or a developing acute/subacute bowel obstruction (dilated loops of bowel with air/fluid levels). While manual disimpaction should be the first intervention attempted, the presence of obstipation with a higher impaction should primarily be managed with enemas to clear the bowel from below. In some cases, the addition of oral osmotic laxatives such as Lactulose can be used to clear the bowel from above. Gastrointestinal lavage solutions have also been proven to be very effective in treating fecal impaction.

Health care professionals should always be observant for the development of complications and especially for the development of complications related to the treatment of obstipation/fecal impaction.

2. Health care professionals should be reminded of the importance of instituting a regular prophylactic bowel regimen at the initiation of opioid therapy for the purpose of preventing the development of constipation.

Components of the regimen should include:

(a) patient education,
(b) counselling and management of toileting activities,
(c) lifestyle factors such as the diet including fluid and fibre content, and
(d) pharmacologic treatment.

3. Health care professionals caring for the elderly in both acute and long-term care facilities should receive ongoing training in:

(a) the definition of constipation in adults,
(b) the clinical conditions and pharmacologic interventions that may put the patient at risk to develop constipation, and
(c) strategies which will allow for the early recognition of constipation.

CASE 2

Issue

1. The use of narcotic analgesia in the elderly.

History

This is the case of an 82-year-old man who was admitted to a LTCF for respite care on October 19, 2005. Within three days, his admission status was changed to permanent and within 10 days, he was dead. Death was attributed to an acute thrombotic occlusion of the circumflex coronary artery in association with acute Fentanyl intoxication.

On transfer to the LTCF, the man was noted to be quite confused and had "depression at separation". In the Committee's experience, it is not unusual for newly admitted residents to a LTCF to exhibit confusion especially if the resident has cognitive impairment which was likely the case in this instance. Of some concern to the Committee was the fact that an antidepressant was prescribed during a period of transition and without definitive evidence of the presence of a major depression such as a high score on a standardized assessment tool such as the Geriatric Depression Scale or criteria to support a DSM IV diagnosis. In the Committee's opinion, the prescribing of an antidepressant was not a factor in the gentleman's death.

Of major concern to the Committee was the fact that the man was diagnosed as having chronic pain while the medical record suggested that the pain was of recent (3 day) onset. From the documentation submitted for review, no examinations or investigations were done in an attempt to detect the cause of the pain. A Fentanyl Patch was prescribed as the initial therapy despite the fact that the United States FDA Approval Label for transdermal Fentanyl emphasizes that the medication is for the use in opioid tolerant patients only. The Label goes on to note that serious life threatening hypoventilation can occur in patients who are not opioid tolerant. Given the gentleman's rapid decline following the application of the transdermal Fentanyl Patch, the Committee suspected that the medication may have contributed to the death.

Recommendations

1. Health care professionals should be reminded of the importance of using caution when making the diagnosis of depression in a resident newly admitted to a licensed long term care home. Recognized valid diagnostic criteria should be used to make the diagnosis of depression.
2. Health care professionals caring for the elderly in the long term care setting should be reminded that the first step in management of any painful condition should be an attempt to identify the cause of the pain.
3. Health care professionals should be reminded that the Fentanyl transderman patch should only be prescribed to opioid tolerant patients. If a patient develops side effects such as unresponsiveness or a decreased level of consciousness, the patch should be removed immediately and consideration should be given to the use of a narcotic antagonist.

CASE 3

Issue

1. Emergency room management of the elderly.

History

This is the case of a 70-year-old woman who underwent a bowel resection with a colostomy in July 2005 for cancer of the rectum (colon). She completed a course of chemotherapy on November 15, 2005, 12 days prior to her first ER visit on November 27, 2005, and was scheduled for radiation on December 5, 2005, the date of her death.

At 0155 hours on November 27, 2005, the woman first presented to the ER of the small local community GH with back pain, constipation, and had not recently urinated. There appeared to be some confusion as to the time of her initial assessment by physician "A" given the times recorded on the ER record. The time of assessment on the ER Record was recorded at 0730 hours when the woman had arrived at 0155 hours, had been registered at 0209 hours, and according to the nursing notes, was awaiting reassessment at 0715 hours with 2 enemas and Lactulose having been given prior to 0730 hours. If the woman had been assessed by physician "A" prior to 0730 hours, the Committee was confused by the apparent focus on her constipation and not on the back pain which was her chief complaint. Orders for pain control were not recorded until after 0730 hours. An order for Tromethamine 60 mg IV was written but this was corrected to 30 mg. When her care was transferred to physician "B" as evidenced by the presence of discharge type prescriptions on the medical record, it would appear that physician "A" was planning to discharge the woman home. Eventually, admission was arranged under physician "C". The woman was appropriately investigated and managed in the GH which resulted in her being discharged on December 1, 2005 with improved pain control, improved bowel function, and no shortness of breath.

Three days later at 0830 hours on December 4, 2005, the woman returned to the ER complaining of increased back pain which had suddenly occurred during the night. The woman was seen by physician "D" who did not document a thorough examination. Notation was made however, that her blood was "OK" and there was no xray evidence of a fracture. The decision was made to discharge her home with instructions to increase the amount of long acting Morphine Sulfate by altering the time interval between doses from 12 hours to 6 hours (bid. to qid. dosing).

Based on a review of the woman's ER record, the Committee was concerned with how she was assessed and managed on this visit. The Committee's concerns included the following:

1. When compared to her previous visit to the ER on November 27, 2005, her vital signs had changed significantly and were abnormal. Her respiratory rate (RR) had increased from 18 to 28. Her blood pressure (BP-155/107) and pulse (P-123 and irregular) were elevated on the prior visit possibly due to the presence of pain. On the present visit, her BP had decreased to 90/60 and her P had decreased to 107. Was consideration given as to why her vital signs had changed and perhaps more importantly, why her BP dropped when she was complaining of increased back pain?
2. Her liver function tests were now elevated and abnormal on the visit of December 4, 2005. Was consideration given as to why the liver function tests had changed?
3. Her renal function tests were now elevated and abnormal to a significant degree given the short time interval between testing. Was consideration given as to why the renal function test had changed?
4. The woman's neutrophil count was now elevated. Given the history of recent chemotherapy and the previous low neutrophil count of 0.2 recorded just 3 days earlier on December 1, 2005, was consideration given to as why her neutrophil count had changed?
5. There was X-ray evidence of the presence of a new pulmonary infiltrate. Was consideration given as to the significant of this new chest xray finding?
6. There was X-ray evidence that the compression fracture of L1 had progressed from an end plate fracture to a 50 per cent loss of vertebral height which was the probably cause of her increased back pain. Was consideration given as to the significance of this interval change?
7. Why was the long acting Morphine Sulfate ordered at *qid.* interval rather than at a *bid.* interval, the interval at which it is intended to be given?
8. Did the treating health care professionals realize the impact that impaired hepatic and renal function would have on this long acting medication?
9. Given the woman's pneumonia as evidenced by the presence of chest X-ray evidence of a new pulmonary infiltrate and her chronic

obstructive pulmonary disease (emphysema), did the treating health care professionals realize the increased potential for this long acting medication to depress respiration?

10. Given the woman's altered clinical condition on December 4, 2005 as compared to her status just a few days earlier, why was consideration not given to re-admitting her to hospital for investigation and treatment?
11. Did the treating health care professional realize that the standard practice to manage pain is to incrementally increase the dosage of short acting analgesics?

The pathologist concluded that the cause of death was consistent with acute morphine intoxication in association with small bowel ischemia and acute bronchopneumonia status post recent colectomy for colonic carcinoma.

The Committee noted that the woman had not been designated as "palliative", did not have a "DNR" (Do Not Resuscitate) order, and had no evidence of recurrent/metastatic cancer. Although there was no documentation on the ER record for the visit of December 4, 2005 to suggest that the woman was terminally ill with cancer, the Committee wondered if the fact that the woman was known to have "cancer" negatively impacted in the health care she received on this visit.

Recommendations

1. Health care professionals working in the emergency room setting should be reminded of the importance of reviewing the results of laboratory and imaging clinical parameters such as vital signs, laboratory, and imaging procedures conducted on elderly patients who present themselves to the emergency room on more than one occasion during the course of an illness. The comparing of results recorded on the present visit with those recorded on previous visits may be invaluable in accurately assessing the elderly patient's clinical condition and the reason for the present visit. Documentation of the entire process on the emergency room health care record should be mandatory.
2. Health care professionals working in the emergency room setting should be reminded of the importance of obtaining an appropriate history, conducting a thorough examination, and judiciously utilizing available

laboratory and imaging resources on elderly patients who present new or changing symptoms.

3. Health care professionals and especially health care professionals working in the emergency room setting should be reminded of the importance of not being negatively influenced by the fact that an elderly patient is "old" or has a diagnostic label such as "cancer".
4. Health care professionals and especially health care professionals working in the emergency room setting should be reminded of the importance of having a full understanding of the pharmacokinetics of narcotics prescribed to control pain.
   For example, the lowest possible dose of short acting narcotics such as Morphine Sulfate should be the initial dose with increasing doses titrated upwards depending on the patient's clinical response.
   The use of long acting narcotics may also be of benefit but their dosage and timing between doses must be carefully monitored and in keeping with recognized medical practice.
5. Health care professionals should be reminded of the importance of watching for the development of side effects of medications prescribed for elderly patients with impaired hepatic or renal function.

Conclusions

While the Committee reviews individual cases and prepares a report with recommendations specific to the circumstances surrounding the death, it is the Committee's annual reports that have been instrumental in the education of health care professionals in an effort to improve care of the elderly in the Province of Ontario and throughout Canada.

The Committee believes their work strongly supports the motto of the Office of the Chief Coroner.

"We speak for the dead to protect the living."

References

Clinical Practice Guideline (2002). The management of persistent pain in older persons, *Journal of the American Geriatric Society*, Vol. 50, No. 6, supplement.

Folden S.L. (2004). Practice Guidelines for the Management of Constipation in Adults, *Association of Rehabilitation Nurses*, p. 51.

Gardner-Nix, J. (2004). Chronic non-cancer pain management in older adults, *Geriatrics and Aging*, Vol. 7, No. 3.

Gibson, Conn D. et al. (2006) National Guidelines for Senior's Mental Health: The Assessment and Treatment Mental Health Issues in Long Term Care Homes (Focus on Mood and Bahaviour Symptoms) *Canadian Coalition for Seniors Mental Health.*

Goldlist, B., Naglie, G. and Gorden M. (1992). Constipation can be deadly, *Canadian Family Physician* Volume, 38.

13

Adult Protection Legislation: From Intent to Practice in Three Canadian Provinces

Joan Harbison, Stephen Coughlan, Jeff Karabanow, Madine Vander Plaat, Sheila Wildeman, Ezra Wexler, and Carla Nassar

Adult protection legislation is one response to what is frequently referred to as problem of 'elder abuse and neglect' which, until recently, has for the most part been characterized in western states as one type of 'family violence' (Straka and Montminy, 2006). The individual provinces and territories that make up the Canadian Federation hold legal jurisdiction over matters pertaining to family life. As a consequence, there is no federal adult protection legislation. However, a number of the provinces and territories have passed legislation dealing with the protection of vulnerable adults who are mentally incapacitated. This paper refers to research carried out in Canada's three Maritime provinces each of which has similar longstanding legislation targeted at adults seen to be in need of protection.

The Social and Historical Context for the Development of Adult Protection Legislation

It has been argued in both North America and Europe that the reasons for the particular trajectory of 'elder abuse and neglect' and its evolution as a social problem lie in its social context (Baumann, 1989; Kosberg et al., 2003; Leroux and Petrunik, 1990; Chappell et al., 2003; Ogg and

Munn-Giddings, 1993). In the 1950s, in both North America and Europe there was an overabundance of workers at the same time as employers wanted to renew their labour force in response to new technologies and new needs (Anetzberger, 2005; Townsend, 1986). This resulted in policies that forced older people to retire. The state pensions that accompanied these retirements changed their status from that of paid worker to recipients and dependents of state support.

A theory of ageing that viewed old age as a gradual disengagement from life (Cumming and Henry, 1961), with retirement as the major step in this disengagement, emerged fortuitously at the same time as the labour market policies described above; indeed "Cumming and Henry argue that ageing cannot be understood separate from the characteristics of the social system in which it is experienced" (Lynott and Lynott, 1996). The Disengagement theory was, from its beginnings, the subject of criticism and dispute among scholars. However, despite this, in Western societies disengagement theory appears to have had a powerful, and continuing, effect on societal perceptions of older people (Lynott and Lynott, 1996), so that in some areas of social life, older adults are expected to withdraw. Indeed, some contemporary sociologists still argue that older adults who are active are refusing to acknowledge the ageing process.

In company with most other Western societies Canada has an ageing population so that the numbers of older people in society are increasing relative to those of other age groups (Gee and Gutman, 2000). In Canada a large proportion live with their spouses or, especially in the case of women who have a greater life span than men, live alone. However, this pattern may vary according to family history and cultural values, especially among immigrants and aboriginal peoples. Despite the fact that most older people are relatively healthy and require little care, Anetzberger (2005) points to a concern by professionals from the 1950s on "that the growing number of mentally impaired older people living alone . . . could not provide for their own care and protection without community intervention" (p. 2).

Thus, the concept of 'elder abuse and neglect', and responses to it were developed in an era when older people were identified as a homogenous group based on chronological age, and were marginalized by an understanding of their capacities that was associated with their exclusion from the labour market and with a perception that their roles in society were limited and subject to decline (Neugarten, 1967).

Baumann (1989) argues unequivocally that 'elder abuse and neglect' was socially constructed by professional 'experts' as part of the development of gerontology as a discipline. Baumann's perspective is coincident with that of Leroux and Petrunik, for whom the idea of 'elder abuse' as a social problem emerged from "the public perception of old age as a social problem", where "old age overrides all other statuses and has the most priority in the characterization of the individual". Based on the perception of old people as frail in mind and body there is "an assumed need to protect the elderly" through professional intervention. Moreover this construction "overrides their status as legally and socially competent adults" (1990, p. 653).

This construction of old people is central to issues arising out of the adult protection legislation that has been widely used in North America as a response to the mistreatment and neglect of older people. For instance, in the United States each state has adult protection legislation. In Canada, as a consequence of constitutional arrangements formal responses to incidences of mistreatment and neglect, whether based on legislation or programmes, are unique to each province. The Atlantic model is one of three intrinsic models (Gordon, 2001). This model pertains to each of the three Maritime provinces included in our discussion. It includes "special adult protection legislation" and has been characterized as similar to the legislation addressing child abuse in that "upon receiving information that an adult is being neglected or abused adult protection service personnel will investigate the case" (Gordon, 2001:119). Concerns have been raised about the extent to which such legislation fosters an ageist perception of older people as vulnerable children rather than as adults with their associated rights.

However, in each Maritime jurisdiction, if, after an investigation by an adult protection worker, the older person is found to be legally mentally competent, they are free to refuse assistance and to choose to remain in a situation which others consider to be not in their 'best interests'. It is noteworthy that many older people do refuse assistance and that this causes considerable frustration among those who seek to offer help (Barer, 1997). Each of the three studies carried out by members of our research team, and discussed below, has shed some light on just how difficult and complex it is to use legislative provisions to facilitate assistance to mistreated and neglected older people.

Methods

All three studies have used a combination of qualitative methods including: (1) a broad based review of the literature relating to elder abuse and neglect and its contextualization within the field of ageing; (2) a comprehensive review of the legislation and legal articles relating to elder abuse and neglect and (3) interviews and focus groups with participants representative of a wide range of formal and informal providers of assistance including adult protection workers; health and social service professionals, police and police safety officers, professional and lay members of non-profit organizations such as women's shelters, the Victorian Order of Nurses and Meals on Wheels, faith leaders, members of seniors' organizations, volunteers and interested individuals, with the addition of members of the judiciary for the first study; (4) telephone and face-to-face consultations with a number of key service providers, advocates and policy experts (Harbison et al., 1995; 2005).

In the first study (Harbison et al., 1995) the interview data was subjected to content analysis including initial coding by the interdisciplinary team. The second and third studies employed "the constant comparative method of data analysis . . . including ongoing coding and analysis by the research team" (Harbison et al., 2005: 236). In all three studies dissemination groups are an integral part of the qualitative methods affording an opportunity both to discuss and amend the findings with our participants.

The Geographic Context

Each of the three provinces under consideration have relatively small populations even within the Canadian context. Nova Scotia has a population of approximately 900,000, New Brunswick 750,000 and Prince Edward Island 135,000. The inhabitants are chiefly white and European immigrants of longstanding, as well as small numbers of indigenous First Nations peoples and African Canadians who have been residents for over two hundred years. We drew the participants for our studies from both urban and rural locations and from those areas that were relatively wealthy and those that were relatively poor.

Findings

Our first study of adult protection legislation was requested in 1992 by the Nova Scotia Government's Department of Community Services. Our research team was asked to explore the reasons for a great deal of dissatisfaction directed at Nova Scotia's Adult Protection Act which had been proclaimed in 1986. We found that criticisms came from the judiciary because the implementation of the legislation raised issues of individual rights. For instance The Canadian Charter of Rights and Freedoms (1982) guarantees equality rights for all Canadians with no discrimination on the basis of age. Judges were concerned that some cases being investigated and brought before them did not fully consider these rights. On the other hand, many professionals and lay people looked to the Act to solve the problem of older people in living situations that did not meet community norms and standards. Many of these mistreated, neglected and/or self-neglecting old people were refusing assistance to change their living conditions, and because they were mentally competent were legally entitled to do so. There was a further reason for referral to adult protection services even where the referee knew that the person was mentally competent and did not fall under the provisions of the Act. That was the hope that such a referral might lead to the provision of much needed services for their clients—services that would not otherwise be supplied because they were in such short supply.

Thus, Adult Protection Services had become a magnet for frustrated helpers, legislation of which the Minister said in 1986 "[it] will, presumably, not require frequent application" (The honourable Edmund Morris, cited in Coughlan et al., 1995, p. 45), by the year 1992–93 dealt with 931cases—the majority involving older people, 141 of which involved court applications.

Our second study was begun six years after the first study in 2001 and completed in 2004. Given that our earlier study demonstrated the limited capacity of the Adult Protection Act to deal with the majority of problems involving mistreatment and neglect we wanted to explore what was happening informally to address the mistreatment and neglect of older people, as opposed to focusing on the formal services based on provisions of the Adult Protection Act. We focused our attention on rural areas because comments by participants in our previous study indicated that rural areas were especially poor in service provision and that lack of transportation increased the rural isolation of older people.

Our findings suggest that in the intervening period from our earlier study a greater understanding of the limitations of the provisions of the Adult Protection Act had developed. The following remarks made by professionals demonstrate this clearly and are typical of what we heard:

> . . . their [Adult Protection] mandates are pretty narrow. Adult Protection has to have just cause . . .They'd have to talk to collateral supports a mile long to get justification to go out because the law says they can't intrude until they have just cause.

and the following

> [the adult protection worker] came in and the thing that he said was, "I'm not the lifestyle police" and it's a great, really great way to characterize Adult Protection.

This clear understanding of the limitations of the adult protection legislation and the rights of older people may well be related to efforts within the departments responsible for adult protection services. For instance, the Adult Protection Services Policy Manual (April 1, 2001) refers to their mandate to provide "services to protect vulnerable adults while respecting the inherent rights of adults to live their lives according to their own beliefs and wishes" (p. 1) and, "[recognizes that] all adults have the right to autonomy and self-determination" (p. 2) [and to] the ability to enjoy the fundamental rights and freedoms prescribed in the Canadian Charter of Rights and Freedoms (p. 3).

However, while on the one hand, we found this clear understanding of the limitations of the adult protection role under the Act, on the other we found a greatly enhanced role for adult protection workers. Among health and social service professionals they were valued for their expertise in understanding abuse, neglect and self-neglect and in finding ways to address it. Inexperienced health and social service workers relied a great deal on consultation from an adult protection worker ". . . most cases I usually would call adult protection and brainstorm with them" (social worker).

Nevertheless, referrals to adult protection were not always benign. As in the previous study, it was suggested that "pressure from the community . . . that people aren't making safe choices" led some workers to make a formal referral to adult protection services even when they knew the situation would not meet the criteria of the Adult Protection Act "... and then [he or she] will go back to the community and say, you know, it's, been referred but at this point they have the right to risk" (statement of home care coordinator). This is an ethically and legally disturbing use of the provisions of the Act, whereby older people's rights are knowingly infringed in order to give primacy to community values and protect the professional reputation of the worker involved.

In contrast, we also found considerable cooperation between many differing groups and individuals seeking to provide assistance that was acceptable to the older person without using a formal referral to adult protection. In addition to formal health and social service providers, police, faith leaders, Meals on Wheels organizers, members of seniors' organizations and interested individuals on occasion combined their efforts to provide help. We heard about many instances when community members came together to generate creative solutions to meet the needs and wishes of older people in a range of difficult and bad circumstances. It appeared as if over time, people had become reconciled to the limitations inherent in adult protection legislation and had been able find other ways to assist the older members of their communities. Once again, however, many people commented on the lack of services to support older people, especially those living in their own homes. Moreover, the only alternative residential accommodation was long-term residential care, often far from the person's community. This alternative was one that most older people refused to contemplate.

The third study referred to in this discussion is currently under way. The choice of the Maritime provinces was based on the parallel provisions of the legislation in each province in that they followed a 'child protection' model (Gordon, 2001; McDonald et al., 1991). The study is aimed at exploring the extent to which the differing provisions of Maritime adult protection legislation may lead to differing patterns and practices in what assistance is provided and how. Our interest in pursuing these questions emerged from the findings of the second study discussed above. This, as we have seen, suggested that in Nova Scotia a wide range of professionals and community members came together to address their concerns about diverse manifestations of what has come to be known as 'elder abuse and neglect', and in doing so transcended the provisions of the Adult Protection Act. Finally, we want to understand whether there are adequate services to assist in resolving older people's situations of mistreatment and neglect.

While our analysis is as yet incomplete one important finding has emerged so far. The comparative study has highlighted a current preoccupation among professionals in all three jurisdictions with whether or not a person is 'mentally competent' and therefore has the right to live at risk. The quotations below illustrate this. A mental health worker says:

> One of the biggest challenges is knowing what we can actually do and what we can't . . . and we need to know when to stop. And those are all . . . frankly stressful kinds of judgment calls that we have to make with high case loads.

An adult protection worker says:

> So if it's a competent person and their living situation is terrible, and they refuse medical treatment, they refuse services and they're competent, then we can't do anything legally.

And acknowledges that this is:

> . . . a very difficult thing for me when they've been declared competent but yet go back to living at risk. And you know everybody's hands are kind of tied at that point.

The following statement from a social worker sums up many of the issues that attend working with older people:

> . . . from my point of view the number one issue . . . legally, is competency. If that person is competent, they are deemed to have the right to live at risk. So competency is a big issue and that's something that we take great pains with . . . Some of the bigger issues are the right to live at risk and we all live at risk. . . We all accept the risks we choose to and some people have lived with a high degree of risk all their lives and just because they're older now doesn't mean that we can say "you don't have a right to do that any more" based on competency.

This social worker recognizes that just because someone is chronologically older, does not mean that their right to live the way they choose should be taken from them. However, it is clear that for many people this acknowledgement of rights is not an easy one and that it is tempered by an ongoing pressure to monitor an older person who is perceived as vulnerable. The words of another adult protection worker reflect this:

> Oh yes, and often I feel like part of my job is to be a vulture, you know, I just kind of sit and hover over the body, waiting . . . like, because we are waiting for something to happen. We're waiting for the person to fall . . . so you're going and you're just monitoring and you're trying to build a relationship and you're trying to get the person to accept some services . . .

This worker may also have captured a key element in just why some older people are so reluctant to engage with formal service providers offering assistance – they anticipate the monitoring that may end in the removal of their rights and their autonomy.

Limitations of the Studies

All of the studies used the qualitative methods that are best suited to the exploration of complex topics without a well-researched knowledge base. Our chief purposes have been the carefully constructed collection of data that will allow us to understand what the issues are and what questions need to be explored with regard to assisting mistreated and neglected older people. The knowledge accumulated from these three sequential studies has given some direction in our findings. At the same time we need "to be careful not to over-interpret their meaning. This is especially so in attempting to apply the findings outside of their immediate cultural and geographic context [and historical timeframe" (Harbison et al., 2005).

Discussion

Adult protection legislation in the Maritime provinces was originally conceived as a means of addressing severe situations of mistreatment and neglect by caregivers of vulnerable mentally incompetent old people—a group that constitutes only a small minority of the old. The legislation was not intended to address the self-neglect which constitutes the majority of referrals under the legislation. Nor was it intended to address financial exploitation now widely acknowledged as the most frequent type of abuse, nor a range of mistreatment perpetrated by family, caregivers, acquaintances and strangers and tolerated by older people for their own reasons. Moreover these situations could be dealt with, by the provision of more services and increased use of other existing legislation including the Criminal Code (Coughlan et al., 1995; National Seniors Council, 2007). A recent report by the National Seniors Council commissioned by the Federal government concluded that "it is important to recognize that legal solutions alone are not as effective in combating elder abuse as social solutions that include the legal community (2007: 12).

However, the very existence of the legislation has, as we have seen, made it the focus of those seeking help for older people, experiencing a range of problems. This has the effect of drawing energy away from the provision of assistance to older people to help them solve their problems. Instead that energy that goes into monitoring whether the older person has the mental capacity to make their own decision to live at risk (Webb, 2006). These practices raise profound questions about the extent to which individual rights and wishes should be paramount in our society, whether older people should be treated as full citizens, or whether the needs of family, community and state to 'protect' should predominate.

Acknowledgement

The authors wish to acknowledge with thanks, their funders. The first study in Nova Scotia was funded by the Nova Scotia Department of Community Services and the Federal Department of Justice. The second study in Nova Scotia was funded by the Nova Scotia Health Research Fund. The study of all three Maritime Provinces is funded by the Social Sciences and Humanities Research Council.

■ References

Adult Protection Act R. S. N. S., 1989, c.2.

Anetzberger, G.J. (ed.) (2005). *The clinical management of elder abuse.* New York: The Haworth Press.

Barer, B.M. (1997). The secret shame of the very old "I've never told this to anyone else". *Journal of Mental Health and Aging*, 3(3), 365–75.

Baumann, E.A. (1989). Research rhetoric and the social construction of elder abuse. In J. Best (ed.), *Images of issues: Typifying contemporary social problems.* New York: Aldine de Gruyter.

Chappell, N. et al. (2003). *Aging in contemporary Canada.* Toronto: Prentice Hall.

Coughlan, S., B. Downe-Wamboldt, R. Elgie, J. Harbison, P. Melanson and M. Morrow (1995). *Mistreating elderly people: Questioning the response to elder abuse and neglect,* (vols. 1 and 2). Halifax, Canada: Dalhousie University, Health Law Institute.

Cumming, E. and W.E. Henry (1961). *Growing old: The process of disengagement.* New York: Basic Books.

Family Services Act 1983, S. N. B. 1980, c. C–2.1.

Gee, E. and G. Gutman (2000). *The overselling of population aging: Apocalyptic demography, intergenerational challenges, and social policy.* Don Mills, Ontario: Oxford University Press.

Gordon, R.M. (2001). Adult protection legislation in Canada, models, issues, and problems. *International Journal of Law and Psychiatry*, 24, 117–34.

Hansen, N.H. (1984). The vulnerable elderly in Nova Scotia: Their abuse and neglect. *The Nova Scotia Medical Bulletin, August/October*, 111–15.

Harbison, J., Coughlan, S., Downe-Wamboldt, B., Elgie, R., Melanson, P. and Morrow, M. (1995). *Mistreating elderly people: Questioning the response to elder abuse and neglect* (vol. 1). Halifax, Canada: Dalhousie University, Health Law Institute.

Harbison, J., S. Coughlan, J. Karabanow and M. Vanderplaat (2005). A clash of cultures: Rural values and service delivery to mistreated and neglected older people in Eastern Canada. *Practice: A Journal of the British Association of Social Workers, 17*(4), 229–46.

Kosberg, J. et al. (2003). Study of elder abuse in diverse cultures. *Journal of Elder Abuse and Neglect*, 75 (3/4), 71–89.

Leroux, T.G. and M. Petrunik (1990). The construction of elder abuse and neglect as a social problem: A Canadian perspective. *International Journal of Health Services, 20*(4), 651–63.

Lynott, R.J. and P.P. Lynott (1996). Tracing the course of the theoretical development in the sociology of aging. *The Gerontologist, 36*(6), 749–60.

McDonald, L.P. et al. (1991). *Elder abuse and neglect in Canada.* Toronto: Butterworths.

National Council of Seniors (November, 2007). *Report of the National Seniors Council on Elder Abuse.* Ottawa: Government of Canada.

Neglected Adults Welfare Act, S. N. 1990, c. N–3.

Neugarten, B. (1967). The aged in American society. In H. Becker (ed.), *Social problems: A modern approach.* New York: Wiley.

Ogg, J. and C. Munn-Giddings (1993). Researching elder abuse. *Ageing and Society*, 13, 13–29.

Straka, S.M. and L. Montminy (2006). Responding to the needs of older women experiencing domestic violence. *Violence Against Women, 12*(3), 251–67.

Townsend, P. (1986). Ageism and social policy. In C. Phillipson and A. Walker (eds.), *Ageing and social policy: A critical assessment.* Aldershot: Gower Publishing Co. Ltd.

Webb, S.A. (2006). *Social work in a risk society: Social and political perspectives.* Basingstoke, Hampshire: Palgrave Macmillan.

14

Elder Abuse and Mistreatment: A Life Span and Cultural Context

Carey Wexler Sherman, Dorrie E. Rosenblatt, and Toni C. Antonucci

Elder abuse is now recognized as a global, social and public health problem threatening older people (Lachs and Pillemer, 2004; WHO, 2002). Older adults constitute the fastest growing segment of the population in the United States and many nations. Demographic projections indicate that there will be 18.2 million adults over the age of 85, or 'oldest old,' in the United States by 2050 (Population Resource Center, 2006). Poverty and disability rates also rise dramatically with age, with disproportionate impact on minority elderly populations and women. It is predicted that rates of dementia, with its attendant needs for long-term family caregiving, will triple in the coming decades (Paveza, Cohen and Eisdorfer et al., 1992; Pillemer and Suitor, 1992; Dyer, Pavlik, Murphy and Hyman, 2002). Given that two-thirds of the ageing world population lives in the rapidly changing developing world (United Nations Population Report, 2007), the World Health Organization and the United Nations have called for an urgent consideration of how these trends may contribute to increasing elder mistreatment risk and incidence in the coming decade so as to improve early detection and facilitate sensitive intervention.

In this paper we consider current cultural understandings of elder abuse from a social relations perspective. Guided by the Convoy model of social relations (Antonucci, 2001; Kahn and Antonucci, 1980), which incorporates a contextual, life span perspective, we examine how cultural expectations of social roles and support of the elderly may contribute to or ameliorate the risks of elder mistreatment.

Evolving Definitions of Elder Abuse

There is no agreed-upon universal definition of elder abuse (Bennett and Kingston, 1993; Wolf and Pillemer, 1989). Generally, elder abuse is understood to include actions of violence or mistreatment committed intentionally or unintentionally, through over abuse or through forms of neglect (Hudson, 1999b). Working definitions also describe types of abuse (e.g., physical, psychological, financial, sexual and neglect), the victim and perpetrator, and the location of abuse (e.g., violence at home or in an institutional setting).

Evolving definitions of elder abuse necessarily reflect the cultural contexts in which they emerge. The World Health Organization and the International Network for the Prevention of Elder Abuse defined elder abuse in the mid-1990s as: "a single, or repeated act, or lack of appropriate action, occurring within any relationship where there is an expectation of trust which causes harm or distress to an older person" (Action on Elder Abuse, 1995). In the United States, the National Research Council (2002) adopted their own definition of elder abuse to include "intentional actions that cause harm or create a serious risk of harm, whether or not intended, to a vulnerable elder by a caregiver or other person who stands in a trust relationship to the elder, or failure by a caregiver to satisfy the elder's basic needs or to protect the elder from harm" (p. 40). The NRC version emphasizes the notion of the vulnerability of the elder victim, but specifically omits financial exploitation as well as self-neglect, which may represent as much as 60 per cent of cases reported to social services charged with the protection of adults in the United States (Duke, 1996). In addition, this definition includes the notion that actions contributing to heightened risk can also be construed as elder abuse and mistreatment.

The violation of a 'trust relationship' is explicitly identified as a defining feature of elder mistreatment (NRC, 2002), and distinguishes mistreatment from other forms of violence or illegal behaviour towards older adults. Trust relationships include "those people who have assumed the responsibility for caregiving or are expected to do so" (p. 41). In most cases, influential trust relationships and their intergenerational dynamics are long-term in nature, and are, therefore, best understood from a life course perspective.

These definitions reflect the values and sensibility of most western social and legal understandings of elder abuse. As such, they provide useful guides for future interventions in the United States and other countries that ascribe to similar value traditions. Nonetheless, culturally specific interpretations of elder abuse are bound to vary between and within distinct groups, (e.g., ethnic, racial, religious) and/or generations. Broad popular engagement in the process of identifying and defining such a complex phenomenon as elder abuse is needed to assure that the legal and programmatic responses based on those definitions, are not "ethically and pragmatically insensitive to the public they are intended to serve" (Hudson and Carlson, 1999, p. 57). It remains critical, therefore, to identify and account for culturally specific conceptions of elder abuse and mistreatment in increasingly diverse societies around the world (Kosberg, Lowenstein, Garcia and Biggs, 2003).

Elder Mistreatment: A Global Public Health Concern

Estimates of reported elder abuse in the population range from 2 to10 per cent (Lachs and Pillemer, 2004) and are based on the few extant large-scale probability non-clinical sample surveys in Boston, MA, (Pillemer and Finkelhor, 1988), Canada (Podnieks, 1992), the Netherlands (Comijs, Penninx, Knipscheer and van Tilberg, 1999), and Finland (Kivela, Kongas-Saviaro, Kesti, Pahkala and Ijas, 1992).

In Sweden, however, national estimates of elder abuse indicate that 13 per cent of men and 16 per cent of women over 65 years report experiencing some form of abuse (Eriksson, 2001). In spite of minimal societal recognition of elder abuse , a recent Chinese study of elders at large urban health centres found that over 35 per cent of elders reported being mistreated or abused (Dong, Simon and Gorbien, 2007). Similar concerns of increased elder abuse and neglect have been voiced in India, where a growing per cent of the total population is elderly and two-thirds of older people live in rural villages far from medical or social services (Jamuna, 2003). In a recent nationally representative self-report study of Jewish and Arab Israeli elders, over 18 per cent of elders indicated that they had experienced at least one form of abuse (Eisikovitz, Winterstein and Lowenstein, 2005). Verbal abuse was the most common type of mistreatment, followed by neglect of primary needs. A separate Israeli study found that while 6 per cent of the elder respondents disclosed being abused, 21 per cent were described by medical staff as showing clear evidence of abuse, and 33 per cent were deemed to be at high risk of abuse (Cohen, Levin, Gagin and Friedman, 2007). This same study found that certain abuse types (i.e., physical, sexual) were more likely to result in disclosure, adding yet another layer of complexity to establishing reliable or comparable prevalence rates.

Effects of Abuse on Morbidity and Mortality

The paucity of reliable global prevalence levels of elder abuse is particularly serious given that the psychological and physical costs to victims can be enormous. Given that elder mistreatment victims are often frail, the injuries from physical abuse or neglect often have severe or long-lasting impact. In a recent longitudinal study of older adults, elder mistreatment victims were found to be over three times more likely to die during a three year period than non-victims, and this trend became more striking over the full 13 years of the study (Lachs, Williams, O'Brian, Pillemer and Charlson, 1998). Studies to date have documented that victims of elder mistreatment have significantly higher levels of psychological distress, and more negative self-perceptions in areas of mastery and self-efficacy than non-victims (Comijs, Penninx, Knipscheer and van Tilberg, 1999).

Methodological Issues

While these studies have shaped the field, findings have been limited by variations in definitional and inclusion criteria that inevitably lower participation by the most vulnerable, such as the frail or cognitively impaired, who are potentially the most likely victims of elder abuse. Overall, experts suspect that problems of elder mistreatment are far more pervasive than currently recognized (Wolf, 2000).

The intrinsic difficulty of accessing vulnerable adults is a substantial hurdle in the field. This concern prompted the United States Congress to call for an American national one year incidence study. That study, conducted by the National Center on Elder Abuse (1998), found nearly 500,000 community-dwelling Americans aged 60 and older were abused, neglected, or exploited. This same study, however, suggested that for every one case reported to Adult Protective Services, at least five additional cases are unreported to social services. Similarly, a separate prevalence study of domestic elder abuse indicated that only 1 in 14 incidents, excluding cases of self-neglect, come to the attention of authorities (Pillemer and Finkelhor, 1988). Rates of underreporting of financial exploitation are assumed to be much higher (Wasik, 2000).

Adaptation of the Convoy of Social Relations: The Case of Elder Abuse

A growing body of research using the Convoy Model of social relations (Kahn and Antonucci, 1980; Antonucci, 2001; Akiyama, Antonucci, Takahashi and Langfahl, 2003) has demonstrated how personal and situational factors affect the structure of one's support network as well as types of support exchanged and perceptions of satisfaction with that support.

Close, trusting and supportive relationships have been shown to be protective in adulthood and old age against a large array of physical and mental illnesses, such as cardiovascular disease and cancer, depression, certain cognitive impairment outcomes and Alzheimer's disease (Antonucci, Fuhrer and Dartigues, 1997; Fratiglioni, Wang, Ericsson, Maytan and Winblad, 2000; Ingersoll-Dayton, Morgan and Antonucci, 1997; see Bowling and Grundy, 1998 for a recent review), and stress-related health disparities (Antonucci et al., 2003; Jackson, Williams and Torres, 2003; Vaillant, Meyer, Mukamal and Soldz, 1998).

At the same time, however, close relations have also been documented as the most common sources of negativity, frustration, conflict, guilt, and ambivalence (Birditt Jackey, Iglesias and Antonucci, 2007; Luescher and Pillemer, 1998; Murphy et al., 1997). Negative exchanges with close network members have been shown to be more strongly or reliably associated with health outcomes than positive relationship quality (Kiecolt-Glaser, et al., 1993; Rook, 1997). In fact, extreme cases of negative relationships may deteriorate into violent, neglectful or exploitative interactions.

Such complex dynamics and outcomes of close social relations and support across the life span have been increasingly considered within a cultural context (Akiyama et al., 2003; Antonucci and Jackson, 2003; Elder,

1998, 2002; van Tilburg et al., 1998). With respect to the complex phenomenon of elder abuse, we consider several macro-level influences, such as cultural values, gender norms, as well as ongoing societal changes that inevitably impact social relations and elder care. We also consider how personal and situational factors, such as gender, health status, and relationship, may influence relationships and the potential for abuse.

Cultural Expectations as Context for Abuse

Despite globalization, distinct cultural value systems, religious orientations and expectations towards older adults, shape attitudes towards elder abuse in different parts of the world (Inglehart and Welzel, 2005). Cross-cultural theorists have indicated that cultures vary on several value dimensions, including individualism/collectivism, relatedness/separateness, traditional/secular, and self-expression/survival and modernism/postmodernism (Hofstede, 1980; Inglehart and Welzel, 2005; Markus and Kitayama, 1991).

Using the World Values Survey, the largest existing study of beliefs and values around the world, Inglehart and Welzel (2005) diagrammed how countries were distributed on traditional/secular and survival/self expression value dimensions. The study included 81 societies, encompassing 85 per cent of the world's population. They found that traditional societies valued obedience to God, religion, one's homeland, family, and social conformity, while secular societies valued science and autonomy. Societies that emphasize survival values are more likely to stress the importance of economic and physical security, promote traditional gender roles, constrain individual autonomy and limit contact with out-group or foreigners. In contrast, societies that value self-expression emphasize human choice, well-being and creativity.

These value dimensions suggest distinct cultural variations in the structure and quality of social relationships in general, and understanding of elder abuse in particular. For example, individualistic cultures, such as the United States, are known to value self expression and focus on maintaining relationships that are beneficial for personal goals. Intergenerational investments in family members may be more psychological than economic. While people in these cultures generally feel obligated to family, these relationships may be perceived as more voluntary in nature, and sustained on the basis of their relational quality (Kagitcibasi, 1996; Oyserman, Coon and Kemmelmeier, 2002). Cultures ascribing to collectivism and relatedness tend to believe that group membership is unchangeable (Oyserman, Coon and Kemmelmeier, 2002). Such societies tend to maintain extended families in which young people provide direct financial help to the elderly. For instance, most Far Eastern countries exemplify these values through strict expectations of filial piety towards elders. The Chinese culture, for example, has historically promoted a strong sense of family peace, dignity, honour and respect for elders (Tam and Neysmith, 2006). While these dimensions are helpful in identifying overarching approaches towards social life in a given country or part of the world, we recognize that gradations of grey are more the rule in the increasingly mobile, interactive, diverse global society. When considering a complex issue like elder abuse, it is critical to recognize both traditional and changing values and circumstances.

To better understand how such value traditions influence elder abuse, a growing number of studies have described cultural and ethnic perceptions and definitions of elder mistreatment. Culturally situated descriptions of elders' role(s) and intergenerational expectations help illuminate why and how perceptions of and responses to elder mistreatment vary between and within different societies (Anetzberger, 1998; Arai, 2006; Brownell and Podneiks, 2005; Moon, 1993; Sanchez, 1999; Tatara, 1999; Tomita, 1999). A comparative study, for example, found that native Americans rated behaviours as more abusive than African Americans, who were in turn, more likely to rate behaviours as abusive than were European Americans (Hudson and Carlson, 1999). Rating the relative severity of different abuse types among African American adults, younger adults rated verbal abuse as a mild form of abuse while older participants described verbal abuse as an extreme form of abuse. Neglect and abandonment were more likely to be considered extreme abuse by women as compared to men across age groups (Tauriac and Scruggs, 2006).

Highlighting inherent heterogeneity within minority groups, another study explored attitudes of elder mistreatment among a sample of four Asian American groups (Moon, Tomita and Jung-Kamei, 2001). The authors found, for example, that American-born participants were more tolerant of verbal abuse, less likely to blame the elder parent for causing abuse and more likely to report incidents than were immigrant-born Asian Americans. On the other hand, overall Korean Americans differed significantly from other Asian groups in their tolerance of financial exploitation, blaming elders, and in reluctance to report.

The Role of Socio-economic Change: Risks for Elder Abuse

Culturally-specific macro-level changes also create potential risk environments for elder abuse. India and China, for example, are currently experiencing massive socio-economic change in the face of rapid industrialization, urbanization and globalization of their economies. Migration out of rural villages to cities for employment and increased rates of women entering the work force can contribute to overt or covert neglect of elders who must increasingly fend for themselves. In India, tradition has called for the elderly to live with the eldest son's family. While young Indian women have been acculturated to provide such care to their mothers-in-law, greater educational and professional attainment among Indian women can threaten this traditional expectation and augment intergenerational conflict. Even among those adult children who wish to provide necessary care, many are required to move to the industrial centres for employment, leaving elders without the traditional safety net of their extended family. Such larger socio-economic changes thus can create or increase potential risk factors for mistreatment of elders (Jamuna, 1992).

In China, which is also undergoing rapid industrialization, recent studies of elder abuse have documented increased caregiver neglect, financial exploitation, and emotional abuse. Indeed, acute loneliness is the leading risk factor associated with elder abuse in China (Dong, Simon, Gorbien, Percak, and Golden, 2007). Similar findings have been reported in Korea, another country with a strong tradition of filial piety toward its elders. With shifts towards a more nuclear family structure and increased participation by women in the work force, older Korean parents are increasingly left alone to care for themselves (Oh, Kim, Martins, and Kim, 2005). In fact, a population-based survey found that sons and daughters-in-law, traditionally responsible for elder care, are now named as the most frequent abusers in Korea, with emotional abuse the most frequent form of mistreatment. Unlike many of the prior studies of abuse in other countries, significantly more Korean men compared with women reported overall abuse, including emotional, economic and verbal abuse (Oh, Kim, Martins, and

Kim, 2005). Whether this gender difference reflects actual abuse directed towards men or a greater willingness to reports remains unclear, and warrants further investigation. Such studies are critical to uncover culturally specific forms and interpretations of types of abuse and mistreatement.

Institutional Forms of Care as Context of Abuse

Specific cultural and medical models of elder care also influence meso level contributors to elder abuse. For example, institutional settings are a well established and accepted, if not optimal, option for the care of frail and infirm elders in many Western countries. While concerns and incidence of elder abuse within such settings have been documented (Hawes, 2002), the availability of institutional care can also serve to protect elders from neglect and other forms of abuse when other resources for care are absent or insufficient. In more traditional societies, however, culture expectations dictate family care and assistance for elders. Such cultures/countries typically have very limited institutional or governmental forms of support and care in place (WHO, 2002). While these cultures do not confront elder abuse in institutional settings, the absence of such alternatives can result in a lack of protective options for elders whose family cannot or do not provide adequate care in the later years.

In the same vein, access to primary and intensive medical care for elders differs widely between diverse countries. In India, for example, access to medical care is severely limited in the villages. Unable to reach adequate health services, many older adults experience insufficient care and/or accept chronic disability as a way of life (Jamuna, 2003). Such significant societal shifts are occurring in much of the developing world, with cascading effects on the level of interaction and care of elders who remain tied to and dependent on traditional life. Unfortunately, those in the developed world who have limited access to such resources are similarly disadvantaged and vulnerable

Studies in ethnically and religiously diverse countries, such as Israel show that they face multiple pressures which may contribute to rising rates of elder abuse. Despite its small population, a large number of language groups are represented. Israel has historically accommodated large scale immigrations of refugees, recently from countries as diverse as Ethiopia and the former Soviet Union. These groups, with their own traditions and cultural histories, have had to rapidly adjust to the pressures and expectations of 21st century, industrialized urban life. Governmental social service agencies, which provide multi-generational assistance to these new immigrants, are over-extended while economic struggles at the national level have resulted in lower pension payments and service overall. Such macro level demands inevitably set the stage for higher risk for vulnerable populations within the larger society.

Finally, historical racial abuse and trauma of certain ethnic/racial groups by a dominant culture also constitute risk factors which can contribute to increased violence against and within a vulnerable or minority groups. High levels of violence in the Native and African American communities in the United States, for example, have been traced, in part, as a response to the systemic abuse of these groups by the government (Griffin, 1998). Immigrant and refugee populations who have suffered personal and collective deprivation, warfare and genocide have also been found to have heightened levels of intergenerational abuse, including elder abuse. While macro level influences on family and elder abuse may be challenging to document, efforts must be made to understand and account for the cultural meanings of such larger historical patterns, before effective interventions and supports can be implemented.

Personal and Situational Factors and Elder Abuse

The Convoy model details how personal (e.g., gender, age) and situational factors (e.g., social roles of parent, child, worker) shape social relations and affect outcomes of well-being (Antonucci, 2001). For example, it has also been noted that "the single most powerful risk marker for becoming a victim of violence is to be a woman" (Walker, 1999). Cultural variation in the life circumstances, social responsibilities, and access to resources by women make them more vulnerable to and less protected from all health problems, including abuse across the life span (Simpson, 2002). Fernandez (2006) describes specific ways in which cultural expectations can play a major role of both perpetration and interpretation of violence against women across the life span. For example, patriarchal conceptions of ownership and ultimate authority over women still persist in many global cultures as well as among specific ethnic and religious groups. In such societies or groups, men are considered legally and economically responsible for their female relatives. The use of physical and psychological control, assault, and even killing of women is condoned as an acceptable means of asserting social values and/or expectations (Kulwicki, 2002; Sagot, 2005). Such cultural or group expectations present notable risks for ageing women who despite disability, live longer, in greater poverty and in greater dependence on family members. Violence against women, however, remains underreported due to the sensitive nature of the subject and potential risk of retribution (Watts and Zimmerman, 2002).

Circumstances affecting either or both members of a victim-perpetrator dyad, such as poverty and its consequences, isolation, alcohol abuse, mental illness, depression, and financial dependence among family members, (Kosberg and Nahmiash, 1996; Simpson, 2002) have also been identified as potential risk factors for elder abuse (Wolf, 2000). Physical and cognitive decline, again on the part of either or both of the abusive dyad, coupled with the demands of chronic caregiving, can further place vulnerable older people at risk of elder mistreatment (Coyne et al., 1993; Dyer, Pavlik, Murphy, and Hyman, 2000; Lachs et al., 1997; Paveza et al., 1992; Pillemer and Suitor, 1992).

Future Directions

The ageing of American and global societies as well as the convergence of demographic trends suggest a clear imperative to address the issue of elder mistreatment. Given the intergenerational effects of elder abuse, it is also clear, that when examining elder abuse, we must consider both structural aspects of relationships and cultural expectations of relationships across the life span. These have important influence on the risk and vulnerability of elders for abuse and mistreatment. Indeed, existing studies have done much to highlight the value of considering ethnic and cultural variation (Kosberg, Lowenstein, Garcia and Biggs, 2003). Further examinations of culturally sensitive studies of changing intergenerational expectations and attitudes towards elders will help identify behaviours that may constitute or contribute to abuse or mistreatment.

In order to accommodate such multi-level examinations, researchers in the elder abuse area must continue to address the methodological limitations that have been constrained in the field. The development of shared definitions and measurements has been noted as a priority for the field by the National Research Council (2002) and others. Paradoxically, specific intervention efforts, such as mandatory reporting, often present unintended barriers to elder abuse research, while lengthy interviews or clinical approaches are sometimes inappropriate or too cumbersome for use in community samples. Accessing those vulnerable adults, who are frail and/or cognitively impaired elders, presents an ongoing research and intervention challenge that needs to be addressed. At the same time, alternative methods must be employed which offer the privacy and confidentiality required for highly sensitive or stigmatized topics, especially among minority communities who have grave apprehensions about agency or formal intervention (Lee and Renzetti, 1990).

In addition to methodological issues, several particularly thorny issues regarding cultural definitions and affiliation must be considered in future research. First, there is the substantial issue of whether, in a given culture or society, elders and/or women who ascribe to the traditional gender roles or intergenerational expectations actually 'feel' abused or mistreated, according to definitions that have emerged in other cultures or legal systems. This issue has been in the forefront of challenges to women who ascribe to traditional practices promoted by strict religious sects, for example. This issue certainly affects levels of elder abuse reporting, and therefore has direct effects on reliable identification of elder abuse prevalence. Similarly, development of effective intervention programmes is not possible without addressing whose definition of abuse is ultimately going to apply in such settings.

A related challenge for future research and intervention efforts is the tremendous heterogeneity within racial, ethnic and religious categories and groups (Jackson, Brown, Antonucci and Daatland, 2005). Levels of affiliation within a given ethnic group, or levels of endorsement of traditional values of a given religion, for example, may be a more meaningful way to proceed in future. Of course, such nuances of affiliation are more complicated to assess, especially as these affiliations can vary within families, across generations, and across the life span. Moving beyond the use of simple categories of race, ethnicity and religion is a perennial problem. However, research of such complex phenomena as elder abuse requires the promotion of culturally sensitive and applicable knowledge in this area of global concern.

Rapid global social changes challenge existing social relations norms and traditions regarding the role and care of elders. We propose that through collaborative, cross-cultural effort, highlighting a life span perspective, researchers and policy makers may be better able to harness the greater access resulting from global interconnectivity to develop innovative approaches for dissemination of information, education and implementation of culturally relevant interventions of elder abuse and mistreatment.

References

Action on Elder Abuse. http://www.elderabuse.org.uk, 1995. Retrieved online 1 March, 2008.

Arai, M. (2006). Elder abuse in Japan. *Educational Gerontology*, 32: 13–23.

Anetzberger, G. (1998). *Psychological abuse and neglect: A cross-cultural concern to older Americans. Understanding and Combating Elder Abuse in Minority Communities.* Archstone Foundation, 141–51.

Antonucci, T.C. (2001). Social relations: An examination of social networks, social support and sense of control. In J.E. Birren and K.W. Schaie (eds.), *Handbook of the psychology of aging* (5th ed.), (pp. 427–53). New York: Academic Press.

Antonucci, T.C., Ajrouch, K.J. and Birditt, K.S.(2006). Social relations in the third age: Assessing strengths and challenges using the Convoy Model. In K.W. Schaie (Series ed.) and J.B. James and P. Wink (vol. eds.), *Annual review of gerontology and geriatrics:* vol. 26. *The crown of life dynamics of the early postretirement period* (pp. 193–209). New York: Springer Publishing Co.

Antonucci, T.C., Fuhrer, R. and Dartigues, J.F. (1997). Social relations and depressive symptomatology in a sample of community-dwelling French older adults. *Psychology & Aging*, 12: 189–95.

Antonucci, T.C. and Jackson, J.S. (2003). Ethnic and cultural differences in intergenerational social support. In V.L. Bengtson and A. Lowenstein (eds.), *International perspectives on families, aging and social support* (pp. 355–70). New York: Aldine de Gruyter Publishing Co.

Akiyama, H., Antonucci, T.C., Takahashi, K. and Langfahl, E.S. (2003). Negative interactions in close relationships across the life span. *The Journals of Gerontology*, 58B(2): 70–79.

Bennett, G. and Kingston P. (1993). *Elder abuse: Concepts, theories and interventions.* London: Chapman & Hall.

Bent-Goodley, T. (2007). Health disparities and violence against women: Why and how cultural and societal influences matter. *Trauma, Violence and Abuse*, 8: 90–104.

Birditt, K.S., Jackey, L.M.H., Iglesias, H.F. and Antonucci, T.C. (2007). *Older but not necessarily nicer: Longitudinal patterns of negativity in adulthood.* Symposium paper presented at annual meeting of Gerontological Society of America, San Francisco, CA.

Bowling, A. and Grundy, E. (1998). The association between social networks and mortality in later life. *Reviews in Clinical Gerontolgy*, 8: 353–61.

Brownell, P. and Podneiks, E. (2005). Long-overdue recognition for the critical issue of elder abuse and neglect: A global policy and practice perspective. *Brief Treatment and Crisis Intervention*, 5: 187–91.

Cohen, M., Levin, S.H., Gagin, R. and Friedman, G. (2007). Elder abuse: Disparities between older people's disclosure of abuse, evident abuse and high risk of abuse. *Journal of American Geriatrics Society*, 55: 1224–30.

Comijs, H.C., Penninx, B.W., Knipscheer, K.P. and van Tilberg, W. (1999). Psychological distress in victims of elder abuse: The effects of social support and coping. *Journal of Gerontology: Social Science*, 54: 240–45.

Coyne, A.C., Reichman, W.E. and Berbig, L.J. (1993). The relationship between dementia and elder abuse. *American Journal of Psychiatry*, 150: 643–46.

Dong, X.Q., Simon, M.A. and Gorbein, M.J. (2007). Elder abuse and neglect in an urban Chinese population. *Journal of Elder Abuse and Neglect*, 19.

Dong, X.Q., Simon, M.A., Gorbein, M.J., Percak, B.A. and Golden, R. (2007). Loneliness in older Chinese adults: A risk factor for elder mistreatment. *Journal of American Geriatrics Society*, 55: 1831–35.

Duke, J. (1996). Self-neglect: The professional's challenge. *National Association of Adult Protective Services Administrators.*

Dyer, C.B., Pavlik, V.N., Murphy, K.P. and Hyman, D.J. (2002). The high prevalence of depression and dementia in elder abuse or neglect. *Journal of American Geriatric Society*, 48: 205–58.

Elder, G.H. (1998). The life course and human development. In *Handbook of Child Psychology*, edited by Richard M. Lerner (Volume 1: Theoretical Models of Human Development), (pp. 939–91). New York: Wiley.

Elder, G.H. (2002). Historical times and lives: A journey through time and space, *Looking at Lives: American Longitudinal Studies of the 20th Century*, (pp. 194–218) in E. Phelps, F. Furstenberg, Jr. and A. Colby, (eds.). New York: Russell Sage Foundation.

Eriksson, H. (2001). *Violence against elderly women and men: A prevalence study.* Sweden: Umea.

Eisikovitz, Z.,Winterstein, T. and Lowenstein, A. (2005). Elder abuse in the multicultural society of Israel. Paper presented at the 18th World Congress of Gerontology, International Association of Gerontology, Brazil.

Fernandez, M.(2006). Cultural beliefs and domestic violence. *Annals of New York Academy of Science*, 1087: 250–60.

Fratiglioni, L., Wang, H., Ericsson, K., Maytan, M. and Winblad, B. (2000). Influence of social network on occurrence of dementia: A community-based longitudinal study. *The Lancet*, 355: 1315–19.

Griffin, L. (1994). Elder maltreatment among rural African-Americans. *Journal of Elder Abuse and Neglect*, 6: 1–27.

Hawes, C. (2002). *Elder Abuse in Residential Long-Term Care Facilities: What Is Known About Prevalence, Causes and Prevention* , U.S. Senate Committee on Finance, (June 18).

Hofsted, G. (1980). *Culture's consequences: International differences in work-related values*. Newbury Park, CA: Sage Publishers.

Hudson, M.F. (1999b). Elder abuse: Some African American views. *Journal of Interpersonal Violence*, 14: 915–39.

Hudson, M.F. and Carlson, J.R. (1999). Elder abuse: Its meaning to Caucasians, African Americans and Native Americans. In Toshio Tatara (ed.), *Understanding elder abuse in minority populations* (pp. 187–204). Philadelphia: Taylor & Francis.

Inglehart, R. and Welzel, C. (2005). *Modernization, cultural change and democracy*. New York and Cambridge: Cambridge University Press.

Ingersoll-Dayton, B., Morgan, D. and Antonucci, T. (1997). The effects of positive and negative social exchanges on aging adults. *Journal of Gerontology: Social Sciences*, 52B: S190–S199.

Jackson, J.S., Brown, E., Antonucci, T.C. and Daatland, S.O. (2005). Ethnic diversity in ageing, multicultural societies. In M.L. Johnson (ed.), *The Cambridge handbook of age and ageing*. New York: Cambridge University Press.

Jamuna, D. (1992). Caring for the disabled elderly: Problems and perspectives. In S.K. Chowdary (ed.), *Problems of the aged and of old age homes*, (pp. 111–16). Bombay: Askhar Pratiroop Ltd.

Jamuna, D. (2003). Issues of elder care and elder abuse in the Indian context. *Journal of Aging and Social Policy*, 15: 125–42.

Kagitcibasi, C. (1996). *Family and human development across cultures: A view from the other side*. Mahwah: Lawrence Erlbaum Associates.

Kahn, R.L. and Antonucci, T.C. (1980). Convoys over the life course: Attachment, roles and social support. (pp. 253–86) In P.B. Baltes and O.G. Brim (eds.), *Life-span development and behavior* (Vol. 3). New York: Academic Press.

Kiecolt-Glaser, J.K. Malarkey, W.B., Chee, M., Newton, J.T., Cacioppo, M., Hsiao-Yin, M. and Glaser, R. (1993). Negative behaviour during marital conflict is associated with immuniological down-regulation. *Psychosomatic Medicine*, 55:395–409.

Kivela, S.L., Kongas-Saviaro, P., Kesti, E., Pahkala, K. and Ijas, M. (1992). Abuse in old age: Epidemiological data from Finland. *Journal of Elder Abuse and Neglect*, 4: 1–18.

Kosberg, J.I., Lowenstein, A., Garcia, J.L. and Biggs, S. (2003). Study of elder abuse within diverse cultures. *Journal of Elder Abuse and Neglect*, 15: 71–89.

Kosberg, J.I., Nahmiash, D. (1996). Characteristics of victims and perpetrators and milieus of abuse and neglect. In L.A. Baumhover and S.C. Beal (eds.), *Abuse, neglect and exploitation of older persons* (pp. 31–50). Baltimore: Health Professions Press.

Kulwicki, A.D. (2002). The practice of honor crimes: A glimpse of domestic violence in the Arab world. *Issues of Mental Health Nursing*, 23: 77–87.

Lachs, M.S. and Pillemer, K. How would you like to be treated when you are 75? *The Lancet*, 364: 1263–72, 2004 Retrieved September 22, 2006, from the PubMed database.

Lachs, M.S., Williams, C.S., O'Brian, S.O., Pillemer, K.A. and Charlson, M.E. (1998). Emergency department utilization by older victims of family violence. *Annals of Emergency Medicine*, 30: 448–54.

Lee, R. and Renzetii, C.M.(1990). The problems of researching sensitive topics. *American Behavioral Scientist*, 33: 510–28.

Luescher, K. and Pillemer, K. (1998). Intergenerational ambivalence: A new approach to the study of parent-child relations in later life. *Journal of Marriage and the Family*, 60: 413–25.

Markus, H.R. and Kitayama, S. (1991). Culture and the self: Implications for cognition, emotion and motivation. *Psychological Review*, 98*:* 224–53.

Moon, A., Tomita, S.K. and Jung-Kamei, S. (2001). Elder mistreatment among four Asian American groups: An exploratory study on tolerance, victim blaming and attitudes toward third-party intervention. In N.G. Choi (ed.), *Social work practice with the Asian American elderly* (pp. 153–68). New York: The Haworth Press, Inc.

Murphy, B., Schofield, H., Nankervis, J., Bloch, S., Herrman, H. and Singh, B.H. (1997). Women with multiple roles: The emotional impact of caring for ageing parents. *Ageing and Society*, 18: 277–91.

National Center on Elder Abuse. (1998). *National Elder Abuse Incidence Study: Final Report.* Washington, DC, American Public Health Services Association.

National Institute of Aging. (2006). Prevalance statistics about Alzheimer's Disease. Retrieved from *www.alzheimers.nia.nih.gov.*

National Research Council. (2002). *Elder Mistreatment: Abuse, Neglect and Exploitation in an Aging America.* R. Bonnie and R.B. Wallace (eds.), National Research Council, The National Academy of Sciences.

Oh, J., Kim, H.S., Martin, D. and Kim, H. (2005). A study of elder abuse in Korea. *International Journal of Nursing Studies*, 43: 203–14.

Oyserman, D., Coon, H.M. and Kemmelmeier, M. (2002). Rethinking individualism and collectivism: Evaluation of theoretical assumptions and meta-analyses. *Psychological Bulletin*, 128: 3–72.

Paveza G., Cohen, D., Eisdorfer, C., Freels, S., Semla, T., Ashford, J.W., Gorelick, P., Hirschman, R., Luchins, D. and Levy, P. (1992). Severe family violence and Alzheimer's disease: Prevalence and risk factors. *The Gerontologist*, 32: 493–97.

Pillemer, K. and Finkelhor, D. (1988). The prevalence of elder abuse: A random sample survey. *The Gerontologist*, 28: 51–57.

Pillemer, K. and Suitor, J.J. (1992). Violence and violent feelings. What causes them among family caregivers? *Journal of Gerontology: Social Sciences*, 47: S165–S172.

Podnieks, E. (1992). National survey on abuse of the elderly in Canada. *Journal of Elder Abuse and Neglect*, 41: 5–58.

Population Resource Center. (2006). *Older Minorities: A Demographic Profile.* Retrieved October 1, 2008 from *http://www.prcdc.org/Older_Minorities.pdf.*

Rook, K.S. (1997). Positive and negative social exchanges: Weighing their effects in later life. *Journal of Gerontology: Social Sciences*, 52B: S167–S169.

Sagot, M. (2005). The critical path of women affected by family violence in Latin America. *Violence Against Women*, 11: 1292–1318.

Sanchez, Y. (1999). Elder mistreatment in Mexican-American Communities: The Nevada and Michigan experience. In T. Tatara (ed.), *Understanding Elder Abuse in Minority Populations* (pp. 67–77). Philadelphia: Taylor & Francis.

Simpson, A. (2005). Cultural issues and elder mistreatment. *Clinical Geriatric Medicine*, 21: 355–64.

Tam, S. and Neysmith, S. (2006). Disrespect and isolation: Elder abuse in Chinese communities. *Canadian Journal of Aging*, 25: 141–51.

Tatara, T. (ed.), (1999).*Understanding elder abuse in minority populations.* Philadelphia: Taylor & Francis.

Tauriac and Scruggs (2006). Elder abuse among African Americans. *Educational Gerontology*, 32: 37–48.

Tomita, S. (1999). Exploration of elder mistreatment among the Japanese. In T. Tatara (ed.), *Understanding elder abuse in minority populations* (pp. 119–139). Philadelphia: Taylor & Francis.

United Nations Population Fund: State of the World Population 2007: on http://www.unfpa.org/. Retrieved online 1 March, 2008.

van Tilburg, T., Gierveld, J., Lecchini, L. and Marsiglia, D. (1998). Social integration and loneliness: A comparative study among older adults in the Netherlands and Tuscany, Italy. *Journal of Social and Personal Relationships*, 15: 740–54.

Vaillant, G.E., Meyer, S.E., Mukamal, K., Soldz, S. (1998). Are social supports in late midlife a cause or result of successful physical aging? *Psychol Med.* 28: 1159–68.

Walker, L.E. (1999). Psychology and domestic violence around the world. *American Psychologist*, 54: 21–19.

Wasik, J.F. (2000) The fleecing of America's elderly. *Consumer Digest*, March/April: 77–81.

Watts, C. and Zimmerman, C. (2002). Violence against women: Global scope and magnitude. *The Lancet*, 359: 1232–37.

Wolf, R. (2000). The nature and scope of elder abuse. *Generations*, 24: 1–7.

Wolf, R.S. and Pillemer, K. (1989). *Helping elderly victims: The reality of elder abuse.* New York: Columbia University Press.

World Health Organization. (2002). *Missing voices: Views of older persons on elder abuse.* Geneva, Switzerland: WHO Press.

World Health Organization. (2002). *Innovative care for chronic conditions: Building blocks for action.* Geneva, Switzerland: WHO Press.

15

Investigating Emotional Reactions to an Elder Abuse: Pilot Study of a Triple Perspective Questionnaire

Christen Erlingsson

Which actions we take when witnessing an elder abuse situation not only depends on existing legislature, verifiable risk factors, or available intervention programmes, but also with how we perceive the situation (Erlingsson, 2007a). Yet perceptions are only partially based on ethical reasoning such as the reasoning reflected in written laws. Our perceptions also have deep roots in our beliefs and emotions (Fridja et al., 2000). Therefore, it is crucial to study not only how potential elder abuse witnesses in society reason and *think* about elder abuse situations but also how potential witnesses *feel* about elder abuse.

Research studies on witnesses' perceptions of elder abuse have primarily involved professionals such as physicians, nurses, and social workers (Erlingsson, 2007b) and found differences in how participants perceive elder abuse related to, e.g., age, gender, profession, and culture (Erlingsson, 2007a). There are only a handful of studies examining perceptions among lay persons (cf Erlingsson et al., 2005; Gebotys et al., 1992; Hudson, 1996; Moon and Williams, 1993). In several studies participants described feeling reluctant to take action when witnessing a situation of suspected elder abuse (Erlingsson, 2007a). However research on how emotional reactions form our perceptions of elder abuse is almost non-existent. An important exception to this is a study conducted by Werner, Eisikovitz and Buchbinder (2005) on lay persons' emotional reactions to elder abuse. One thing all these studies have in common is that participants are reporting how they themselves perceive elder abuse. But can we content ourselves with only exploring the complex phenomena of elder abuse through a single lens perspective, i.e., through the lens of "I perceive"?

Our actions are also affected by what we assume other actors in the drama are experiencing. Beliefs about what others are feeling and why they are feeling as they do, influence our experiences of emotions and how we react to our emotions (Clark and Brissette, 2000). It seems likely that it is a combination of perception perspectives that guides actions. The aim of this present study was to examine lay persons' emotional reactions to a potential elder abuse situation from the triple perspective of (1) how they themselves feel (2) they perceive the potential abuser feels, and (3) how they perceived the potential victim feels.

Method

The executive branch of the European Union, the European Commission, founded the European "Night of the Researcher" in 2006. As part of this initiative, the University of Kalmar held a two hour long exhibition, open to the public where Kalmar researchers presented projects and provided information about their areas of study. Persons walking by or visiting my booth exhibiting elder abuse research were asked if they wanted to be on-the-spot participants in an elder abuse study and invited to participate in the pilot study. Children were requested to first ask for permission from their parents or accompanying adult before participating. Participants represented both the general public and people associated with the University of Kalmar. My four assistants and I provided information about the study and instructions on how to fill in the questionnaire.

Questionnaires investigated emotional reactions to an elder abuse situation and were based on an instrument used by Werner et al. (2005) examining lay persons' self-experienced emotional reactions to a vignette concerning a situation of potential elder abuse. On the first page of the questionnaire participants were asked to respond about demographics (age, gender, occupation, education, marital/cohabitation status, and number of children). Participants then were to read and respond to items related to the vignette. Lastly participants were asked if they had perceived the vignette as an elder abuse situation and if they had personal experience of a situation where an older person had been abused. If answered positively there were follow-up questions about the relationship between the abused person, the victim, and the participant.

Questionnaires were based on two versions of the same vignette. The questionnaire used in Kalmar named the potential victim as either suffering from Alzheimer's disease (Ques-Alz) or rheumatism (Ques-Rh) (see Table 1 for explanation of abbreviations). The face validity of the vignette was first assessed by five teachers in the School of Human Sciences, University of Kalmar before questionnaires were piloted. In the current pilot study, 69 questionnaires were completed (33 included the vignette where the wife suffers from Alzheimer's disease, and 36 included the vignette where the wife suffers from rheumatism).

In order to examine emotional reactions, participants were to first read the following vignette:

> Sara Larsson is your 78 year old neighbour. She lives with Karl, her husband for the last 54 years. The couple has a son who lives nearby and provides assistance with everything his parents need help with. You know that Sara suffers from Alzheimer's disease (rheumatism). That is why home care personnel visit the couple twice weekly to help Sara take a shower and with other activities. Yesterday you met the couple near their home and noticed that Sara has several bruises on her arms and face. When you ask her what happened to her, Karl answered that she fell at home. Sara shouted, "I was beaten! I was beaten!"

After reading the vignette, participants rated 33 items. This entailed rating 11 alternative endings to each of three statements about emotional reactions. In the first statement, participants were to respond from their own, self-experienced perspective ("When I read this vignette I feel . . ."). Participants were then to respond to same 11 alternative endings but from the perspective of what the husband in the vignette would feel ("When I read this vignette I believe Karl feels . . ."). In the third statement participants were to respond from the perspective of what the wife in the vignette would feel ("When I read this vignette I believe Sara feels . . ."). Participants were to rate the same eleven alternative endings under each statement. These 11 alternative endings were "Anger", "Impatient", "Shame", "Disgust",

"Concern", "Embarrassment", "Compassion", "Irritation", "A desire to help", "Insecure", and "Frightened". Participants rated each item on a four-level Likert scale (Do not agree, Agree to a low extent, Mostly agree, Agree to a high extent).

Responses were analysed using computer software SPSS 15 for descriptive statistics, examining frequencies and cross-tabulations. Data was explored to see if sub-groups could be formed that would elucidate variations in the data and still represent adequate group size. Small sample size (see Table 2) and diversity in participants' age, number of children, type of employment, and years of schooling limited using these variables in formation of sub-groups. Questionnaire version

Table 1 Response Classifications and Abbreviations Used for Questionnaire Versions and Participant Sub-group Descriptions

Response classifications;

A = **Agreement** with the statement-specific item (Alternatives "Agree to a high extent" + "Mostly agree" > 70%)

(A) = **Agreeing more than disagreeing** with the statement-specific item (Alternatives "Agree to a high extent" + "Mostly agree" > 60% – < 69% of responses)

+/– = **Neither agreeing nor disagreeing** with the statement-specific item (Alternatives "Agree to a high extent" + "Mostly agree" and response alternatives "Agree to a low extent" + "Do not agree" are both between 41%–59% of responses)

(D) = **Disagreeing more than agreeing** with the statement-specific item (Alternatives "Agree to a low extent" + "Do not agree" > 60% – < 69% of responses)

D = **Disagreement** with the statement-specific item (Alternatives "Agree to a low extent" + "Do not agree" > 70%)

Questionnaire version abbreviations;

Ques-Alz;
Questionnaire version based on vignette specifying Alzheimer's disease

Ques-Rh;
Questionnaire version based on vignette specifying rheumatism

Participant sub-group abbreviations;

Cohab B&: Males, married or cohabitating
Cohab @&: Females, married or cohabitating
Single B&: Males, unmarried and not cohabitating
Single @&: Females, unmarried not cohabitating

(Ques-Alz or Ques-Rh) and participant's gender were variables that provided sufficient sub-group size. On closer scrutiny it could be seen that layering the cross-tabulations of questionnaire version/participants' gender with data on marital/cohabitation status revealed clear variations. Eight sub-groups were formed based on participants' gender, marital/cohabitation status, and questionnaire version (see Table 1). It must be reiterated and strongly emphasized that this was an extremely small sample and that this was a pilot study of an untested questionnaire. As such, results are only indicative of possible directions for further development and utilization of the questionnaire. Having said as much let us still take a look at some interesting results.

Table 2 Age Range and Number of Participants in Total Sample and Sub-groups

	Age range	Number of participants: In total sample	Ques-Alz	Ques-Rh
Total sample		69	33	36
	10–19 years	22	12	10
	20–39 years	25	12	13
	40–e"65 years	18	6	12
Sub-groups		65*		
CohabB&	25– e"65 years	15	6	9
SingleB&	10–e"65 years	15	9	6
Cohab@&	20–64 years	20	8	12
Single@&	10– 44 years	15	7	8

* Missing values for age, gender, or marital/cohabitation status for four participants

Results

Results were classified (see Table 1) according to the level of agreement or disagreement (A, (A), +/–, (D), or D) and are presented on the level of total sample, questionnaire version, participant sub-group, statement, and statement-specific items (see Table 3). Results were further explored by ranking items according to number of A or D responses (see Table 4), and comparing percentages of A or D responses among participant sub-groups (see Table 5). The reasoning behind reporting results in this manner is that potential trends in responding to the questionnaires, within and between groups, could become more visible.

In response to the query if the vignette was describing a situation of elder abuse, 80 per cent answered yes in the total sample (79 per cent in Ques-Alz and 81 per cent in Ques-Rh), 10 per cent answered no, and 10 per cent had unclear or no response.

Discussion

First, some of the noteworthy results of the pilot study will be highlighted. Following this the methodology of the questionnaire is considered and, lastly, conclusions about future use of this questionnaire are discussed.

Pilot Study Results

The classification of responses as A or as D indicates results where participants were responding very similarly to each other. Responses classified as (A), +/–, or (D) reveal instead a diversity in participants' response patterns. One reasonable hypothesis is that A or D response patterns indicate items, participants could respond to in a confident manner. Results classified as A or D can be considered as representing an opinion held generally by the participants. It follows that the reverse situation, diverse response patterns, could be indicating items that are more difficult to take a stand on, i.e., items where participants were less certain of how to respond. In total sample results for example, it would seem that participants were most confident in their responses in connection to items in the emotion "Concern" and least confident response pattern for items in connection to the emotion "Disgust" (see Table 3 and Table 4).

When it came to revealing the diversity of response patterns in the data, total sample results however did not tell "the whole story". As can be seen in Table 3, results classified +/– in the total sample were either, 1) confirmed in sub-groups by the majority of responses classified as +/–, (A) or (D), or 2) due to opposite responses in Ques-Alz and Ques-Rh within the same sub-group. "I feel angry" exemplifies the first case showing how diversity in sub-groups' responses supported +/– in the total sample. Item "Sara feels shame" exemplifies the second case, showing how opposite

Table 3 Level of Agreement or Disagreement with Items in Total Sample, Questionnaire Versions, and Participant Sub-groups

		Total Sample (QuesAlz + QuesRh)	**Total sample**		**Cohab.**	**Cohab.**	**Single**	**Single**			
			Ques Alz	Ques Rh	Ques Alz	Ques Rh	Ques Alz	Ques Rh	Ques Alz	Ques Rh	Ques Alz	Ques Rh
Angry	I feel	+/–	+/–	(A)	+/–	(A)	D	A	(A)	(A)	+/–	+/–
	Karl feels	(A)	A	+/–	+/–	+/–	A	A	+/–	(A)	(A)	+/–
	Sara feels	A	A	(A)	+/–	(D)	A	A	A	(A)	+/–	A
Impatient	I feel	(D)	D	(D)	+/–	(A)	D	D	D	(A)	+/–	D
	Karl feels	+/–	(A)	(D)	+/–	(D)	A	A	+/–	(D)	+/–	D
	Sara feels	+/–	(A)	+/–	(D)	+/–	A	D	A	+/–	+/–	A
Shame	I feel	D	D	(D)	D	+/–	D	D	D	D	+/–	(D)
	Karl feels	A	(A)	A	(A)	A	+/–	A	(A)	+/–	A	A
	Sara feels	+/–	(D)	(A)	+/–	A	D	A	+/–	(A)	D	(D)
Disgust	I feel	(A)	+/–	A	+/–	+/–	+/–	A	+/–	(D)	+/–	+/–
	Karl feels	(D)	D	+/–	D	+/–	D	(D)	(D)	(A)	(D)	+/–
	Sara feels	(A)	+/–	(A)	+/–	A	+/–	+/–	A	A	+/–	A
Concern	I feel	A	A	A	A	A	A	A	A	A	(A)	A
	Karl feels	A	A	A	A	A	+/–	A	A	(A)	+/–	A
	Sara feels	A	A	A	(A)	A	A	A	A	A	(A)	A
Embarrass -ment	I feel	D	(D)	D	D	(D)	D	(D)	D	D	+/–	D
	Karl feels	(A)	(A)	+/–	+/–	A	D	(D)	A	D	A	A
	Sara feels	+/–	(D)	+/–	(D)	+/–	+/–	(D)	+/–	(A)	D	+/–

Contd.

Contd.

Compassion	I feel	A	A	A	(A)	A	A	A	A	A	(A)	(A)
	Karl feels	(D)	+/–	D	(D)	D	A	D	(D)	D	(A)	+/–
	Sara feels	D	D	D	D	D	D	D	D	D	D	D
Irritation	I feel	+/–	(D)	+/–	(D)	A	+/–	D	(D)	(A)	+/–	+/–
	Karl feels	A	A	(A)	A	A	A	+/–	A	+/–	(A)	A
	Sara feels	A	A	(A)	A	+/–	A	A	A	(D)	+/–	A
Desire to help	I feel	A	A	A	+/–	A	A	A	(A)	+/–	A	A
	Karl feels	+/–	(A)	D	(D)	D	+/–	D	(A)	(D)	A	D
	Sara feels	A	A	A	A	A	A	A	A	A	A	A
Insecure	I feel	D	D	D	D	D	D	D	(D)	D	+/–	D
	Karl feels	(A)	+/–	(A)	+/–	A	D	+/–	(A)	(A)	(A)	D
	Sara feels	A	A	A	A	A	A	A	A	A	A	A
Frightened	I feel	D	D	D	D	D	D	D	+/–	D	+/–	D
	Karl feels	A	(A)	A	(A)	A	+/–	A	(A)	(A)	(A)	A
	Sara feels	A	A	A	A	A	A	A	A	A	A	A

Table 4 Emotions Ranked from Greatest Number of A or D responses to Fewest A or D Responses in the Total Sample and Statement-specific Items

		Statement-specific items		
	Total Sample	"I feel..."	"Karl feels..."	"Sara feels..."
Greatest #	- *Concern*	- Concern	- Concern	- *Compassion/*
of A or D	- *Frightened*	- *Insecure/*	- *Irritation*	*Desire to help/*
responses	- *Desire to help*	*Frightened*	- Embarrassment	*Insecure/*
⇩	*Compassion*	- *Compassion/*	- Shame	- *Frightened*
⇩	- Insecure	*Desire to help*	- Frightened	- Concern
⇩	- Shame	- *Shame/*	- *Compassion/*	- Irritation
⇩	- Irritation	*Embarrassment*	*Desire to help*	- *Angry*
⇩	- Embarrassment	- Impatient	- *Disgust/*	- *Shame*
Fewest #	- Angry	- *Angry/*	*Angry*	*Impatient/*
of A or D	- Impatient	*Irritation*	- *Insecure/*	*Disgust*
responses	- Disgust	- Disgust	*Impatient*	- Embarrassment

Note: Marked items in *italics* share same rank

responses in or between sub-groups supported +/– in the total sample. This lack of correspondence was frequently observable between total sample results, questionnaire version results, and participant sub-group results, and points to how valuable it is to view results through different lenses of questionnaire version and participant sub-groups.

One-third of the items in the total sample results, showed confident response patterns, i.e., results classified as either A or D. These were "I feel concern", "Karl feels concern", "Sara feels concern", "I feel compassion", "Sara feels compassion", "I feel a desire to help", "Sara feels a desire to help", "I feel insecure", "Sara feels insecure", "I feel frightened", "Sara feels frightened". When considering total sample results together with participant sub-group results, only four of these items showed exclusively A or D responses both for the total sample and participant sub-groups; "Sara feels compassion", "Sara feels desire to help", "Sara feels insecure", "Sara feels frightened" (see Table 3). It is interesting to note that there was only one "Karl feels . . ." item classified as A or D in the total sample and no "Karl feels . . ." item among items with responses classified exclusively as A or D in the total sample and participant sub-groups results taken together.

When ranking responses in the total sample and statement specific items, it was also "Karl feels . . ." items that most strongly diverged from ranking patterns otherwise observable in the "I feel . . ." items, and "Sara feels . . ." items, and in the total sample results. This was especially clear when considering three items; "Karl feels irritation", "Karl feels embarrassment" (more A or D responses than in total sample or other sub-groups), and "Karl feels insecure" (fewer A or D responses than in total sample or other sub-groups) (see Table 4). Responses to statements connected to "Karl feels . . ." also showed the lowest percentage of A or D responses compared to statements connected to "I feel . . ." and "Sara feels . . ." (see Table 5). This diversity and divergence in response to items concerning how Karl feels

Table 5 Comparison of Percentages of Items Classified A or D in Total Sample and Sub-groups Regarding Questionnaire Version and Statement ("I feel", "Karl feels", and "Sara feels")

			% of items classified A or D	% of items classified A or D in each of the three % of items		
Sub-groups				"I feel . . ."	"Karl feels . . ."	"Sara feels . . ."
Cohab	Ques-Alz + Ques-Rh		51 %	50 %	50 %	55 %
		Ques-Alz	39 %	45 %	27 %	45 %
		Ques-Rh	64 %	55 %	73 %	64 %
Cohab	Ques-Alz + Ques-Rh		77 %	82 %	64 %	82 %
		Ques-Alz	76 %	82 %	64 %	82 %
		Ques-Rh	79 %	91 %	64 %	82 %
Single	Ques-Alz + Ques-Rh		47 %	50 %	23 %	68 %
		Ques-Alz	52 %	45 %	27 %	82 %
		Ques-Rh	42 %	55 %	18 %	55 %
Single	Ques-Alz + Ques-Rh		50 %	32 %	50 %	68 %
		Ques-Alz	30 %	9 %	27 %	55 %
		Ques-Rh	70 %	55 %	73 %	82 %
Average in Sub-groups	Ques-Alz + Ques-Rh		56 %	54 %	47 %	68 %
		Ques-Alz	49 %	45 %	36 %	66 %
		Ques-Rh	64 %	64 %	57 %	70 %
Total sample	% of items classified A or D	"I feel . . ."	"Karl feels . . ."	"Sara feels . . ."		
	Average in total sample		54 %	64 %	36 %	64 %
		Ques-Alz	54 %	64 %	36 %	64 %
		Ques-Rh	51 %	64 %	45 %	64 %

could signify that it was either (1) generally difficult to put oneself in Karl's position, or (2) that participant's personal situation (e.g., gender, age, or marital/cohabitation status) affect how participant's believe Karl feels.

Karl's role in the vignette is kept purposely vague so that each participant must decide if Karl is an abuser or a harried caregiver. Earlier research on perceptions of abusers describes how both lay persons (Erlingsson et al., 2005; Grafström et al., 1993) and professionals (Erlingsson et al., 2006; Limandri and Tilden, 1996; Saveman et al., 1993) see caregivers from several perspectives simultaneously and have difficulties seeing the caregiver only as a villainous abuser. Diverse and divergent responses to "Karl feels . . ." items also indicate that this decision was difficult for participants to make and, perhaps, that participants considered Karl both a harried caregiver and abuser.

Participant sub-group Single B& showed the most diverse response pattern of any sub-group (47 per cent items classified as A or D responses). This was especially noticeable in that Single B& had only 23 per cent A or D responses to items under "Karl feels . . .". The sub-group Cohab @& was most confident in rating items as can be seen in the high percentages of responses classified as A or D (77 per cent). Confident rating was especially visible in items connected to statement "I feel . . ." and "Sara feels . . ." (82 per cent of sub-group's responses to each statement classified as A or D) (see Table 5). Why single men showed lowest percentages of A or D responses while Cohab @& showed the most confident response patterns will be an interesting avenue for further investigation.

Another interesting result is seen in items connected to the emotion "Concern". All three perspectives ("I feel . . .", "Karl feels . . .", "Sara feels . . .") had results classified as A or (A) both in the total sample and in participant sub-groups, with the fewest number of responses classified +/–, and no D or (D) results (see Table 3). In comparison with other emotions in the questionnaire, "Concern" also stands out as one of the least value-laden items, carrying a fairly neutral meaning. One may feel concern in situations involving either love, hate, violence, caring, or sickness. Taking this into account, "Concern" should perhaps be changed in future versions of the questionnaire to "Unconcerned". Another approach would be to include in the questionnaire a question asking participants if they would agree to a follow-up telephone interview during which researchers could further investigate what had motivated a participant's response.

Response patterns to an emotion frequently differed, both in the total sample as well as in all sub-groups, according to whether participants were responding to the "I feel . . .", "Karl feels . . ." or "Sara feels . . ." perspective. One example of this is "Compassion" where the item "I feel compassion" had responses classified only as A or (A) while participants only disagreed with the item "Sara feels compassion". The opposite could be observed in "Frightened" where participants mostly disagreed with the item "I feel frightened" but exclusively agreed with the item "Sara feels frightened" (see Table 3). These results, showing differences in reported emotional reactions from the same participants when taking different perspectives, once more raises questions concerning what it is that motivates witnesses to take action in cases of suspected elder abuse. Do we act based on how we ourselves feel or based on how we think the abused or the abuser are feeling ? These results and reflections raise the question of whether a questionnaire item, currently absent from the questionnaire, needs to be included; i.e., a specific question at the end of the questionnaire asking if and/or what action the participant would take if actually witnessing a situation as described in the vignette.

Response patterns also differed depending on whether participants were responding to the Ques-Alz or Ques-Rh. These differences were especially noticeable in three statement-specific items; "Sara feels shame", "Karl feels compassion", and "Karl feels a desire to help". These questionnaire-version-dependent differences were consistent both in the total sample and participant sub-groups. In item "Sara feels shame" there was a trend to agree more with this item in Ques-Rh than in Ques-Alz. In two other items "Karl feels compassion" and "Karl feels a desire to help", there was a trend to disagree more with the item in Ques-Rh than in Ques-Alz (see Table 3).

Consistently higher percentages of responses were classified as A or D in the Ques-Rh than in Ques-Alz (see Table 5). The only two exceptions to this were responses to items in connection to "Karl feels . . ." and "Sara feels . . ." from sub-group Single B&. Cohab B& and Single @& were the two sub-groups with greatest difference in percentages of items classified as A or D between the two questionnaire versions. This is especially marked in Single@& ratings with 30 per cent items classified as A or D in the Ques-Alz but 70 per cent of items classified as A or D in the Ques-Rh. As a sub-group Single@& had only 9 per cent A or D responses to "I feel . . ." items in Ques-Alz compared to 55 per cent in Ques-Rh. (see Table 5).

Most dramatic differences between Ques-Alz and Ques-Rh could be seen when opposite responses for the same item were seen within the same sub-group. Opposite responses to the same items in Ques-Rh and Ques-Alz from the same sub-group were observed six times; in the sub-group Cohab @& ("I feel angry", "Sara feels impatient", "Sara feels shame", "Karl feels compassion"), in the sub-group Single B& ("Karl feels embarrassment"), and in the sub-group Single @& ("Karl feels a desire to help"). That the sub-group Cohab @& was at times responding differently depending on the questionnaire version while the sub-group Cohab B & did not, is an area needing further investigation. Earlier research, such as the study by Childs et al. (2000), has found that gender and age play a role in how we perceive elder abuse. An extremely interesting line of investigation would be to test whether it is primarily age, gender or experience of living in a marriage-like relationship that affects how we react emotionally to the vignettes and items in the two questionnaire versions.

Methodological Aspects of the Pilot Questionnaire

Results from the pilot questionnaire indicated several areas for questionnaire improvement. As mentioned earlier, some of the included emotions need to be reconsidered. Pilot results have also prompted the idea that an additional question should be added to the end of the questionnaire specifically asking if and/or what action the participant would take if actually witnessing a situation as described in the vignette. A second idea generated by pilot results is to include a question asking participants if they would agree to a follow-up telephone interview during which researchers could further investigate what had motivated a participant's response.

Another methodological issue is that it remains unknown whether participants were responding as they thought Karl or Sara *actually* feel, or were participants responding as they thought Karl and Sara *ought to* feel? This ambiguity must be addressed in a revised questionnaire by including additional clarification. An interesting modification of this questionnaire would be to expand from three basic questions to six questions, e.g., "I actually feel . . .", "I ought to feel . . .", "Karl actually feels . . .", "Karl ought to feel . . .", "Sara actually feels . . .", and "Sara ought to feel . . .". The advantage with this is that it would both clarify which question the participant is responding to and shed light on ethical reasoning behind how participants have responded. The obvious disadvantage is that 33 items in the pilot questionnaire would triple to 99. Lengthening the questionnaire increases the risk that participants tire, lose interest and leave the questionnaire unanswered. This risk is especially high if an impersonal, postal distribution is chosen. A second disadvantage of lengthening the questionnaire is that the number of participants required for adequate power in order to, e.g., conduct factor analysis greatly increases(Polit and Beck, 2008). These aspects will need to be weighed before constructing the next version of the questionnaire.

The motivation for using a four-point Likert scale in the pilot questionnaire was to "force" participants away from choosing a neutral response. Results of the pilot and of earlier studies (Werner et al., 2005) indicate however that a neutral response could be a result in itself, i.e., that the situation didn't elicit any especially strong emotion. Emotions can be confusing experiences and although some may be easier to grade on a black and white, "either/or" four-point scale, there are perhaps those emotions that need the midpoint/neutral answer alternative. This suggests that further development of the questionnaire will involve utilizing a five-point Likert scale. A second motivation for using a five-point Likert in future utilization of this questionnaire is that it will facilitate comparison to earlier studies of lay person's reactions to elder abuse (cf Werner et al., 2005).

Future Use of the Questionnaire

The results of the questionnaire pilot clearly showed that it is a fruitful effort to use two versions of the questionnaire and a triple perspective for examining emotional reactions to a vignette about a potential elder abuse situation. Results also show that analysing responses through the different lenses of participant sub-groups and layered by questionnaire version provides valuable information.

Several results suggest ways to improve the questionnaire and point to possible avenues for future research. For example, why did single men show the most diverse answering patterns while married/cohabitating women the most confident response patterns? And why did married/cohabitating women sometimes respond differently depending on questionnaire version whiles the married/cohabitating men did not? An extremely interesting line of investigation will be to test whether it is primarily age, gender or experience of living in a marriage-like relationship, that affects how we react emotionally to the vignettes. Most importantly though, will be to investigate on a larger scale lay persons' and professionals' emotional reactions to elder abuse and how these reactions and feelings affect our actions or inaction as witnesses to elder abuse.

References

Childs, H.W., B. Hayslip, Jr., L.M. Radika and J.A. Reinberg (2000). Young and middle-aged adults' perceptions of elder abuse. *Gerontologist* 40, 75–85.

Clark, M. and I. Brissette (2000). Relationship beliefs and emotion: Reciprocal effects. In *Emotions and beliefs: How feelings influence thoughts* (N. Frijda, A. Mantead and S. Bem, eds.). Cambridge University Press, Cambridge, pp. 212–40.

Erlingsson, C. (2007a). Elder abuse explored through a prism of perceptions: Perspectives of potential witnesses. PhD thesis from the Faculty of Medicine, University of Umeå. Umeå, Sweden.

——. (2007b). Searching for elder abuse: A systematic review of database citations. *J Elder Abuse Negl* 19, 59–78.

Erlingsson C., S. Carlson and B.I. Saveman (2006). Perceptions of elder abuse: Voices of professionals and volunteers in Sweden – An exploratory study. *Scand J Caring Sci* 20, 151–59.

Erlingsson C., B.I. Saveman and A. Berg (2005). Perceptions of elder abuse in Sweden: Voices of older persons. *Brief Treatment and Crisis Intervention* 5, 1–15.

Fridja, N., A. Mantead and S. Bem (2000). *Emotions and beliefs: How feelings influence thoughts.* Cambridge University Press, Cambridge.

Gebotys, R.J., D. O'Connor and K.J. Mair (1992). Public perceptions of elder physical mistreatment. *J Elder Abuse Negl* 4, 151–71.

Grafström, M., A. Nordberg and B. Winblad (1993). *Abuse is in the eye of the beholder.* Report by family members about abuse of demented persons in home care. A total population-based study. *Scand J Soc Med* 21, 247–55.

Hudson, M.F. (1996). Expert and public perspectives in defining elder abuse and neglect. In *Advances in bioethics: Violence, neglect and the elderly* (L.B. Cebik, G.C. Graber and F.H. Marsh, eds.). JAI Press, Greenwich, CT, pp. 1–21.

Limandri, B. and V. Tilden (1996). Nurses' reasoning in the assessment of family violence. *J Nurs Scholarsh* 28, 247–52.

Moon, A. and O. Williams (1993). Perceptions of elder abuse and help-seeking patterns among African-American, Caucasian American and Korean-American elderly women. *Gerontologist* 33, 386–95.

Polit, D. and C.T. Beck (2008). *Nursing research: Generating and assessing evidence for nursing practice*, 8th ed. Lippincott, Williams and Wilkins, Philadelphia.

Saveman, B.I., I.R. Hallberg and A. Norberg (1993). Identifying and defining abuse of elderly people, as seen by witnesses. *J Adv Nurs* 18, 1393–1400.

Werner, P., Z. Eisikovits and E. Buchbinder (2005). Lay persons' emotional reactions toward an abused elderly person. *J Elder Abuse Negl* 17, 63–76.

16

Intergenerational Justice: An Israeli Perspective

Ariela Lowenstein and Israel Doron

The intergenerational contract is an ancient concept. Today, demographic changes in the Western world and the postmodern approach to the study of social reality challenge us to rethink the concepts of social solidarity, obligation, and mutuality between generations. The concept of generational equity or intergenerational justice has developed as a result of the ageing of the population, shortfalls in the government's budget, a crisis in health services, and inequality of incomes.

Intergenerational equity is an important component of various gerontological theories and of gerontological literature in general. It makes the social construction of old age, with its implications for policy, possible. Generational equity refers to the concept that different generations should be treated in similar ways and should have similar opportunities. However, this debate stems from the growing rate of elders in the population and is usually related to the conflict approach—division of economic resources between generations—'generational negotiation' for resources (Collard, 2001) and in the manner of each generation activating power and social control (Dunham and Bengtson, 1986).

Fairness in the distribution of resources between different age groups influences the privatization of services and changes in social policy. Nonetheless, when various aspects of the concept, and the degree to which it is implemented in social policy, are examined in the Israeli context, a complex and interesting picture, in which it is hard to find consistency or clear uniformity, is revealed.

In this paper, we shall examine changes in Israeli welfare policy with regard to questions of intergenerational justice and intergenerational transfers, in light of the ways in which the concept of the welfare state has changed. It has three parts: the first is a brief sketch of the main theoretical approaches to intergenerational justice accompanied with empirical findings from the world at large and from Israel. In the second part we shall examine the trends now developing in Israel in this respect, on the basis of data relating to the extent of poverty among various age groups, to the transition from a public, pay-as-you-go, pension system to a privatized, defined contribution, pension system, and to the controversy about retirement age. The third, concluding section, deals with the implications of these changes for social fabric and social solidarity in Israel.

Principal Approaches and Empirical Data on Intergenerational Transfers

Intergenerational transfers are an integral part of one's own life cycle and his or her family's life cycle. Hence, the patterns of consumption and saving of each individual are determined not only by him or her self, but by other individuals that surround them, most importantly, his or her familial transfers. Further, the family differs from the labour market or the welfare system in that it is a social framework for the preservation of rights and their transmission from one member of the family to another. The recent research on family transfers—both inter vivos and as bequests—demonstrates that transfers are considerable, that they occur mostly in the generational lineage, and that they flow mostly downwards, from the older to the younger generations (Kohli, 1999). There may be expectations of reciprocity, or other strings attached, but by and large, parents are motivated by altruism or feelings of unconditional obligation, and direct their gifts to situations of need.

Three main approaches to intergenerational family transfers are presented in the literature: the normative approach, the altruistic approach, and the strategic approach.

The *normative approach* views intergenerational transfers as exchanges of 'functions': the descendant transfers functions to his/her parents, just as they transferred theirs to their parents. This approach calls for an analysis of the social/historical process of intergenerational transfers over a specified period of time. The intergenerational transfer is conceived of, as a key component in the continuity of the process of preserving family solidarity, and it has long-term social implications. On the macro level, this procedure constitutes a normative contract, similar, for example, to that established by the Social Insurance Law. At the level of the family it is a complex of values, norms, and family obligations. Research in Israel and four European countries (Norway, England, Germany and Spain) —the Oasis research project[1] shows that most of the respondents (1,200 in each country, 6,000 in all) in every country spoke of a relatively high degree of normative obligation, though this was highest in Israel, Spain and Germany. Nonetheless, even in countries such as Norway, which is still a comprehensive welfare state, the fact that there is a wide range of social services did not impair family responsibility and obligation—filial duty between the generations (Lowenstein, Katz and Daatland, 2004; Lowenstein and Daatland, 2006). Similar results, highlighting the importance of intergenerational norms and relationships among young and old alike, have been obtained in Europe (Walker, 1993) and the US (Bengton and Roberts, 1991).

The *altruistic approach* conceives of intergenerational transfers as the result of a special type of feeling of obligation, as distinct from considerations of advantage for individuals. The concept of altruism embraces love, concern, and solicitousness of each generation for the other. According to this approach, the 'strong' individual in the family takes on him or her self the care for the others, as a result of love and concern. This approach matches the concept of 'role reversal': in the early stage of the life cycle the parent is the altruist, but during old age the descendant takes on him or her self the role of the carer, from similar altruistic motives. Logan and Spitze's (1995) findings demonstrate the presence of altruism, as opposed to expediency, and emphasize the strength and importance of altruistic norms in the framework of filial responsibility in different groups defined by origin, gender and age. It is of some interest that the findings show that support for these norms is consistently higher among the younger age groups than older. This is in contrast to the "generational stake phenomenon" which reflects a pattern in which older generations perceive intergenerational relations in a more positive light than do younger generations. This pattern is explained by the developmental imperative of older generations to emphasize continuity with younger generations and of younger generations to emphasize autonomy from older generations.

According to the *strategic approach*, social interaction is based on the fact that individuals' expectations (which determine their concrete actions) are influenced by the actions of others. Transfers are part of an extended process of exchange. On this view, intergenerational transfers are subject to rational considerations, according to which both parties profit, or at the least, neither is harmed. Mutuality plays a decisive part in this approach, like exchange transactions in sociological theories based on the work of Homans (Homans, 1960), or in the theory of conflict solution in social psychology (Thilbaut and Kelley, 1959). Such mutuality or reciprocity is to be found for example in the Oasis research project (Lowenstein, Katz and Gur-Yaish, 2007).

Transfers may also be conceived of, as family transactions. There may be four types of intergenerational transfers within the family: those which can be classified as insurance transactions; those which can be classified as capital transactions—economic/financial transfers; those which can be classified as labour transactions—transfer of time or working services, as when physical care is required; and transfers which are mainly in the affective sphere of emotional aid and support.

As a result of the development of the capital market and systems of assurance of income and pension, the economic/financial situation of a number of old people (even though a relatively small proportion of them) is no worse than that of the rest of the population, since those in this group have invested in insurance and pension schemes during their working life. On the other hand, technological and medical developments have led to the existence of a relatively long period of 'handicapped living' in the course of which the old person needs help in his/her daily activities. As a result, the main requirements of old people, and particularly the 'old-old' (aged 75 and above) are connected with the deterioration of their functional capabilities and the need for tangible services and support. Thus, the public generational contract is partly balanced by a private one in the opposite direction. The family transfers function to some extent as an informal insurance system for periods of special needs.

It should be, however, acknowledged that the potential for distributional conflicts among generations exists and is fuelled by the current challenges of public finances and demography. In view of all this, it is not surprising that financial transfers from descendants to the old constitutes a small proportion of their income. The findings of the Oasis survey moreover show that older parents in four of the countries (Norway, England, Germany and Israel) except Spain also provided financial assistance to their children (Lowenstein, Katz and Gur-Yaish, 2007). On the other hand, transfers in terms of time and labour constitute a decisive proportion of the support which old people receive from their adult children, despite the development of formal services, particularly in Israel under the aegis of the Israeli Community-Based Nursing Insurance Law.

Controversy Concerning Intergenerational Equity

It is generally accepted today that the very act of raising the topic of intergenerational equality or justice, serves to create a social construct in which interest groups, social groups and policy-makers endeavour to justify the 'deterioration' or 'retreat' in the extent of the welfare services, play a role. This includes the endorsement of ideologies such as that of individualism, the competitive market, and the transfer of responsibility from the state to the family also in matters of care for the aged. It is claimed that these processes increase social inequality.

Moreover, a major limitation of the generational equity frame is that it provides a rationale to base policy on age or age cohort and to discount other forms of equity based on race, ethnicity, class, gender, and sexual orientation. As Norman Daniels has argued, "Justice between age groups is a problem best solved if we stop thinking of the old and the young as distinct groups. We age. The young become the old. As we age, we pass through institutions that affect our well-being at each stage of life, from infancy to very old age" (p. 18). Also, the perspective on generational equity is usually restricted to public resource flows, and neglects the private side—the transfers between family generations (Kohli, 2005).

In the US an organization known as AGE (Americans for Generational Equity) and, in parallel, an organization known as Generations United, have been set up. The latter is a coalition of more than a hundred health and welfare organizations which support an intergenerational policy approach.

In fact, an overall analysis of social inequality entails consideration of the labour market, the welfare system, and the family set-up. When the welfare system abandons its function of reducing the dangers to which the populations which it encompasses are exposed, this disturbs the delicate balance between these three systems. It increases the importance of the family as a social system which combats the dangers threatening its members; as a result, the state can 'shrug off' its responsibility for the weak sectors within it.

In the opinion of Binney and Estes (1988), the approach to the unequal allocation of resources between the generations with respect to the welfare services has rested on two mistaken assumptions made by economists, demographers, politicians and the media. One is connected with the old age dependency ratio. This assumption is based on a comparison between employed and retired populations, which does not take into account the 'institution of retirement', or the fact that the economic system does not provide employment for every individual. The other assumption is connected with the 'zero-sum' concept, which relates to the belief that goods and services are limited, and that benefits are provided for one generation at the expense of another. In the context of this paper, this means that the provision of grants and pensions for the ageing population reduces the benefits enjoyed by younger generations. This is reflected in the statistics of poverty among children, compared with the rise in the standard of living of the old.

However, these statistics ignore the fact that a high proportion of the expenditure connected with old people—for instance, retirement funds and pensions—is not financed by the state, but by the workers and their employers. According to Israeli statistics, the level of income of some 70 per cent of the old population is less than three quarters of the average wage in the economy; and the situation of old immigrants is even worse. In addition, about 30 per cent of the old have only their old-age or survivor's pension to live on, and are, therefore, below the poverty line. Inequality continues to increase and to spread, and recent economic restrictions have been particularly hard on old people. The statistics about the level of income of poor families are similar. Even if old people have recently been less hard hit than, for instance, single parent families, in the long run the impact of the adjustment of pensions, will lead to a reduction of the pension to 13 per cent of the average wage, and by 2020 to no more than a tenth. In the words of Gal, the result will be 'a sharp reduction of the principal stable basis of income for old people'.

In addition, the Oasis project and other researches in Israel and elsewhere have shown that younger age-groups give active support to their old, even at the expense of their own future economic situation (Lowenstein and Daatland, 2006). In effect, the efforts of the young on behalf of the old will enable the young themselves to grow old without fear for the future. Binney and Estes claim that the expression 'generational equity' enables the government to shrug off its responsibility for individuals in need, and to transfer resources to sectors with high incomes. They suggest that the universal right of the individual to the satisfaction of basic human needs which the welfare system should supply throughout his/her life cycle should be taken into account (Binney and Estes, 1988).

Trends in Welfare Policy in Israel

Despite the complex situation described above, it may be said that, at a certain level, there are indications that in various spheres welfare policy in Israel has moved from the concept of intergenerational equity in the sense of generational obligation in the direction of a policy whereby old age is separated from the generation preceding or succeeding it. This situation can be described as 'lack of intergenerational obligation', or 'the beginning of the end of intergenerational justice'. We shall illustrate this trend by the use of two examples.

Change from Funded to Private Pensions

Ensuring the social security of the ageing population is one of the most important challenges of social welfare policy. One of the ethical and moral principles which can be used to justify the social obligation to ensure the social security of the old and to resist the poverty which threatens to engulf them is the obligation of intergenerational justice. This argument is based on the supposition that when the younger generation is of working age it has 'enjoyed'—during the period of childhood and adolescence—the 'fruits' of the productivity and economic activity of those who are now old. Therefore, those 'young people' who have now matured and are able to work, should 'return' the benefits they have been given, and repay those who made it possible for them to grow and develop in a society with the resources for their education and training. The repayment for these benefits is also based on the assumption that in the future, when these 'young' people grow old, the coming generation, which is as yet unborn or in its infancy, will itself repay the present generation, and thereby close the circle of intergenerational reciprocity (Chen, 1998).

Traditionally, social security during old age, which was based on arrangements for funded pensions (also known as "pay-as-you-go" pensions), was based precisely on this supposition: the principle of intergenerational ethical and economic obligation. The reason for this is that the funded pension is so organized that the employer and employee do not contribute from current income to the fund for the future pension; and, therefore, the pension which is paid today to pensioners in workplaces with funded pensions is, in effect, financed by the work, the produce and the services of those who are currently at work. In other words, in the system of funded pensions, today's workers are 'carrying on their shoulders, yesterday's workers. The reason they are prepared to do this is the knowledge and the promise that tomorrow's workers will 'carry' those of today. Again, it is the values of mutuality and continuity which enable the system to exist.

Of recent years, however, Israeli society has seen a significant retreat from the approach of the funded pension. As a result of recent economic emergency plans (although the general trend could already be discerned in the 1990s), it is no longer possible to join funded pension plans, and, in fact new workers in many parts of the economy in which funded pensions were the rule—such as the civil service or local authorities—have all been transferred to a system of private, defined-contribution (DC) pensions schemes (Doron, 2004; Pelleg, 2006).

Unlike a funded pension, private pension scheme is based on personal accounts, through which the worker and the employer each make payments directly to a pension fund, which manages each worker's pension separately at an individual level. The private DC pension has virtually very little direct connection with or dependence on intergenerational relationships, and there is practically little link or obligation between the different generations. Every generation and every individual has to care, for him or her self, in the framework of personal 'pension plans', independently of their colleagues, and whether or not they are of the same generation (Munnell, Sunden and Lidstone, 2002).

Although there are many reasons and arguments which led to the desire to bring the system of funded pensions to an end, there is no doubt that the ideological, political and ethical dimensions of the question of intergenerational relationships played an important part in Israel's readiness to adopt this change in policy. The adoption of a different set of values concerning the relationships between the generations is far more than a simple 'technical' transition from one system to another.

Raising of the Retirement Age

One of the classical arguments on the question of raising, and even abolition of the compulsory retirement age, is connected with the implications of the extension of working life on the level of unemployment, and the opportunities of the young to obtain work and promotion. One of the main reasons for the institution of compulsory retirement was the idea of refreshing the working force, and 'freeing' places of work for young people at the beginning of their path in life, so that they could advance their careers. Here again, just as in the case of the funded pension, it was assumed that old people would be prepared to cease working, even if they were able and willing to continue to work, as a result of their understanding that it is right and proper to do so in order to allow the younger generation to find work and develop their careers. Here, too, the basic assumption is that the old people of today 'profited' in their youth from the fact that veteran workers retired and vacated their places of employment (Shnit, 1978/9).

Just as in the case of funded pensions, here, too, over the past few years this concept has been eroded and resisted. An important expression of this is to be found in the amendment to the Law of Equal Opportunities of Employment, 1988, which was adopted in 1995. This amendment added 'age' to the provisions forbidding discrimination not only in recruiting workers but in a range of conditions of employment, promotion, wages and retirement. Another, no less important, expression was seen very recently, in the enactment of a law raising the age of compulsory retirement for men to 67, and for women, by stages, to 62 and then to 64. At a certain level it can be argued that the practical significance of this legislation is a reduction in the opportunities for employment and promotion of young people, as a result of the postponement of the retirement of the old. Clearly, this situation will become even more serious if this general trend persists and the American system, whereby compulsory retirement on the grounds of chronological age has been completely abolished, is adopted (Doron, 2004).

It would be possible to adduce more examples which appear to support the contention that one of the characteristics of social policy regarding the old has been the direct or indirect undermining of intergenerational obligations and relationships. Thus, for instance, a similar point could be made about the Law for Community-Based Nursing Care, 1988 which gives preference to formal instrumental care by salaried professionals over the informal care of relatives based on personal obligation (Borowski and Schmid, 2000); about the Patients' Rights Law 1996, which gives no preference or status to relatives in medical decisions about old patients who are no longer legally competent to make decisions about their own bodies; about the rescinding of tax credits for relatives who accommodate aged parents requiring constant care in their own homes and care for them; or even about the method in which various protective laws, such as the Law of Legal Competence and Guardianship, which 'suspects' relatives of a conflict of interests in matters concerning the economic affairs of aged parents or relatives who are no longer of sound mind, are applied (Doron, 2004a).

Discussion and Conclusions

Each of the examples adduced above can be explained by economic or political considerations which are not necessarily linked with the complexity of intergenerational relationships. This is because each of the measures described above has been justified on the basis of economic reasoning, which ostensibly has no connection with intergenerational relationships or intergenerational justice. On the other hand, these developments can be interpreted in a much broader context of social ethics. If we are turning into a society in which the individual is the focus of attention, and the social groupings round him, such as the family, the community, or previous and succeeding generations, are irrelevant to the definition of his/her rights and duties, for old people this process means the abolition or severance of intergenerational relationships and obligations.

This trend is part of the general inclination to adopt the neo-liberal world outlook, with its exaltation of individualism and capitalism. But in concrete terms, this trend has special, and complex, implications for the old. On the one hand, this development can be viewed as a component of the 'liberation' or emancipation of the aged population from the historical 'bonds' which tied them in their relationships with other generations. Old people are no longer economically dependent on the young of today; they no longer have to cease working against their will at the age of 65 in order to 'sacrifice' themselves for the benefit of the unemployed young; and they are no longer automatically 'abandoned' to the care and concern of their children or some other representative of the younger generation.

On the other hand, this development is open to criticism, and points to a number of shortcomings. When the young are 'freed' from the concern for or obligation to the old, how is it possible to ensure the functioning of social insurance programmes intended to preclude poverty among those old people who have not succeeded in arranging a personal pension scheme for themselves? How will it be possible to prevent the steady erosion of the level of social benefits and social programmes which support informal family care of the old—care which is the principal basis of support for frail old people with limited means, who live within the community—at a time when the state increasingly shrugs off its responsibility, and lays it on the family?

Research data show that the family is in fact the main social framework for the distribution of resources in society. When the welfare state has difficulty in providing a universal safety network, the family becomes even more important. In this connection, the impact on weaker families is to some extent more serious; and this takes into account that there is proof of intergenerational continuity of inequality between the resources of the family of origin and the status of the families established by its children.

From many points of view, old people as a minority group are still dependent on combined political power with the younger generations in order to realize their legal rights. The cessation of this moral and social relationship will force them to fight independently in the political arena for their part in the attenuated aggregate of resources, while the forces arrayed against them are far stronger and more influential. In the final analysis this process will not bring about an improvement, but will weaken and impair the social and legal rights of the old in society.

The definition of policy questions in terms of generational equity leads to old people becoming scapegoats and being sacrificed to those who are interested in limiting the public sector and expanding privatization.

Generational equity means that all the generations in society should have equal levels of burdens and resources. Undoubtedly, there are difficulties in carrying out the contract for intergenerational transfers when the process of long-term justice has to be taken into account. Nonetheless, the view that a person must insure his old age on his own account leads to privatization and a cut in expenditures. Further, the concept that it is impossible to continue to execute social programmes because assets which are granted to a certain sector of the community are given 'at the expense' of the assets of another sector, expresses a mistaken dichotomy which perpetuates class inequality between populations and erodes intergenerational obligations.

Issues for Discussion and Policy Recommendations

We have shown that generational equity is not necessarily the fundamental criterion for policy or fairness, and that it may be preferable to aim at the reduction of inequality between populations with low incomes and those with high incomes. In accordance with this approach, a number of central issues must be delineated if we are to continue the discussion and deal with policy-making:

1. The first major issue is whether the discussion should be based on a description of the competitive and conflictual relationships between different age-groups, or on an approach that emphasizes mutual dependence between generations.
2. A related issue is the question of whether a major criterion in policy-making should be generational equity or the aspiration to greater equality between weaker and stronger sections of the population.
3. The concept of the welfare state must be considered, since it is a redistributory system, and can change the state of inequality between individuals and families to a certain extent.
4. It is important to examine the significance of the 'retreat' of the welfare state for the balance between the three above-mentioned systems—the welfare system, the labour market, and the family system. How is it that disturbance of this balance primarily influences the weaker social strata? Does this disturbance add even more to the significance of intergenerational equality or justice?
5. Another issue is the question of whether we should also aim at equality

in relation to private transfers—time and money invested by parents in their children—since the family is today the main mechanism for the transfer of care for children and the disabled.

6. Another central question is: do the monies paid to the National Insurance Institute, for instance for the financing of old-age pensions, constitute a tax with whose receipts the government can do what it wants, or does the payment by the workers 'afford them rights' over this money, on which they have learned to rely?

Regarding policy recommendations, according to the normative approach, it is important to strengthen intergenerational relationships and obligations, and to try to achieve a balance between the three systems—the market, the welfare system and the family.

The altruistic approach will advocate the development of a policy which will act directly on the variables which determine the behaviour of the old person, such as fixing a low (subsidized) price for services, increased income, and direct provision of services, as well as the development of interventions which will work through their influence on the behaviour of the offspring whose duty it is to care for a disabled parent: by granting tax reductions to increase their income, or by developing work friendly policies such as shortening their hours of work without reducing their income. In this way an adult child will receive a raise in income or payment for the hours in which [s]he assists her/his parent, on condition that [s]he is indeed an altruist who transfers resources to the parent. Intervention of this sort must take into account that parents and offspring constitute an economic unit which functions in accordance with its total resources, and the interventions will lead to a decline in transfers within the family.

According to the strategic approach, it is important to ensure a low price for services, additional income for the parent, direct supply of services, and added income for the adult child. Furthermore, it is important to encourage productive ageing, employment and involvement in the community as well as intergenerational programmes such as 'kindergarten grandpas'. It is important to develop a welfare policy based on a concept of the whole life course. Younger generations should be encouraged to make arrangements for their old age: to invest more in private pensions and saving schemes, and, in parallel, to strengthen intergenerational ties on the basis of the concept of generational mutuality and mutual dependence, what has been termed the interdependence of generations (Attias-Donfut and Wolff, 2005). From a life course perspective, it follows that an alternative formulation of generational equity is generational interdependence. Kingson, Hirshorn and Cornman (1986) discuss the "ties that bind" generations together and stress the high degree of inter-dependence between individuals and between generations within society. This view emphasizes what different generations have to offer one another as opposed to what one consumes at the expense of the other (Johnson, 2005).

Those who established the level of pensionable age did not consider the long years of leisure and their implications for intergenerational support and transfers. Therefore, it is important to reconsider the significance of egalitarianism, and to what extent it can be realized. The issues of retirement, financial transfers such as legacies, and the significance of two or three decades of life outside the labour system should be considered. It may be that we should consider the initiation of a flexible retirement age, between the ages of 55 and 75.

Note

1 Oasis—'Autonomy in Old Age: The function of service systems and intergenerational family solidarity, is a research project financed by the European Community, Contract QLK6–CT–1999–02182.

References

Attias-Donfut, C. and Wolff, F.C. (2005). Generational memory and family relationships. In Johnson, M.L. *The Cambridge handbook of age and ageing.* (pp. 443–454). Cambridge: Cambridge.

Bengtson, V.L. (1993). Is the 'contract across generations' changing? Effects of population aging on obligations and expectations across age groups. In V.L. Bengtson and W. A. Achenbaum (eds), *The changing contract across generations* (pp. 3–23). New York: Aldine de Gruyter.

Bengtson, V.L. and Roberts, R.E.L. (1991). Intergenerational solidarity in aging families: An example of formal theory construction. *Journal of Marriage and the Family*, 53, 856–870.

Binney, E. A. and Estes, C.L. (1988). The retreat of the state and its transfer of responsibility: The intergenerational war. *Journal of Health Services*, 18(1), 83–96.

Borowski, A. and Schmid, H. (2000). Israel's long-term care insurance law after a decade of implementation. *Journal of Ageing and Social Policy*, 12(1), 49–71.

Chen, Y.P. (1998). Economic security: Strengthening social security. In J.S. Steckenrider and T.M. Parrott (eds), *New directions in old-age policies* (pp. 37–49). Albany, NY: State University of New York Press.

Collard, D. (2001). The generational bargain. *Journal of Social Welfare*, 10, 54–65.

Doron, I. (2004). Old age and social and economic rights. In Y. Rabin, Y. Shany (eds) *Economic, social and cultural rights in Israel* (pp. 893–940). Tel Aviv: Ramot—Tel Aviv University Press.

Doron, I. (2004a). Ageing in the shadow of law: Elder guardianship in Israel. *Journal of Ageing and Social Policy*, 16(4), 59–77.

Dunham, C.C. and Bengtson, V.L. (1986). "Conceptual and Theoretical Perspectives on Generational Relations". In N. Datan. A.L. Greene, H.W. Reese. *Life-span developmental psychology intergenerational relations.* (pp. 2–27. Hillsdale, New Jersey: Lawrence Erlbaum Associates, Publishers.

Homans, G.C. (1961). *Social behavior: Its elementary forms.* New York: Harcourt, Brace and World.

Johnson, M.L. (2005). *The Cambridge handbook of age and ageing.* Cambridge: Cambridge University Press.

Kingson, E. R., Hirshorn, B.A., and Cornman, J.M. (1986). *Ties that bind.* Washington, DC: Seven Locks Press.

Kohli, M. (2005). Generational changes and generational equity. In Johnson, M. L. *The Cambridge Handbook of Age and Ageing.* (pp. 518–526). Cambridge: Cambridge University Press.

Logan, J. R., and Spitze, G.D. (1995). Self-interest and altruism in intergenerational relations. *Demography*, 32(3), 353–364.

Lowenstein, Katz, R. and Daatland, S.O. (2004). Filial norms and intergenerational support in a comparative cross-national perspective. In M. Silverstein (Guest Editor.), *Annual Review of Gerontology and Geriatrics*, vol. 24, 200–224.

Lowenstein, A. and Daatland, S.O. (2006). Filial norms and family support to the old-old (75+) in a comparative cross-national context (the OASIS study). *Ageing and Society*, 26, 1–21.

Lowenstein, A., Katz, R. and Gur-Yaish, N. (2007). Reciprocity in parent-child exchange and life satisfaction among the elderly in cross-national perspective. *Journal of Social Issue*, 63(4), 865–883.

Munnell, A.H., Sunden, A. and Lidstone, E. (2002). *How Important Are Private Pensions?* Boston College Issue Brief 8. Boston: Center for Retirement Research.

Pelleg, D. (2006). Pension system reforms in Israel: 2002–2004. Social Security, 71, 84–108.

Shnit, D. (1978/9). Age discrimination in employment. *Tel Aviv University Studies in Law*, 4, 168–218.

Thibaut, J.W. and Kelley, H. (1959). *The social psychology of groups*. New York: Wiley.

Walker, A. (1993). Intergenerational relations and welfare restructuring: The social construction of an intergenerational problem. In V.L. Bengtson and W.A. Achenbaum (eds), *The changing contract across generations*. (pp. 141–165). Hawthorne, NY: Aldine de Gruyter.

17

Elder Abuse in a Cross-Cultural Context: Assessment, Policy, and Practice

Rashmi Gupta and Anoshua Chaudhuri

With the global population of older persons expected to triple from 672 million in 2005 to 1.9 billion in 2050, it is becoming increasingly important to focus on policies and practices that support and enhance the wellbeing of the older population in later life. One sad reality for many seniors in later life and an increasing cause for concern, is elder abuse. It is extremely difficult to exactly quantify the extent of elder abuse, neglect and exploitation because many such cases go undetected and under-reported. According to a 1998 study, for every case of elder abuse that gets reported to authorities, about five more go unreported in the United States (National Center on Elder Abuse ,1998). Definitions of elder abuse vary as well. There are wide cultural variations in what gets considered as abuse both by the victim as well as the perpetrator. Further, there is no uniform reporting system because of which state level statistics vary widely and there is lack of comprehensive national level statistics in the United States as well as in other countries. According to the best available estimates, between 1 and 2 million Americans aged 65 and older have been injured, mistreated and exploited by people they depend on for protection and care (National Research Council, 2003). In the year 2000 alone, there have been 472,813 reports received on elder/adult mistreatment in various states in the US (NCEA, 2003). Almost 500,000 older people in the UK are abused every year (London Department of Health, 2000). The ageing of populations with a shift away from institutional care in the developed world has increased demands on the family member for the care of the older person. This along with an uncertainty in the availability of health and social services could potentially increase elder abuse in the developed world. In the developing world too, increased longevity of the older population has created a strain on households with limited resources, particularly in the absence of formal social support systems. In countries that have introduced pension for older and retired adults such as Taiwan and South Africa, household compositions have changed that have left the older people vulnerable to potential exploitation. The consequences of elder abuse on the victim, perpetrator as well as families and communities are serious. Abuse can exacerbate chronic and disabling conditions of the older person and make the person more dependent, vulnerable and marginalized. For abusers, it may result in social rejection, broken family ties and embarrassment. Abusive workers are at risk for dismissal. Family members and communities lose out when the victim can no longer positively contribute and participate fully. All of this results in short run and long run financial costs to society. It has therefore become critical to understand the extent of prevalence of elder abuse, identify and mitigate the risk factors and provide prevention strategies to reduce incidences of elder abuse.

In this paper, we provide an assessment of what constitutes elder abuse in a cross-cultural context with a special focus on older South Asians living in the United States. We also discuss various prevention and intervention strategies to help mitigate incidences of elder abuse among this population.

What is Elder Abuse?

> "Elder abuse is a term referring to any knowing, intentional, or negligent act by a caregiver or any other person that causes harm or a serious risk of harm to a vulnerable adult" (National Center on Elder Abuse).

Elder abuse can be broadly categorized into self-abuse, domestic elder abuse, and institutional elder abuse. Self-abuse or self-neglect is the result of the older persons' unwillingness to look after themselves as a result of depression from loss of spouse, loneliness, chronic pain, financial worry and loss of independence. Domestic and institutional abuse can be broken down into different categories:

- **Physical Abuse**—Inflicting, or threatening to inflict, physical pain or injury on a vulnerable elder, or depriving them of a basic need.
- **Emotional Abuse**—Inflicting mental pain, anguish, or distress on an elder person through verbal or nonverbal acts.
- **Sexual Abuse**—Non-consensual sexual contact of any kind.
- **Exploitation**—Illegal taking, misuse, or concealment of funds, property, or assets of a vulnerable elder.
- **Neglect**—Refusal or failure by those responsible to provide food, shelter, health care or protection for a vulnerable elder.
- **Abandonment**—The desertion of a vulnerable elder by anyone who has assumed the responsibility for care or custody of that person. (NCEA, 2008)

It is difficult to detect victims of abuse and both older men and women are at risk of being abused. Evidence from empirical and clinical studies confirms that a large proportion of elder abuse takes place in shared living arrangements. Those who live alone are more prone to financial abuse. Further elder patients with dementia are at risk for physical abuse. Social isolation, pathological characteristics of perpetrators such as mental illness and alcoholism, and total dependency of the victim are other factors that lead to elder abuse (Lachs and Pillemer, 2004). Abuse of the elderly takes place in various settings including their homes, hospitals, assisted living facilities and nursing homes.

Theoretical Explanations of Elder Abuse

Various theories have been presented to explain elder abuse. Each of the explanations is not mutually exclusive in explaining causes of elder mistreatment because mistreatment results from multiple factors. Characteristics of the elderly victim and caregiver, and societal factors are the main causes of elder abuse.

Characteristics of the Elderly Victim

Demographic characteristics such as older age (such as those in the old-old category), being female, being widowed, low income (Holt, 1994; Pritchard, 1993) and low educational attainment are associated with higher incidences of elder abuse. Further, total dependency as a result of disability, limitations in activities of daily living and dementia increases the risk of abuse.

Characteristics of the Caregiver

Researchers have found that caregiver stress may lead to incidences of elder abuse (Phillips, 1983; Giordano and Giordano, 1984; Steinmetz, 1983). Further, pathological conditions of the abuser in the form of poor impulse control, poor anger management, alcoholism are potential risk factors. The 'learned violence' hypothesis (Gordon and Brill, 2001) has explained that children who are maltreated or witness to violence, are likely perpetrators of elder abuse. However, evidence for this hypothesis is weak.

Societal Factors

Although the 'modernization hypothesis' has not been proven empirically, it is a factor that is used extensively to discuss elder abuse in developing countries or among immigrant populations that are in the process of a social transition. Kosberg and Garcia (1995) discuss the socio-economic problems that stem from modernization and conclude that in modern society, the younger generation follows individualistic values, have geographic mobility and do not share the same values as their elderly parents. Some of the elderly parent-child relationship existing among immigrant Asian populations is based on social exchange whereby the younger generation supports the older adult financially and emotionally, in exchange of housekeeping or childcare services (Le, 1997).

It has been also argued that elderly who are tied to diverse social support networks are less likely to be abused compared to those in dense networks (Kosberg, 1988). The elderly that are part of a diverse network have a buffer from possible abuse as they have ties to both formal and informal support systems, hence the chances of abuse getting identified and reported is much higher.

Incidence and Nature of Elder Abuse: Cross-Cultural Evidence

Although it is extremely hard to detect elder abuse, recent estimates of elder abuse in a variety of international settings are available from various sources. Studies with various sampling and survey methodologies have come up with a range of estimated frequency of elder abuse. A study of non-institutionalized elder in the metropolitan area of Boston, a frequency of 3.2 per cent (Pillemer and Finkelhor, 1988), a national random sample survey from Canada measured that 4 per cent reported maltreatment after reaching the age of 65 (Podnieks, 1992), a Dutch study measured elder abuse at a rate of 5.8 per cent (Comijs, Pennix, Knipscheer and Tileberg, 1999) while a study from Denmark and Sweden recorded a rate of 8 per cent (Tornstarn, 1989). A study conducted to investigate elder abuse in residential settings in Sweden (Saveman et al., 1999) found that 11 per cent of respondents who were nursing staff were aware of abusive incidents, and 2 per cent admitted to abusive acts. Abusers were considered to be tired, burned out or short-tempered and the victims were mostly reported as mentally or physically handicapped and usually over 80 years old. The incidence rate of elder abuse from a study in Finland (Kivela, Kongas-Saviaro and Kesti, 1992) found that 3 per cent of the men and 9 per cent of the women interviewed indicated that they had been abused. The most common types of abuse were physical and psychological, and the home was the most common place of occurrence. Patients of four aged care assessment teams in Perth, Brisbane, Sydney, and New South Wales in Australia were studied to assess prevalence and incidence of elder abuse. This study identified a 1.2 per cent prevalence rate with psychological abuse as the most common form of mistreatment amongst this population (Kurrle, Sadler, Lockwood and Cameron, 1997).

Elder abuse was considered by the Japanese to be a 'foreign' problem as late as 1987 and the subject still remains relatively invisible, with no elder abuse reporting agency in the country. A study (Tsukada, 2001) using data from 1999 Nihon University Japanese Longitudinal Study of Ageing to assess the awareness and perceptions of elder abuse indicated that only 51 per cent of respondents were aware of elder abuse. In a study of 355 Hong Kong seniors (aged 65 and over), 21 per cent of study participants were found to have experienced at least one instance of abuse (predominantly verbal abuse) within the past year (Yan and So-Kum, 2001). Researchers suspected that the Chinese tradition of preserving the privacy of the family may contribute to an underestimation of elder abuse. A study that explored the nature of elder abuse within the traditional Arab community (Sharon and Zoabi, 1997) residing in Israel found an incidence rate of 2.53 per cent for Arab elders. In urban areas, higher incidence rates were reported. While characteristics of abuse victims were similar to those in developed nations, a notable difference was that sons, rather than spouses, were found to be the most common perpetrators.

A study that examined the role of culture in the perception of various types of elder abuse showed that Americans found physical abuse to be more offensive whereas Koreans found psychological abuse as more offensive (Malley-Morrison, You and Mills, 2000). Hence, cultural factors impact perceptions of elder abuse and hence reporting of elder abuse.

Within a diverse country like the United States, there are substantial ethnic and cultural differences in the nature of elder abuse. In general, non-white ethnic elderly and recent immigrants are more prone to abuse. Studies focusing on Mexican-Americans who are the largest Latino population in America, have found elder mistreatment in the form of denial of shelter (Sanchez, 1998a). Normative *familismo* along with *verguenza* (shame) is a barrier to reporting abuse and neglect amongst Latinos (Sanchez, 1998b). Financial exploitations, psychological intimidations, silence, avoidance and isolation are the main forms of elder abuse amongst Asian American communities such as those of Korean (Moon, 1998) and Vietnamese (Le, 1997) origin. The tendency to value family over individuals, fearing family shame, and avoiding conflict are the reasons for Asian elders' reluctance to seek formal services in addressing abuse.

In 2002, the World Health Organization recognized the need to develop a global strategy to cope with elder abuse and working partnerships between the WHO Ageing and Life Course unit of the Department of Chronic Diseases and Health Promotion, the WHO Department of Injuries and Violence Prevention, the International Network for the Prevention of Elder Abuse (INPEA), HelpAge International and partners from academic institutions in a range of countries were envisioned to develop this strategy (WHO, 2002). While most of the elder abuse literature has pointed to elder abuse as an individual and familial problem, hence an issue to be dealt within the family, the WHO report was the first to point out elder abuse as a societal problem, especially in the context of the developing world. Country reports were commissioned in Argentina, Brazil, India, Kenya and Lebanon and the emerging theme was the discomfort in talking about or acknowledging the presence of elder abuse. Particularly in India, 'abuse' was mostly understood as an extreme form of physical violence and its existence was denied. 'Abuse' supposedly did not exist but elder mistreatment was mostly construed as disrespect, loss of dignity, lack of emotional support and neglect by family members. Gender and socio-economic status were the key factors that led to elder abuse in India. Older, widowed and childless women were the most affected as well as those elders who were poor. Older persons in most of these countries, including India, blamed change in social roles, lack of governmental policies, and lack of health and social services as the real reasons for an increase in the incidences of elder abuse.

Abuse among South Asians Living in the United States: How is it Different ?

South Asian elderly constitute those who are 65 years or older originally from countries such as Bangladesh, Bhutan, India, Pakistan, Myanmar, Nepal and Sri Lanka. They constitute the third largest immigrant group in the United States growing at a rate of more than 100 per cent over the last decade. This group is very diverse because of different languages, religions, food habits and socio-economic status. However, the common factor that binds this group together is the common cultural and social context of the Indian subcontinent (Diwan, Jonnalagadda and Gupta, 2004). Respect for elders, financial and emotional support from sons in later life, and shared living with son's family are part of the social fabric (Gupta, 2002).

Psychological abuse, exploitation and neglect were found to be the main forms of abuse amongst South Asian seniors (Nagpaul, 1997; Pablo and Braun, 1997). Personal shame, family honour and protecting family members were main reasons for not reporting such experiences. In the course of practising in the field, several cases of elder abuse were brought up in community meetings with the South Asian seniors in Dallas-Fort Worth area. The following case studies are illustrations of abuse among South Asian seniors (Gupta, 2005).

Case 1

Mrs. Y was 65 years old when she came to the US as her son and daughter-in-law were going to have a baby and they needed assistance with the new born. As soon as Mrs. Y came to the US she had to assume the responsibility of taking care of her newborn grandchild but also perform all the cooking and cleaning as her daughter-in-law went back to work after three weeks. All day Mrs. Y was confined to the house with the baby. Only on rare occasions did her son take her to the mosque. Mrs. Y felt lonely most of the time and would cry, as she felt like a prisoner. When Mrs. Y became sick and her stomach pain did not subside after two months, her son sent her back home for a couple of months. Over the years Mrs. Y had lived in the US for more than 15 years. She was receiving Social Security Income and Medicaid. Mrs. Y's son would use the money she was receiving from the SSI for his own use. When Mrs. Y was sick her son would get some over-the-counter medication instead of taking her to a physician. Mrs. Y's son had also sold her home in Bangladesh, so when she felt she was not becoming well wanted to go back, she did not have a place to go back to. Although her daughter and son-in-law were in a high income bracket, yet they did not seek basic care for her but instead shipped her back. Within a few months Mrs. Y died as her stomach cancer was diagnosed at a much later stage.

Case 2

Mr. and Mrs. X came to the US as their son insisted that they would have a better life in the US. Within a few days of their arrival Mr. and Mrs. X were asked to do janitorial work as their son and his wife were motel owners. The elderly Mr. and Mrs. X had never cleaned toilets as they were mill owners in India. They felt demeaned having to do menial labor. Their daughter-in-law would verbally abuse them when some of the motel patrons complained about the dirty sheets. They wanted to go back, but their son would not let them. Each evening the older couple would sit alone to eat dinner as his son's family would eat early. Some of the time the older couple would go hungry as they were vegetarian and the son's family ate meat. One day when Mr. X asked his grandchildren some simple things like how to start the microwave, his grandchildren imitated his accent and laughed at him.

A number of times Mrs. X would witness his grandchild and his girlfriend fooling around and when the older couple objected to this inappropriate behaviour, they were verbally insulted. Over time Mrs. X had a stroke and Mr. X Parkinson's disease and he lost some of his hearing and sight and was unable to function at a fast pace. About two years ago the older couple was placed in a nursing home.

An attitude that is uniquely common among South Asian families is the ageist attitude that allows younger people to shun older adults. The latent belief among South Asians that *sathiyana* (sixtyishness), resulting in mentally unstable behaviours, forgetfulness, feelings of sadness, and physical limitations, is a normative part of the ageing process, convinces adult children against the necessity to get medical help for their elderly relatives. The lack of timely intervention prevents early initiation for treatment of chronic diseases such as diabetes, heart disease and cancer. This ageist attitude is one of the causes of perpetuation of prejudice and neglect of older adults. Some South Asian elderly are reluctant to seek physical and mental health services because they feel like a burden on their adult children.

Strategies for Prevention of Abuse amongst the South Asian Elderly Population

Prevention of abuse is a three stage approach. Primary prevention measures include promoting awareness about elder abuse as well as providing services to protect elders against abuse. For example, primary prevention strategies include using governmental agencies for creating awareness and advocating for elderly who are at risk of being abused, providing services to strengthen caregiver and elderly person's interpersonal skills, manage conflict, and confer other relationship and life skills to foster emotional resiliency. These services are provided for the most part, by health professionals and public health agencies.

In addition, the elderly need to be educated about their legal rights, safety, and the effect of abuse on health and mental health. Confidential telephone hotlines in ethnic languages should be provided so that the elderly have a voice to express their concerns. As one of the main reasons for elder abuse is caregiver stress (Gupta, 1999), overnight relief with nursing care and adult day services need to be created within the community that would provide respite for the caregivers. Encouraging medical professionals such as physicians, nurses and social workers to provide primary care services through free weekly clinics, improving health literacy through Health Fairs are other primary prevention strategies.

The goal of *secondary prevention* is to identify elder abuse in its earliest stages, before noticeable symptoms develop, and when it is most likely to be treated successfully. With early detection and diagnosis, it may be possible to prevent elder abuse. Secondary prevention also aims to prevent the spread of elder abuse. Early identification and treatment of victims of elder abuse, not only provides secondary prevention for those who are abused but also primary prevention for those who are potential victims.

Like primary prevention, individual health care practitioners, public health agencies and non-governmental organizations perform secondary prevention. Physical and mental health screenings to identify elders at the risk of abuse, and identifying stressed and emotionally unstable caregivers are some of the secondary prevention strategies. Hospitals, medical clinics, and physicians play an important role in secondary prevention where they can often conduct screenings and detect abusive relationships in their earliest stages. Table 1 contains a guide to the various signs and symptoms of elder abuse identified by Action on Elder Abuse (2007).

Table 1 Signs and Symptoms of Elder Abuse

Physical Abuse	
The older person has	Untreated injuries that are in various stages of healing or are not properly treated including cuts, lacerations, puncture or open wounds, bruises, welts, discoloration, burns, bone fracture or breaks; Has poor skin condition or hygiene; Shows signs of dehydration, malnutrition or weight loss that are unrelated to illness; Has soiled clothing including bedclothes; Reports having been hit, slapped, kicked or mistreated; Shows signs such as broken eyeglasses or having been punished, or having been restrained; Shows signs of having used medication inappropriately, including signs of overdose or under dose.

Contd.

Contd.

Psychological Abuse	
The older person	Shows signs of helplessness, confusion or disorientation, emotional upset or agitation, unexplained fear or anger without apparent cause; Claims verbal or emotional abuse; Displays sudden changes in behaviour or unusual behaviour such as sucking, biting or rocking; Denies situations or tells implausible stories; Hesitates to talk openly; Shows sign of extreme withdrawal, a lack of response and communication.
Neglect	
The older person	Has poor personal hygiene or rashes or sores or lice; Has inadequate clothing; Shows signs of dehydration, malnutrition or untreated medical conditions; Shows signs of over or under medicated; Lacks assistance when eating or drinking.
Familial Abuse	
The older person	Is forbidden to speak for him or herself or from seeing others when alone; Is the object of indifference, anger or aggressive behaviour such as threats, insults or harassment or is blamed inappropriately for example for being incontinent; Is isolated from other family members or is restricted from being fully active or shows signs of unusual confinement; Offers accounts of incidents that differ from those of family members; Shows signs of having lacked assistance or attendance.
Financial Abuse	Signatures on the older person's cheques do not resemble those of the older person's or signed when the older person cannot write; There is a sudden change in the older person's bank account, including unexplained withdrawal by others or the addition of new names, or there is an unexplained sudden transfer of assets from the older person to family members or others; There are unexplained disappearances of funds or valuable possessions from the older person;

Contd.

Contd.

	There is an abrupt change in or a sudden establishment of the older person's will; Previously uninvolved related appeal suddenly to claim an interest in the older person's affairs or unusual concern is expressed by family members or others about the amount spent on the older person's care; The older person has numerous unpaid bills or overdue rent, when there are supposed to have been paid by others; The older person lacks affordable amenities such as personal grooming items or appropriate clothing; The older person is deliberately isolated from friends and family, giving caregivers full control.

Source: Adapted from Box 1 in Gerard Cronin, "Elder Abuse: The Same Old Story", *Emergency Nurse*, Vol. 15 No. 3 (2007).

Unlike primary and secondary prevention, *tertiary prevention* involves actual treatment for both the elderly victim and the caregiver. Elders who are admitted to the hospital for physical injuries as well as elders participating in community events can be checked for signs and symptoms of elder abuse. A thorough needs assessment of the older person would be crucial. The practitioner should create a supportive environment where the elder feels safe to disclose information about being abused. The practitioner also needs to obtain information about health status, mental health and behavioural problems of the older person. After assessing the emotional stability of the caregiver, history of violence in the family, availability of support network of extended family and friends, the family members should be approached separately to get a comprehensive picture about the dynamics of family functioning. While making an assessment clinicians and practitioners need to be culturally sensitive to understand elder abuse within various ethnicities, cultures and language groups. Tertiary prevention measures also include outreach programmes that monitor older vulnerable persons who live in the community to ensure that their needs are being met by their caregivers. Such programmes have demonstrated efficacy in reducing elder abuse.

Practitioners and physicians are mandated by law to report elder abuse. It is not necessary that the report of abuse come directly from the victim or abuser, for it to be considered valid. A report from the third party who suspects abuse can be sufficient (Welfel, Danzinger and Santoro, 2000).

Failure to report can result in a misdemeanour or in some states the licence to practice might be revoked. In an institutional setting elder abuse can be prevented if relatives and family members of the nursing home residents become eyes and ears, not only for their loved one, but also report abuse when they witness psychological, physical or verbal abuse meted out to another resident.

According to a 2005 report by American Bar Association Commission on Law and Ageing (NCEA, 2008), there are three categories of laws that protect elder abuse in the United States: adult protective services, institutional abuse and the long term care ombudsman programme. Criminal laws and other laws in a jurisdiction may also authorize services for older abused persons. For example, in instances of physical abuse, domestic violence laws with tools such as restraining orders can be invoked to help older adults. Further, regulations and policies as well as power of attorney and state laws on guardianship are important for elder abuse. Although federal laws for domestic violence and child abuse fund programmes and shelters for victims, there are no comparable laws on elder abuse. The Federal Older Americans Act provides definitions for elder abuse and authorizes the National Center on Elder Abuse as well as supports some state-level programmes and activities. However, it does not fund services and shelters for abused older persons.

The Adult Protective Services laws have helped establish a system of reporting and investigation of older abuse and provide services for helping and sustaining the victims. All fifty states and territories of the United States have enacted legislation authorizing adult protective services (APS) to deal with elder abuse. State APS laws vary widely regarding age of eligibility, type and location of abuse, reporting (mandatory or voluntary), investigation procedures and remedies.

In some states such as Georgia, Delaware and Illinois amongst others, separate laws address elder abuse and mistreatment in institutions and have agencies other than APS deal with these cases. Some other states such as California and New York do not make any distinctions between domestic and institutional abuse and places all cases under the jurisdiction of APS agencies. Currently, all but five states mandate reporting suspected abuse. The states that do not require mandatory reporting are Colorado, North and South Dakota, Pennsylvania and Wisconsin (NCEA, 2008). In all states the older person can refuse protective services.

Additionally, all states have laws authorizing the Long Term Care Ombudsman Programme (LTCOP) which is mandatory for states to institute in order to receive federal funds. The LTCOP acts as an advocate for long term care residents, who experience abusive situations, refer these cases to the APS or other agency, local law enforcement agency or the agency responsible for licensing the long term care facility. Sometimes, LTCOP fulfils the APS function and has the legal authority to carry out an investigation in response to reports of abuse in a long term care facility.

At this stage of intervention where the practitioner reports abuse, the elderly may be removed from the private home and placed in a residential facility. Many older adults wish to remain in their homes even after being abused. Therefore service providers need to intervene with both the victim and the abusive caregiver. Abusive caregivers need to be held accountable for their inappropriate behaviours (Schwiebert, Myers and Dice, 2000) and assisted in confronting the root cause so that the cycle of abuse could be broken. If the abusive behaviour of caregivers cannot be changed, the older person needs to be removed to a safe place.

Other ways to stop abusive behaviours of family members and caregivers is, by educating them about the services that are available to them (Quinn and Tomita, 1997). Assistance to caregivers are available in the form of respite care, volunteer visitors programmes, books and videos on how to perform care giving tasks, support groups and various other existing community resources. Treatment of conflict, strain, depression, anxiety, anger issues can also help to mitigate abusive behaviour (Reay and Browne, 2002).

Other Suggested Community Level Interventions

The most common form of intervention is psychological treatment that includes family therapy, individual therapy and relationship counselling that requires behavioural skills training, cognitive restructuring and emotional impulse control (Papadopoulos and Lafontaine, 2000). Caregivers of the elder need to be empowered by recognizing that they need personal time, assistance like respite care, education and guidance on how to deal with behaviour problems of the elderly. Positive reminiscence is a technique that can be used effectively as it entails enhancing compassion and attachment between the adult child caregiver and the elderly (Browne and Herbert, 1997). Intervention also needs to address depression, sadness, shame and guilt experienced by victims of elder abuse.

Intervention strategies should focus on enhancing and supporting the strengths and survival skills of victims. For example, South Asian elders formed a seniors group at the local Hindu temple where they would meet once a month for a senior citizen meeting. At these meetings, the seniors would decide whether they should have picnics, celebrate holidays together, and plan off-season international travel. Some of the seniors raised enough money to have small houses built near the temple so that they could live independently. Seniors who knew English found part-time jobs which assisted them in having some discretionary money. Other older South Asians designed a day care so that young couples could leave their young children in their care.

Psycho-educational seminars need to be conducted in the community that are aimed at educating both elderly and potential or current caregivers regarding the factors and challenges involved with caregiving and the possibility of abuse. Information on the challenges involved in becoming a caregiver of elderly parents, of available social support services including health services should be easily accessible. The social context has to be understood before encouraging parents to immigrate to a new country.

At the community level affordable housing for older adults, foster care, group living should be offered as a substitute for family care. It is important that family caregivers are able to access in-home support services, adult day care, and senior centers with recreational activities. Social support networks for both the elderly and the caregivers are needed to lessen the incidences of elder abuse and neglect. Informal support groups can be started so that caregivers can share ideas that will assist them in venting and releasing tension. An added advantage is that such support groups may help them in pooling resources and providing relief to each other.

Conclusion

Each year hundreds of thousands of older persons are abused, neglected, and exploited by family members and others in the United States. The victimized are often people who are frail, helpless, and vulnerable and depend on others to meet their basic needs. Legislatures in all the 50 states have passed some form of elder abuse prevention laws. Laws and definitions of terms vary considerably from one state to another, but all states have established reporting systems. Generally, Adult Protective Services (APS) agencies receive and investigate reports of suspected elder abuse. The 2004 Survey of State Adult Protective Services, funded by the Administration on Ageing, found that there was a 19.7 per cent increase from 2000 to 2004 in the total cases of elder and vulnerable adult abuse and neglect, and a 15.6 per cent increase in substantiated cases. Twenty states reported that more than two in five victims (42.8 per cent) were aged 80 years or older. Most alleged perpetrators in 2003 were adult children (32.6 per cent), followed by other family members (21.5 per cent) and spouses/intimate partners (11.3 per cent) in 11 states that reported older abuse.

Unlike the long history of successful legislation in the US on domestic abuse and child abuse, legislation around prevention of elder abuse has been fraught with failure. Therefore without any assistance from the federal government, the states made their own laws and reporting procedures. Out of 52 states, about 17 used more than one type of law to address elder abuse. For example California used its own elder abuse reporting laws. Other states like Georgia, Missouri and Oregon had laws protecting the elderly against abuse in long term care facilities only. Many parts of the US were not able to identify and devise laws to respond to elder maltreatment for lack of funds. After decades of failed legislation and denial of funding to the states, the Congress using the Family Violence Prevention and Services Act of 1992 (P.L. 102-295), mandated a national study of the incidence of neglect, abuse and exploitation of elderly people (NEAIS, 1998). The Administration of Children and Families (AF) joined forces with Administration on Ageing (AoA) and jointly funded the National Center on Elder Abuse (NCEA) which is a national resource centre dedicated to prevention of elder abuse. Since there is a lack of uniformity in the policy and practice of elder abuse prevention in the United States, it is even more important for community level efforts to recognize and encourage elder abuse awareness in a culturally sensitive context.

Acknowledgements

This research was supported in part by Research Infrastructure for Minority Institutions grant (RIMI). We acknowledge James Wiley, Ph.D., Programme

Director Public Research Institute for his comments and suggestions. We are grateful to Dr. Gerald Eisman Director of the Institute for Community and Civic Engagement for his continued support.

References

Browne, K. and M. Herbert (1997). *Preventing family violence.* London: Wiley.

Comijs, H.C., B.W. Penninx, K.P. Knipscheer and W. van Tileberg (1999). Psychological distress in victims of elder abuse: The effects of social support and coping. *Journals of Gerontology Series B: Psychological Sciences and Social Sciences,* 54(4), P240–P245.

Department of Health. (2000). No secrets: Guidance on developing and implementing multi-agency policies and procedures to protect vulnerable adults from abuse. The Stationary Office, London.

Diwan, S., S. Jonnalagadda and R. Gupta (2004). Structural differences in depressive symptoms among English and Non-English speaking older Asian Indian immigrants to the US. *Journal of Applied Gerontology,* 23(4), 370–84.

Giordano, N. and J.A. Giordano (1984). Elder abuse: A review of the literature. *Social Work,* 29(3), 232–36.

Gordon, Robert and Deborah Brill (2001). The abuse and neglect of the elderly. *Journal of Law and Psychiatry,* 24(2–3), 183–97.

Gupta, R. (July, 1999). The revised caregiver burden scale: A preliminary validation. *Research on Social Work Practice,* 9(4), 508–20.

——. (2002). Consideration of nursing home care placement for South Asian elderly. *Journal of Immigrant Health,* 4(1), 47–58.

——. (2005). Factors that contribute to caregiver burden and uplifts among caregivers of the elderly in India. 58th Annual Meeting. *The Gerontological Society of America,* Orlando, Florida.

Holt, M. (1994). Elder abuse in Britain. *Journal of Elder Abuse and Neglect,* 5(1), 33–39.

Kivela, S., P. Kongas-Saviaro and E. Kesti (1992). Abuse in old age: Epidemiological data from Finland. *Journal of Elder Abuse and Neglect,* 4(3), 1–18.

Kosberg, J.I. and J. L. Garcia (1995). *Confronting the maltreatment of elders by their family.* Thousand Oaks, GA: Sage Publishers.

Kosberg, J.I. (1988). Preventing elder abuse: Identification of risk factors prior to placement decision. *Gerontologist,* 28, 43–49.

Kurrle, S., P. Sadler, K. Lockwood and I. Cameron (1997). Elder abuse: Prevalence, intervention, and outcomes in patients referred to four aged care assessment teams. *Medical Journal of Australia,* 166 (3), 119–22.

Lachs, Mark S. and K. Pillemer (2004). Elder abuse, *The Lancet,* vol. 364.

Le, Q.K. (1997). Mistreatment of Vietnamese elderly by their families in the United States. *Journal of Elder Abuse and Neglect*, 9(2), 51.

Malley-Morrison, K., H.S. You and R. Mills (2000). Young adult attachment styles and perceptions of elder abuse: A cross-cultural study. *Journal of Cross-Cultural Gerontology*, 15, 163–84.

Moon, A. (1998). Elder Abuse and neglect among the Korean elderly in the United States. In T. Tatara (ed.), *Understanding elder abuse in minority populations.* (pp. 109–18). PA: Brunner/Mazel—Taylor & Francis.

National Center on Elder Abuse. (1998). National Elder Abuse Incidence Study: Washington, DC: National Center on Elder Abuse at American Public Human Services Association.

National Center on Elder Abuse. (2003). A response to the abuse of vulnerable adults: The 2000 Survey of State Adult Protective Services, Washington, DC: National Center on Elder Abuse.

National Center on Elder Abuse. (2008). *http://www.ncea.aoa.gov/ncearoot/Main_Site/About/What_We_Do.aspx.* Department of Aging. Retrieved March 21, 2008.

National Research Council. (2003). Elder mistreatment: Abuse, Neglect and exploitation in an Aging America, Washington, DC: National Research Council Panel to review risk and prevalence of Elder Abuse and Neglect.

Papadopolous, A. and J. LaFontaine (2000). *Elder abuse: Therapeutic perspectives in practice.* Bicester, United Kingdom: Winslow.

Phillips, L. (1983). Abuse and neglect of the frail elderly at home: An exploration of theoretical relationships. *Journal of Advanced Nursing*, 8(1), 379–92.

Pillemer, K. and D. Finkelhor, (1988). The prevalence of elder abuse: A random sample survey, *Gerontologist*, 28, 51–57.

Podnieks, E. (1992). National survey on abuse of elderly in Canada. *Journal of Elder Abuse and Neglect*, 41, 5–58.

Pritchard, I. (1993). Dispelling some myths. *Journal of Elder Abuse and Neglect*, 5(2), 27–36.

Quinn, M.J. and S.K. Tomita (1997). *Elder abuse and neglect.* New York: Springer.

Reay, G.A. and K.D. Browne (2002). The effectiveness of psychological interventions with individuals who physically abuse or neglect their elderly dependents. *Journal of Interpersonal Violence*, 17, 416–31.

Sanchez, Y. (1998a). Elder Mistreatment in Mexican-American communities: The Nevada and Michigan experiences. In T. Tatara (eds.), *Understanding elder abuse in minority populations.* (pp. 67–77). PA: Brunner/Mazel-Taylor & Francis Group.

—— (1998b). Elder abuse in the Puerto Rican context. In T. Tatara (ed.), *Understanding elder abuse in minority populations.* (pp. 93–105). PA: Brunner/Mazel—Taylor & Francis.

Saveman, B., S. Astrom, G. Bucht and A. Norberg (1999). Elder Abuse in Residential Settings in Sweden. *Journal of Elder abuse and neglect,* 10(1/2), 43–60. (Co-published simultaneously in *Elder abuse and neglect in residential settings: Different national backgrounds and similar responses,* F. Glendenning and P. Kingston, eds. New York: The Haworth Press, Inc.

Schwiebert, V.L, J.E. Myers and G. Dice (2000). Ethical guidelines for counselors working with older adults. *Journal of Counseling and Development,* 78, 123–29.

Sharon, N. and S. Zoabi (1997). Elder Abuse in a Land of Tradition: The Case of Israel's Arabs. *Journal of Elder Abuse and Neglect,* 8(4), 43–58.

Steinmetz, S.K. (1983). Dependency, stress and violence between middle aged caregivers and their elderly parents. In J.I. Kosberg (ed.), *Abuse and mistreatment of the elderly: Causes and interventions.* (pp. 134–149). London: PSG.

Tornstarn, L. (1989). Abuse of the elderly in Denmark and Sweden: Results from a population study. *Journal of Elder Abuse and Neglect,* 1, 35–44.

Tsukada, N., Y. Saito and T. Tatara (2001). Japanese Older People's Perceptions of "Elder Abuse". *Journal of Elder Abuse and Neglect,* 13(1).

Welfel, E.R., P.R. Danzinger and S. Santoro (2000). Mandated reporting of abuse/maltreatment of older adults: A primer for counselors. *Journal of Counseling and Development,* 78, 284–92.

WHO/INPEA. (2002). Missing Voices: Views of Older persons on Elder Abuse, Geneva, World Health Organization.

Yan, E. and C. So-Kum Tang (2001). Prevalence and Psychological Impact of Chinese Elder Abuse. *Journal of Interpersonal Violence,* 16(11), 1158–74.

18

Resolving Elder Abuse Complaints in Homes for the Aged: Relevance of Ombudsman Programme

Varsha Pandya

Homes for the aged whose family may not be able to provide care for them are a growing phenomenon in India. The internet exploration showed the listing of homes for the aged in four southern states of Kerala, Tamil Nadu, Karnataka, Andhra Pradesh and the City of Delhi (list of old age homes, retrieved on July 2, 2008). It is believed that the growth of such homes in these states is because of increased migration of the younger generation in pursuit of better economic opportunities compared to other states. Karmayog (retrieved on February 7, 2008) detailed the four types of old age homes in Maharashtra based on monthly charges : (1) old people without any support—free, (2) based on the income of elderly persons, (3) charging less than Rs. 1000 per month, (4) charging more than Rs. 1000 per month. According to Roy (n.d.), the Government of India has initiated the setting up of 603 old age homes for India's 21 million destitute who are 60 years and older—one in each district of the country. The Ministry of Social Justice and Empowerment will provide a grant of Rs. 20 million to state governments for constructing each home that would accommodate not less than 150 destitute senior citizens.

Sawhney (n.d.) reports that the traditional belief that the elderly are well taken care of in a joint family system is quickly becoming a myth as shown by some cases and ethnographic studies. These studies found that even though the elderly may be living with their son's family, sometimes their needs are neglected. Old age homes are set-up for elderly members who do not have appropriate caregivers immediately available and who cannot care for themselves. The guiding principle for these homes in India is to provide an opportunity to such elders to spend the "evening of their lives" with dignity and respect (Sawhney, n.d., p. 11).

Concerned citizens, gerontology professionals, and the government need to take proactive steps to address the issues related to sub-standard care, neglect of residents, and possible abuse that are likely to occur in growing numbers of homes for the aged (HfA) in India. In western countries, where residential care facilities for older adults have existed for more than four decades, the maltreatment of elders in these facilities was observed in a variety of forms that compromised human dignity and worth. These included serious neglect of physical care required, overmedication, unnecessary use of restraints, and verbal, physical, sexual, and financial abuse (Monk, Kaye and Litwin, 1984). Wilson (1978) observed that the residents whose rights are curtailed or who have been victims of abuse and neglect in residential facilities often times did not come forward to complain and seek justice and restoration because of their frailty, isolation from the community and families, lack of physical and psychological energy for combativeness required in the face of adversarial relationship that might result in HfA, lack of financial resources and legal assistance, and small value on injury to those in the evening of their life. A study done by Gottsman and Bourestom (1974, as cited in Monk et al., 1984) confirmed a positive relationship between the rate of visitors in such facilities and quality of care provided to its residents. Ombudsmen, who are third party visitors with certain investigative, advocating, and reconciliatory resolution powers, have been adopted as a fairly successful mechanism in the western world to address the violation of bill of rights and abuse of residents of HfA.

The objective of this paper is to provide information on the Ombudsman programme for consideration of Indian entities that might be interested in developing a proactive system to address the potential issues of elder abuse and maltreatment in HfA. Monk et al. (1984), though an old reference, have been frequently used in this paper for the comprehensiveness of the information and that it was written during the times when Ombudsman programmes were still in the developmental stages in the United States.

What is an Ombudsman Programme ?

An Ombudsman programme is assigned responsibility to investigate complaints made by or on behalf of older persons in long-term care facilities or HfA (Lehigh county office of Ageing and Adult Services, n.d.). The Ombudsman also assists in resolution of the substantiated complaints. This is the minimum role that an ombudsman is required to play; but there are several other responsibilities that an ombudsman programme can be assigned and tasks that its staff or volunteers may perform.

Models of Ombudsman Programme

Monk et al. (1984) identify three models of Ombudsman programme: classical, executive and hybrid.

Classical : This model was developed in the Scandinavian countries in late 19th and early 20th centuries to investigate complaints against the administration. An independent, non-partisan office of the legislature was assigned the task to investigate complaints from the public against administrative injustice and maladministration. This office had power to investigate, criticize, and publicize, but not to reverse any administrative action.

Executive : The Ombudsman is an appointed officer by the executive branch of the government who develops and oversees a system to receive, investigate, and dispose complaints received from or on behalf of the residents in HfA.

Hybrid : The Ombudsman in this model is a specialist employed within a system, (e.g., prison, hospital, HfA) who acts as a mediator between the consumer (client), community, and the system. The person attempts to see all sides of the dispute and bring it to a satisfactory and reconciliatory resolution.

Besides these models, there are three systemic designs found in literature (e.g., Monk et al., 1984): salaried professionals only, volunteers only, and a mix of salaried ombudsmen and volunteers. Three types of functions that ombudsmen can carry out investigating, advocating for the residents, and liaisoning between the community, HfA, and the oversight authority in the government. Though all types of ombudsmen programmes are found to be useful in resolving complaints in HfA, there are certain disadvantages associated with each of these designs and expectations placed on Ombudsmen. Certain tasks have an inherent conflict. A partisan (one advocating for the resident) ombudsman may be biased when investigating a complaint. Certain investigative tasks may be vulnerable to fallacy, should the matter go to the judicial system. A volunteer ombudsman may not have the needed specialized knowledge to investigate complaints related to over-medication, unnecessary restraints, or other lapses in professional care and victimization. On one hand, the ombudsman programme may find it difficult to demand accountability from volunteers who may just leave. On the other hand, the ombudsman employed in the system may not be non-partial in the investigation of the complaints.

An alternative "Board of Visitors" model comprising of family and friends of the residents and community leaders also can be found in literature (Monk et al., 1984). A pilot of such a board had investigative and some judicial powers in all complaints of elder abuse in HfA. The board was able to subpoena the witnesses and record their testimony under oath, as well as require production of documents relevant to investigation. The findings of such boards were systematically noted and were, in most instances accurate and substantive. The major drawback however was that such a board did not have any sanctioning power, and oftentimes authorities ignored their findings, minimizing their work as "not professional", "done by volunteers" and burying their reports without instituting pertinent changes and sanctioning the persons responsible or guilty of offending against the elder resident (Monk et al., 1984).

The US Ombudsman Programme

The Ombudsman programme in the US began as a demonstration programme in 1972 and is currently established in all states of the US under the Older Americans Act, administered by the Administration on Ageing (AoA). In the year 2000 there were about 1000 paid and 8000 certified volunteer ombudsmen (Administration on Ageing, retrieved on March 13, 2008). The US adopted the executive model of Ombudsman programme, using a mix of staffed employees and volunteers, where volunteers are trained and certified to carry out all the three functions of investigator, advocate, and community liaison (AoA, retrieved 03/13/08; Monk et al., 1984). It must be noted though that there are variations in the programme structure and function in different states because the executive powers to implement the Ombudsman programme is vested in the states (AoA, n.d., American Association of Retired Persons [AARP], n.d.). Several national studies (e.g., Monk et al., 1984; Pearson, 2004) identified roles performed by Ombudsmen across the country. The paid Ombudsman staff generally performed the role of training and supervising volunteer ombudsmen, assisting them in conducting investigation, and serving as a liaison between the volunteers, residential facility administrators and the oversight agency of the government. The volunteers identified their primary role as being friendly visitors to the residential facilities with empathy for the residents. Some volunteers saw their role as a mediator when the residents had grievances whereas some identified themselves as advocates for the residents (Pearson, 2004). Resident abuse cases, when substantiated were then referred to the appropriate governmental or judicial authorities for their resolution whereas ombudsman could mediate, advocate and resolve issues related to violation of the residents' rights, discrimination in health care, mental health needs, relationship issues, and participation in the governance of the facility. Monk et al. (1984) reported several tasks assigned to the Ombudsman programme across the states, which can also be found in more recent literature available on the AoA and AARP websites (see additional resources in the reference section). These tasks are: (1) to establish a better relationship between the HfA and the community to facilitate informal oversight that can prevent isolation of the residents and prevent abuse of residents; (2) to facilitate involvement of the residents and their family and friends in the governance of the facility; (3) to establish a mechanism for speedy resolution of residents' complaints; (4) to file a complaint on behalf of the residents or their families when they cannot do so; (5) to provide public education on long-term care; and (6) to provide information to legislature and programme planners for needed changes in policies and programmes for the long-term care of the elderly.

Monk et al. (1984) studied issues that different Ombudsmen programmes considered for the development of their own programmes. Based on their findings, they suggested a model pathway for programme development that may be considered by decision-makers in India if

- Goal / mission
  (emphasize residents' rights or promotion of quality of life)
- Objectives (investigative, supportive etc.)
- Foucs (advocacy or mediation)
- Identification of targets constituents

External organizational issues

- Sanction/mandate (statutory empowerment, informal cooperation)
- Organizational placement (governmental, non-governmental)
- Funding (public, private)
- Scope (state wide, district wide, Taluka based, or single home focused)

Internal management issues

- Staffing pattern (paid and volunteers)
- Recruitment and training (emphasis: education, orientation)
- Supervisory mechanisms
- Record-keeping
- Procedures for resolution of different types of complaints/grievances

Figure 1 Issues for Programme Development Guiding Philosophy of the Programme

they choose to develop an Ombudsmen type of programme. Figure 1 outlines some of the issues that may be considered for the development of Ombudsman type of programme in countries like India where HfA as a mainstream caregiving mechanism for elderly is a more recent phenomenon. As is evident in the chart, issues are identified from the literature on programme administration and management whereas details of each issue are picked out from the specific discussion about the programme, I have presented so far in this paper. The next section discusses the issues in implementation process of the Ombudsman programme.

Issues in Implementation of Ombudsman Programme

The issues in implementation of Ombudsman programme are mainly identified from the experience of Pennsylvania state report where the author currently resides. But as the readers will note these issues can be generalized to any situation wanting to design and implement such a programme. First and foremost, the issue of housing of the ombudsman office must be decided. Having the office of the paid executive of the programme in appropriate department of the state government will provide the much needed decision-making and sanctioning authority to the programme. This executive can supervise paid employees at district offices or can contract with non-governmental organizations (NGO) to execute the tasks and responsibilities of the Ombudsman programme at the district level. Whether an employee of the government or an NGO, mechanisms, procedures and processes for investigation, intervention, and resolution must be clearly stated and adequate decision-making and sanctioning authority be vested in a district level or even Taluka level officer. A clear guideline must be developed about what routes for resolution may be used under what types of situations or findings: litigation route, mediation and collaborative corrective action route, or dismissal of the complaint. Depending on what route is chosen, who will be best trained to play that role effectively? An advisory board comprising of multidisciplinary experts (e.g., lawyer, social worker, psychologist, physician etc.) to provide the needed guidance during the process of investigation and resolution can be very effective.

Pennsylvania Advocates for Better Care (1979) reported the usefulness of an advisory committee during the development years of the Ombudsman programme. The board had 50 per cent membership of allied professionals (physicians, nurses, social workers, lawyers, etc.) and 50 per cent membership of consumers, citizens and service providers (representatives of residents, family members, HfA administrators and staff, and community leaders). The advisory committee was found to be very useful in diffusing conflicts, devise creative solutions to problems, and assistance in the development of educational material. The only, but important limitation observed was the minority representation of consumers on such advisory committees. The consumers' voice was generally overpowered by the service providers and the allied professionals. The report recommended increasing representation of the consumers on such a committee.

Complaint Resolution Procedures

Oftentimes the residents do not complain because either they are incapacitated or they feel vulnerable and powerless, or both (Huber, Borders, Netting and Nelson, 2001; Monk et al., 1984; Pennsylvania Advocates for Better Care, 1979; Walshe, 2001). Huber et al. (2001) found in their study that even when a complaint was made on behalf of the vulnerable population like members of the racial minority groups, a lower percentage of those were resolved compared to the complaints received on behalf of the racial majority group. Indians should also be cognizant of this fact and ensure that the poor, women, and persons from the scheduled castes, tribes, and lower castes are treated fairly in HfA. Huber et al. (2001) also found that men were more vulnerable to physical abuse and women were more vulnerable to sexual abuse in HfA.

There are three ways in which an Ombudsman can note complaints: (1) when the Ombudsman visits HfA, the residents can tell him about the difficulties they are experiencing; (2) other people may call the Ombudsman to lodge a complaint; and (3) during the visit the Ombudsman may notice an abusive situation or violation of patients' rights or compromised care of a resident, and may note a complaint. The Ombudsman may be able to resolve some complaints at the facility level either through mediation between the aggrieved party and the accused party or by involving the advisory committee. Other complaints, once verified or substantiated, may need referral to the health department, prosecutor's office, or another relevant agency. When the complaint is referred elsewhere for its resolution the Ombudsmen office may keep the case open and monitor its progress or may close the case (Huber et al., 2001) after that agency becomes actively involved.

It is important to determine the maximum time limit within which the verification of the complaint must be completed and a disposition determined. Besides, if hiring volunteers, Linnane (1977) and Monk et al. (1984) suggest that emphasis may be put on training the ombudsman on the following skills: developing a macro-micro view of the presenting problem, investigative skills, interviewing skills, tact, firmness, knowledge of government and ability to work through bureaucracies, patience, conflict resolution, mediation, advocacy, ability to listen to many sides and make an objective assessment, ability to solve a problem, and a sense of humour. Keith (2000), in a survey of volunteer ombudsmen training, found that the availability of training and certification to become an ombudsman volunteer in the communities were more effective in recruitment, retention, and effectiveness of volunteer ombudsman than the in-service training provided after recruiting the volunteers. The former attracted those individuals who saw volunteerism as their second career. The findings of the study of Keith also suggested that volunteer ombudsmen preferred access to written manuals and other references and resources that could help them understand the needs of older people in HfA, and successfully carry out their roles. Ombudsmen also preferred that more time was allotted to hands-on experience that provided opportunities for them to learn and practice the skills and techniques required by their responsibilities and tasks. They also expressed a need for attending conferences and workshops for continuing education as well as interaction with other Ombudsmen.

Concluding Remarks

Due to the growing number of homes for the aged in India, a clear need to prevent and address elder neglect and abuse in these homes, is established. Ombudsman programmes in the US and European countries provide a framework for the Indian stakeholders in development of Homes for the Aged to meet this need. In my opinion, questioning the need for such a programme is not up for debate here, but the question "what type of responsive programme does India want to have to address this potential problem of neglect and abuse in homes for the aged" definitely needs to be asked. The article provides alternative models, processes, and potential pitfalls of these to guide the decision-making for the programme development similar to the Ombudsman programme in India. Training and employment of paraprofessional workforce instead of voluntary ombudsmen may be worth considering for the Indian situation. It is hoped that such a process will be prompted or enhanced as a result of this writing.

References

Administration on Aging (retrieved, on March 13, 2008). The long-term care ombudsman Program. http://www.aoa.gov/prof/aoaprog/elder_rights/LTCombudsman/ombudsman.pdf

Huber, R., K. Borders, F.E. Nettong and H.W. Nelson (2001). Data from long-term care ombudsman programs in six states: The implications of collecting resident demographics. *The Gerontologist*, 41(1), 61–68.

Karmayog. http://www.karmayog.com/lists/oah.htm Retrieved on February 7, 2008.

Keith, P.M. (2000). Training and educational activities, efficacy, and worry among volunteer ombudsmen in nursing facilities. *Educational Gerontology*, 26, 249–60.

Lehigh County Office of Aging and Adult Services (n.d.) Information Pamphlet.

Linnane, P. (1977). *Ombudsman for nursing homes: Structure and process.* DHEW publication No. (OHD) 78–20293. Wahsington DC, US Government Printing Office.

List of old age homes. http://www.accommodationtimes.com/freesection/ageoldhomes.htm. Retrieved on February 7, 2008.

Monk, A., L.W. Kaye and H. Litwin (1984). *Resolving grievances in the nursing home: A study of the ombudsman program.* New York: Columbia University Press.

Pearson, D.I. (2004). Volunteer ombudsmen in the nursing home: Obstacles to retention. *Journal of Aging Studies,* 18(2), 205–14.

Pennsylvania Advocates for Better Care. (1979). *Nursing Home Ombudsman Project: The Pennsylvania Experience.* Final Report. Harrisburg, PA: Pennsylvania Advocates for better care.

Roy, R.R. (no date). http://in.news.yahoo.com/indiaabroad/20080207/r_t_ians_nl_politics/tnl-coming-up-603-homes-for-india-s-elde-a4b7bec.html Retrieved February 7, 2008.

Sawhney, M. (no date). www.helpageindia.com. Retrieved on February 7, 2008.

Walshe, K. (2001). Regulating US nursing homes: Are we learning from experience? *Health Affairs,* 20(6), 128–44.

Additional Resources:

Administration on Aging, US: http://www.aoa.gov.

American Association of Retired Persons: www.aarp.org.

Locating State Ombudsman Program: http://www.ltcombudsman.org.

National Long Term Care Ombudsman Resource Center, US: www.nccnhr.org

19

The Abuse of Older People: The English Scenario

Arup K. Banerjee

Whilst the maltreatment and abuse of children are very well recognized, attracting lots of public and media attention, mistreatment and neglect of older vulnerable individuals do not usually arouse the full interest and attention of the society at large. Only extreme cases are reported in the newspapers as incidents of a criminal nature.

Unfortunately, there is a paucity of high quality research in this field and, as such, anecdotes abound. As far as my recollection goes Dr Geoffrey Burston, a Bristol geriatrician had reported in the *British Medical Journal* the first case of 'Granny Battering' in this country, frustrated carers being blamed for this (Burston, 1975). The descriptive title was chosen presumably to compare it with 'baby battering', i.e., abuse of children. In the last three decades, there has been many enquiries, reports, guidelines and advisory legislations; the general attitude of the community as a whole, however, has not altered all that much, the alleged 'incidents' are still not taken seriously and often remain un-investigated and un-actioned.

The abuse of the older people has been defined by the WHO (2002) in their Toronto Declaration, for international usage, as

> A single or repeated act or lack of appropriate action occurring within any relationship where there is an expectation of trust, which causes harm or distress to an older person.

Although this is a good starting point, unfortunately the emerging picture is much more complex than that; furthermore this definition does not include 'neglect' i.e., failure of provision of basic necessities for survival: food, heat, hygiene and Appropriate Health Care (Correct Diagnosis and Treatment of Proven Value). Human Rights issues do come into this as well.

The overall qualities of research in this field, as mentioned already, have not been of the highest order in both their depth and expanse. The study undertaken by Ogg and Bennett (1992) in conjunction with the OPCS Omnibus survey had looked only at the 65–74 year age group living in the community and detected abuse of various types: physical in 2 per cent, financial in 2 per cent and verbal in 5 per cent. It had been extrapolated that at any one time, about 5,00,000 older people in this country are being abused in some form. Unfortunately, this study had not included more frail and also mentally infirm elderly residents of care homes and hospitals ; accordingly no definitive conclusion on the incidence of elder abuse could be drawn. In another study published a bit earlier (Garner and Evans, 2000) in each year approximately 1,000 cases of 'abuse' were said to be reported to the UK Central Council of Nursing consisting of verbal, physical and sexual nature. In 2003, an enquiry among the district nurses revealed that 88 per cent of them had encountered some form of abuse in their professional contacts (Potter, 2003). More recently (2004) the UK Department of Health enquiry into total referrals for 'adult protection cases' established that nearly 30 per cent of such cases related to older subjects. To summarize the situation, therefore, the true incidence of elder abuse in own homes, care homes and in hospitals remains largely unknown; hopefully the current 'Protection of Vulnerable Adults' (POVA) scheme launched by the government (DOH, 2000) would shed further light and 'protect' the vulnerable from the perpetrators.

One of the main difficulties in these issues affecting the old and the vulnerable seems to be a general lack of public awareness intermixed with an element of 'dismissiveness'. Whilst abuse of children attracts wide attention, publicity and a very tight regulatory approach, there is nothing yet, similar to those targeting the old. Other forms of domestic violence also receive a significant degree of public interest, even production of movies, e.g., provoked, with famous Bollywood stars! Perhaps this reflects the overall social attitude to ageing ; the old, unless rich, still remain undervalued.

There is a feeling in this country that the people in the East are much more respectful towards their elders and the old are treated with dignity. I am currently not adequately qualified to comment on this. Sadly one reads the odd sad tales of 'neglect' of the old, in Indian newspapers from time to time. It is important that further social and socio-medical research and surveys are undertaken to measure the true incidence of this evil practice in India.

Another important factor is training or the lack of it. In the UK, geriatric medicine and nursing are established 'specialist' areas ; even then, many 'trained' people remain appallingly ignorant and ill-prepared on 'abuse' cases. Handling of 'suspected' cases tends to be amateurish. Assessment is inadequate and fragmented and follow up poor.

To tackle the situation more thoroughly, the health care establishment is now setting up a variety of measures on the assessment process, further management protocols and most importantly, a proper infrastructure with a protection coordinator in each district. Health care agencies are now being directed not to appoint any one with a poor record, to the services for older people. Such employee screening has been applicable to childcare areas for many years.

Guidelines are being issued with regular training sessions involving all categories of health and social care professionals and care staff. Police authorities are beginning to show an interest and hopefully in another few years, good and effective multi-disciplinary protection teams will be fully operational in all the health districts.

From the existing experience, the principal 'risks' tend to remain with:

People living with others (e.g., spouse or relatives) are more vulnerable to verbal and physical types; people living alone are more likely to be at financial risk.

Individuals with dementing illnesses and behavioural disorders are more likely to be abused physically.

Abuse of all types are commoner in the socially isolated.

As regards the perpetrators, those who 'financially depend' on the older person, frequently under the influence of alcohol or drugs or are mentally unstable themselves, are more likely to be abusive. Despite 'frustration and tiredness', ordinary carer-stress has not been found to be a cause of abusive behaviour.

For a 'prevention' strategy, such risk factors are extremely important and should be identified, and corrective measures taken at an early stage, before it is too late.

Recognition of any form of abuse is not always easy. Whether the bruises are due to recurrent falls or from physical abuse, can be a bit tricky to establish, against 'denials' from many corners. Verbal berating, psychological pressure, financial misappropriation, etc., need to be explored by a properly experienced and trained multidisciplinary team of professionals. When the 'culprit' happens to be the only available support for the frail old person, it is unlikely that the 'victim' would speak out! The doctor cannot do it alone. Clinical interest and involvement along with a degree of leadership from the family doctors, however, is very useful and, therefore, to be encouraged.

In this country, a number of well-organized charities are doing sterling work in the field ; the best known specialized organization is 'Action on Elder Abuse' (www.elderabuse.org.uk). A close look at their official website would provide detailed information about their activities on training, research, service provision needs, programmes for seminars, networking with other similar organizations both in this country and abroad, etc. They are probably the most authoritative source of information in this country at this moment. Other age-charities, e.g., Age Concern (www.ageconcern.org.uk) and Help the Aged (www.helpthe aged.org.uk) also have experts to advise on the subject. The specialist medical body 'British Geriatrics Society' has a 'policy' statement (BGS, 2007) on elder-abuse, updated every three years (www.bgs.org.uk). The reader is advised to look at these web sites for further detailed information which cannot possibly be all provided in a small article such as this.

Elder abuse is beginning to be recognized in this country, as an entity warranting proper attention of the local statutory agencies and the national government (DOH, 2000). This process has commenced but will not be fully operational overnight. The media and public interest will be a driving force and everyone will be watching. Whether the incidence of elder-abuse will increase is difficult to predict as its causation happens to be multi-factorial intermixed with many social and health care issues (Fox et al., 2007)

There is enormous scope for both medical and social research. The South Asian community of the very first generation immigrants are now in their old age. New research into the pattern and incidence of abuse in that cohort of population would be very useful when assessing their service needs. A comparative study of such occurrences in the older folks in the subcontinent and those living abroad, would be very interesting. Let's hope this special issue of *Indian Journal of Gentrology* will stimulate such interest among its readers.

References

Action on Elder Abuse. (2004). *Hidden voices: Older people's experience of abuse.* London, Help the Aged.

British Geriatrics Society. (2007). Compendium of Guidelines . London BGS.

Burston, G.R. (1975). Granny Battering. *BMJ* 3, 592.

Department of Health. (2000). No Secrets, London, DOH.

——. (2006) Guidance for the Protection of Vulnerable Adults (POVA) Scheme, London.

Fox, G., A. Cracknell and P. Belfield (2007). Elder abuse: A practical guide and literature review. *CME Journal on Geriatric Medicine*, 9(3): 99–104.

Garner, J. and S. Evans (2007). Institutional abuse of older people, Royal College of Psychiatrists, London.

Ogg, J. and G. Bennett (1992). Elder abuse in Britain, *BMJ*, 305: 998–99.

Potter, J. (2003). Findings in relation to the community and district nursing association survey examining the issue of elder abuse, London CDNA.

World Health Organisation. (2002). The Toronto Declaration on the global prevention of elder abuse. Geneva, WHO.

20

Determinants of Elder Abuse in Rajshahi City Corporation, Bangladesh: Evidence from a Micro-Level Survey

Md. Ismail Tareque, Towfiqua Mahfuza Islam, and Md. Mostafizur Rahman

Data regarding elder abuse are difficult to find and interpret because elder abuse is a relatively recently recognized phenomenon, has a wide variety of definitions from state to state, and is subject to cultural interpretation (Wolf, 1997). According to National Center on Elder Abuse (NCEA) (2008), elder abuse is a term referring to any knowing, intentional, or negligent act by a caregiver or any other person that causes harm or a serious risk of harm to a vulnerable adult. The specificity of laws varies from state to state, but broadly defined, abuse may be: (1) *physical abuse:* inflicting, or threatening to inflict, physical pain or injury on a vulnerable elder, or depriving them of a basic need, (2) *emotional abuse:* infl icting mental pain, anguish, or distress on an elder person through verbal or nonverbal acts, (3) *sexual abuse:* non-consensual sexual contact of any kind, (4) *exploitation:* illegal taking, misuse, or concealment of funds, property, or assets of a vulnerable elder, (5) neglect: refusal or failure by those responsible to provide food, shelter, health care or protection for a vulnerable elder, and (6) *abandonment*: the desertion of a vulnerable elder by anyone who has assumed the responsibility for care or custody of that person.

Elder abuse may be domestic, taking place in the home of the abused or in the home of a caregiver, or it may be institutional, taking place in a residential facility for the elderly (e.g., a nursing home). Elder abuse may be intentional (active) or unintentional (passive) (Wolf, 1997). Physical abuse is only one among many sub-types of elder abuse, which includes psychologic abuse, financial abuse, sexual abuse, and neglect. Although these sub-types are discrete entities, they are often closely related and interdependent. In an extensive study, neglect was found to be the most common form of abuse, followed by psychological abuse, financial exploitation, physical abuse, abandonment, and sexual abuse. In the home, two-thirds of abusers are spouses and adult children (AOA, 1998).

Many characteristics of the perpetrator and the victim have been cited as potential risk factors for elder abuse. A shared living arrangement lends itself to an increased risk of abuse due to the proximity of the abused and the abuser, and greater risk has been noted if the patient resides with immediate family but without a spouse (Paveza et al., 1992). Characteristics of the perpetrator that increase the risk of abuse include a history of mental illness, substance abuse, or dependence on the victim for fi nancial assistance, housing or other needs (Pillemer, 1988). Perception of stress by the caregiver, not the stress level, was correlated with increased abuse (Wolf, 1997). Characteristics of the elder, including frailty, poor health, and functional impairments, have been shown to be associated with an increased probability of mistreatment, although these data are controversial (Wolf, 1997; Lachs et al., 1997). An elder's aggressive behaviour towards caregivers has been shown to increase the probability of physical abuse (Paveza et al., 1992). Elderly persons most susceptible to neglect were those in poorer health, more socially isolated and without contacts to call for help (Pillemer and Finkelhor 1988).

In the advanced countries, studies have shown that most elderly are neither safe nor happy at home as well as in institutional setting (Pillemer and Tinkelhor, 1987; Kosberg and Gracia, 1995). It was during 1980s that elder abuse gained rapid recognition in the USA and the UK. It is estimated that every year around 0.5 to 2.5 million elderly are subjected to physical violence alone in the USA. We lack such statistics for Bangladesh. Thus, this study makes an attempt to determine the important factors of elder abuse and neglect in Rajshahi City Corporation, Bangladesh.

Materials and Methods

The study is based on the data of 87 abused persons out of 495 persons, aged 60 years and over who were purposively interviewed in Rajshahi City Corporation during September 6, 2008 to September 16, 2008.

We found three types of abuse—mental, economical and physical, in the study area. A score was developed to measure how much per cent an elder was abused. Firstly mental abuse is scored 1, economical abuse is scored 2 and physical abuse is scored 3. So, the total score was 6. Then each score was divided by the total score and multiplied by 100. Thus on this basis if an elder was mentally abused, it was scored 16 per cent, if economically then 33 per cent and so on. Point bi-serial correlation was used to investigate the relationship between the causes of abuse (according to the respondent's statement) and the score. And finally the score was used as a dependent variable to determine the important factors related to elderly abuse by analysis of variance named as General Linear Model (GLM) Univariate Analysis of Variance.

Salient Features

Before presenting the major findings of the study an account of the societal characteristics of the respondents may be in order. Table 1 presents the data in this regard.

Table 1 shows that majority of the abused elderly are young old, i.e., between 60 and 69 years. This is somewhat contradictory to the prevailing view, which suggests that oldest of the old are the most vulnerable group who receive ill treatment. This unexpected result can be explained by the fact that many oldest elderly respondents possibly felt ashamed of or became embarrassed to admit their ill-treatment openly even to their next door neighbours. Or, may be, they were too afraid to disclose their woes and miseries because of the fear of being thrown out or abandoned.

Female elderly who were widowed are more susceptible to ill treatment as 80 per cent of them reported to have suffered from abusive behaviour while the corresponding figure for male elderly is 16.2 per cent only. Since the life expectancy for females is higher than that of males and age at marriage for females is less than that of males, more males exist in married status after 60+ years than females.

The study revealed that four-fifth of the abused female elderly were illiterate and most of the study respondents were Muslim.

Data also show that half of the abused elderly lived with married children. Relatively more female than male, abused elderly lived alone. About two-third of the families were male headed and only one-third families's monthly income was more than 5000 takas.

Table 1 Demographic and Socio-economic Characteristics of the Respondents

Characteristics	Male		Female		Total	
	Freq.	%age	Freq.	%age	Freq.	%age
Age group (in years)						
Young Old (60-69)	24	64.9	40	80.0	64	73.6
Adult Old (70-79)	6	16.2	5	10.0	11	12.6
Oldest old (80+)	7	18.9	5	10.0	12	13.8
Marital Status						
Married	30	81.1	9	18.0	2	2.3
Unmarried	1	2.7	1	2.0	39	44.8
Widowed/Widower	6	16.2	40	80.0	46	52.9
Educational Qualification						
Illiterate	13	35.1	40	80.0	53	60.9
Literate	24	64.9	10	20.0	34	39.1
Religion						
Islam	35	94.6	48	96.0	83	95.4
Hindu	2	5.4	2	4.0	4	4.6
Living Arrangements						
Living alone	4	10.8	15	30.0	19	21.8
Living with spouse	9	24.3	2	4.0	11	12.6
Living with unmarried children	5	13.5	8	16.0	13	14.9
Living with married children	19	51.4	24	48.0	43	49.4
Living with others	-	-	1	2.0	1	1.1
Family Head						
Male	32	86.5	30	60.0	62	71.3
Female	5	13.5	20	40.0	25	28.7
Family Income						
≤2500	9	24.3	25	50.0	34	39.1
2501 – 5000	11	29.7	14	28.0	25	28.7
5001+	17	45.9	11	22.0	28	32.2
Total	**37**	**100.0**	**50**	**100.0**	**87**	**100.0**

Physical Conditions and Causes behind Elder Abuse

Table 2 shows the self-stated physical conditions and causes behind elder abuse. According to the study respondents, 48 per cent female elderly were unhealthy while the corresponding figure for male was 21.6 per cent. Approximately 67 per cent of the abused had been suffering from some disease or the other, during the six months before the survey.

Table 2 also revealed the viewpoints for being abused. According to the abused elderly, the causes behind the abuse were mainly poverty, inability to do any thing and dependency. They also identifi ed property distribution to the children and their physical illness as causes for getting abusive behaviour.

Table 2 Self-stated Physical Conditions and Reasons for Abuse

Characteristics	Male		Female		Total	
	Freq.	%age	Freq.	%age	Freq.	%age
Present physical condition						
Healthy	13	35.1	9	18.0	22	25.3
Fairly healthy	16	43.2	17	34.0	33	37.9
Unhealthy	8	21.6	24	48.0	32	36.8
Suffered from some disease during last 6 months						
No	13	35.1	16	32.0	29	33.3
Yes	24	64.9	34	68.0	58	66.7
Reasons for abuse — Poverty						
No	18	48.6	15	30.0	33	37.9
Yes	19	51.4	35	70.0	54	62.1
Reasons for abuse— Inability						
No	22	59.5	28	56.0	50	57.5
Yes	15	40.5	22	44.0	37	42.5
Reasons for abuse — Dependency						
No	33	89.2	23	46.0	56	64.4
Yes	4	10.8	27	54.0	31	35.6
Reasons for abuse — Property distribution						
No	35	94.6	46	92.0	81	93.1
Yes	2	5.4	4	8.0	6	6.9
Reasons for abuse — Illness						
No	33	89.2	47	94.0	80	92.0
Yes	4	10.8	3	6.0	7	8.0
Total	37	100.0	50	100.0	87	100.0

Correlation between Score and Reasons for Elder Abouse

Though we observed the cause of elder abuse according to the study respondents in Table 2, in order to find out the degree of the relationship between score (non-dichotomous) and the reasons (dichotomous), point bi-serial correlation was used (see Table 3).

Table 3 Correlation Analysis between Score and the Reasons of Elder Abouse

Reasons	Score		
	Male	Female	Total
Poverty	+0.02	+0.2	+0.13
	(0.937816)	(0.504491)	(0.675498)
Inability	-0.27	-0.15	-0.19
	(0.417363)	(0.620129)	(0.541560)
Dependency	**-0.62**	+0	-0.29
	(0.042601)	(0.992200)	(0.343451)
Property Distribution	-0.52	-0.41	-0.45
	(0.100496)	(0.149505)	(0.109241)
Illness	**-0.54**	-0.43	**-0.46**
	(0.067508)	(0.124853)	**(0.097033)**

Notes: Parentheses indicate the p-value .

From Table 3 we observed that score is positively related with poverty but negatively with other reasons for all respondents, except the dependency for female elderly. Remarkably, we found dependency and illness for male and illnesses for total respondents are significantly related with the score of elder abuse.

Determinats of Elder Abuse: Application of GLM Univariate Analysis of variance

Considering the score of elder abuse as dependent variable and Q12, Q30, Q37 and Q38 as covariates we determine the factors important for elder abuse where Q4 is treated as random factor and Q10 as fi xed factor. The results are presented in Tables 4, 5 and 6 for male, female and total respondents respectively.

Table 4 Effects for Male Dependent Variable: SCORE

Source	Type III	Sum of Squares	df	Mean Square	F	Sig.
Intercept	Hypothesis	29.664	1	29.664	0.118	0.735
	Error	4499.476	17.873	251.744		
Q12	**Hypothesis**	**2790.907**	**1**	**2790.907**	**11.234**	**0.004**
	Error	3975.000	16	248.438		
Q30	Hypothesis	11.523	1	11.523	0.046	0.832
	Error	3975.000	16	248.438		
Q37	**Hypothesis**	**915.442**	**1**	**915.442**	**3.685**	**0.073**
	Error	3975.000	16	248.438		
Q38	Hypothesis	22.785	1	22.785	0.092	0.766
	Error	3975.000	16	248.438		
Q10	Hypothesis	4073.090	3	1357.697	2.368	0.186
	Error	2909.663	5.075	573.351		
Q4	Hypothesis	2772.991	9	308.110	0.507	0.821
	Error	2839.821	4.669	608.241		
Q10 * Q4	**Hypothesis**	**2757.546**	**4**	**689.387**	**2.775**	**0.063**
	Error	3975.000	16	248.438		

Notes: Q4 = educational qualification, Q10 = living arrangements, Q12 = family head, Q30 = family's monthly income, Q37 = present physical condition, Q38 = suffer from any disease during last 6 months.

The more important fi ndings from Table 4 revealed that family headship, present physical condition and the interaction between living arrangement and educational qualifi cation of the elder are signifi cantly related with elder abuse, i.e., score of elder abuse. But we did not get any signifi cant factor for female elder abuse in Table 5. In Table 6, for total elderly we again found that interaction between living arrangement and educational qualifi cation is a signifi cant factor for elder abuse. In addition we identifi ed suffering from any disease during the six months before the survey, as an important factor for elder abuse for total respondents

Conclusion and Policy Recommendations

Though most of the abuse will remain unreported because people are too frightened, ashamed or embarrassed to bring it to light, we found out that

Table 5 Effects for Female Dependent Variable: SCORE

Source		Type III Sum of Squares	df	Mean Square	F	Sig.
Intercept	Hypothesis	1118.064	1	1118.064	4.906	0.035
	Error	6646.901	29.165	227.910		
Q12	Hypothesis	.653	1	.653	0.003	0.956
	Error	7346.190	35	209.891		
Q30	Hypothesis	160.494	1	160.494	0.765	0.388
	Error	7346.190	35	209.891		
Q37	Hypothesis	44.266	1	44.266	0.211	0.649
	Error	7346.190	35	209.891		
Q38	Hypothesis	121.797	1	121.797	0.580	0.451
	Error	7346.190	35	209.891		
Q10	Hypothesis	5201.520	4	1300.380	2.279	0.372
	Error	888.543	1.558	570.489		
Q4	Hypothesis	1719.716	4	429.929	0.876	0.599
	Error	933.131	1.902	490.682		
Q10 * Q4	Hypothesis	949.768	2	474.884	2.263	0.119
	Error	7346.190	35	209.891		

Table 6 Effects for Total Dependent Variable: SORE

Source		Type III Sum of Squares	df	Mean Square	F	Sig.
Intercept	**Hypothesis**	**1709.106**	**1**	**1709.106**	**6.640**	**0.012**
	Error	18301.687	71.104	257.395		
Q12	Hypothesis	409.946	1	409.946	1.613	0.209
	Error	15248.048	60	254.134		
Q30	Hypothesis	25.517	1	25.517	0.100	0.752
	Error	15248.048	60	254.134		
Q37	Hypothesis	2.591	1	2.591	0.010	0.920
	Error	15248.048	60	254.134		
Q38	**Hypothesis**	**813.880**	**1**	**813.880**	**3.203**	**0.079**
	Error	15248.048	60	254.134		
Q10	Hypothesis	4985.188	4	1246.297	2.270	0.140
	Error	4990.304	9.090	548.978		
Q4	Hypothesis	2459.806	11	223.619	0.438	0.905
	Error	5290.982	10.366	510.414		
Q10*Q4	**Hypothesis**	**4593.657**	**7**	**656.237**	**2.582**	**0.021**
	Error	15248.048	60	254.134		

87 abused elderly out of 495 aged 60+ years, i.e., 17 per cent. It was also found that most of the abused elderly were young old. Females who were widows and illiterate were more vulnerable to abuse.

It is obvious from the study that elder abuse has to be taken as an urgent issue. The overall fi nding seems to suggest a close relationship of abuse with the family head, his physical condition, living arrangements and educational background and this piece of information needs to be scientifi cally utilized in developing suitable programmes addressing the elderly in the country. The government really needs to introduce various social packages for the elderly, apart from increasing the literacy level and employment opportunities for the aged, making the older persons real assets rather than liabilities.

References

AOA (1998). *The National Elder Abuse Incidence Study*: final report. Washington, DC 7.

Kosberg, J.L. and J.L. Gracia (1995). Elder abuse: International and cross-cultural perspectives. *Journal of Elder Abuse and Neglect*, Special Issue 6 (3 and 4): 1–12.

Lachs, M.S., C. Williams, S. O'Brien et al. (1997). Risk factors for reported elder abuse and neglect: A nine year observational cohort study. *Gerontologist* 37: 469–74.

Paveza, G.J., D. Cohen, C. Eisdorfer et al. (1992). Severe family violence and Alzheimer's disease: Prevalence and risk factors. *Gerontologist* 32: 493–97.

Pillemer, K. and K. Tinkelhor (1987). Domestic violence against the elderly: A discussion paper. In *Encyclopedia of ageing*, New York: Springer Publishing Company.

Pillemer, K. and D. Finkelhor (1988). The prevalence of elder abuse: A random sample survey. *Gerontologist* 28: 51.

Wolf, R. (1997). Elder abuse and neglect: Causes and consequences. *J Geriatr Psychiatry* 30: 153–74.

21

Critical Understanding of Prevalence of Elder Abuse and the Combating Strategies with Specific Reference to India

Mala Kapur Shankardass

In India, as in many other developing countries, traditionally the responsibility of taking care of older persons and protecting them, falls on individuals in the family and the community. Yet, family and community are now increasingly being viewed as shying away from their role of 'caring for elders' and are being held responsible for perpetuating elder abuse, neglect and violence, even though defining these words is controversial. Indeed, there is no consensus about the definition of 'elder abuse'. Its meaning is still rather obscure with regard to its forms and the settings in which it occurs.

Many families, certain community and religious leaders as well as politicians claim that while occasional neglect of older people and crime against them may occur in Indian society, or old parents may at times be disrespected, but historically and at present there is no substantial evidence to treat 'abuse' of old parents and elders in the family and the community as a major social problem. They argue that 'elder abuse' equated with very violent physical behaviour is a concept associated with Western societies. It is asserted that 'abuse' is a strong word for behaviour or action that does not generally happen to older people in 'our' society, in 'our' families and communities as there is practice of taking care of elders by families—near and distant, or religious bodies, philanthropic individuals, charitable agencies and government as well as community-based organizations (WHO, 2002; Shankardass, 2003[b]).

In fact, there is a history of old age homes, *ashrams* (residential place provided by a religious or philanthropic group for individuals without family members), in other words, there are institutions which provide care to older people when it is non available from kith and kin (Shankardass, 2000). In general, as is often stated in public discourses, Indians show reverence to older people implicitly or explicitly in various ways, despite certain plays, films, and fiction over the years depicting neglect of older parents by sons, daughters-in-law, even daughters and grand children.

There is also the recent legislation promoted by the government, namely, the the Maintenance and Welfare of Parents and Senior Citizens Bill which provides an understanding of 'elder abuse' in the Indian context, without actually defining it. The legislation, popularly called as the Maintenance Bill, was approved by the Cabinet in December 2007. It is viewed as a social welfare mechanism to protect adults, parents and 'senior citizens', defined as 60 years of age or older. It refers to the challenges being posed in society in the context of care of the growing number of older people and the declining ability of families, communities and governments to deal with the issues. It views neglect of older people as a concern and its understanding in terms of mistreatment is similar to that voiced by the World Health Organization (WHO, 2002), where it is seen as a manifestation of the timeless phenomenon of interpersonal violence, but only now in the 21st century is it achieving due recognition. Clearly, perceptions and definitions of abuse/neglect of older persons and violence against them vary in time and place and between groups across and within families, communities, classes and societies.

Understanding through Definitions, Typology and Contextualization

Report of the Secretary General of United Nations on Abuse of Older Persons (2002) submitted to the Commission for Social Development which acted as the preparatory committee for Second World Assembly on Ageing stated that there is lack of clear and transposable definitions in both developed and developing countries. Yet, there is global evidence of abuse of older persons based on studies conducted in the past 20 years.

There is documentation of older people's perception and experience of abuse which encompasses neglect, violence, maltreatment, exploitation, deprivation, abandonment, etc., though there is deficiency of reliable and valid data and also there are shortcomings of methodology in documentation. Nonetheless, internationally growing attention to human rights and increasing awareness of the rights of older men and women have led to viewing abuse of older persons as a human rights issue, a framework appropriate to view elder abuse as a political, economic, social and health concern requiring adequate and effective combating strategies. Indeed, older persons' vulnerability to abuse may increase when their rights as guaranteed in international covenants and embodied in the United Nations Principles for Older Persons are violated. Thus, if older person's, independence, participation, care, self-fulfilment and dignity are hampered and they are denied choices and opportunities, then indications of abusive practices against older people are prevalent and we need to document it by establishing valid and robust definitions which provide a better knowledge base for developing strategies to combat it.

Significantly, 'elder abuse' as a term does not find place in the dictionary. But, due to concern with issues of care of older persons, and probably because of growing evidence of abuse of older persons, the term 'elder care' has gained popularity and is getting included as a specific new agenda in policies and programmes across the countries. In 2004, Oxford, the most trusted name in references, included 'elder care' in its publication on 'New Words'. This is a volume of record of words for which no dictionary at hand provides any help. But, due to public comprehension of words, they survive, gain importance and get defined by lexicographers as a response to changes in human activities over a period of time (Hargraves, 2004). Preoccupation of our times with care of older people and rather growing lack of it resulting in abuse/neglect of older people gives recognition to the word 'elder care' in the context of its usage and general currency across the world. It sets the ground for outlining the rights of older people in matters of their independence, participation, care, self-fulfilment and dignity, i.e., the UN Principles for Older Persons.

In India, as in many other parts of the world, there is growing evidence that 'elder care' defined in the *Dictionary of New Words* as "care of the elderly or infirm, provided by residential institutions, by paid daily help in the home, or by family members" is increasingly lacking or is inadequate and inappropriate. As few studies conducted since the 1990s, the years since when the subject started to receive substantial research attention (Padmasree, 1991; Mahajan, 1992; Shah et al., 1995; Bambawale, 1996, 1997; Vaithi, 1996; Dandekar, 1997; Ushasree and Basha, 1999; Bakshi, 2000; Mehta, 2000; Bose and Shankardass, 2004, Puri, 2004; Shankardass, 2002, 2003[a] & [b], 2004), and my ongoing research on older people residing in institutions and at home indicates that often their health, emotional, financial and social needs are not met and consequently they feel neglected, abandoned, disrespected, maltreated, threatened, exploited and emotionally blackmailed.

The recent legislation, The Maintenance and Welfare of Parents and Senior Citizens Bill, is also based on the premise that there may be children, biological or adopted or grand children who fail in caring for their aged parent/grandparent (GoI, 2007). The Bill, strives for ensuring financial, emotional and social security to the 'uncared' senior citizens by their families (Shankardass, 2007). The Maintenance Bill, which was in its formulating stage termed as The Older Persons (Maintenance, Care and Health) Bill, observed that even if parents are residing with children, recent trends of erosion of values of respect for senior citizens, changing roles and lifestyles at the household and work level, shortage of space in residential dwellings in urban areas, and emergence of greater emphasis on 'individualism' by the children, is leading to severance of family ties and parents being deprived of their culturally accepted dependency on children, resulting in growing financial and social insecurity among the older people (GoI, 2005). The National Policy on Older Persons announced in 1999 also acknowledged these changes which are leading to a number of senior citizens being left to live alone, with insufficient resources to meet even their most basic requirements of food, clothing, housing and medical care.

The *Oxford Dictionary* (2006) defines 'abuse' as treatment with cruelty or violence, for a bad purpose, addressing in an insulting and offensive way. Other dictionaries, for instance, Webster's include in the meaning of abuse also reproach, to disparage a person in the most violent terms, to take unfair or undue advantage of, to injure, hurt and damage and treat without consideration or fairness, to be physically harmful and maltreat. Clearly, the ever present face of violence, both overt and covert, physical and non-physical, generally associated with abuse of women and children, now also has overwhelming influence on our understanding of abuse of older people. 'Neglect' in contrast is seen as careless behaviour resulting in failure to give proper attention to care, which may result in isolation and social exclusion without any strong social censure. This may include self neglect, a set of behaviours that threaten the health and safety of an older person and lead to limited capacity for self care and health seeking behaviour. Significantly, the legislation The Maintenance and Welfare of Parents and Senior Citizens Bill intends to protect adults, parents and 'senior citizens' from neglect by their children (GoI, 2007), but does not mention the term abuse. Also, while it outlines besides families, the role of old age homes and hospitals in providing for elderly care, the Bill does not consider the possibility of institutional abuse, which is increasingly being associated with institutional care provisions in countries where it is available.

A typology of elder abuse that has gained ground universally, identifies four categories of abuse, namely, physical, emotional, financial exploitation, and neglect (Tatara, 1995; United Nations, 2002; WHO/INPEA, 2002). In recent times, sexual abuse, spousal abuse and medication abuse have been expanded in the typology (Shankardass, 1997; Ushasree and Basha, 1999; DWARF, 2002, 2003). Scientific literature recognizes also other specific forms of elder abuse, primarily, loss of respect, scapegoating—identifying and blaming older people, usually women, for ills befalling the community. In India and in many other third world countries incidents have been reported about older women, generally widows being ostracized, tortured, maimed or even killed in order to gain control over their assets [Shankardass, 2003(b); Puri, 2007].

Development agenda (United Nations, 1995), in particular, voices the need for identifying also systemic abuse as a form of elder abuse in so far as there is marginalization of older persons in institutions, or by social and economic policies and their implementation, and leads to inequitable resource allocation and discrimination in service provisions and delivery. This form of abuse becomes specifically significant with reference to ageing societies such as India.

In the first ever united work on elder abuse undertaken by the international community including World Health Organization (WHO), International Network for Prevention of Elder Abuse (INPEA), HelpAge International and researchers, scholars from academic institutions in a range of countries, namely Argentina, Austria, Brazil, Canada, India,

Kenya, Lebanon and Sweden it is recognized that elder abuse is perceived by older people under three broad areas: (1) neglect including isolation, abandonment and social exclusion; (2) violation of human, legal and medical rights; and (3) deprivation of choices, decisions, status, finances and respect. All of this in some form or the other occurs in both developing and developed countries across the continents.

Recent studies on marginalization of older people have also documented instances of elder neglect and abuse emerging from political violence, armed conflict, displacement, disasters and emergencies, whereby needs of older people are rarely provided for in relief plans and rehabilitation programmes. A review of recent disaster management programmes in India indicated that during earthquakes and tsunami, higher proportions of older people were left out from aid provisions as few agencies at the national and community level included them in the target population for assistance (Shankardass, 2005). Significantly, the 11th Five-Year Plan as part of its development agenda identifies an inclusive approach and notes the vulnerability of older people along with other groups, which require special attention.

United Nations, after taking into account variations in the definition of elder abuse among the member countries, adopts an approach based on the British Charity Action on Abuse of Older Persons which reads as "a single or repeated act, or lack of appropriate action occurring within any relationship where there is an expectation of trust, which causes harm or distress to an older person" (United Nations, 2002). The critical level of defining elder abuse in such a manner lies in the socio-cultural understanding of its experience both at the level of the individual and the social group. Importantly, the break down of 'trust' can occur within family, community and institutional settings, through social interactions, contractual relationships or those established even with intruders. Such an understanding facilitates recognition of elder abuse in diverse forms as economic, social, community and political violence against older people, provided greater attention is paid to its manifestations. Recognition of indicators and manifest effects of abuse are essential for detecting elder abuse, which in turn reveals its prevalence.

Detection Necessary for Understanding Prevalence

While theoretically abuse can be easily classified in terms of neglect, violation and deprivation, the problem in understanding it comes when we try to identify its occurrence, relate it with the reporting mechanisms and seek justice for the grieved party. The question arises, what kind of behaviour and action can be termed as abuse and how can it be detected, given the variability of factors in providing care, such as poverty, lack of education and awareness of old age problems, economic and social constraints. Gender inequality and structural disadvantages seen in many developing societies, including India add another aspect which requires consideration in our understanding of prevalence of elder abuse. Further, if we include certain societal forms of deprivations and violations of rights associated with older persons without governments and communities and at times older persons themselves perceiving them as abuse, we confront terminological confusion.

Problems with detecting 'elder abuse' relates to lack of clarity about its definition and this arises from the fact that in our country the issue is still under recognized and not sufficiently acknowledged as a societal concern. For any consensus on the definition, it is essential that 'elder abuse' be first recognized as a social problem of significance. In the UK and European countries, reference to the problem of elder abuse started to appear around the 1970s (Burston, 1975), and later through the seminal work of Mervyn Eastman (1984) the issue received attention for developing socio-political and legislative action to tackle abuse. In America, even though little legislative attention has been paid to the social problem of elder abuse at the federal level (Brownell, 2003), there exists some amount of terminological understanding. It is defined in terms of its physical, financial or psychological impact (Wolf and Pillemer, 1984), as mistreatment (Hudson, 1989) or active even passive neglect or self neglect. In Australia, abuse and neglect of older people by family members started and soon there was a confirmation of it as a social, medical and legal problem in both residential care and the community (Kurrle, 2003).

In India, as per review of research studies, articles and books, 'elder abuse' as an academic concern started to surface in the 1990s though as a subject worthy of serious inquiry and concerted action, it has begun to receive attention only at the turn to the 21st century when the rapidly growing numbers and proportions of older persons in the populations are gradually being acknowledged as a significant group having rights, requiring care, services and programmes for living a life of dignity and respect (Shankardass, 2003[b]).

In India, as it is in all other societies too, elder abuse is difficult to document and quantify since it occurs primarily in the privacy of the home. Reporting system for elder abuse was almost absent till recently. The police as its drive to combat crime against older people have improved mechanisms to report and record cases of elder abuse and neglect. The Maintenance Bill gives power to third party to report neglect of older people and the tribunals set up to deal with maintenance issues can take action without any plea from the victims of such neglect.

In terms of neglect of older people, elder abuse and violence against older persons, invariably it is seen that while neglect gets ignored by the concerned parties (Shankardass, 2003[a], [b]), abuse and violence against older people "may become known to authorities through a third party" (Mahajan and Madhurima, 1995). But, by and large, cases of abuse have often gone unnoticed and unreported, with only the most severe cases commanding attention. There is no mandatory mechanism to report mistreatment, neglect or abuse of older people in Indian society unlike in some western countries. Older people are reluctant to speak of their trauma of violence, abuse and neglect and a concern with the family's reputation coupled with dependence on those who may be abusive and violent but supposedly responsible for taking care, restricts them from acknowledging it publicly, especially in the case of women and those living in institutions. In fact, those experiencing and observing it remain generally silent and indifferent. Researchers have faced difficulties in discussing the subject with respondents as often there is persistent denial by family members that abuse takes place in their homes. Many people deny its existence, or camouflage it with other terms considered to be less severe. As a result, there is absence of valid statistics and systematic collection of facts related to the problem. The limited studies conducted are small scale, thus there is inadequate documentation notwithstanding lack of conceptual and definitional clarity. Definitional dispute about what may constitute abuse is linked to the fact of its obscurity. Consequently, it is difficult to accurately measure the national extent of the problem.

How Prevailing is the Problem

Based on certain studies on elder abuse conducted in India UN Secretary General in the report presented at the Second World Assembly (United

Nations, 2002) revealed that in a sample of 1,000 older persons, 4 per cent claimed to be physically abused and in another smaller sample of 50 persons aged 70 years and over living in an urban area, 20 per cent said they had been neglected in their households. There are estimates that elder abuse in India, in all communities and across all sections of the society, is on the rise. Increasing media coverage, stories filed by journalists (Verma, 1996; Mitra, 1998; Paul, 1998), newspaper clippings (Menon, 1998; Martyris, 1999; Mehta, 2000; Sharma, 2001; Sangwan, 2004; Shoma, 2004; *Hindustan Times Metro*, 2006; Gomes, 2006; Choks, 2008), TV coverage in serials, discussions and news, films, literary stories, some published autobiographical account, small scale qualitative studies (Mahajan, 1992; Vaithi, 1996; Bambawale, 1997; Prasad, 1997; Shankardass, 1997, 2002, 2004; Ushasree and Basha, 1999), and NGO activities[1] directed towards addressing the multitude of issues related to the abuse, all depict abuse of older persons in some form or the other.

There is also now increasing evidence from crime records and court proceedings which indicate that elder abuse is no longer a hushed affair. Older people who, because of question of family shame and regard for their adult children, were earlier suffering in silence are gradually coming out in the public with their 'horror and disgraceful' stories, their loss of dignity. For instance, Senior's Cell at police headquarters in Delhi in June 2007 reported to be on a daily contact with 50 senior citizens through their helpline and analysis of distress calls made by older people in 2006 and half year of 2007 revealed 4 per cent complains related to property and tenant dispute, 7 per cent to harassment by other people other than family, 39 per cent complained of family disputes, 7 per cent sought police assistance, 12 per cent complained of public nuisance in neighbourhood, 2 per cent had problems with civic agencies and the rest were termed as miscellaneous (Singh, 2007). An analysis of actual complaints received at the Cell indicated 43 per cent older people having disputes with family members, 11 per cent with neighbours, and other 11 per cent were threatened or harassed by others, 4 per cent complained about being cheated, while another 4 per cent complained about disputes with tenants or landlord and 8 per cent had property disputes with others. Similarly, 8 per cent had complained about problems with authorities and 8 per cent complaints were termed as miscellaneous, while 2 per cent were against police assistance.

Evidence of growing incidence and prevalence is also being estimated by increase of old age homes and demand for institutional care and care providers/givers from outside the family. Institutional provisions in the form of old age homes are no longer viewed as unacceptable places as they were before and are now being seen as possible alternative and necessity by some older people and their families (Flash, 2001; Chauhan, 2006). The emerging concept of senior citizens complexes or retirement retreats is a testimony to this growing phenomenon. However, this raises another dimension of elder abuse, so far overlooked, that is, of elder abuse in community and institutional settings and this has emerged as a growing concern in India.

Some though point out that even in the past there were instances of marginalization of older persons, of neglect and deprivation, but these were rare and generally associated with lower economic strata. In fact for some, the practice of older persons retiring to ashrams was not always because of choice and it would be wrong to assume that it was only for religious considerations. As observed the idea of renouncing the world, isolating oneself from worldly goods, possessions, relations, etc., is probably due to lack of connectedness with the family, community and other agencies in the society (Shankardass, 2000).

Certain reports from different parts of the country characterize neglect/abuse as habitual scolding, nagging, non-communication, as well as feigned ignorance about their needs and ailments, material and sexual exploitation [Bambawale, 1997; Bose and Shankardass, 2004; Dandekar, 1996; Karlekar, Agarwal and Ganjoo, 1995; Karlekar, 2003; Mehta, 2000; Shankardass, 1997, 2002, 2003(a), (b)]. A report brought out by the women's organization *Karmika* argues that many forms of neglect/abuse could be sometimes worse than physical injury (MARG, 1996).

Some of these studies also indicate the experience of physical assault by older people. Media reports in the last few years, 2000 onwards in particular, point towards the existence of many forms of abuse of older persons, including physical, emotional, psychological, financial, spousal and sexual abuse. Newspaper reporting on an elderly person or a couple being murdered or thrown out of the house, deprived of their property and income are now almost a regular feature in national dailies. Material exploitation at the societal level and also in the family is the commonest type of abuse of the elderly which is reported by the media and also seen through crime record reports.

My research with older people has many narrations of elder abuse living in difficult situations and being constantly exposed to abusive environments. Some older people have stated on a few occasions to being hit, or more specifically slapped, by their sons, daughters-in-law and even daughters. A few narrate, things being thrown at them when they have not done as desired by their children. Instances of burning, scalding, being pushed around have also been narrated. A few narrate being pushed around and experiencing rough handling. Spitting on them is a common expression of showing disregard. The threat of being physically assaulted is faced by many older people in vulnerable situations. It is a step adopted by children for making the old parents do something against their wishes. There are narratives of older persons being excessively restrained through various means from doing things undesired by their children. Many older persons experience undue pressure to do things against their wishes. Controlling the older person from spending the money or participating in activities according to their own wishes is another form of abusive behaviour experienced. In more subtle forms abuse is visible in the form of putting the health of the older person at risk and many older people do not realize this. Another form of abuse is when poor or limited care is provided for the older person. There are also narrations of older persons from different socio-economic groups experiencing on a regular or occasional basis, humiliating behaviour. They are forced to eat unappetizing/unwanted food and often treated like a servant. Also in certain cases when old parents are hospitalized, there is failure to serve appetizing, nutritious food and provide adequate personal care. Some experience excessive physical restraints, for instance, not letting them move out of the room, or in some cases medications are administered to subdue them so that they do not make any demands and remain tucked away in a corner.

Also a few NGOs, for instance, Development, Welfare and Research Foundation (DWARF, 2002, 2003), working with older people have documented stories, experiences of physical assault, material exploitation, verbal humiliation, excessive restraint, putting older persons' health at risk, poor or no care, putting undue pressure on the older persons, and exposing them to humiliating behaviour, institutionalizing them on the face of it for their benefit but actually putting them in another kind of abusive environment. Studies of old age homes indicate that older people residing there, are seldom visited by family members, and trained staff to take care are not available. Many old age homes are seen to be lacking in meeting the needs of older people, especially in terms of long term and acute care (Dandekar, 1996; Shankardass, 2000).

While it is true that in India there is little well documented and statistically analysed national level information on attitudes and behaviour of young people in families and communities at large towards older people, a few studies on family inter and intra generational relationships, support networks and review of concerns emerging out of ageing of the population (Shankardass and Kumar, 1996; Bose and Shankardass, 2004; Karlekar, 1995, 2003; Puri, 2004; Shankardass, 1996, 1998, 1999) establish that a situation of dependency on the younger generation is a risk factor for neglect and in some cases, ill-treatment, and different forms of violence against older people in all kinds of settings, for instance, in families, communities, neighbourhoods, and in institutions.

Government Recognition of the Issue of Elder Abuse

The National Policy on Older Persons formulated in January 1999 by the Ministry of Social Justice and Empowerment does not refer specifically to the incidence and prevalence of elder abuse, but does acknowledge it as a concern which emerges due to "pressures and fissures in living arrangements of older persons" as a consequence of demographic ageing of the population in the country (GoI, 1999). The policy, on the one hand, under the section on implications of demographic trends, which are seen at the macro and the household level, stresses that family ties in India are strong with an overwhelming majority of older persons living with their sons or being supported by them and also that working couples find the presence of old parents emotionally bonding and of great help in managing the household and caring for children. It, nonetheless, acknowledges that due to the operation of several forces, the position of a large number of older persons has become vulnerable. They cannot take it for granted that their children will be able to look after them when they need care in old age, especially in view of the longer life span implying an extended period of dependency and higher costs to meet health and other needs (para 10).

Further, the policy document outlines: "Much higher costs of bringing up and educating children and pressures for gratification of their own desires affects the transfer of a share of income for the care of the parents." In understanding the changes in values and lifestyles which impact the lives of older persons negatively, the policy refers to shortage of space in dwellings in urban areas and high rents whereby migrants prefer to leave their parents in their native place. It further elaborates, "Changing roles and expectations of women, their concept of privacy and space, desire not to be encumbered by caring responsibilities of old people for long periods, career ambitions, and employment outside the home implies considerably reduced time for care giving. Also, adoption of small family norm by a growing number of people implies the availability of fewer caregivers especially since in an increasing number of families, daughters, too, are fully occupied, pursuing their educational or work career". The concern in the policy is more visible with regard to the older women as attention is brought to their greater vulnerability as single individuals since few people are willing to take care of non-lineal relatives, especially widows who have no independent source of income, do not own assets and are totally dependent (para 11).

Even after considering the strains and constrains in family relationships and its impact on the care of older persons, the policy document advocates for the care of older people by families and outlines certain modalities for supporting the care mechanisms in the community. The Policy Statement under the section on 'Principal Areas of Intervention and Action Strategies' refers to assisting voluntary organizations and associations of older persons in providing protective services and help to older persons through helpline services, legal aid and other measures. Further, it directs the police to keep a vigil on older couples and more specifically on old single persons, especially those living alone, and to strengthen the neighbourhood watch system. It however does not outline the mechanisms by which there could be institutionalization of processes through which primary service systems relevant to the prevention, early detection and intervention of elder abuse or neglect or mistreatment, whatever may be the term, can be put in place to serve older adults and their families. It nonetheless takes recourse in suggesting a legal framework for tackling deprivation and exploitation of older people.

The Policy Statement under section 'Principal Areas of Intervention and Action Strategies' notes that "old persons have become soft targets for criminal elements". It gives a hope of combating the problem by providing under the section on 'Protection of Life and Property' a promise for the introduction of a clause in the Indian Penal Code which shall protect older persons from domestic violence, specifically in the context of deprivation of their rights of inheritance, occupancy, etc.

In recent times, legislation on domestic violence has been put in place after recognizing that statistics of crime are irrefutably confirming that women, including those who are older, are victims of domestic violence. Certain social scientists have also documented older women as victims of domestic violence (Shankardass, 1997). While the Protection of Women from Domestic Violence Act, 2005 which was passed by the Lok Sabha on 24th August, 2005 and by Rajya Sabha on 29th August, 2005 and it received the assent of the President of India on 13th September 2005 to come on the Statute Book as Act 43 of 2005, in spirit and intent, is for the protection of women, it also recognizes violence towards older persons, which occur in the context of a breakdown in social relations between persons and their family. These are manifested through a continuum of multiple and often inter-related factors. It can vary from the most private, in spaces of domestic and matrimonial relationships, considered distinctly sacred (Jaising and Sakhrani, 2007). The Protection of Women from Domestic Violence Act enacted in 2005 is a law specifically meant to address the issue of domestic violence by providing for civil relief with a view to ensuring immediate and emergency relief to those facing violence in intimate relationships.

Significantly, the Planning Commission of India, in the 11th Five-Year Plan, recognizes the marginalization of older persons and consequently recommends a specific Health Care Plan for the Elderly, which could reduce their neglect and abuse in society. It calls for the training of medical and nursing professionals, para-medicals and other categories of caregivers in geriatrics in order to provide for the growing need for such services. It also suggests opening of geriatric clinics and hospitals in cities and at the district level. Lack of health care provisions makes older people vulnerable to neglect, mistreatment and abuse.

Clearly, in India, as in many other countries, there is age discrimination, the usual low pensions, marginalization of older people due to structural adjustment programmes in social and economic policy, and all these do result in violation of human rights and socio-economic deprivations. A significant issue is—will the neglect, isolation and deprivation of older people resulting out of these factors be termed as 'abuse' and our societies as 'abusive environments'? If so, what models do we adopt to combat abuse and reduce abusive conditions, when the word 'abusive' as an adjective includes in its meaning, improper use or action, tending to deceive, cheat, damage, weaken, be physically injurious and also involve illegality, besides employing harsh insulting language.

Addressing the Issue of Elder Abuse: Some Dilemmas

Understanding the prevalence of abuse is linked to identifying the different systems in which this social problem is addressed. For instance, if we define elder abuse within the parameters of social service system response then the growth of agencies on ageing, such as not-for-profit community-based services to older adults and increased provisions for adult protective service programmes mandated by state can provide us clue about its incidence and prevalence. Similarly, if we regard abuse as a mental health issue, then growth and utilization of counselling centres, training programmes, stress relief interventions can provide indications about abuse. Similarly if we view abuse as a legal issue, the response from the criminal justice system, the police, the courts, lawyers, judges, etc. become our guide to understand the incidence and prevalence of abuse, whichever way it is defined.

Each system, social services, health and criminal justice system, under which we define and give form to understanding abuse, generates its own remedies. The social services system tackles strained relationships but has limited powers to protect older victims who are mentally or physically impaired and are refused care. Health and mental care systems provide medical and psychiatric care to impaired older adults, but may not be prepared to diagnose stress-related health problems or undernourishment among older patients as related to psychological or financial abuse. The criminal justice system may generate legal remedies, but be unprepared for or unaware of the social consequence of these remedies (Shankardass, 2007). For example, a legal solution of older people separating from their adult children is probably not the answer to tackle their requirement for care.

In addition to differing categories of elder abuse, and different service systems serving older adults and their families that may come into contact with elder abuse and neglect, there are also two primary settings in which abuse or neglect can occur, each with its own legislative and reporting mandates, remedies and constraints. These are domestic or community settings and institutional settings. For instance, institutional abuse is tackled legally in terms of the liability of those who organize and run institutions/old age homes with an obligation to care for the residents. However, there is little awareness about the fact that institutions involved with caring for older persons do have legal liability and obligation to perform their task through the Indian Contract Act 1872 and the Law of "Torts" whereby, for any mistreatment and failure in caring, a civil suit can be filed against the management of the institution for the breach in contract to care, even though there might not be a written contract and damages can be claimed for the wrong done (Bakshi, 2000; Shankardass, 2003 [b]). Institutions for meeting the needs of older persons have not so far been brought under legal purview in order to alleviate elder abuse but there is need to take seriously the provision in the Indian Penal Code under which breach of contract may attract criminal liability (DWARF, 2002).

Professionals working with elder abuse victims and their families are challenged to confront professional ethical mandates to respect the autonomy of their clients or patients. For instance, while providing service such as counselling it might not be within the mandate of the professional or the concerned organization to report the case of abuse to the police. The professional can only advise and suggest reporting to police as a remedial action but it is the prerogative of the victim to take action. The state is judicious in defining the circumstances in which and the extent to which it can intervene into the private lives of individuals and families. Two areas of intervention legislated to date are: (1) when a serious crime has been committed against one family member by another, and (2) when victims lack the capacity to protect themselves from harm. Overriding the autonomy of unimpaired abuse victims because of their age alone is a matter of serious consideration for professionals and lawmakers. However, not to attempt to prevent or detect at an early stage suspected or known instances of elder abuse is also troubling, particularly for those in the helping professions.

Prevention Programme Models

While there are difficulties in establishing a nationally uniform response system to elder abuse and neglect as a significant social problem of concern, some innovative elder abuse prevention programmes and initiatives can be developed within social service, health and mental health, and criminal justice frames.

- Community-based services for older people including nutrition programmes, transportation, case management, selected home care, information and referral, advocacy, and other services intended to empower older people to be self-directing for as long as possible can be useful.
- Public education campaigns that define elder abuse and neglect and explain how older adults can protect themselves from abuse and neglect have an important role to play.
- Developing caregivers' support programmes which are intended to educate and provide emotional support to caregivers of older people can help prevent abuse and neglect.
- Establishing 'Respite Care' services to enable caregivers to get a break from the pressure of caregiving, particularly if the older adult being cared for, is an Alzheimer's patient, can help to prevent abuse and neglect.
- Encouraging counselling for family members who may have unresolved conflicts with older adult family members and are at risk of becoming abusive is a necessary tool to prevent abuse and neglect.
- In the health care field elder abuse prevention can be prompted by initiatives, such as, education of physicians and nurses on elder abuse and abuse prevention. It is important that the health care system develop and implement prevention strategies as well as detection and intervention strategies to address elder abuse and neglect among patients.
- Preventive criminal justice programmes can include distribution of handbooks that include information on older peoples' rights as a means for elder abuse prevention.
- The courts can become active in fraud and abuse prevention by tackling cases in time, without delay.
- Community policing initiatives have been developed that target prevention of elder abuse that rises to the level of a crime and these need to be strengthened and have wider coverage.
- In some states, legislations have been passed to strengthen state-based elder abuse prevention efforts. These need to be encouraged in other states too.

- But more than legislations, community education programmes can be effective in prevention of abuse and neglect.
- Finally, to extend the service needs of elder abuse victims beyond the traditional ageing service networks.

Conclusion

If combating elder abuse is the goal, which is increasingly being recognized by societies, then the target of services must be extended beyond older people to include the larger networks and community. Education and outreach, and engaging community organizations are essential. Besides, in developing preventive and combating strategies, mechanisms to regulate care and monitor it in the family, community and institutional settings is necessary. What programmes and initiatives can be undertaken requires an understanding within which they can operate. What measures need to be adopted from the social service, health and criminal justice perspectives require outlining and debating upon. The lack of a common definition that transcends the cultural and institutional and boundaries of agencies, institutions, countries and state limits the ability of policymakers, advocates, gerontologists and researchers to understand current trends in elder abuse and neglect. As a result, it is difficult to project future trends, recommend preventive measures, and plan for the kinds of services needed to understand and reduce the prevalence of elder abuse and neglect.

Given the circumstances there is definitely a need for dialogue, consciousness and societal response to tackle the issue of understanding prevalence of elder abuse in India especially since we observe abusive situations in many different settings and circumstances.

Note

1 Many non-government, voluntary and charitable organizations working at national, regional and local levels, for instance, Age Care India; Centre for the Welfare of the Aged; Development, Welfare and Research Foundation; Dignity Dialogue; Harmony Foundation; HelpAge India; Heritage Trust; OutrEach; Indian Gerontological Association etc. have been working for the cause of older persons and bringing about awareness of the issue.

References

Bakshi, P.M. (2000). 'Homes for the aged—legal aspects'. In P.C. Bhatla (ed.), *Lecture Series in Geriatrics*, Health Care Promotion Trust, New Delhi: National Institute of Primary Health Care, pp. 416–17.

Bambawale, Usha (1996). 'Abuse of the Aged.' In V. Kumar (ed.), *Aging: Indian perspectives and global scenario*. New Delhi: AIIMS, 298–302.

——. (1997). 'The abused elderly'. *Indian Journal of Medical Research*, 106, October, pp. 389–95.

Bose, Ashish and Mala Kapur Shankardass (2004). *Growing old in India: Voices reveal and statistics speak*, India: B.R. Publishing Co.

Brownell. 2003, Systems of Prevention and Early Detection of Elder Abuse and Neglect in the United States of America, in *Understanding the Early Detection and Early Intervention in Elder Abuse in Developed and Developing Countries and Efforts to Develop Measures for Combating Elder Abuse in Asian Countries: A Status Report*, Symposists' Papers, The 7th Asia / Oceania Regional Congress of Gerontology, Tokyo, Japan.

Burston, G.R. (1975). 'Granny Battering'. *British Medical Journal*, 3(6) p. 592.

Chauhan, Chetan (2006). 'More and more elders are opting for a happy life independent of their children'. *Hindustan Times*, Tuesday, 13 June.

Choks, Mansi (2008). '92 year old beaten, thrown out of home in Mumbai', *The Times of India*, 6 April.

Dandekar, K. (1996). *The elderly in India*. New Delhi: Sage Publications.

DWARF (2002), *Research brief: Abuse of the elderly—Concerns and response*. Prepared by Mala Kapur Shankardass, New Delhi: Development, Welfare and Research Foundation, November.

——. (2003). *Research brief: Ageing women and abuse—Concerns and Need for Action*, Prepared by Mala Kapur Shankardass, New Delhi: Development, Welfare and Research Foundation, April.

Eastman, Mervyn (1984). *Old age abuse*. London: Age Concern England.

Flash Newspaper. (2001). 'Charity Begins at Home for Old Age Home'. *Neighborhood News*, 28 October–3 November.

GoI (1999). *The National Policy on Older Persons*. Government of India, Ministry of Social Justice and Empowerment, New Delhi.

——. (2005). 'The Older Persons (Maintenance, Care and Health) Bill' http://ncw.nic.in/olderpersonMaintenancebill.pdf.

——. (2007). The Maintenance and Welfare of Parents and Senior Citizens Bill, Bill No. 40 of 2007 as introduced in Lok Sabha.

Gomes. (2006). 'In her last days, family deserted Kaushalya'. *The Times of India*, 26 August.

Hargraves, Orin (ed.), (2004). *New words*. New York: Oxford University Press.

HT Correspondent. (2006). 'Targets at Twilight'. *Hindustan Times, Metro* 26 August.

Hudson, T. (1989). 'An analysis of the concepts of elder mistreatment, abuse and neglect'. *Journal of Elder Abuse and Neglect*, 1, 5–25.

Jaising, Indira and Monica Sakhrani (2007). *Law of domestic violence.* New Delhi: Universal Law Publishing Co. Pvt. Ltd.

Karlekar, Malavika, Anuja Agarwal and Maithali Ganjoo (1995). 'No Safe Spaces', Report on a Workshop on Violence against Women, New Delhi: Centre for Women's Development Studies.

Karlekar, Malavika (2003). 'Domestic Violence'. In Veena Das (ed.), *The Oxford Indian companion to sociology and social anthropolgy.* New York: Oxford University Press.

Kurrle, Susan (2003). The Systems of Prevention and Detection of Abuse in Australia, *Symposists' Papers, Invited Symposia on Elder Abuse*, Executive Editor, Toshio Tatara, *Tokyo International Forum*, Japan.

Mahajan, A. (1992). 'Social dependency and abuse of the elderly'. In P. Krishnan and K. Mahadevan (eds.), *The elderly population in developed and developing world.* New Delhi: B.R. Publishing Corporation, pp. 414–23.

Mahajan, Amarjit and Madhurima (1995). *Family violence and abuse in India.* New Delhi: Deep & Deep Publications.

MARG (1996). *Within four walls: A profile of domestic violence.* New Delhi: Multiple Action Research Group.

Martyris, Nina (1999). 'Help is just a phone-call away'. *The Times of India*, February 28.

Mehta, Rajul (2000). 'Exploitation and neglect are indicators of abuse'. *The Times of India*, January 15.

Menon, Leela (1998). 'In forward-looking Kerala, there is no future for the aged'. *Indian Express*, Special Report.

Mitra, Sumit (1998). 'Old parents unlovingly yours'. *India Today*, July 13.

Padmasree, V. (1991). *A study of incidence of elder abuse and some factors related to abuse.* Unpublished Master Thesis, S.V. University, Tirupati.

Paul, Sumita (1998). 'With a little help from friends'. *The Sunday Times of India*, April 5.

Prasad, B. Devi (1997). 'Elder Abuse and Neglect: A review of research and programs'. Paper presented at the National Seminar on Globalization and the Ageing: Implications for Gerontological Social Work, organized by Tata Institute of Social Sciences and Family Welfare Agency, Mumbai, December 22–24.

Puri, Kiran (2004). Preventing and Managing Neglect of Older People: The Importance of Reducing Burden of Care in Metropolitan Cities. Paper presented at the National Seminar on Abuse of the Elderly, 29–30 November 2004, Thiruvananthapuram.

Puri, Kiran (2007). 'The Maintenance and Welfare of Parents and Senior Citizen's Bill 2007 and the Ageing Women and Widows'. *Research and Development Journal*, Special Edition, Vol. 13, No. 3, October.

Sangwan, Soni (2004). 'Loneliness can be killing for the elderly'. *Hindustan Times*, 26 January.

Shah, Gita, Rosamma Veedon and Sabiha Vasi (1995). 'Elder abuse in India'. *Journal of Elder Abuse and Neglect*, 6, (3 and 4), pp. 101–08.

Shankardass, Mala Kapur (1996). 'Strengthening Care of the Aged in their Family Set-Up'. *Proceedings of the Seminar on Services for the Aged: A National Commitment*, NIPHC and HCPT Publication.

—— (1997). 'The Plight of Older Women: Victims of Domestic Violence'. In K. Bagchi (ed.), *Elderly females in India: Their Status and Suffering*. New Delhi: Society for Gerontological Research and HelpAge India, pp. 79–88.

—— (1998). 'Perspectives on Key Policy Issues Relating to the Elderly'. In *Population Ageing: Improving the Lives of Older Persons*, Report of The ICPD + 5 Technical meeting On Population Aging, UNFPA, Technical and Policy Division, December.

—— (1999). 'Older People and the Family: Focus on Relationships of Restraints and Constraints'. In P.C. Bhatla (ed.), *Planning for a comfortable retirement in old age*. New Delhi: Health Care Promotion Trust Publication.

—— (2000). Societal Response. *Seminar*, 488, April.

—— (2002). 'Voices of older poor in India'. In *Situation and voices: The older poor and excluded in South Africa and India*. Population and Development Strategies Series, 2, UNFPA, New York.

—— (2003[a]). 'Concern for Ageing Women in India'. In *Quarterly Journal of the International Institute on Ageing*, United Nations, Malta, May.

—— 2003[b] 'Combating Elder Abuse in India: An Emerging Social, Legal and Public Health Concern'. In *Understanding the Early Detection and Early Intervention in Elder Abuse in Developed and Developing Countries and Efforts to Develop Measures for Combating Elder Abuse in Asian Countries: A Status Report*, Symposists' Papers, The 7th Asia/Oceania Regional Congress of Gerontology, Tokyo, Japan.

—— (2004). 'Voices Reveal'. In Ashish Bose, and Mala Kapur Shankardass, *Growing old in India: Voices reveal and statistics speak*. New Delhi: B.R. Publishing House

—— (2005). 'Older People and Disaster Management: Risks and Vulnerabilities'. *Meeting nature's upheavals: A holistic look at disaster mitigation*, India Habitat Centre.

—— (2007). 'Maintenance and Welfare Bill, 2007 as Adult Protection Legislation: A Critical Assessment'. *Research and Development Journal*, Special Edition, Vol. 13, No. 3, October.

Shankardass, Mala Kapur and V. Kumar (1996). 'Sociological Analysis of Support Network in Old Age'. In V. Kumar (ed.), *Indian aging: Indian perspective and global scenario.* New Delhi: All India Institute of Medical Sciences.

Sharma, Neeta (2001). 'Son throws out parents from their own house'. *Hindustan Times*, 17 March.

Shoma (2004). 'Aging Parents: A Socio-Legal Problem?' *Alive*, March.

Singh, S.B.K. (2007). Safety and Security of Senior Citizens: Role of Police, paper presented at Second World Elder Abuse Awareness Day (WEAAD) organized by Development, Welfare and Research Foundation (DWARF) and International Network for Prevention of Elder Abuse (INPEA) in New Delhi, India on 15 June.

Tatara, T. (1995). 'Elder Abuse'. In R.L. Edwards (ed.), *Encyclopedia of Social Work*, 19th Edition, Washington, DC: NASW Press, 834–42.

United Nations. (1995). *Report of the World Summit for Social Development*, Copenhagen, UN Publication Sales No. 96, V 8.

—— (2002). Report by United Nations Secretary-General Kofi Annan released at the Second World Assembly on Ageing, Madrid, Spain 8–12 April 2002. Published by the UN Department of Public Information DPI/2264 March 2002.

Ushasree, S. and S. Azmal Basha (1999) 'Domestic abuse among the elderly'. *Indian Journal of Gerontology*, 13 (3 and 4), pp. 99–104.

Vaithi, Savithri (1996). 'Elder Abuse'. Paper presented at the National Workshop on Elder Abuse, organized by the Centre for the Welfare of the Aged (CEWA), Madras, March 16–17.

Verma, C.D. (1996). 'Unwanted both by kin and society'. *Hindustan Times*, June 9.

WHO/INPEA (2002). *Missing Voices: Views of older persons on elder abuse.* Geneva: World Health Organization. WHO/NMH/VIP/02.1WHO/NMH/NPH/02.2.

Wolf, R. and K. Pillemer, (1984). *Working with the abused elderly: Assessment, advocacy and intervention.* Wooster, Massachusetts: University Center on Aging, University of Massachusetts Medical Center.

22

Elder Abuse: Outcome of Changing Family Dynamics

U.C. Jain

The traditional welfare institutions and higher socio-cultural values of Indian society provided respect and care for the elderly people. The aged in the families were generally taken care of, by the family itself (Raju, 2002). But increasing industrialization, modernization and urbanization have had negative impact on the traditional institutions and socio-cultural values of the families (Mishra, 1979). These have resulted in breaking of the joint family system and migration of children in search of jobs leading to the deterioration of the higher socio-cultural values of Indian society, and rapid transition in the structure and functioning of the family.

The structure in the family refers to the type of family (i.e., joint, nuclear and extended) and functioning denotes the dynamics of interaction, interpersonal relations and communication between family members. Healthy interaction between family members leads to healthy relationships created and reinforced by positive communication. But due to structural changes in the family the relations and the communication patterns have inevitably changed. This transition in all the three components is a serious threat for healthy ageing at the level of the family.

Increasing individualism in youths has resulted in asserting strongly for individual self, and they are in a great hurry to have every source of pleasure ignoring others' consideration totally. Such attitudes may lead to indignity, disgracefulness, embarrassment, dishonour, disheartening, disregard, indifference, injustice, lack of care, psychological torture and unlimited hostility towards elders (Khan, 2004). Presently, older people cannot take it for granted that their children will be able to look after them when they need care in their old age (Reddy, 2002).

In India, about 90 per cent of the elderly stay with the family (Radkar and Kaulageker, 2006). However, there are no sufficient data to show the quality of their care. Those 10 per cent who are living alone or in old age homes can tell us the reasons for not living with the family and suffering from psychological pains.

The social and cultural heritage of the family as an institution of care of elders has already entered the risk zone. The dynamics of relations in the family are undergoing unprecedented changes. The emotional bondage—the source of keeping the family intact, united and fully functioning are changing not only in joint families but also in nuclear families.

Migration out of the family in search of a good source of living is debasing the dynamics of families. It leads to break down of the family system and creates emotional deprivation among family members, particularly in elders who had a different outlook on the family system, having a strong bondage of emotional relations and care of each other. The satisfaction of emotional needs of the individual in the family requires closer interaction.

Elderly people are encountering both physical and psychological distancing in families. They feel isolated and side tracked (Bajpai, 1998). These changes at the family level and unhealthy approaches some times hurt them and encourage them to relocate themselves in old age homes. Some times their family members force them to shift to old age homes. But, elders usually prefer to derive a sense of meaning of connectedness to their homes, their neighbourhoods and their natural environment (Prakash, 2004). For this they are usually ready to make compromises, which tax their physical and mental well being. Depression and emotional shocks are common among them. They develop negative emotions towards themselves due to lack of employment, low income and failing health, the newly added worries and feeling of neglect, loss of importance in the family, feeling of inadequacy, loneliness and of being unwanted (Bose, 1990). This in turn makes them sensitive to the physical and psychological world. A glimpse of abuses and changes in the family dynamics can be had from the selected stories of elderly persons, being presented in the subsequent paragraphs.

Case I

Rajeev Ranjan (name changed) is 71 years old, a resident of Bhopal, married and staying with his wife in an old age home for the last 8 years. He was a professor and held a government job in a reputed college as head of the department. His wife was a primary school teacher. Other family members are a son and a daughter, both married and settled and staying with their respective families. Recalling his early days, Ranjan said that when his children were young, they all stayed in government accommodation allotted to him. He said that he was very happy and contended at that time. He provided the best of everything to his children to the best of his abilities. Being a good father and husband, he had full faith in his children and wife regarding all financial, personal and social matters. He followed the advice given by them, especially by his wife, as he had confidence in their decisions. They all took a joint decision to build their beautiful house.

His children were bright so they achieved success very early in life. His daughter got married in a reputed family of Gwalior. His son also was married in a respected family known to them. Ranjan and his wife were very affectionate and considerate towards their daughter-in-law and her parents, who would often come and stay in their house.

Before marriage, his son was very close to his father and very considerate too. But after his marriage, unfortunately, his relation with his parents changed. Ranjan maintained a close relationship with his daughter and started consulting her on various family matters. Due to some reasons, his son resented this, so the atmosphere at home became tense. After his retirement, the relationship with his son worsened and his daughter-in-law was to a large extent responsible for this. He realized that his wife, who was his better half, was now dancing to the tunes of his son, because he was more materialistically sound and influential. Without realizing the implication he was persuaded to sign on papers related to property. His son sold the property and invested the returns in his own name. The daughter-in-law and her parents resented even his presence and started insulting him. The situation worsened when his son manipulated the property. He forced Mr. and Mrs. Ranjan to leave their home.

All this disturbed both of them. Their health suffered a lot in the following years due to emotional stress. They both decided to live in an old age home to get care from others. Their pension is their only support.

They suffered abuse of psychological, physical and financial nature by their own family members. Having been victims of prolonged stress, they realized the need for spiritual health and relaxation technique. But, they are apprehensive about what will happen when one of them dies. There is no caregiver in sight. Their greatest need and desire is for love and respect from their family members.

Case II

Mrs. Radhika (changed name) is a 68 years old woman, widow, staying alone in an old age home for the last 12 years. Her husband was a high court judge. They lived a very happy and prosperous life with their three sons, who were very obedient and sincere in their childhood. Their hard work and the blessings of their elders made them successful in their life. Her elder son is a doctor and married with a girl of the same profession. They have their own nursing home at Raipur. They both are busy in their business so they refused to take care of their parents.

Her second son is a director of a well-known NGO working for rural development. He is also married in a reputed family. He was obedient but could not stand against his wife's decision that they could not take care of their parents. So her younger son, who is a professor by profession and stays in Bhopal with his family, takes care of his parents. Everything was cool and they lived healthy life. But the sudden departure of her husband changed the entire scenario. Mrs. Radhika sensed that her status was reduced and her daughter-in-law was displeased with her presence, although she actively participated in household chores like cooking, escorting her grandchildren to school in the morning and to park in the evening, shopping, etc. One day in the presence of her son, her daughter-in-law slapped her after a serious argument. Then her son himself locked her in a dark room and refused to serve meals to her.

After three days, in the absence of her son and daughter-in-law, one of their servants opened the door and advised her to leave the house. He also gave her some money. Then she left the house and joined an old age home. She has been staying there for the last 12 years. Her sons did not even try to search for their mother. Now she feels cheated and abused by her own family members. She gets the pension of her husband for livelihood.

Case III

Charanjeet Singh, a 70 years old man, is father of two worthy sons and a daughter. He lives on the ground floor of a two-storey building with his married elder son. His younger son occupies the upper portion of the building, which he himself built in his prime time. Mrs, Charanjeet Singh stays with the younger son.

Describing his problem, Charanjeet Singh said, "The relations between my two sons and their families are not cordial. They did not allow me to talk to my wife, who lives with my younger son in the upper portion of my house. We get only two meals from our sons. They do not even entertain my guests. We don't have any say in the family affairs. I am living a very embarrassing life".

Case IV

Mrs. Roshini, a 68-year-old lady, who lived her entire life with dignity and prosperity, was forced by her family members to live in the outhouse of their house. This happened when she handed her entire property to her son-in-law. A maid was kept for her support. But after the death of the maid, she cooks her own food. The daughter and the son-in-law do not care her in any way and she feels lonely and rejected.

Case V

Hasan, aged 69, unmarried, eldest among six siblings. He lives in an old age home. He lost his parents vary early in his life and all responsibilities fell on his shoulder. He somehow completed his graduation and got job in a bank. He poured all his earning in education of his three younger sisters and two brothers. After completion of their studies all of them settled and got married. Now all are busy with their respective families and there is no one to take care of him. He is very upset and curses himself for supporting the family members who rejected him.

These case studies give us a glimpse of elderly abuse prevalent in Indian society and its effect on the mental health of elderly persons. These case studies suggest that abuse of the elderly in the family is increasing from psychological torture to physical torture including insults, humiliation and partial or total denial of food, clothing, shelter and medical help and emotional support. It is more pronounced in the case of those who are dependent on their family members for every type of support, having nothing or very little to contribute to the family either physically or materially and are in constant need of care. In these examples poverty is not the major cause of abuse. Old people are abused in affluent families as well.

These case studies tend to suggest the 'motive for self' as overriding the family values and being the sole basis of untimely ageing. Each member of the family wants to have their own choice of living. The youth particularly, have started asserting strongly for the individual self, and they are in a great hurry to have every source of pleasure regardless of its legitimacy. Everybody in the family strives for individual freedom and prefers to live with individualized liking, thinking, eating and moving around. They hardly care for the personal, physical and emotional needs of the elderly members. Sometimes family members fail to meet the physical, social and/or emotional needs of the elderly persons.

The severity of elderly abuse is increasing day by day. The worst sufferers in the society are elderly people (Khan, 2004) but there is big gap between the problems of the aged and the available resources. Although voluntary organizations are engaged in taking care of the elderly, their limitations disable them from addressing the magnitude of the problem.

Under such circumstances, what should be the responsibility of the government ? Can older people claim it to be their right to be looked after fully in families for healthy ageing? Can a society reconcile the emerging individualism of the youth with compassion and care for the elderly ? Can any government policy address a problem of such high magnitude and complexity? Can any formal institution replace the family care most needed by the Indian aged people?

No, no institution can replace the family. Therefore, the demand is to find a care model which supports elderly care while living in the family. This needs some community services to help the family in changing its mindset and provide low cost care for the elders. WHO, India is involved in developing models for community based health care for the elderly for which projects have been conducted in Chennai, Jodhpur and Mizoram. Efforts have been made to utilize health workers engaged in other health-related or social service activities with additional nominal remuneration. Similarly ICMR has conducted a long project in rural south India and has offered a feasible model for the total health care of the rural aged within the existing infrastructure with some extra inputs. Other efforts are to be made in this direction to take care of the elderly in their families by providing community care. We offer some tentative suggestions which can be initiated to help the aged for positive ageing, while living in the family:

1. Children, while going through the socialization process and education, should be made sensitive to the needs of their elders.
2. The government needs to start some training programmes for elders, for the facilitation of positive and productive ageing with the help of NGOs.
3. There must be some law against elderly abuse. Grown up sons and daughters must be forced by the law to take care of their aged parents and to meet their physical and psychological needs.
4. Realistic portrayal of old age and awareness and facilitation of positive and productive ageing through various media channels is essential.
5. Joint activities, involving all age groups, related to community development, must be organized with the support of local government.
6. Essential training for assertiveness must be given to all elderly people.
7. Elders must be made to feel that they are desirable for the community.
8. Adequate training programme may be organized for caretakers, so that they can meet the demands of elders.
9. Visits of higher authorities to old age homes are strongly recommended as it helps in maintaining requisite standards of these places.
10. Grown-up sons and daughters should be forced to visit old age homes on auspicious occasions, if it becomes necessary for them to relocate their parents there.

The aforesaid suggestions are not exhaustive and more can be added to the list. The strategies for the needed care of the aged have to depend on the basic assumption that, in the Indian context, the care has to be based in the families and old age homes cannot serve as an alternative of the family system. Old age homes, however, may serve those who do not have families to look after them.

References

Arora, S. (1993). Concept of aging and problems of the aged: Some observations. *Man in India*, vol. 73, no. 3, 251–57.

Bajpai, P.K. (1998). Generation gap: Implication on the aged. In P.K. Bajpai (ed.), *Social work perspective on health*, Jaipur: Rawat Publications.

Bose, A. (1990). Aspect of aging in India, *Social Action* 32, 2–9.

Khan, A.M. (2004). Decay in family dynamics of interaction, relation and communication as determinant of growing vulnerability amongst elders. *Indian Journal of Gerontology*, vol. 18, no. 2, 173–86.

Mishra, S. (1979). Social adjustment in old age: Case study of retired government employees living in Chandigarh. *Indian Dissertation Abstracts*, vol. 30, no. 2, 217–35.

Prakash, Indira Jai (2004). Aging in place: Possibilities and problems. *Indian Journal of Gerontology*, vol. 18, no.1, 95–102.

Radkar, A. and A. Kaulagekar (2006). Living conditions of elderly in India. *Indian Journal of Gerontology*, 20, 250–63.

Raju, S.S. (2002). Meeting the needs of older poor and excluded in India. Situation and Voices, The Older Poor and Excluded in South Africa and India. *UNFPA, Population and Developmental Strategies*, vol. 2, 93–110.

Reddy, C.G. (2002). Interactive sessions on active participation of older persons in economic social and political life. *Indian Research and Development Journal*, vol. 9, no. 2, 5–9.

Sandhu, P. and R. Bakhshi (2004). Views of elderly women on their social and mental well being in modern society. *Indian Journal of Gerontology*, vol. 18, no. 1, 135–44.

Sonar, G.B. (2004). Old age pensioners: a socio-psychological study. *Indian Journal of Gerontology*, vol. 18, no. 2, 187–200.

23

Caregiving and Caregiver Stress: A Case Report

Roopalekha Jathanna P.N. and K.S. Latha

The family constitutes the major caregiving response to the needs of the elderly who are no longer self-sufficient. These caregivers are often wives or daughters who have chosen to keep the patient at home with them. On an average, three-quarters of the caregiver's day is devoted to the patient, a proportion that tends to increase linearly as the disease progresses. Caring for a person with disabilities can be physically demanding, especially for older caregivers, who make up half of all caregivers. Caring for a person with dementia at home can be overwhelming. The caregiver must cope with declining abilities and difficult behaviour. Basic activities of daily living often become hard to manage for both the care-receiver and the caregiver. As the disease worsens, the care-receiver usually needs 24-hour care.

A large body of research now suggests that caring for an elderly family member with dementia can impose chronic stress that may harm the caregiver's emotional and physical health (Stone, 1994). Dementia has been studied as a risk factor for elder abuse. Conflicting data exist regarding this relationship. An observational cohort study of 68 elderly patients in New Haven, Connecticut demonstrated that older age, minority status, poor social networks, and functional (but not cognitive) disability based on Mental Status Questionnaire errors were risk factors for abuse (Lachs et al., 1994). Many theories have been developed to explain abusive behaviour towards elderly people. Theories of the origin of mistreatment of elders have been divided into four major categories, as follows: physical and mental impairment of the patient, caregiver stress, trans-generational violence, and psychopathology in the abuser. Clearly, no single answer exists to explain behaviour in an abusive relationship. A number of psycho-social and cultural factors are involved.

Abuse may consist of single or repeated acts. It may be physical, verbal or psychological; it may be an act of neglect or an omission to act; or it may occur when a vulnerable person is persuaded to enter into a financial or sexual transaction to which he or she has not consented, or cannot consent. Abuse can occur in any relationship and may result in significant harm to, or exploitation of, the person subjected to it. The most typical informal caregiving involves the provision of assistance to elderly persons who, because of chronic illness and/or disability, need help with everyday activities. Abuse occurs in all social classes, and anyone is capable of becoming an abuser when he is under persistent and unrelenting stress.

Research has suggested that caregivers experience greater levels of emotional distress than the general population (Kiecolt-Glaser, 2001), such as higher levels of depression (Rosenthal, Sulman and Marshall, 1993), with studies reporting the rate of depression in caregivers at 22 per cent compared with 11 per cent for older people generally (Vitaliano, 2003). A recent British study of dementia sufferers living in the community found that disturbed behaviour was relatively infrequent. Only 10 per cent of the markedly demented, community-resident persons were described by their caregivers as noisy, 5 per cent as aggressive and 6 per cent as prone to wandering. When these problems arose, however, they were strongly associated with caregiver stress (O'Connor et al., 1990).

It must be recognized that many caregivers in this situation are themselves elderly and at risk of abuse at the hands of the dementia sufferer. Some studies estimate that more than half of dementia sufferers manifest some form of aggressive behaviour—that is, verbal outbursts, physical threats or violence (Paveza et al., 1992). In developing countries, where most of the world's older persons live—most of them are poor and there have not yet been many studies or systematic collection of statistics done on the stress of caregiving and elder abuse. Even so, there is ample evidence from crime records, news reports filed by journalists, social welfare records and some small studies, that elder abuse—physical, emotional and financial, is widespread.

There is paucity of literature dealing with elder developmental stage abuse. There is a debate over the treatment of elders in a child-like manner when they have regressed on the developmental scale, as with Alzheimer's disease. Most published researchers agree that an elder's lifestyle must be limited if their physical and mental abilities have deteriorated (Key et al., 2000). However, there are limited developmental scale assessment instruments.

This paper examines the extent of elder abuse in a caregiver setting of patients with dementia in the light of available data of a long-term project by the authors and suggests its implications. Also discussed are the problems, stresses, and strains of caregivers of the persons with dementia.

Materials and Methods

Informal caregivers of persons with dementia fulfilling diagnostic criteria according to (ICD-10) were included. Four cases were selected from the fifteen cases seen, where there was a mention of abuse by the care receipient as well as the caregiver.

The information was collected in the home environment during home visits by the first author with the questionnaires for both strain and other details. Caregiver Strain Index was used to quantify the strain. The Caregiver Strain Index (CSI) Zarit et al. (1980) is a tool that can be used to quickly identify families with potential caregiving concerns. It is a 13-question tool that measures strain related to care provision. There is at least one item for each of the following major domains: employment, financial, physical, social and time. Positive responses to seven or more items on the index indicate a greater level of strain. This instrument can be used to assess individuals of any age who have assumed the role of caregiver for an older adult.

Socio-demographic data and other details were collected in a semi-structured interview and correlated with related variables.

Case 1

The caregiver, a 50-year-old daughter, with financial constraints has been made to look after her father aged 85 for the last 7 years. The caregiver complains of physical abuse by the patient like hitting on the head with whatever he lays his hands on whenever agitated. She also complains of his suspicious nature due to which he indulges in verbal abuse (using obscene words) in front of other family members, which embarrasses her, her relatives and neighbours. For this, she would argue with other family members, which is very disturbing and finds her self emotionally upset. She also vents out her financial problems as her husband works in a small hotel in Mumbai and has to look after four children, and that she cannot make both the ends meet.

She complains of being trapped by the family members who promised to support her and her family financially. She becomes touchy whenever spoken to and is easily moved to tears and expresses helplessness.

Caregiver variables	Patient variables
Caregiver: Daughter	Patient: Mr. A
Age: 50	Age: 85
Education: Primary	Education: Nil
Occupation: Nil	Occupation: Farmer
Years of caregiving: 7 years	Religion: Hindu
Patients relationship: Father	Marital status: Married
Strain experienced: 11/13	Family type: Nuclear

Women in the lower economic class, homemakers, faced a different problem of being victimized by another family member, who is financially sound. They are being burdened to look after the older people who are difficult to handle. In the current case, the daughter was summoned to look after her ill father and was manipulated into taking up the responsibility forever. Her old father, who is a victim of dementia, subjected her to verbal and physical abuse. Financial support, which they promised, was denied and 'the maid-like' attitude towards, her disturbed her mind.

Case 2

The 53-year-old wife is the informal caregiver of the patient. She narrates about how the patient is becoming a burden on the family members by his disturbing behaviour like getting up at night, wandering, etc. She also narrates how their son can only control him by scolding and sometimes beating him. "He doesn't listen to any one in the house and we females cannot control him. Only my son can control him by scolding, and sometimes it requires some hitting to put him to sleep."

Caregiver variables	Patient variables
Caregiver: wife	Patient: Mr. B
Age: 53	Age: 63
Education: Primary	Education: Graduate
Occupation: House wife	Occupation: Retired Bank Officer
Years of caregiving: 2 years	Religion: Hindu
Patient's relationship: Husband	Family type: Extended
Strain experienced: 9/13	

In this case his well-educated son who is a doctor abuses the patient who is a victim of Alzheimer's disease. Verbal and physical abuse has become a part of caregiving whenever a patient shows non-cooperation.

Case 3

In this case, the narrator is a 34-years-old daughter- in-law who is looking after her 80-years-old mother-in-law. The caregiver says she is not much strained looking after her mother-in-law. The narrator showed her hostility towards other family members who did not share the responsibility of caregiving. The patient has two sons and two daughters who at present are not staying with their mother except the elder son, the narrator's husband. She be meaned "Her other children are enjoying life without any responsibility. I am trapped here in this house looking after her and cannot leave her and go anywhere. I feel mentally tortured and some times show my frustration by abusing her verbally".

Caregiver variables	Patient variables
Caregiver: Daughter-in-law	Patient: Mrs. C
Age: 34	Age: 80
Education: SSLC	Education: Nil
Occupation: Housewife	Occupation: Nil
Years of caregiving: 4 years	Religion: Hindu
Patient's relationship: Mother-in-law	Marital status: Widow
Strain experienced: 4/13	Family type: Nuclear

Here the caregiver looked very frustrated by the burden of caregiving. The attitude towards her mother-in-law is a result of such frustration. Here the patient, depending on her family for care, is emotionally abused and humiliated, but remains powerless to stop it, due to her dependent situation.

Case 4

Mrs.C's caregiver is her youngest daughter. She is unmarried and lives with her mother, taking care of her. In the process she is getting exposed to a high level of stress looking after a mother who has been suffering from dementia for the last three years and who is exhibiting disturbing behaviour like wandering, depression and incontinence. The other family members, after their marriage, left her with their mother and live separately with their own families. She could not find any servant or social support as she resides in a rural area. She looks after her mother without complaining as she thinks that it is her fate. She has a suicidal tendency as she says, "I feel like ending my life sometimes. My mother doesn't show any emotions and she is like a child herself. I live because of her and I am afraid of what lies ahead for us". She does not want to disclose any kind of abuse towards the patient during the interview.

Among caregivers of dementia, there is a gender-biased pattern of familial transmission of responsibility for care of relatives suffering from dementia and such responsibility becomes an important source of burden if the patient shows problematic behaviour as is evidenced from this case vignette.

Caregiver variables	Patient variables
Caregiver: Daughter	Patient Mrs. C
Age: 26	Age: 60
Education: Graduate	Education: Primary
Occupation: Business	Occupation: Nil
Years of caregiving: 3 years	Religion: Hindu
Patient's relationship: Mother	Marital status: Widow
Strain experienced: 10/13	Family type: Nuclear

Result and Discussion

The largest area of unidentified elder abuse and neglect is in the elderly population that remains in their own homes. Included in this area of abuse is also self-neglect (Tumosa, 1999). Unfortunately, signs that may be interpreted as abuse by a caregiver or family member may also be a sign of self-neglect by the elder. Failure of health care personnel to report suspected cases of elder abuse may cause loss of license and/or fines (Marshall et al., 2000).

The four focus pairs selected varied from lower to higher strata of society and in the age range of 26 to 85 years. The participants, i.e., informal caregivers initially talked about 'emotional problems', 'lack of emotional support', 'neglect by other family members', 'feelings of insecurity', as reason for abuse in both the ways. However, not a single person was willing to label it as 'abuse'. They linked abuse to acts of violence, which they all seemed to agree was normal. In the current study defining abuse and its conceptualization was a problem.

In fact, there was a general uneasiness among the carers and a genuine attempt was made to evade the issue. On being forceful about the specific issues of physical abuse, verbal abuse and financial abuse, the carers agreed to the existence of such happenings in the community, at least within their own.

Taking advantage of the financial situation (case 1), family members are victimized by their own siblings or parents. This is a very uneasy situation for any outsider/researcher/social worker to intervene in and come up with the solutions even though the 'abused' implied for some kind of support or relief. Financial abuse was linked with people of the low-income group, especially women in the family who were dependent. The daughter was made to look after the sick father who abused her both physically and verbally, and her own close family relatives abused her.

One example at this point would be of Ms. D (case study 4) who never disclosed any kind of abuse of her mother. The avoidance of the issue is very evident which also points to the fact that whatever happened she was not willing to discuss.

Even physical abuse was sighted in one of the cases (case no 2). The symptoms such as restlessness, wandering and agitation exhibited by these patients led to verbal and the physical abuse by the caregiver which is an alarming trend of ignorance about the disease pattern which has to be taken up as a serious issue for discussion in all levels of society.

Another major factor was the fact that the older parents themselves were unaware of the abuse which they were facing and were inhibited to discuss this matter with the investigators to justify "neglect" in the existing circumstances. Whatever be the cause, carers were sympathetic towards their parents. The reason could be emotional bonding with the parents.

In case of Mrs C the daughter-in-law, who was frustrated in the family situation did not mention any evidence of abuse towards her mother-in-law other than verbal abuse, for which she was blaming other family members. This incident depicts the negative side of the Indian tradition where the daughters-in-law are still the weaker part of the family.

Woman in the present day Indian scenario has a traditional role entrusted to her as a caregiver in a largely patriarchal society, with no financial independence, and if she happens to be financially unsound (case 1 and 4), the world may not be a very nice place to live in.

There is substantial support for the idea that abuse is associated with personality problems of the caregiver, rather than characteristics of the elderly victim (Pillemer and Finkelhor, 1989). The present study also indicated that females make up a greater proportion of caregivers than do adult males.

Informal supporters provide the bulk of long-term care to chronically disabled elders. Care giving has been recognized as an activity with perceived benefits and burdens. Caregivers may be prone to depression, grief, fatigue and changes in social relationships (Nelis et al., 2007). They may also experience physical health problems and fatigue. Perceived caregiver burden has been associated with premature institutionalization and patient reports of unmet needs. Screening tools are useful to identify families who would benefit from a more comprehensive assessment of the caregiving experience.

Mona Baumgarten et al. (1994) in their study of health of family members caring for elderly persons with dementia, suggest that the economic impact of dementia is a particular issue for families living in developing countries, and the combination of reduced family incomes and increased family expenditure on care is particularly stressful.

The reluctance to intervene in family affairs, difficulty in knowing how to cope with the problem when it is identified, and defining the problem are reasons given for why elder abuse has been ignored.

Conclusion

Dementia and elder abuse are relatively common and under-diagnosed geriatric syndromes. If risk factors for abuse are identified, the health care provider has the opportunity to intervene to prevent abuse. The success of primary prevention of elder abuse rests on the ability of the health care provider to make assessments and interventions and to maintain a consistent relationship with patients and caregivers. Education of the caregiver and attention to caregiver stress, including depression, may prevent the onset and perpetuation of abuse.

References

Key, S.W., D.J. DeNoon and S. Boyles (August, 1999). Study says Alzheimer's mirrors child development. *World Disease Weekly Plus*, 11–13.

Kiecolt-Glaser, J.K. and R. Glaser (2001). Stress and immunity: Age enhances the risks. *Current Directions in Psychological Science*, 10(1): 18–21.

Lachs, M.S., L. Berkman and T. Fulmer (1994). A prospective community-based pilot study of risk factors for the investigation of elder mistreatment. *J Am Geriatr Soc*, 42: pp. 169–73.

Marshall, C.E., D. Benton and J.M. Braizer (2000). Elder abuse: Using clinical tools to identify clues of mistreatment. *Geriatrics*, 55(2): 42–53.

Mona Baumgarten, M., Hanley A. James, C.I. Revard, Battista N. Renaldo, R. Becker and S. Gauthier (1994). Health of Family Members Caring for Elderly Persons With Dementia: A Longitudinal Study. *Annals of Internal Medicine*, 120(2): 126–32.

Nelis, S.M., C. Quinn and L. Clare (2007). Information and support interventions for informal caregivers of people with dementia. (Protocol), Issue 2. 10.1002/14651858.CD006440. *Cochrane Database of Systematic Reviews*.

O'Connor, D.W., P.A. Pollitt, J.B. Hyde, J.L. Fellows, N.D. Miller and M.A. Roth follow-up study of dementia diagnosed in the community using the Cambridge mental disorders of the elderly examination. *Acta Psychiatr Scand*, 81: 78–82.

Paveza, G.J., D. Cohen, C. Eisdorfer et al. (1992), Severe family violence and Alzheimer's disease: Prevalence and risk factors. *Gerontologist*, 32(4): 493–97.

Pillemer, K. and D. Finkelhor (1989). Causes of elder abuse: Caregiver stress versus problem relatives. *American Journal of Orthopsychiatry*, 59(2): 179–87.

Rosenthal, C.J., J. Sulman and V.W. Marshall (1993). Depressive symptoms in family caregivers of long–stay patients. *Gerontologist*, 33(2): 249–57.

Stone, R., G.L. Cafferata and J. Sangl (1987). Caregivers of the frail elderly: A national profile. *The Gerentologist*, 31: 770–77.

Tumosa, N. (1999). Injury prevention for the elderly: Preventing elder abuse, preventing suicide and depression. *The Gerontologist*, 39(3): 380–81.

Vitaliano, P.P., J.P. Zhang and J.M. Scanlan (2003). Is caregiving hazardous to one's physical health? A meta-analysis. *Psychological Bulletin*, 129(6): 946–72.

Zarit, S.H., K.E. Reever and J. Bach-Peterson (1980). Relatives of the impaired elderly: Correlates of feelings of burden. *Gerontologist*, 20: 649–55.

24

Elder Abuse and Neglect: A Review

K.S. Latha

Abuse of old people is an uncomfortable concept for health professionals. Elder abuse and neglect is a critical health care issue that must be brought to the attention of health care providers and older adults' family members. Adults older than 65 who live at home or in long-term care facilities may be at risk for abuse.

Although elder abuse and neglect has occurred for centuries, it is the most recent form of family violence to come to the attention of modern societies. Despite the efforts of health and social-care professionals to draw attention to the topic since the issue was first raised in the late 1970s, it is only since 1988 that the issues related to elder abuse and neglect have begun to be addressed. Elder abuse has received increasing attention over the past decade as a common problem with serious consequences for the health and well-being of old people. Health and social-care professionals have not viewed work with older people very positively.

The proportion of older people in the world population is on the increase. The most striking effects of population ageing are seen in the most rapidly developing regions such as China, India and Latin America. Due to the unprecedented pace of demographic ageing, these societies will have comparatively little time to develop social and healthcare policies to deal with the healthcare needs of the elderly in their population (Randal and German, 1999).

Elder abuse in family settings has increased in recent years for a variety of reasons, including the increasing proportion of older adults in the total population, the related increase in chronic disabling diseases, and the increasing involvement of families in caregiving relationships with elders.

Elder abuse has been recorded since the 19th century, but it was not brought to the forefront until 1980. Each year approximately 10 per cent of adults, 65 years and older are abused, and 4 per cent experience moderate to severe abuse (Greenberg, 1996; Weiler and Buckwalter, 1992). Mistreatment of older people—referred to as "elder abuse"—was first described in British scientific journals in 1975 under the term 'granny battering' (Baker, 1975; Burston, 1975). Apart from the distress caused to the subject while alive, it is alarming to read in a recent article that elder mistreatment is associated with shorter survival, even after adjusting for other factors associated with increased mortality in older adults (Lachs et al., 1998).

Elder abuse is an often overlooked and under-diagnosed malady (Collins, 2006; Cohen et al., 2006; Rodriguez et al., 2006). Between 1 per cent and 10 per cent of elders are victims of abuse at some time (Cohen et al., 2006). These individuals frequently present to the emergency department and often have multiple visits before abuse is uncovered (Lachs et al., 1997).

Abuse varies in form and includes physical, sexual, and psychological maltreatment, financial exploitation, and neglect (Collins, 2006; Cohen et al., 2006; Rodriguez et al., 2006; Wei and Herbers, 2004).

Although elder abuse was first identified in developed countries, where most of the existing research has been conducted, anecdotal evidence and other reports from some developing countries have shown that it is a universal phenomenon. That elder abuse is being taken far more seriously now reflects the growing worldwide concern about human rights and gender equality, as well as about domestic violence and population ageing. In the West where 'older age' begins is not precisely defined, which makes comparisons between studies and between countries difficult.

Concept of Elder Abuse

Elder abuse has been used as an all-inclusive term that is often used to represent physical abuse. Therefore, that already indicates that there are differences in the way elder abuse is interpreted. It may involve relationships between spouses, adult children, other relatives, may be friends, and anyone else in whom the older person has placed trust. Other behaviour that is considered abusive may depend on its duration, its frequency, its intensity, its intentionality, and the consequences.

Elder abuse thus encompasses the physical, sexual, or emotional abuse of an elderly person, usually one who is disabled or frail.

Elder abuse is an umbrella term used to describe one or more of the following:

Physical abuse is the willful infliction of physical pain or injury, such as slapping, bruising, sexually molesting, or restraining.

Sexual abuse is the infliction of non-consensual sexual contact of any kind.

Emotional or psychological abuse is the infliction of mental or emotional anguish, such as humiliating, intimidating, or threatening. *Psychological abuse* may include threats, insults, harassment, harsh orders, and behaviour designed to increase social isolation. Stealing pension checks, not using funds for support of the elder, and/or inappropriate use of the elder's personal property constitute *financial and material abuse.* This latter form of abuse/neglect could also be alleged in the current case since the caretaker was using the decedent's funds, but not for her support. *Violations of rights* occur when the caregiver deprives the individual of his or her inalienable rights, such as freedom of choice, life, or privacy.

Financial or material exploitation is the improper act or process of an individual, using the resources of an older person, without their consent, for someone else's benefit.

Neglect is the failure of a caretaker to provide goods or services necessary to avoid physical harm, mental anguish or mental illness, such as abandonment, denial of food or health related services. *Neglect* is one of the more common forms of abuse and is characterised by a failure of the caregiver to provide the goods or services that are necessary for optimal functioning or to avoid harm. *Medical neglect* is the form of neglect where there is failure to seek medical care appropriate for the patient's condition.

Self-neglect is characterized as the behaviour of an elderly person that threatens their own health or safety.

In 1987, the American Medical Association's Council on Scientific Affairs defined *elder abuse* as an act or omission that results in harm or threatened harm to the health or welfare of an elderly person. Elder abuse can be classified into six categories: (1) physical abuse, (2) sexual abuse, (3) neglect, (4) psychological abuse, (5) financial and material exploitation, and (6) violation of rights (AARP, 1993).

Often, several types of abuse occur simultaneously. A family member who may initially take in an elderly patient may not be aware of the work and sacrifice involved and may become subject to the stress of the situation, which can lead to neglect or abuse (Schor et al., 1995).

Elder Abuse and Neglect

While the term 'elder abuse and neglect' is commonly used to describe acts of commission or omission that result in harm or threatened harm to the health or welfare of an older adult, many authorities prefer to use the term 'elder mistreatment'. Mistreatment of the elderly person may include physical, psychological, or financial abuse or neglect, and it may be intentional or unintentional. Intentional mistreatment involves a conscious and deliberate attempt to inflict harm or injury, such as verbal abuse or battering; unintentional mistreatment occurs when an inadvertent action results in harm to the elderly person. Unintentional mistreatment is usually due to ignorance, inexperience, or a lack of ability or desire of the caretaker to provide proper care.

Reasons for Not Reporting Elder Abuse

Elder abuse is a hidden, tragic secret for many. Sometimes victims simply do not have the capacity to report it. Whether a victim is unable or unwilling, some of the barriers to revealing elder abuse include:

Fear

- of being punished for reporting,
- of institutionalisation,
- of rejection or abandonment by other family members,
- of losing their caregiver,
- of losing access to family members, including grandchildren that the disclosure will reflect poorly upon their family.
- Love for the abuser.

- The senior may care deeply for his/her abuser, leading to conflicting feelings about revealing the abuse. The victim is likely reluctant to see the abusers criticized or face consequences for the behaviour.
- *Lack of understanding or impairment.* A victim may be unable to report the abuse because of cognitive impairment or other disability. A mental impairment or inappropriate medication may also keep a victim from revealing the abuse.
- *Shame and /or guilt.* Victims of elder abuse often blame themselves for violence and neglect they are subjected to. They are often reluctant to report the abuse because they are ashamed of what the family member did to them or embarrassed that they placed their trust in that person. The senior may also believe that it was something they did that brought on the abuse.
- *Unaware of resource options.* Victims are often unaware of the community supports and services available to assist them.
- *Acceptance of abuse or neglect as normal.* If abuse has been a prevalent or typical pattern of behaviour in a family, both the abusers and the victims may accept it as "normal" behaviour. For many victims suffering at the hands of an abuser, violence and neglect are simply a way of life. Additionally, as violence is an accepted form of expressing rage in our society, the abuse may be dismissed and go unreported by others.

Besides, health professionals may ignore signs and symptoms of elder mistreatment because they are unaware of the extent of the problem and uncomfortable with the responsibility of further assessment and action, also their poor training in recognizing the condition, the subtle presentation of symptoms and signs, inherent unfavorable attitudes towards the elderly (ageism), reluctance to recognize that a problem exists, and fear of confronting or reporting the offender.

Characteristics of the Abused Victim and the Abuser

The abused elder most often has a cognitive impairment, lives in close proximity to the abuser, lives in social isolation, and is older than 75 years (Lett, 1995). An impaired patient—mentally or physically—is at greatest risk of mistreatment—particularly someone in need of assistance with feeding (Lachs et al., 1994). Characteristics of the abuser often include a history of mental illness and/or substance abuse, excessive dependence on the elder for financial support, and a history of violence or antisocial behaviour outside the family (Lett, 1995).

Caregivers experience 'burnout' and frustration, which can lead to abuse of their ward. Alcohol abuse (by the patient or the caregiver) increases the risk of physical abuse and neglect. Finally, the personality and psychological character of the caregiver, as well as that of the patient, can play a causative role in situations involving mistreatment.

In a study to determine the family physicians' perceptions of barriers and strategies in the effective detection and appropriate management of abused elderly people, physicians identified the barriers as denial of abuse, resistance to intervention, not knowing where to call for help, lack of protocols to assess and respond to abuse, lack of guidelines about confidentiality, fear of reprisal, and lack of knowledge of the prevalence and definition of elder abuse (Krueger, et al., 1997).

Awareness of these factors can assist health care workers in identifying the individuals at risk.

The following factors should be considered when evaluating a potential case of elder mistreatment:

- Elder mistreatment occurs among men and women of all racial, ethnic and socioeconomic groups.
- The perpetrator of neglect is often the spouse or an adult child of the older person, but paid or informal caregivers may also be involved.
- Physical, functional, or cognitive problems in caregivers may prevent them from providing proper care
- Mental illness, alcoholism, or drug abuse in the older person or the caregiver may be associated with abuse and neglect.
- Social isolation and dependence of the elderly person may increase the risk for mistreatment.
- A past history of abusive relationships may predispose the victim to future mistreatment. Financial or other family problems may impair the ability to provide adequate care.
- Inadequate housing or unsafe conditions in the home may increase the likelihood of elder mistreatment.
- Victims often experience several forms of elder mistreatment at the same time.

Etiological Factors Related to Elder Abuse: Theories

There have been attempts to elucidate risk factors for elder mistreatment for both older adults and their caretakers. These factors are based on etiologic theories for the occurrence of elder abuse and neglect. Unfortunately, none of these theories has been substantiated with good clinical data. However, awareness of such factors, and the theories underlying them, may help physicians understand, anticipate and prevent situations in which elder mistreatment may occur.

The transgenerational or family violence theory asserts that violence is a learned behaviour. Individuals who have witnessed or have been victims of family violence may deal with their problems in a like manner. A second theory implicates the psychopathology of the caretaker in some cases of elder mistreatment. Alcoholism, drug addiction, or severe emotional problems on the part of the caretaker may predispose him to abusive behaviour. A third theory argues that medical, functional, or cognitive disability of elderly persons increases their dependency and vulnerability, and therefore their risk for abuse or neglect. Other authorities point out that the caretaker may be dependent, especially economically, on the older patient. This dependency may lead to resentment and, when combined with other factors, may predispose to mistreatment. Other theories emphasize stress as an important factor in elder mistreatment. Although the caregiving role is inherently stressful, outside situations such as economic pressures, lack of community support, or increasing care needs may heighten tensions and produce frustrations that lead to abusive behaviour. While one theory will not explain all or even a majority of cases of elder mistreatment, it is useful for clinicians to view the interaction of these factors as contributing to the overall behaviour pattern.

Manifestations of Elder Abuse

Potential elder abuse can be detected through the elderly person's (1) fear of a family member or caregiver, (2) unexplained injuries, (3) very poor hygiene, and (4) appearance of elder neglect or mistreatment. Signs of physical restraint were also considered, but cases of financial abuse were not evident.

Elder abuse is mainly associated with a poor social network, and secondarily with some characteristics of the elderly senior. Abused elders are likely to have a poor social support system and numerous conflicts with family. They become isolated and often feel lonely. These seniors also have at least one of these characteristics: short-term memory loss, psychiatric illness, and problems with alcohol.

Abuse is like disease—if it is not considered in the differential diagnosis, it probably will not be diagnosed (Lett, 1995). Recognition of elder abuse/neglect is difficult for several reasons, such as the lack of structured training in screening for abuse and the discomfort of discussing the topic with patients. Many of these elders will even deny help. Elders may deny abuse because they are ashamed of being abused or fear reprisal (Lett, 1995).

There was no association between elder abuse or elder neglect and age, sex, marital status, or education. Studies have shown that elderly people of all backgrounds may be vulnerable to abuse, which often goes undetected.

Diagnosing Elder Abuse/Mistreatment

A careful history is imperative, although older adults may have difficulty in giving accurate information due to memory impairment. Sometimes they are reticent, being afraid of retaliation by the offender—either in the form of physical abuse or threats of abandonment. Sometimes the fear of being moved to a nursing home, may repress reports of mistreatment.

Physical symptoms may be the dominant presenting complaints. The physician must ask directly about rough/harsh treatment, confinement or verbal abuse. Sometimes the information from the patient may be disguised or confused, or only given when the patient is away from the home, i.e., at the doctor's office or the nursing home. Usually, the patient should be interviewed alone in privacy. A good rapport is crucial in uncovering the information related to abuse. Questions should be directed towards the patient's view of daily life, covering such topics as meals, medication, and trips to the shops or park. There should be some questions about the relationship with the caregiver, e.g., "How do you and Ms X get along?" and "Does Ms X take good care of you?" Likely signs of depression or alcohol abuse should be sought, and it may be appropriate to discuss finances.

If any issues of mistreatment are raised, the caregiver should be interviewed as well. Great care must be taken not to over-interpret the patient's complaints, especially if there is cognitive impairment.

Information from several sources—relatives, friends and neighbors may be helpful and throw light on instances of abuse/mistreatment.

Medical assessment of the victim should include a complete history, complete physical examination, and documentation of all injuries. Multiple injuries at various stages of healing, unexplained injuries, delays between illness or injury onset and treatment, 'doctor hopping', and multiple emergency department visits are a few of the findings. Pressure ulcers are often present in the elderly who are ill, and these should be thoroughly examined with all the dressings removed. Evidence of foul-smelling or necrotic pressure ulcers that have not been brought to the attention of the physician should raise suspicion of neglect (Schor, 1995).

Results of the physical examination must be carefully and accurately recorded, as they may be needed as legal evidence of mistreatment. Signs of injury should be noted (traumatic alopecia, hematomas, burns, fractures or signs of previous fractures). Evidence of neglect may include unkempt appearance, weight loss, dehydration, poor oral hygiene, decubitus ulcers, inguinal rash, and fecal impaction. Any suspicious findings in the history or physical exam should be confirmed with laboratory and radiological exams, as this would be valuable. Thus, dehydration and malnutrition can be established with simple lab tests such as a complete blood count, blood urea nitrogen, creatinine, and total protein and albumin, and cholesterol levels. Results of all such tests should accompany the documentation of abuse/mistreatment.

Management

Abuse of the elderly occurs all over the world, and education is the key to detection. Elder abuse is often difficult to identify and occurs in all races and all socioeconomic groups. Knowledge of the risk factors can assist in preventing elder mistreatment, if the persons involved are prepared to address them. Screening patients and caregivers before placement, if feasible, can be helpful. Adequate frequency of physician visits and availability of social community support will help avoid the circumstances leading to mistreatment.

One of the most important developments in addressing elder abuse/mistreatment in recent years has been the use of multidisciplinary teams in hospitals and communities. Specialists in geriatrics, social work, nursing, psychiatry, and other fields offer insight that can help the primary care physician to develop an appropriate intervention plan. These specialists may have important referral information for patients or family members, support groups and other services in the community that focus on ageing parents, home care, substance abuse, family violence, and financial and legal planning. Perhaps most important, physicians need to become familiar with long-term care and in-home health service options in their communities. Caring for an elderly parent at home is inherently stressful, and abusive situations can be prevented by providing support to overburdened caregivers.

Prevention of Elder Abuse: Strategies

At the most basic level, greater importance must be attached to primary prevention. This requires building a society in which older people are allowed to live out their lives in dignity, adequately provided with the necessities of life and with genuine opportunities for self-fulfillment. For those societies overwhelmed by poverty, the challenge is enormous. Prevention starts with awareness. One important way to raise awareness—both among the public and concerned professionals—is through education and training. Those providing health care and social services at all levels, both in the community and in institutional settings, should receive basic training on the detection of elder abuse. The media are a second powerful tool for raising awareness of the problem and its possible solutions, among the public as well as the authorities.

Programmes, in which older people themselves play a leading role, for preventing abuse of the elderly in their homes include:

- recruiting and training older people to serve as visitors or companions to other older people who are isolated;
- creating support groups for victims of elder abuse;
- setting up community programmes to stimulate social interaction and participation among the elderly;
- building social networks of older people in villages, neighbourhoods or housing units;
- working with older people to create "self-help" programmes that enable them to be productive.

Preventing elder abuse by helping abusers, particularly adult children, to resolve their own problems is a difficult task. Measures that may be useful include:

- offering services for the treatment of mental health problems and substance abuse;
- making jobs and education available;
- finding new ways of resolving conflict, especially where the traditional role of older people in conflict resolution has been eroded.

Much can also be done to prevent abuse of the elderly in institutional settings. Measures that may be useful include:

- the development and implementation of comprehensive care plans;
- training for staff;
- policies and programmes to address work related stress among staff;
- the development of policies and programmes to improve the physical and social environment of the institution.

Conclusion

The problem of elder abuse cannot be solved if the essential needs of older people—for food, shelter, security and access to health care—are not met. The nations of the world must create an environment in which ageing is accepted as a natural part of the life cycle, where anti-ageing attitudes are discouraged, where older people are given the right to live in dignity—free of abuse and exploitation—and are given opportunities to participate fully in educational, cultural, spiritual and economic activities (Randal and German, 1999).

References

Baker, A.A. (1975). Granny battering. *Modern Geriatrics*, 5: 20–24.

Burston, G.R. (1975). Granny battering. *British Medical Journal*, 3: 592.

Cohen, M., S. Halevi-Levin, R. Gagin and G. Friedman (2006). Development of a screening tool for identifying elderly people at risk of abuse by their caregivers. *J Aging Health*, 18: 660–85.

Collins, K.A. (2006). Elder maltreatment: A review. *Arch Pathol Lab Med,* 130: 1290–96.

Greenberg, E.M.(1996). Violence and the older adult: The role of the acute care nurse practitioners. *Crit Care Nurs Q,* August 19: 76–84.

Krueger, P., C. Patterson and Hamilton-Wentworth (1997). Research Subcommittee of the Elder Abuse and Self-Neglect Task Force of Detecting and managing elder abuse: Challenges in primary care. *Canadian Medical Association Journal,* 157(8): 1095–00.

Lachs, M.S., L. Berkman, T. Fulmer and R.I. Horwitz (1994). A prospective community-based pilot study of risk factors for the investigation of elder mistreatment. *J Am Geriatr Soc.,* 42: 169–73.

Lachs, M.S., C.S. Williams, S. O'Brien et al. (1998). The mortality of elder mistreatment. *JAMA,* 280: 428–32.

Lett, J.E. (1995). Abuse of the elderly. *J Fla Med Assoc.,* 82: 675–78.

Program Resources Department, American Association of Retired Persons (AARP) and Administration on Aging (AoA), US Department of Health and Human Services. A Profile of Older Americans. Washington, DC: American Association of Retired Persons, 1993.

Randal, J. and T. German (1999). *The ageing and development report: Poverty, independence and the world's people.* London: Help Age International.

Rodriguez, M.A., S.P. Wallace, N.H. Woolf and C.M. Mangione (2006). Mandatory reporting of elder abuse: Between a rock and a hard place. *Ann Fam Med.,* 4: 403–09.

Schor, J.D., A. Selby and C.A. Bertone (1995). Geriatric assessment in the diagnosis and treatment of elder abuse. *N J Med.,* 92: 108–10.

Wei, G.S. and J.E. Herbers Jr. (2004). Reporting elder abuse: a medical, legal, and ethical overview. *J Am Med Women's Assoc,* 59: 248–54.

Weiler, K. and K.C. Buckwalter (1992). Abuse among rural mentally ill. *J Psychosoc Nurs Ment.,* Health Serv. September 30: 32–36.

25

Narratives of Aged Widows on Abuse

Anupriyo Mallick

The proportion of the elderly in the Indian population has been rising steadily over the last four decades, and the gender difference is sharply evident in the old age groups, with women outnumbering men. In India, out of the 73 million elderly people, 33 million are widows. Among 60+ population the proportion of widows in female population is 60 per cent while only 19.4 per cent of the men are widowers in this age group. This was even more sharply defined among those who were above 70 years. About 77.6 per cent of the women are widows compared to 21.7 per cent of their male counterparts (Chakravarty, 2001). Widows are considered to be a marginalized group in India because they occupy a very low social status in society. They are viewed as inauspicious and taboo in several social situations and rituals. Older widows are doubly affected due to the combined effects of ageing and widowhood (Jamuna, 1989).

Conceptualizing the Widowhood: Widowhood as Social Death

Widowhood in India is a state of "social death"(Chakravarti, 2000). The widow's social death stems from her alienation from reproduction and sexuality following the loss of her husband and her exclusion from the functioning social unit of the family. Once a woman ceases to be wife (especially if she is childless) she ceases to be a 'person', daughter or a daughter-in-law. The problem posed by patriarchy therefore is this: since the wife has no social existence outside of her husband and his family, who, or what, is she as a widow? The problem itself simply stated is that although the widow is socially dead, she remains as an element in society. The question is how to retain her in the main stream of society as an integral element. Another could be to retain her in society but place her on its margin and then institutionalize her marginality. This is what patriarchy did with the widow. The widow's institutionalized marginality, a liminal state between being physically alive but socially dead was the ultimate cultural outcome of the deprivation of the widow of her sexuality as well as her personhood.

The widow's marginal state means that she is, in a manner of speaking, functionally incorporated into the household while being considered an outsider. Thus while she is functionally incorporated either into the natal or affinal family, the widow is, especially in her affinal household a 'domestic enemy'. At the sametime she is the 'insider' who has fallen, one who has ceased to belong and been expelled from normal participation in the community (for failing to prevent the death of her husband). This is how widowhood is conceived.

The death of a woman's husband marked the transition from wife to widow taking the woman from a central place in the family to its margin; thenceforth she was regarded as someone who was physically alive but socially dead. Desai's (1997) case studies of institutionalized elderly women showed that the elderly women's status changed not just due to chronological ageing but when they lost their husbands. Until their husbands were alive they had a place to live. Even for women who earned more than their husbands, a house was not an inalienable resource, to call her own in old age. Thus widowhood leads to social, emotional and financial insecurity. A woman is recognized as a person, an auspicious social entity only when she is with her husband. Together with her husband she performs rituals and procreates a son or many sons (Kane, 1941). These two acts define her as a social being and, for both, the presence of the husband (who makes her complete) is imperative. Without the husband, the wife has no recognized existence in Hindu patriarchy. Thus, the state of widowhood is a great calamity in a patriarchal and traditional society like the Indian society and patriarchy has played the biggest role in the total marginalization of widows.

The Gender Lens: Widow Abuse

Feminist analysis starts with the gender. The gender represents a social construction (Berger and Luckman, 1966). That is, it relates to the roles, tasks, positions and assumptions associated with male and female within a particular social context. These roles and assumptions are internalized by those brought up within that society. Acting according to the ways a society prescribes or inhibits resistance to oppression and recreates the social construction of gender.

Power is, of course, central to the issue of the gender. The marginalization of older people and, in particular, older women (widows) in society is to be taken into account. The patriarchal context sees men as having access to greater power over the more vulnerable and less powerful and being protected by societal norms. The social construction of ageing as negative and stigmatizing is important (Bytheway, 1994).

Older women (widows) are marginalized in society on account of gender and age. The negative connotations of ageism and ideas of dependency and impairment aggregate in the negotiations of power within society. Ageism, sexism and structural divisions combine to create power imbalances that are predicated on the notion of women as being of inferior status. This facilitates the conditions in which abuse flourishes and militates against an easy or quick resolution. The socialization of individuals in families is created by the wider social structures and cultural factors and, in turn, recreates them by subscribing to the gender and power games advanced. All these interact to produce individual experiences and behaviours, some of which are fundamentally abusive and proscribed by society, some which are neither condoned nor proscribed, and some which are perpetuated within the existing social fabric. This is often internalized by individuals who then add to the maintenance and development of a gendered and unequal society.

Methodology

In the present study a broad definition of abuse was used, adapted from Article 1 of the United Nations Declaration on the Elimination of Violence Against Women. "Any acts of gender-based violence or threats of such acts, coercion or arbitrary deprivation of liberty, that results in, or is likely to result in harm or suffering to older women, including: physical abuse, psychological abuse, financial abuse, neglect, sexual assault, and violation of human rights" (United Nations,1993). Obviously, there is nothing in this statement which implies that women of any age are excluded from this definition.

The operational definition of 'aged widow' for this study included all widows 60 years old or older. Age 60 was chosen, recognizing the particular difficulties like social, economic, and emotional faced by widows who, because of advanced age and ageist attitude find great difficulty in adjustment in family.

The position of a widow in society is a crucial topic which sociologists, social workers; social researchers have to discuss and elucidate. The treatment women receive is often an index to the attitudes of society towards widows as a class. The sufferings of the widows are their own. Some other factors that affect the mental and physical health of the widows are loneliness, neglect, economic instability and illness. There is no uniform pattern of widowhood either in terms of conditions leading to such a phenomenon or in terms of any pattern of consequences. There is also no uniform lifestyle for widows. Lifestyles vary not only according to the location in the social system, be it in upper class area or a middle class area, or the slum, urban or rural areas, but also by the women's own combination of characteristics. Widowhood necessitates establishment of new relations within the family, with the kin-group and with the community. If such new relationships appear difficult to emerge, widows often have to take refuge into old age homes (Ranjan, 2001). In the light of the context of widowhood in India, a study to explore the links between widowhood and abuse was undertaken.

The specific objectives of this study were:

1. to find out the socio-economic condition of the aged widow;
2. to find out the role and status of the aged widow and her inter-personal relations in the family;
3. to study the nature and extent of abuse;
4. to identify the major social and psychological variables associated with being abuser or abused;
5. to find out socio-psychological problems faced by the abused widow;
6. to analyse the coping mechanisms available to the widows to improve their situation in the family.

Design of the Study

In order to understand the phenomenon of abuse towards the widows, a qualitative research approach was found to be suitable. A qualitative approach provides a flexible framework and that is why a qualitative method was more appropriate in understanding the meaning of the problem of abuse experienced by the widows from their close kith and kin. The study was undertaken within the interpretative framework, conducted from a case study perspective, meaning that research was conducted to illuminate issues from the standpoint of the widows themselves and to capture complex, real life events and processes and following Yin's (1989) perspective on case studies to answer "how" questions, rather than "why" questions.

Sample

The researcher identified and selected the cases of abuse towards widows from and among the different Old Age Homes in and around Kolkata (W.B.). In West Bengal there are 733 widows in every thousand elderly females (Chakravarty, 2001). Over 42 per cent women in Kolkata are widows and most of them (65 per cent) have no support (*The Hindustan Times*, September 1, 2004). In one of the surveys, conducted by the Indian Society for Welfare of Senior Citizens, it was found that a large percentage of these destitute widows (45 per cent) have children, but have been driven out of their home (*The Hindustan Times*, September 1, 2004). The justification behind selecting the cases from Old Age Homes supports the fact that abuse of widows is a serious "social malaise", though it remains largely hidden within the four walls of a house and is seldom reported. As a result, incidents like these are never highlighted and discussed because Indian culture and ethos do not sanction such behaviour to happen in a family. Hence, keeping in mind this limitation, the researcher did not select the cases from the family set-up and realized that once the widows are outside the family, they would feel more relaxed to articulate their life's experiences and feelings more candidly without any kind of 'fear'. Thus, the cases were identified through purposive sampling technique and subsequently selected by applying the snowball method.

The researcher selected the cases on the basis of the criteria used by Goetz and Le Compte (1984), viz.,

- Degree of mutual respect;
- Love, affection and attention;
- Physical closeness;
- Consulted when decisions are taken in the family;
- Time spent by family members with them;
- Allowed to move freely in the family;
- Have command over their day to day activities;
- Consulted on the major decisions of the family;
- Any change noticed in the interaction pattern with the son before and after his marriage;
- Children cooperate in feeling the life; and
- Treatment before and after the husband's demise.

Data Collection

In the present study data was collected from 'primary' as well as 'secondary' sources. The primary sources constituted of the widows 60 years and above and were victims of abuse and neglect. Secondary sources include census reports, articles, newspaper reports, journals and books.

As the study was qualitative in nature, an *in-depth interview* (unstructured in form) was the primary tool for data collection,

The interviews were conducted according to 'Interview Topic Guide' which consisted of six broad items like:

1. Socio-economic condition,
2. Role and status and interpersonal relations,
3. Nature and extent of abuse,
4. Social and psychological variables,
5. Socio-psychological problems,
6. Coping mechanisms.

All the six broad items were divided into sub items and were open-ended in nature without any alternatives in order to facilitate in providing richer data.

The Contents of Data Analysis

The data obtained during the interviews were in the form of 'linguistic narration'or were of a qualitative in nature. The content of each interview was carefully analysed on the basis of the responses given by each respondent. The writes of analysis were how individuals recounted their histories—what they emphasize and omitted, their stance as protagonists or victims, the relationship the story established between the teller and the audience—all shape what an individual can claim of their own lives. Personal stories are not merely a way of telling someone (or oneself) about one's life; they are the means by which identities may be fashioned.

Presentation of Cases

Case Study I

Mrs. Sangeeta Baidya is a 70 years old Hindu widow, formerly a resident of Kumilla district of Bangladesh, and came to West Bengal after the partition of India. She had a small and a happy family of four members consisting of her husband, who was an Ayurvedic doctor, two children (a daughter and a son) and herself. She had no formal education but can read and write Bengali and a little bit of English. She is an avid lover of reading Bengali novels. Basically she is a homemaker. The widow belongs to a lower middle class family and both her parents were from Bangladesh. She is the only daughter of her parents and her father owns some agricultural land of around two bighas, which sustains the family. At a young age of 19 years her parents got her married to a young 27 years old Ayurvedic doctor. After a year of marriage the first child, a daughter was born to them. The family had been carrying on well. Suddenly, because of political unrest in Bangladesh they were forced to migrate to West Bengal and settled in a place called Barrackpore in 24 Parganas (North). Her husband purchased some land where he built a two-room house and started living there. They admitted their daughter to a Bengali medium girls school nearby from where she completed her secondary level in the first division. "She was very good at studies. Always spent time with books", the mother remarked. Mrs. S and her husband wanted their daughter to become a doctor but the daughter cherished the dream of becoming a teacher. Meanwhile, she again becomes pregnant and this times a son was born to them. Both she and her husband were delighted and thought that in old age he would be a succor to them. In the month of February, the year she could not recollect, while practising in his chamber, her husband started feeling pain in his chest. In the beginning the pain was very mild but towards noon it became unbearable. Mrs. S was immediately informed. She became very panicky and with the help of her neighbours she took her husband to a local nursing home. Hearing the news of his brother-in-law's illness her brother rushed to the nursing home. The doctors attended on him as an emergency case. Her two small children were dumb struck and shocked. The widow revealed that she had also got the feeling that her husband might not live anymore and therefore whenever she used to visit her husband she became very nervous. In spite of that, the widow recalled that she could take courage and served her husband in the best possible manner. She also prayed to God for his speedy recovery but unfortunately on the 8th day of her husband's illness, suddenly his condition deteriorated and he started having intense pain in the chest. She was beside him at that time along with her two children. She recalled that on seeing her husband screaming with pain she at once called the doctor. The doctors came and started checking him up. But soon after that he became unconscious and never regained consciousness. At that time she was just 40 years old. The widow said that she felt very sorry for not being able to talk to her husband at the last moment. When she reached home she fainted. "My husband was a great support to me, I didn't know what would happen to me", said the widow. Her only brother who stays in Kolkata and is an employee of the central government, consoled her and gave her moral as well as financial help. The expenses of the funeral ceremony and for the first 13 days of mourning were borne by him. She shouldered the responsibility of bringing up her children without any kind of financial help or moral support from her husband's family, although her husband's relatives stayed nearby. She educated all of them up to the graduation level and now they hold salaried jobs in the organized sector. She has not received any share from her in-laws property. She did not get any share from the property of her parents as well. The widow did not want to discuss this issue with any person because she was not interested in such a matter. She managed her family from the monthly income scheme (MIS) in the post office, into which her husband had invested for her sake, which was around Rs.2,500 per month. She was pulling on well and managing the affairs of her family. She never made her children feel the absence of their father. In fact, she thought that shaping her children's life would make her happy and secure in old age. Her daughter successfully passed her M.A. in Geography and obtained a good salaried job as a school teacher in an English medium school in Kolkata. She spent the major part of her salary in the maintainance of the family and on the education of her brother. After completion of her son's education the widow got her daughter married to a well-established engineer and both went to settle in New York. During this period, her son got a job in a State Bank in Kolkata. Both mother and son were living happily. And, one day his son came to his mother with a girl who worked in the same office with him and told her that they wanted to marry. The widow felt relieved thinking that since her daughter was far away from her, there was no body with whom she could talk and share her feelings, as his son came late in the evening. Eventually her son got married and the widow handed over the household responsibility with full confidence to her daughter-in-law. But the confidence was broken within six months of marriage. Petty quarrels started on issues like the widow's habit of rising early in the morning, bathing and sitting for the "*pooja*" which her daughter-in-law did not like at all as it disturbed their sleep. She is a strict vegetarian. Her cooking utensils were separate and she did her cooking in a separate area. But her daughter-in-law told her there could not be two sets of utensils in the same house and no separate arrangement for her cooking could be made. She had to adjust with them. This hurt her tremendously. She called her son and told the whole incident but he told her to do what his wife was telling her to do. There was agony and frustration on her face during the conversation while narrating these incidents. She is a patient of asthma and during the winter her breathing trouble gets worse. During one such winter she had a severe attack of asthama and she fell seriously ill. Her son took her to a doctor, bought the medicines for her, but her daughter-in-law was very indifferent to what was happening in the house. The doctor's fee and the cost of medicines were borne by the widow herself. Her son did not spend on his mother's treatment. Even during her period of illness she cooked her own meal. Her daughter-in-law never bothered to look after her. She recalled, one day when she was reading "The Gita" in her room she heard a conversation between her son and daughter-in-law. Her daughter-in-law was pestering her husband to send her away to an old age home. Hearing such comment she felt very depressed and sad. Her husband had willed his property and savings to her. She managed her own financial affairs. One fine morning her son came to her and began pressing her to transfer the property to his name and go to an old age home, as the family members were increasing and there was paucity of space. Meanwhile the widow became a grandmother and relatives from the daughter-in-law's side started coming and staying with them. She refused to comply with her son's proposal which led to conflict and tension all around. "He is a violent man and hit me with a leather belt when I turned down his demand". As the situation worsened, feelings of insecurity, suspiciousness, and fear intensified, especially in the absence of a sympathetic ear to share her troubles. Above all, all her money was in a joint account with her son who refused to part with the passbook and bank statements. The old lady felt helpless. She approached her brother who stayed in the Shyam Bazaar area in Kolkata and described the whole incident and sought his advice. He tried to resolve the matters in vain. Her son was adamant . Finding no other way her brother suggested making a complaint to the police.She sued her son. He was suspended from his job also. The case continued for two years and ultimately the mother won and now she is regularly receiving alimony on a monthly basis as stipulated by the court. This case is very uncommon in its nature because parents seldom sue their children for maintenance. Her daughter who stays in New York came to know of the incident through a newspaper report. Immediately she flew from New York and came to her mother. She was ready to take her to America, but her mother did not agreed to go. She told her daughter, a mother should not stay in a married daughter's house. If she had not have been married, her mother could have stayed with her. This case illustrates that widows are considered a 'liability' by their children. If the widows are owners of property the chances of being victims of abuse are more, as the perpetrators always try to usurp it. But widows can fight with courage and confidence if they get support and help from somewhere.

Case Study II

Mrs. Anju Seal is an old Hindu widow who has been staying in an old age home for four years. She hails from Dandakaranya in Bihar, but has been living in Kolkata for the past 30 years after her marriage. She is literate and was a homemaker. The widow comes from a middle income Hindu family. She was the eldest daughter of her parents. She could not study further because her parents married her off at the age of 14. "During those days early marriage was prevalent in the society", remarked the widow. Her husband was a central government employee in Bihar. He had a shifting duty; sometimes he had to work in the night shift also. Life was moving smoothly. During this period she gave birth to two children—a son and a daughter. Her son passed his secondary and higher secondary examination from Bihar Board. She became a widow at the age of 44 when her two children were 18 and 12 years old respectively. Her husband died during his service period, as a result of which the government gave her a job which she passed on to her son thinking that it would be difficult for him to get a job on his own merit and qualification as he had Hindi medium.

After the death of her husband the family came to Kolkata and started staying in a rented house. She was surviving on her husband's pension, which amounted to Rs. 2000 per month and her son also earning and providing financial support to the family. All her in-laws stayed in Kolkata but after the death of her husband nobody from her in-laws' family approached the distressed family with any kind of support. When her elder brother came to know about her crisis he took her with him and arranged a rented accommodation for her near his house. He took the entire responsibility of looking after her daughter's education. Her daughter completed graduation and took up a job in the private sector. Economically the family was now in a more stable condition. Her sister-in- laws' husband now gave her information about a piece of land which was around 5.5 katha and was on sale. She purchased the land with the financial help of her elder brother.

After working for a few years her son told her that he wanted to get married. She said he could not get married before his sister. He started shouting and abusing her. Tired and helpless she gave him her consent to marry the girl of his own choice.

From some source she came to know that her son had married this girl in the hope that in the future he might acquire a handsome property. The widow and her daughter started staying in the same house without any kind of communication with her son and daughter-in-law. After a few months of marriage the son started pressurizing the mother for money. He took more than he had contributed to the family by putting pressure on the mother. The widow anticipated that after the birth of her grandchildren the requirement for money would increase and simultaneously more emotional torture would be caused to her. Hence, she stopped taking money from him and they separated the kitchen. After a few years her daughter got married with an executive agriculture engineer. In the meanwhile the landlord raised the rent of the house and she was not financially sound enough to pay it. So, she moved to stay with her daughter, and her son too started living separately in a single rented room. Both of them were staying separately at different places in the city.

One day the son came to the mother and told her to transfer the 5.5 katha plot of land in his name as he was planning to build a house and would keep her with him in his new house. If the money was not arranged he would not get a house loan from his office. At the same time he also threatened her that if she did not transfer the land in his name the mother–son relationship would not exist any more. She complied with his demand. Once the land was transferred in his name he told her that it would take some more time to get the house loan from the office and demanded some more money from the maternal uncle. Thus, the demand for money increased. Being a mother she could not turn down the son's demand. She managed to get the money and also gave away all her savings; in the hope that he would keep her with him. The construction of the house was completed and she moved to her son's newly constructed house and started living with him. As there was only one room, she had to live in '*verandah*'. But her kitchen was separate. She cooked her own food. Her daughter-in-law was least interested in her. Her neglect continued silently. She could not protest fearing that if she did so she would be out of the house. When her grandson started to grow-up their behaviour became worse. Her staying was no more required and ultimately the situation became so complicated that she was compelled to leave the house, and started living in a rented house arranged by her daughter. Nobody spoke to her. Even if her grandson spent time with her, her daughter-in-law abused her saying that she was spoiling her son. One day her daughter-in-law even beat her. The widow felt the absence of her husband and was very lonely. After she left the house her son took loans from the bank for a further extension of the house.

Her daughter arranged an old age home for her for the rest of her life. Her son never visited there on the pretext that travelling in a bus caused suffocation. One day her daughter-in-law phoned her seeking some more money in order to build another floor and saying she would give the ground floor on rent and allot the first floor to her. This time she strongly rejected the proposal and told her daughter-in-law that she was quite happy in the old age home. She feels very dejected about the young generation's selfish attitude towards the old people.

The above narration shows that materialistic and individualistic attitudes are the top priorities for the younger people of today's generation.

The philosophy of "WE" has been replaced by "I", Values like sacrifice are fast declining.

Case Study III

Mrs. Moly Dey, a 77 years old Hindu widow, has been an inmate of old age home for six years. She was the youngest child of her parents. Her father was a school teacher. As he was poor, he kept her with her uncle who brought her up. She was educated up to the 7th standard. She was married at the age of 18. She used to stay in Dhaka. After marriage she came with her husband to West Bengal. Her husband was a diploma engineer and was employed as a schoolteacher for two years, and later joined a private company. She had a son and a daughter. After her marriage, she started staying with her husband's elder brother in Kolkata whose wife died when his son was 5 years old. Mrs. M. brought him up and never made him feel the absence of his mother. She led a happy life till she lost her husband at the age of 54 years. After a few years of her husband's death, she married of her daughter to an engineer who worked in a reputed multinational company. After their marriage they went to settle in Mumbai. Her son had a business and took great care of her.

The widow recalls the rainy days in a pathetic manner. "It was during rainy days that God mercilessly snatched away my son. I have lost all my happiness since then." The widow said that her son was returning home on his motorcycle at 7 in the evening when his motorcycle skidded on a slippery road and he received a head injury and become unconscious. When his condition started deteriorating, her husband's elder brother's son (her nephew) started withdrawing from the situation and avoided her, recalled she.

After suffering painfully for two days her son breathed his last. All the expense of the funeral were borne by her daughter and her son-in-law as she was financially exhausted during the treatment. Since the widow was staying with her nephew in a rented house, after his marriage they moved to a new house built by her nephew. It consisted of two rooms, one kitchen and a bathroom. The widow suggested to him to build another room for her stay, but her nephew's wife rejected her proposal.

During this period her nephew lost his job as the company where he worked was closed down. The family was passing through a very disturbing phase. He tried hard to get a job but when he failed he started coaching school children in the morning and in the evening his wife ran a dance class. The coaching classes and the dance classes were held in the same room where Moly was staying. She could not sleep till the classes were over. She had no access to the other room. So silently she had to bear the torture. She was not allowed to do any household work. Her nephew's wife made cutting remarks, shouted at her husband and often used foul language.

One day her nephew approached her and told her that he had found a place where she could live peacefully. The place was an old age home. Initially, she was a little bit reluctant to go, but ultimately thought that old age home would be far better than where she was staying. She agreed to the suggestion and moved to the old age home. The expenses were borne by the nephew. He paid visits to her and during Durga Pooja he comes to give new clothes.

Asked about her expectation, she said, "women should be economically independent and should take their own decisions in life. At the same time she said that if she had been a working woman such situation might not arise. The government must come up with some programmes for poor widows like me."

The inference from this case is that the kind of treatment and respect of a widow in a family depends on the attitude of the people with whom she is staying and the amount of property she possesses. If she had been owner of some property, her kith and kin would perhaps have taken care of her. On the other hand, if she had been educated it would have been easy to take her own decision about her life.

Case Study IV

Mrs. Mukti Dev, a 62 years old Hindu widow has been an inmate of an old age home since 2001. She belongs to rural area of West Bengal. She studied up to primary level. She knows cutting and tailoring but had never used her skills to earn her livelihood. The reason was that she has a eyesight problem from childhood as a result of which the doctor had advised her not to do any activities which could strain the eyes. She has an elder brother and an elder sister. Her elder sister was married and is in North Bengal but her elder brother remained unmarried. He owns a petty grocery shop. She got married at the age of 27 years. Her husband was a graduate and was employed as a Superintendent in Kolkata Telephone Department. They had no children. As she had some gynaecological problem, she could not conceive.

She was living in a joint family, where she had a father-in-law and a sister-in-law, who is a spinster and is employed in a private school as a teacher. The whole family used to stay in a rented house in South Kolkata. "My father-in-law used to work in a private company. Whatever savings he had were spent in the treatment of my mother-in-law who had cancer. My husband lost his mother when he was 32. From that time, my husband shouldered the responsibility of the family, taking care of his father and sister", recalled the widow. She came into the family after the death of her mother-in-law. After marriage when she came to her in-laws' house, from the very first day of her entry, she observed that her sister-in-law behaved towards her in a very 'strange' manner. She reasoned that it was because she belonged to a poor family and could not bring enough dowry with her. Also she was from rural background. For no reason the sister-in-law would find fault in her work, though she tried to do her best. "As I was a simple rural woman, sometimes I failed to understand the 'knitty gritty' of the urban mode of life." The complexity of the urban life is hard to understand. She was dominating in nature and got a lot of importance in the family from her husband and father-in-law. If any major or minor decisions were to be taken my husband and my father-in-law always consulted her. "They never involved me in the process", laments the widow. She felt neglected and thought that her position in the family was no better than that of a 'maid'. The ill treatment meted out to her started from that time.

In a massive heart attack in 1998, she lost her husband. The ill treatment towards her increased. Her sister-in-law made her do all the household work like cooking, washing of clothes and utensils, cleaning of the house and looking after her father-in-law. She was even forced to cook meat though she was a Hindu widow. From morning till night she was engaged in work. She hardly got any leisure. She retired at night fully exhausted. Her advancing age did not permit her to do the kind of work she used to do. Her father-in-law observed the behaviour of his daughter but could not speak out, as he was terminally old. When her sister-in- law went out for work she prepared a list of work she needed to be done that day by Mukti. The emotional torture continued. One day due to inhuman physical exertion she fell seriously ill. Her sister-in-law immediately moved her to a government hospital and informed her elder brother. All the expenses of her medical treatment were borne by her brother. For some days her brother kept her with him. When she had completely recovered she was sent to her husband's house. But her sister–in-law, this time, did not allow her to enter the house. She was humiliated and insulted. She went to her elder sister's house in North Bengal. There she stayed for a few months. There too she was ill treated by her nephew who always coerced her for money, which she got as her husband's pension. When she resisted he hurled foul language at her. She returned to Kolkata and decided in consultation with her brother to take respite in an old age home. She no more wanted to be a burden on any body. "As I am financially sound I can lead my own life" was the reply given by her to her brother when he gave her the proposal to stay with him. She receives a family pension of around Rs. 2000.

Her life has been full of agony after the demise of her husband. Psychologically she feels very lonely in life. But at the same time she is satisfied and happy in the old age home. She feels that a woman's life becomes 'a living hell' after the death of the husband.

The case above shows that after the death of the husband a woman looses her identity and respect in the family, especially if she is childless. However, financial independence does not put an end to abuse and neglect. It is the mindset of the people, which determines the status and condition of widows in society.

Case Study V

Mrs. Nayantara Moitra is a 69 years old Hindu Brahmin widow living in an old age home for 15 years. She belongs to an upper middle class family. She did her B.A. in Bengali and is good at writing Bengali poetry. Her inclination towards writing poetry started to grow from her school days and still at the age of 69 she continues to compose. She got married at the age of 21 years. Her husband was an engineer by profession but instead of taking up a job he started his own independent business. Her in-laws were a joint family. But she could not stay in a joint family because of her husband's business. They used to live outside Kolkata in a place called Jhargram in West Bengal. Jhargram is a rural area in West Bengal. Her husband built a house there. Her husband was an owner of a huge property and assets. Thus, financially the family was in an extremely sound state.

Within two years of marriage she gave birth to three children—two sons and a daughter. She took over all the responsibility of bringing up her children. As her husband was preoccupied with his business, he hardly got any time to look after the children. The mother met all the needs of the children. She was a competent, efficient and active lady. Her two sons are well settled in their life. The elder one works in a Bank and the younger one is employed in the private sector. Her only daughter died when she was 17 years of age. Her death was very unfortunate. She went with her friends for swimming where she drowned. The loss of the daughter was a shock to her and her entire family. It took several months to overcome that shock. It had a tremendous impact on her husband. His health started deteriorating and he fell ill. During that period her two sons looked after the family business.

In course of time they got married and continued to live with their parents. In 1980 her husband died of cardiac arrest. The two deaths affected her mentally but she never expressed her emotions to her children and daughters-in-law.

After the death of her husband the situation in the house started changing. The two sons decided to live separately. They purchased a flat jointly and started living with their mother. But after the birth of their children problems arose. The daughters-in-law told their husbands that they would not take any responsibility for their mother. She had to manage on her own. She was made to cook her own food and do all her work by herself. She even washed her own clothes though they had a housemaid. Her daughters-in-law were always complaining about her to their husbands. "If I cooked, I spent more and became difficult for them to maintain the monthly expenses", said the widow. She had no communication with her daughters-in-law. If she asked any question they replied in a disrespectful tone. If some relatives visited her, the daughters-in-law simply insulted her in front of them with out any reason. If she had to do any thing in the house she had to take their permission. Sometimes they passed derogatory remarks about her. As the days passed the intensity of abuse and neglect increased. She could not stay with her sons any more. One day after consulting her sons she moved to an old age home. Her sons never opposed her decision of going there. As financially she had no problem she could look after herself.

She was forced to change her life first climbing down the social hierarchy and then compromising with the new style of life. "Once I had the control and the authority over the whole family, now after widowhood I have lost all", laments the widow. She does not blame her daughters-in- law or her sons. According to her it is the 'generation gap' that separates them from the old. At the same time nobody wants to take the responsibility of old people.

She used to pay money for her stay with her sons' families. After the demise of her husband she disposed of her house and the money she received was deposited in her bank account. With the interest she pays for her own upkeep in the home. Her husband had willed all his property and assets to her. She wishes to divide the property in equal portion between her sons before her death.

The above case clearly shows that selfish and individualistic attitude of the young people takes precedence over the old in terms of love, respect, attention and affection.

Conclusion and Suggestions

The meaning and extent of older widows in India and the implications of policy and programming can be viewed from two levels:

(a) occurrence of psychological pain/neglect as a result of the widow's own response and lack of adjustment to changing social and economic systems; and

(b) occurrence of neglect, abuse, and exploitation when (compromises are made) by the younger generation in the basic values and in the treatment of elders to attain personal gains. No elder abuse reporting or adult protective service laws exist in India, nor are any research data available on the nature and scope of widow abuse here. However, mistreatment of elderly widows is frequently reported as a news item and is often reflected in the mass media. Research and development of a database on Indian aged widows experiencing widow abuse is needed to quantify the problem as well as to validate and advocate the need for funding to develop essential services.

Suggestions on the Basis of the Study

The major suggestions that emerged from the analysis of the above mentioned case studies can be grouped together as follows:

Awareness and education: People need to be educated to perceive widows more favourably as positive contributors to society. They need to be encouraged to form closer relationships with older adults/women. This education needs to start very early, in primary school. The general population also need to be aware that elder abuse happens and is a problem. Widows need to be aware of the problem and of their rights, as well as about available services and resources.

Intergenerational relationships: There is a need to encourage a closer and more positive contact between generations. The social isolation and neglect of widows need to be broken, through intergenerational relationships, amongst others. Also, most of the cases mentioned the perceived negative attitudes and values of the younger generation and the disrespect they show to the older generation. All of these issues need to be addressed through education and through different programmes to build positive relationships.

Empowerment of widows: There is a need for widows to act for themselves and on their own behalf. Many participants felt strongly about the need for older adults/women to exercise their rights and advocate for their own interests.

Role of the media: The media was often blamed as one of the sources of the negative images of widows in society. It was seen as important to work with the media to change these negative images, to raise awareness and to educate the population about elder abuse and particularly the abuse of widows.

Recreation facilities: The loneliness of widows was a persistent theme throughout most of the narratives. One problem, especially in developing countries, is the lack of adequate recreation facilities. A need for recreational facilities was identified.

Structural solutions: These suggestions were less direct than some of the others, but centered around the need for strong protective laws, improved health care plans, and similar structural issues.

Counselling Services: Family focused case management and counselling with a goal to empower and support family solidarity needs to be developed.

Research: In the absence of reliable data about incidence and different forms of abuse of elderly widows, there is a need for research using large and representative samples, which has scope for arriving at estimates of incidence and prevalence rates of abuse and provide deeper insights into the problem of abuse of elderly widows.

Support services: Alternate, affordable, and adequate living facilities and support services like home delivered meals, domestic help, home visits by social workers, home nursing care, mobile geriatric services and so on are required.

The National Policy on Older Persons has given equal attention to the rights of elderly women. The National Policy assures the older persons that their concerns are national concerns and it aims to strengthen a legitimate place to older persons in the society. The policy visualizes that the state will extend support in the areas of (1) financial security, (2) health care, (3) shelter, (4) welfare, (5) protection against abuse and exploitation, and (6) Opportunities for the development of older person's potential. The policy also gives special attention to older women. The recently passed Act by the central government (Maintenance of Parents and Senior Citizens Act) recognizes that the rights of inheritance, occupancy and disposal by the widows are at times violated by their own children and relatives. It is important that protection is available to older persons. It assures to consider the introduction of special provisions in IPC to protect older persons from domestic violence.

References

Berger, P. and T. Luckman, (1966). *The social construction of reality*, London: Allen Lane.

Bytheway, B. (2001). *Ageism*, Buckingham: Open University Press.

Chakarvati, U. (1998). Gender, caste and labour: Ideological and material structure of widowhood. In Martha Alter Chen (ed.), *Widows in India: Social neglect and public action*, India: Sage.

Chakravarty, I. (2001). Combating problems of widows: Ageing and society, *The Indian Journal of Gerontology*, Vol. 1, No. 2, pp. 53–66.

Desai, M. (1997). 'Imposed Disengagement: Family Case Studies of Institutionalized Elderly Women' paper presented at the National Seminar on Research on Ageing in India, organized by M.S. University of Baroda.

Goetz, J.P. and M.D. Le Compte, (1984). *Ethnography and qualitative design in educational research*, Orlando: Academic Press.

Jamuna, D. (1989). Psychological perspectives of the problems of rural elderly women. In R.N. Pati and B. Jena (eds.), *Aged in India*, New Delhi: Ashish Publishing House, pp. 199–212.

Kane, P.V. (1941). *History of Dhamasastra*, Vol. II, Part I, Poona: Bhandarkar Oriental Research Institute.

Ranjan, Alka (2001). Determinants of well-being among widows: An exploratory study in Varanasi, *Economic and Political Weekly*, October 27, pp. 4088–94.

Yin, R. (1989). *Case study research: Design and methods* (Rev. ed.) Beverly Hills CA: Sage Publishing.

26

Elderly Widows as Victims of Physical Abuse: A Qualitative Study in the State of Punjab

Madhurima

Since the middle of the 20th century, a major demographic revolution has occurred throughout the world. The number of people aged 60 and over is growing faster than all other age groups. Between 1950 and 2050, it is expected to increase from 200 million to 2 billion. The rise in the proportion of the aged has posed new challenges for many nations, both developed and developing. The ageing trends vary between countries and regions. The speed at which population in developing countries is ageing faster than in the industrialized ones. Old age dependency poses an increasing problem in the developing world. India has the second largest number of elderly persons after China. At present, it is 82 million and it is assumed that by 2050, 25 per cent of India's population will be over 60 years of age. In developing countries like India, the problem of ageing is a recent phenomenon. In traditional Indian society, old people played a dominant role in the family and community. But, the changed age pyramids, new mode of production, urban way of life, formal education have brought about changes in the familial network of relationships. These changes have also affected the status and role of the aged, which has attracted the attention of social scientists in India.

An aspect of the ageing problem, the number of widows among the elderly is about three-and-a-half times more than the number of widowers in India (National Human Development Report, 2001). There are 19 million elderly women in India who are widows. Madigan (1957) hypothesized that fundamental biological differences account for male-female mortality differences in the 20th century. Gjonca et al. (1999) mentioned behavioural factors such as smoking as well as medical care, account for some of the male-female differences in mortality at adult age. Others have suggested that the different social roles of the two sexes affect their respective mortality rates with particular emphasis on the fact that males tend to be employed in more dangerous, harmful, stressful or difficult occupations than women. Men die earlier than women because their lifestyle (occupations, recreations) and constitution (hormones) predispose them to more traumatic situations and to more degenerative diseases or to their earlier onset (Solomos, 2000).

Older women are more likely than men to lack basic literacy and numeric skills. Majority of them belong to unorganized sectors with no pension plans, provident fund or medical cover as security in trying times. A large part of the economic contribution of the women is through household and informal economic activity. These elderly widows are often denied access to or control over resources. Also, women's inheritance rights are poorly established. The husband's resources, including house, land and money are distributed among sons. In India, widowhood is usually accompanied by a loss of status and therefore more than the loss of the husband it also means the loss of a separate identity. The older women's issues have been generally overlooked by battered women's movement. Being a woman and that too aged is a twin misfortune in the Indian context. Gender specific research in Gerontology is very significant. Aitken and Griffin (1996) argued that lack of will to intervene in elder abuse of aged women is due to the fact that older women are a disenfranchised group.

Punjab ranks among the most developed of Indian states with a high per capita income, high GDP and low levels of poverty. However, it is characterized by a highly patriarchal and feudal society wherein women are regarded as inferior beings 50 years after independence, Punjabi women continue to feel the burden of womanhood deprived not only of access to basic facilities but even the basic right to be born. The deeply engrained patriarchal ethos limits and confines women to a subordinate role. Punjab has emerged as the most developed but least gender sensitive state of India. The state of Punjab does not carry a soft corner for the female sex. Due to patriarchal values female neglect and abuse is prevalent in all age groups. Hence, it will be sheer optimism to expect holistic care of these widows in this part of the country. Punjab is fast turning into a land of old people. After Kerala, Punjab is the second state with the highest percentage of aged persons. In Punjab, the average age of women is 71 years whereas the national average is 68.01 years at present (Census, 2001). The rapid increase in the aged population has been posing new challenges at the level of the family, community, region and nation as the survival of more and more people to old age has serious demographic and socio-economic implications. When there is increased longevity and fall in infant mortality and child mortality, it results in increased dependency ratio and it adversely affects the status of the aged in the society.

Abuse and Neglect of Elderly Widows

The WHO and the International Network for the Prevention of Elder Abuse (INPEA) define elder abuse as "a single or repeated act or lack of appropriate action, occurring within any relationship where there is an expectation of trust which causes harm or distress to an older person".

Researchers in the West have tried to make a distinction between active and passive neglect while others have viewed neglect and abuse differently. Reluctance to speak of their trauma and a concern with the family's reputation coupled with a dependence on others has meant that "elder abuse becomes known to the authorities through a third party" (Mahajan and Madhurima, 1995).

In a study of 749 elderly in Haryana, 30 per cent of all respondents admitted that quite often or sometimes they were abused by family members. Inability to work, lack of finances and failing health accounted for ill treatment (Mahajan and Madhurima, 1995). According to Kelly (2004), those elderly most likely to be abused are: (1) women, (2) very old, (3) socially isolated in their homes, (4) perceived as burdens to their families, (5) living with abusers, (6) in poor physical conditions, and (7) likely to have become dependent on others suddenly. The abusers are characterized as (1) family caregivers, (2) likely to be unemployed, (3) poor and in need of money, (4) feeling burdened by caregiving, and (5) the depressed.

The aged widows faced greater problems vis-à-vis those who had their spouses living with them. Women's status is dependent upon their husbands. After the death of their husbands they are not treated well (Nair, 1980, Mahadevan and Sumangala, 1986). Death of the spouse is a critical aspect of the ageing experience. Schutz (1979) proposed three basic interpersonal needs for which an individual goes for marriage, namely inclusion, affection and control. With the death of the spouse the wife is not able to transfer her needs elsewhere easily.

Older women, in particular widows, are subject to harmful practices in a number of countries, which can involve both the family and community. Due to socio-technological changes, loss of joint family, changing values, dual career families, etc., the position of elderly women has become deplorable (Ramamurthy, 2003). A study conducted in Ghana found that many poor, often elderly women were accused of witchcraft. Some were murdered by male relatives and those who survived were subjected to a range of physical, sexual and economic abuses (Adinkrah, 2004). Chen and Dreze (1995) observed that marginalization, social as well as physical, was usual and the widow remains highly vulnerable to neglect resulting in poor health and high mortality rates. The food discrimination, inadequate healthcare, lack of living space and excessive expectations as far as domestic work is concerned make the elderly women's situation extremely tenuous. When these are combined with lack of access to property and assets, the elderly widow's situation deteriorates. Dyer et al. (2000) reported that elderly abused widows have a higher occurrence of dementia and depression. Moreover, elderly persons known to have been abused physically or mentally have a significant higher mortality rates than those who have not been abused.

Theoretical Background

The belief that the dependency of elderly individuals is a major cause of abuse, is widely held in literature. This largely developed from recent gerontological research on the strains on families taking care of elderly relatives. Dependency is typically defined as requiring assistance from another person or persons to continue living in the community (Pillemer, 1985). The dependency may be physical, economic, social or psychological.

Steinmetz (1988) argued that families undergo 'generational inversion', in which the elderly person becomes dependent upon their children for financial, physical and/or emotional support. This places the caregiver under severe stress: " As the economic, physical, social and emotional dependency needs of the vulnerable elderly increase, the potential for abuse increases unless adequate resources are available." This is echoed by King (1989) who claims that the "dependency is the most common precondition in domestic abuse".

However, this form of dependency does not provide an adequate explanation of elder abuse. Since many of the elderly are quite dependent on their relatives, the question arises as to why some of these dependent elderly are abused and others are not. Because abuse occurs in only a small proportion of families, no direct correlation between dependency of an old person and abuse can be assumed. The reason can be the dependency of children on their elderly parents. To be free from such economic dependency the children may abuse or coerce their parents to transfer property in their names. As soon as they get their parents' property, they again start abusing them because their parents have been reduced to the status of economic dependency. One may raise the question as to how it is that the elderly assume the status of economic dependency in spite of having sufficient economic resources. They do so because of their emotional dependency on their children. Thus they transfer the property in the names of their sons in the hope that they will be treated better if they fulfil the desires of their children.

The present paper tries to find out the relationship between dependency and abuse whether of the elderly or the caregiver. The paper has the following important features:

- First, it focuses only on physical violence. One reason for restricting the analysis to physical violence is that it is theoretically and practically distinct from other harmful coercive acts.
- Second, it is the elderly widows who are the focus of analysis.
- Third and most important, the present paper focuses on a case study analysis. For the present paper, six cases of elderly widows have been analysed.

Objectives

- To highlight the severity of physical violence against elderly women in the family;
- To explore the reasons for the occurrence of physical violence against elderly women;

- To analyse the repercussions of such violence on the victims; and
- To suggest remedial measures to minimize the occurrence of violence against elderly in the family.

Methodology

Research on abuse of the elderly widows is sparse because the problem is extremely sensitive. It becomes really difficult for the researcher to probe the personal lives of the respondents as it is kept hidden. The present paper is based on the case study method. Three cases were staying in an old age home and three elderly have been killed. On the basis of information from different family members, police records, their case histories have been prepared.

Case I

This is a case where the caregiver manipulated to reduce the elderly mother from the status of economic independence to dependency. Mrs. D is a 75 years old widow. She has two sons and three daughters. All the children are well educated and well placed in society. Her husband during his life time divided his property into four equal shares, i.e., one for each son, one for himself and one for Mrs. D. They had a house in Chandigarh, but after the death of her husband, her sons sold that house and divided the money between themselves. Her sons bought a new house and for that purpose Mrs. D's share as well as the share of her husband was transferred in their names. Mrs. D was treated well till her share of the property was not transferred. Once the formality was completed, she was reduced to the status of a maid servant. On small issues, she was abused verbally. It was when they started beating her physically that she decided to leave the house and seek shelter in an old age home. Her daughters are providing her the financial help. She is happy in the old age home. Her sons hardly visit her. In spite of her bitterness for her sons, her only wish is that her last rites should be performed by them.

Case II

Ms. LD is an 80 years old widow who is the mother of five sons and three daughters. She lost her husband in an accident when her children were very small. Her husband had agricultural land, she was able to take care of her children properly. Her sons were not interested in agriculture and after attaining education took up services in the cities. Two of her sons went abroad and settled there. Three sons who were staying in different parts of Punjab compelled her to sell her land. She distributed the money equally among the three younger sons. Since none of her sons took upon him to fully support her, she was forced to stay with all her sons turn by turn for a few months. She used to work in their houses but was not treated properly. The attitude of her youngest daughter-in-law was very abusive. She used to beat her off and on. Her son always sided with his wife. Once she beat her so badly that she got a fracture on her right wrist. Till date she hasn't recovered fully. She cannot use her right hand. She refused to stay with her youngest daughter-in-law. Her other two daughters-in-law got very upset with this. They have put her in the old age home. She is bed-ridden. Her sons are least bothered about her well being. She spends most of her time in reciting Gurbani and lying on the bed waiting for her death.

Case III

Ms. KK is a 70 years old widow and mother of two sons. She lost her husband 17 years back. Her sons are well settled. They were not staying with her even when her husband was alive. After his death, she continued to stay alone and was getting the pension of her husband. Four years back, she met with an accident. Her hip bone got fractured. She had to stay with her younger son and his family. She spent 6 months with them. She was completely bed ridden. Her son and daughter-in-law found it difficult to take care of her and they decided to put her in an old age home. She stayed there for three months but felt miserable. She begged her other son to take her to his house. After lot of persuasion he decided to take her to his home. She is completely bed-ridden. She is kept in complete isolation and is not allowed to talk to anyone. A maid comes and does her chores. All her finances are controlled by her son. She is abused and physically beaten whenever she asks for money. Now she feels that she was better off when she was in the old age home as she was not abused there.

Case IV

Ms. SK was 77 years old and staying with her husband in a small town in Ludhiana district. They had four daughters and a son, all married and settled. Ms. SK's son was after his parents to transfer the land to his name. However, they did not adhere to his demands. He was living separately in the village but used to come to his parents house quite often and quarrelled with the old couple. Their daughters tried to intervene but the son terminated his ties with them. On and off quarrels culminated in physical violence against the couple. Many times, the neighbours intervened. The couple registered a criminal case against their son. He was taken to the police station but later the police let him off with a warning after his wife came and pleaded. The couple continued to live under fear. The son would threaten his father and would borrow huge amounts of money at the time of harvesting. His misbehaviour continued in spite of intervention by relatives, friends and neighbours. Ms. SK's husband died after a brief illness. Her son's behaviour became all the more troublesome. She warned him but he did not bother and continued with his waywardness. One night when Ms. SK was alone at home her son came. They had an argument. She was thrown down the stairs. She got severely injured with multiple fractures. Her son managed to escape. The whole night she kept on crying in pain. The neighbours contacted her daughters. In the morning when the daughters came, they took her to the hospital in the city where she succumbed to her injuries due to excessive blood loss. The daughters filed a police case. The police registered a case under section 302 IPC. The son was arrested but denied the allegation and had no regret for his actions.

Case V

Ms. JK was a 65 year old widow who was staying with her younger son in a village of Ropar district of Punjab. She was illiterate and worked on her small piece of land. She had two sons and a daughter. Her husband had died due to alcoholism. Her children did not study and also worked as labourers. Her elder son became a drug addict, did not work and always wanted financial help from her. Whenever JK refused, the accused used to fight with her. After the death of her husband, the small piece of land was transferred to her name by her in-laws. She married of all her children. But because of his addiction to drugs, the elder son's wife soon left him. JK decided to transfer the land to her sons. However, her elder son wanted a bigger share in the family property. JK refused to change her will and this made her elder son furious. He brought a country made pistol and shot his mother and injured his younger brother. JK died on the spot while the younger son sustained serious injuries. After this the elder son managed to escape but was later caught by the police. Criminal cases under section 302/25/54/59 IPC were registered against him.

Case VI

Ms. BK, aged 78, belonged to Pakistan and migrated to Amritsar after the partition. Her husband was a small cloth merchant. She had two sons. They were not keen on getting educated and started working at the shop with their father. When they came of marriageable age, they chose their own life partners. Their marriages created a gulf between BK and her sons. As her husband was physically fit and working, it was not possible for the sons to abuse them directly. However, when BK's husband passed away due to heart attack, the sons took over the shop. The daughters-in-law started harassing her every now and then. They made her do all the household work. Whenever her sons tried to intervene, it would lead to fight and her daughters-in-law ill-treated her all the more. She was physically abused whenever she failed to complete the household work on time. She continued to work for 8 years after her husband's death. When she became frail and could not work any longer, her sons decided to send her to an old age home. The sons did not maintain any contact with her after she came to the old age home. She has become extremely weak. Her hearing has impaired and she has been abandoned by her sons. However, she does not carry any ill feelings for them.

Analysis

From the six cases listed above, it becomes abundantly clear that familial relationships are no more based on love, affection and care. Instead there is an emergence of contractual and utilitarian relationships. Sons look after their aged mothers not out of a sense of respect but out of selfish motives to get hold of their property/money. As soon as they got hold over it, they started behaving differently. Whenever they were not able to get it, they resorted to homicide. It can be said that from a status of economic independence the elderly women were reduced to the status of economic dependence. As and when they became old and redundant they were thrown out of their homes.

In the present context it is to be noted that some of the elderly women became dependant on their sons merely out of love, not because their financial condition demanded it. After the death of their husbands, they expected social support from their sons. Their investment in the ideals of the family was quite high. It came as a shock to them when they had to leave their family and seek support from formal agencies as a last resort.

In Indian household the mother-in-law has a dominant role to play. She has influence on the selection of the daughter-in-law as most of the marriages are arranged. She dominates her daughter-in-law to a large extent. However, there is another side of the picture as well. When the mother-in-law becomes dependent on the daughter-in-law she also becomes a victim of her revenge. Such a situation is more evident in cases where the old lady is physically weak and has lost her husband. There are frequent intergenerational conflicts between the two. The son generally sides with his wife because it is she with whom he has to spend his later life and she also looks after his children. Thus the elderly mother feels neglected due to constant tension and conflict, either she leaves the family or is abandoned by the family members.

In extreme situations sons do not hesitate to beat their mothers. Physical violence against elderly parents often goes unreported since the elderly are isolated from the mainstream of the society. This isolation allows violent behaviour to continue unimpeded. In a majority of cases, however, elder abuse becomes known to the authorities through a third party. Due to societal attitudes, many elderly women are too embarrassed to admit that they have raised a child capable of such behaviour.

In a number of studies it has been contended that the family no more acts as a support system to the elderly because the younger generation can ill-afford the burden of dependent elderly kinsmen as they themselves are not financially well placed (Chowdhary, 1968; Mahajan, 1987). In the present study it was noted that not only economically dependent elderly widows but also those who had property in their name were abused. The study endorses the fact that the family in India is losing one of its important functions as a support system for the elderly. A few researchers have depicted pitiable conditions of widows because of their economic, social and psychological dependency on their children (Steinmetz, 1988). The present study supports the above findings. Stoller (1983) reported that married daughters are coming forward to assume the responsibility of providing support to their elderly parents when they are abandoned by the sons. In the present study daughters showed concern for the elderly mothers. However, due to their own familial obligations they could not take care of their mothers. It is interesting to note that in all the cases it was the sons and daughters-in-law who abused their mothers. Since elderly women in Punjab have traditional sex role orientation, they are bound to suffer because of their social dependency on their male children. There is, however, a ray of hope. Keeping in view the reluctance of the male children to perform their filial responsibilities, it is quite likely that peoples' attitude towards the female child will change and thus bring about a change in the sex ratio in Punjab.

These findings lead to two important questions:

- What are the causes of abusers' dependency?
- Why do not elderly abused women terminate the relationship?

With regard to the first question, it can be assumed that consumerism generated by the media has played a very important role in materialistic relationships making. Thus, we can speculate that value orientation among the younger generation is more towards materialism than filial piety. Moreover, emergence of the problem of drug addiction and alcoholism in the state of Punjab is taking its toll on the youth, who under the influence of drugs and alcohol fail to distinguish between right and wrong. They do not mind killing even their own mothers for the sake of money.

The dependency theory furnishes some plausible answers to the second question. Again while definitive data is not available, the most commonly given reasons for staying with an abusive dependent relative implies that no other choice was available. These elderly women have suffered because of their social dependence on their male children whom they raised as insurance for old age. The results indicate that elderly abused mothers perceive themselves as being on the loosing end of the bargain, where they are giving much and receiving very little. Most felt trapped by a sense of family obligation and therefore did not terminate the relationship.

What can be done to prevent elder abuse?

The impact that physical and psychological violence have on the health of an older person is exacerbated by the ageing process and diseases of old age. It is more difficult for the elderly to end an abusive relationship or to make correct decisions because of the physical and cognitive impairments that usually come with old age. In India, kinship obligations and the use of the extended family network to resolve difficulties may also lessen the ability of older people, particularly women, to escape from dangerous situations. Often, the abuser may be the abused person's only source of companionship. Because of these and other considerations, preventing elder abuse presents a whole host of problems. In most cases, the greatest dilemma is how to balance the older person's right to self-determination with the need to take action to end the abuse.

Recommendations

Although abuse of the elderly by family members, caregivers and others is better understood today than it was 25 years ago, a firmer base of knowledge is needed for policy, planning and programming purposes. Many aspects of the problem remain unknown, including its causes and consequences, and even the extent to which it occurs. Research on the effectiveness of interventions has to date yielded almost no useful or reliable results. Perhaps the most insidious form of abuse against the elderly lies in the negative attitudes towards, and stereotypes of, older people and the process of ageing itself, attitudes that are reflected in the frequent glorification of youth. As long as older people are devalued and marginalized by society, they will suffer from loss of self-identity and remain highly susceptible to discrimination and all forms of abuse.

References

Adinkrah, M. (2004). Witchcraft accusations and female homicide victimization in contemporary Ghana. *Violence Against Women*, 10(4): 325–56.

Aitken, L. and G. Griffin (1996). *Gender issues in elder abuse*, London: Sage Publishers.

Chen, M.A. and Jean Dreze (1995). Widowhood and well being in north India, In Monica Das Gupta et al. (eds.), *Women's health in India: Risk and vulnerability*, Delhi: Oxford University Press.

Chowdhary, D.P. (1987). The aged and the infirm, quoted by A. Mahajan in *Problems of aged in unorganized sector*, New Delhi: Mittal Publications.

Dyer, C.B., V.N. Pavlik, K.P. Murphy and D.J. Hyman (2000). The high prevalence of depression and dementia in elder abuse or neglect, *Journal of American Geriatrics Society*, 48(2): 205–08.

Gjonca, A., C. Tomassini and J.W. Vaupel. Male female differences in mortality in developed world, MPIDR working paper, 1999–2001, July.

Kelly, V.A.(2004). Psychological abuse of women: A review of literature. *The Family Journal: Counseling and therapy for couples and families.* 12(4): 383–88.

King, N.R. (1989). Exploitation and abuse of the elderly family members. In J.J. Costa (ed.), *Abuse of the elderly*, Lexington, MA: Lexington Books.

Madigan, F.C. (1957). Are sex mortality differentials biologically caused?, *Millbank Memorial Fund Quarterly*, 25: 202–23.

Mahajan, A. and M. Madhurima (1995). *Family violence and abuse in India*, New Delhi: Deep and Deep Publications.

Mahajan, A. (1987). *Problems of aged in unorganized sector*, New Delhi: Mittal Publications.

Mahadevan, K. and P. Sumangala (1986). *Analytical framework and conceptual model on policy oriented research for the welfare of the elderly.* A paper presented at 11th World Congress of Sociology, New Delhi, 18–22 August.

Nair, T.K. (1980). *Older people in rural Tamil Nadu*, Madras School of Social Work.

Pillemer, K. (1985). The degree of dependency: New findings on domestic violence against the elderly, *Social Problems*, 33(2), December.

Ramamurthy, M. (2003). Empowering the older persons in India. *Research and Development Journal*, 9(2): 5–8.

Schutz, W. (1979). The interpersonal underworld, quoted by A.W. Russel, *The ageing experience*, New York: Lippincott Company.

Solomos, N.W. (2000). Demographic and nutritional trends among the elderly in developed and developing regions. *European Journal of Clinical Nutrition*, 54(3): 2–14.

Steinmetz, S.K. (1988). *Duty bound elder abuse and family care*, Newbury Park: Sage.

Stoller, E.P. (1983). Parental care giving by adult children. *Journal of Marriage and Family*, 45(4).

List of Contributors

Anoshua Chaudhuri, Assistant Professor of Economics, San Francisco State University, San Francisco.

Anupriyo Mallick, Associate Professor, Department of Social Work, Vivekanand Institute of Social Work & Social Sciences, Utkal University, Bhubaneswar.

Ariela Lowenstein, Professor, Graduate Department of Aging Studies and Head, Center for Research and Study of Aging, Faculty of Welfare and Health Studies, University of Haifa, Israel.

Arup K. Banerjee, OBE, FRCP former Professor of Medicine and past President, British Geriatric Society, Egerton Bolton.

B. Devi Prasad, Department of Social Work, Andhra University, Visakhapatnam, Andhra Pradesh.

Barry Goldlist, Professor and Director of Geriatric Medicine, Faculty of Medicine, University of Toronto.

Carey Wexler Sherman, Life Course Development Program, Institute for Social Research, University of Michigan, Ann Arbor, MI, USA.

Carla Nassar, Research Scholar at Dalhousie University, Halifax, Nova Scotia, Canada.

Christen Erlingsson, Assistant Professor of Nursing, School of Human Sciences, University of Kalmar, Kalmar, Sweden.

D. Jamuna, Professor, Center for Research on Ageing, Department of Psychology, S.V. University, Tirupati.

Dephne Nahmiash, recently retired from teaching in gerontology and social work at Laval University and McGill University in Montreal, Canada.

Dorrie E. Rosenblatt, Department of Internal Medicine, Division of Geriatrics, University of Michigan, Ann Arbor, MI, USA.

Douglas McConatha, Department of Sociology, West Chester University of Pennsylvania, West Chester, Pennsylvania, USA.

Ezra Wexler, Research Scholar, Dalhousie University, Halifax, Nova Scotia, Canada.

Indira Jai Prakash, former Professor, Department of Psychology, Bangalore University, Bangalore.

Israel Doron, Department of Gerontology and the Center for Research and Study of Ageing, Haifa University, Haifa, Israel.

Jane Roberts, School of Social Work, University of South Florida, USA.

Jasmin Tahmaseb McConatha, Department of Psychology, West Chester University of Pennsylvania, West Chester, Pennsylvania, USA.

Jeff Karabanow, Faculty member, Dalhousie University School of Social Work, Halifax, Nova Scotia, Canada.

Joan Harbison, Faculty member, Dalhousie University School of Social Work, Halifax, Nova Scotia, Canada.

Joan K. Davitt, School of Social Policy and Practice, University of Pennsylvania, Philadelphia, USA.

John Williamson, Professor, Department of Sociology, Boston College, USA.

K.L. Sharma, Founder, Indian Gerontological Association and Editor, *Indian Journal of Gerontology.*

K.S. Latha, Associate Professor, Department of Psychiatry, Kasturba Medical College, Manipal University, Manipal.

Kelly Joyce, Associate Professor, Department of Sociology, College of William and Mary, USA.

Laura Mamo, Professor, Department of Sociology, University of Maryland, USA.

Lynn McDonald is a professor in the Faculty of Social Work and Director of the Institute for Human Development, Life Course and Aging at the University of Toronto, Canada.

Madhurima, Reader in Sociology, Department of Correspondence Studies, Punjab University, Chandigarh.

Madine Vander Plaat, Faculty Member at Saint Mary's University, Halifax, Nova Scotia, Canada.

Mala Kapur Shankardass, Associate Professor, Department of Sociology, Maitreyi College, University of Delhi, Delhi.

Md. Ismail Tareque, Lecturer, Department of Population Science and Human Resource Development, University of Rajshahi, Rajshahi, Bangladesh.

Md. Mostafizur Rahman, Assistant Professor, Department of Population Science and Human Resource Development, University of Rajshahi, Rajshahi, Bangladesh.

N. Indira Rani, Department of Social Work, Andhra University, Visakhapatnam.

P.V. Ramamurti, former Professor, Center for Research on Aging, Department of Psychology, S. V. University, Tirupati.

Peter Clark, member of Geriatric/Long Term Care Review Committee to the Chief Coroner for the Province of Ontario, Canada.

Rashmi Gupta, Assistant Professor, School of Social Work, San Francisco State University, San Francisco, USA.

Rhonda Schwartz, Member, Notre-Dame de Grace Community Committee on Elder Abuse, Montreal, Quebec, Canada.

Roopalekha Jathanna P.N., Associate Professor, Department of Health Information Management, Manipal College of Allied Health Sciences, Manipal University, Manipal.

Sheila Wildeman, Faculty member, Dalhousie University School of Social Work, Halifax, Nova Scotia, Canada.

Stephen Coughlan, Faculty Member, Dalhousie University School of Social Work, Halifax, Nova Scotia, Canada.

Toni C. Antonucci, Professor of Psychology and Senior Research Scientist at the Institute for Social Research Life Course Development Program at Wayne State University, USA .

Towfiqua Mahfuza Islam, Department of Population Science and Human Resource Development, University of Rajshahi, Rajshahi, Bangladesh.

U.C. Jain, former Professor of Psychology, Barkatullah University, Bhopal and former Vice Chancellor, MPS University, Rewa (Madhya Pradesh).

Varsha Pandya, Associate Professor, College of Liberal Arts and Sciences, Department of Social Work, Kutztown University, Pennsylvania, USA.

Yeon Shim Lee, School of Social Work, San Francisco State University, San Francisco.

Index